MW01282862

JAPANESE
SECRET PROJECTS
EXPERIMENTAL AIRCRAFT OF THE IJA AND IJN 1939-1945

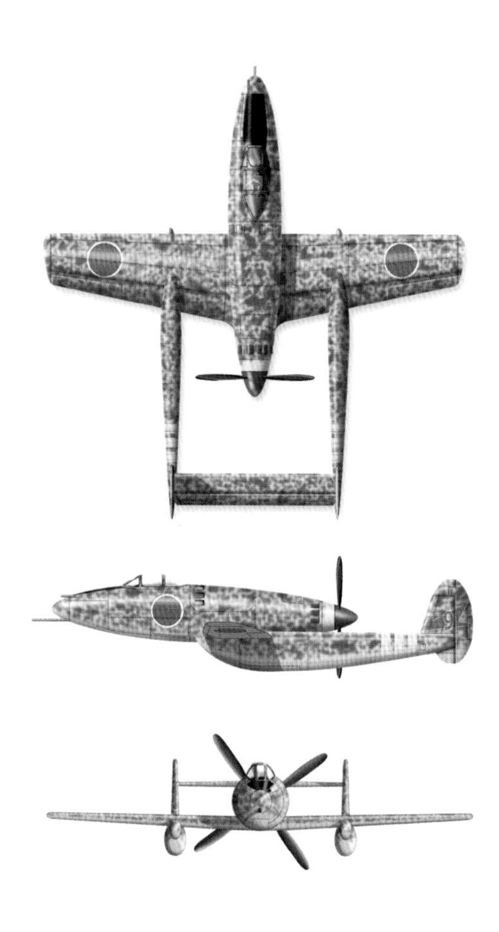

MIDLAND
An imprint of
Ian Allan Publishing

JAPANESE SECRET PROJECTS

EXPERIMENTAL AIRCRAFT OF THE IJA AND IJN 1939-1945

Edwin M Dyer

Japanese Secret Projects: Experimental Aircraft of the IJA and IJN 1939-1945

First published 2009

ISBN 978 1857803 174

Midland Publishing is an imprint of Ian Allan Publishing Ltd, Hersham, Surrey KT12 4RG.
Printed by Ian Allan Printing Ltd,
Hersham, Surrey KT12 4RG.

Visit the Ian Allan Publishing website at
www.ianallanpublishing.com

With effect from 1st February 2010 distribution of all Ian Allan Publishing Ltd titles in the United States of America and Canada will be undertaken by BookMasters Distribution Services Inc,
20 Amberwood Parkway, Ashland, Ohio 44805.

Half-title: **Profile art of the Manshū Ki-98.** Peter Allen
Title page: **Manshū Ki-98 in action.** Ronnie Olsthoorn

Contents

Preface

If you browse any major book seller, you tend to see a good many works on the experimental aircraft developed by Germany both before and, particularly, during World War 2. Also, you'd find a fine selection of books on the topic of American experimental planes. From time to time, you could find mention of such 'X-planes' of other nations amongst the text describing more well known aircraft. But you did not often see, if at all, books dedicated to Japanese experimental aircraft. Usually, one had to visit specialty book dealers, hobby shops, or be fortunate enough to be able to read another language in order to find books on the subject of Japanese X-planes.

I was first exposed to the world of Japanese experimental aircraft in 1988 through the classic book *Japanese Aircraft of the Pacific War* by René J. Francillon. I found the book on the shelf in your typical mall bookstore. Sure, before then, I knew about the classic Japanese planes such as the Mitsubishi A6M Reisen and the Nakajima Ki-43 Hayabusa. But Francillon's book brought to me such planes as the Nakajima Kitsuka, Mitsubishi J8M Syūsui and the Tachikawa Ki-94.

My interest in military technology sat on the kerb through my college years but afterwards it slowly ramped back up. I found that I focused my reading on the military machine of Germany and the sheer breadth of technological innovation their engineers and scientists churned out. Small arms, armour, artillery, missiles, submarines, aircraft, rocketry and much more – no stone was left unturned by Germany's scientists. It was during my studies of German aviation that I would see the Japanese pop up from time to time. Most often, it was the acquisition of German technology for development in Japan, or German plane designs offered for the Japanese to purchase. This piqued my interest in learning about what the Japanese had brewing in their aviation cauldron.

By this time, the World Wide Web was becoming the engine of information that it is today. While I was able to find bits of information regarding Japanese X-planes, it was never anything substantive. Stops into the local hobby shop or major book retailers did not turn up anything above and beyond what I already knew. I found a rather large gap in the online data pool on Japanese X-planes, at least in English, and so I sought about correcting that.

In 1998, I began to assemble a website inspired by Dan Johnson's Luft '46 which started in 1997 as a one-stop site about German X-planes. In 1999, my site, Hikoki: 1946, went live to the world. During its first few years, Hikoki: 1946 expanded to encompass 31 Japanese experimental aircraft and sections on engine specifications, German aircraft the Japanese were interested in or bought, missiles and more. Support for the site was great. Such people as artist Ted Nomura, Polish author Tadeusz Januszewski and J-Aircraft.com contributors Mike Goodwin, George Elephtheriou and D. Karacay helped the site by providing both artwork and data on some of the planes presented. By 2002, I felt that I'd exhausted what there was on the subject and the site entered a state of finality with no further updates having been done since.

Fast forward to the fall of 2007. Jay Slater of Ian Allan Publishing e-mailed me to discuss the prospect of writing a book on Japanese experimental aircraft. This was not the first time someone had approached me to do so. But unlike the others, Jay had a well known publisher behind him who had a number of X-plane books in print, many of which I had in my own library. It seemed natural to him that a book on Japanese X-planes would be a welcome complement to their existing titles as well as providing the English aviation historian or enthusiast with a ready source of dedicated information on Japanese X-planes. I certainly agreed.

The work you hold is not simply my Hikoki: 1946 website in book form. Yes, some of the aircraft in these pages can be found on the site but the information here has been further researched and revised. This means the data in these pages is far more up to date than the site. And for sure, the outstanding artwork provided makes this a spectacular publication and investment for your library.

Because of the constraints on the number of pages, there had to be a process of selecting aircraft for inclusion. The planes selected for this volume have been chosen based on several factors. The first was the nature of the plane in terms of being a conventional or a more radical design. Thus, while the Kūgishō D3Y Myōjō may be a relatively obscure plane of which only two were built, it was a very conventional aircraft in terms of design. The same applied to the Mitsubishi Ki-83. Therefore, these more conventional designs or prototypes received a lower selection priority over more advanced concepts. Another factor concerned aircraft which were derivatives of established production planes in the Japanese arsenal. As such, designs such as the Ki-116, which was derived from the Nakajima Ki-84 Hayate, are also excluded. A third factor revolved around the pool of information available for a certain design. The more obscure or unknown the design was, the higher it was considered over other planes. For example, the scope of the Rikugun Kogiken designs were of far more interest and of a lesser known nature than the prototypes of the Nakajima G8N Renzan or the Aichi S1A Denko of which more information is readily available. Finally, X-planes that were purely research aircraft such as the Kawasaki Ki-78, those experimental planes constructed prior to the start of the war, and most of the non-combat aircraft (transports, gliders and the like) were generally excluded from contention. Perhaps in a future publication, those designs that did not make the cut for this book will get their chance.

It may appear that few aircraft remained with such pruning but it still left a significant number of planes to choose from, from the historically important Nakajima Kitsuka and Mitsubishi J8M Syūsui, to more unknown types such as the Kūgishō Tenga and Kawanishi K-200.

In so far as the book layout, aircraft are separated by service (IJA and IJN) and then alphabetised by manufacturer. Those aircraft that were not of either service (or were joint projects) are listed last. Missiles and a selection of some of the more interesting aircraft munitions that were deployed or were in development are included along with a brief discourse on German technical exchange with Japan before and during World War 2. A feature in each aircraft chapter is the inclusion of a 'Contemporaries' section. The purpose of this is to illustrate to the reader that designs didn't occur in a vacuum and similar concepts could be found in other Allied nations as well as Axis ones. This section should not in any way be construed as pointing to the Japanese as simply copying the work of other nations. While it is true that the Japanese air forces prior to the war were very keen on obtaining as much information on aviation technology as possible (and, in some cases, built and flew versions of foreign aircraft), once hostilities began Japan knew she could no longer rely on outside assistance for their aircraft industry and ensured it could stand on its own. This it did, producing many successful aircraft that were indigenous. The influx of German technology during the war can be viewed as another means by which Japanese aviation technology was boosted through a wartime ally, but more often than not it was an expediency to rapidly increase the capability of Japanese aircraft in the face of a worsening war situation and ever improving Allied fighters and bombers. It is hoped the information in this section will be a catalyst to learn more about the aircraft presented to expand one's knowledge of aviation by other nations. Also keep in mind that this section does not list each and every plane that could be considered a contemporary. Instead, I have picked the more interesting and have intentionally listed only the aircraft name(s) in order to not take away from the main topic at hand. The reader will also find with certain aircraft a section called 'Survivors'. Listed here are those aircraft that survived the war and what their fates were, either being scrapped or escaping the cutting torch. Where known, the Hepburn Romanisation system is utilised for Japanese words.

Every attempt has been made to ensure accuracy in the information provided in this book. Even as the writing of the book was underway, I was acquiring additional sources and checking and rechecking data to make sure nothing was amiss. Of course, at some point I had to 'let it go'. If I held on to chapters waiting on the next titbit of information to appear, the book would never get finished and you wouldn't be holding it in your hands. Thus, invariably, there is the risk of omitting something, interpreting a translation or source incorrectly, or just plain making an error. To that end, corrections, new information and any and all comments can be directed to the author at the e-mail address below.

I hope you, the reader, enjoy the book and find it a worthwhile addition to your library as a ready resource on some of the most interesting Japanese airplanes of the war.

Regards,

Edwin M. Dyer III
japanesesecretprojects@gmail.com

Acknowledgements

This book would not be what it is without the assistance and support of a good number of individuals and I would like to recognise them here.

First and foremost, Jay Slater and his team at Ian Allan Publishing. It was Jay who reached out to me and first proposed this book and through him it became a reality.

To the artists whose work you will see in this publication: Peter Allen, Kelcey Faulkner, Muneo Hosaka, Gino Marcomini, Ted Nomura, Ronnie Olsthoorn and Daniel Uhr. Through their hard work, the aircraft within these pages come to life in spectacular fashion. To Tim Hortman who graciously provided his photographs of the Kyūshū J7W1 Shinden, Nakajima Ki-115 Ko Tsurugi and the Nakajima Kitsuka currently in store at the National Air and Space Museum and which are no longer available to the public.

During the information gathering phase of the book, research support and material was provided by several individuals. Their assistance helped to confirm or deny data, provided a sounding board for theories, offered comments on the information or brought new information to the table. These folks are Shorzoe Abe, David Aiken, Paul Deweer, Tadeusz Januszewski, James Long, Robert C. Mikesh, Nicholas Millman, Ronnie Olsthoorn, Masafumi Sawa and Akio Takahashi. As some of the works used in researching the book were in Japanese, Ryuki Arceno, Nanae Konno, Lara Law and Tekla Munobe provided translations. For those works in Polish, Michal Sporzyński was the key translator.

Last but certainly not least, my parents, Edwin and Margaret, for their support and encouragement. Also to Gail Lashley for always making sure I had my nose to the grindstone.

Abbreviations and Glossary

AOAMC Atlantic Overseas Air Material Centre in Newark, New Jersey.

FE Foreign Equipment. FE numbers were used by the USAAF to mark captured aircraft for tracking and documentation purposes.

Ha Abbreviation for the Japanese word for engine, *hatsudoki*. For example, the Nakajima [Ha-35] 25 14-cylinder radial engine. This was used as a designator for all engines used by the IJA while the IJN used their own system. Eventually, the two systems were combined. In the example above, the '3' was the engine type (14-cylinder, double-row radial), the '5' the bore/stroke (130mm/150mm) while the '25' was the model number, taken from the IJN system.

IJA Imperial Japanese Army (Dai-Nippon Teikoku Rikugun). In this book, IJA refers to the Imperial Japanese Army Air Service (Teikoku Rikugun Kōkūtai).

IJN Imperial Japanese Navy (Dai-Nippon Teikoku Kaigun). In this book, IJN refers to the Imperial Japanese Navy Air Service (Dai-Nippon Teikoku Kaigun Koku Hombu).

K.K. Stands for Kabushiki Kaisha, which translates as Company, Limited. For example, Fuji Kokuki K.K. would be Fuji Aircraft Co Ltd.

Ken Abbreviation for *kensan*, meaning 'research'.

Ki The IJA utilised Ki numbers for aircraft. Ki was the abbreviation for *kitai* which means 'airframe'. The number following the abbreviation was the project number for the aircraft under development regardless of the manufacturer or aircraft type. For example, the Mitsubishi Ki-73.

Ku Abbreviation for *kakku*, meaning 'to glide'.

MAMA Middleton Air Material Area at Olmstead Field in Middleton, Pennsylvania. This was where captured Japanese aircraft were shipped by the USAAF.

NA Not Available. In regards to specifications, NA means that at the time of the book printing, the information on the spec was unknown and not available.

NAS Naval Air Station.

NASM National Air and Space Museum.

Ne Abbreviation for *Nensho Rocketto*, meaning 'burning rocket' in Japanese. Ne was used on Japanese jet engine designations. For example, the Ne 330.

TAIC Technical Air Intelligence Center located in Washington DC at NAS Anacostia. This was where data on enemy aircraft was collected and maintained. Captured aircraft were evaluated at NAS Patuxent River, Maryland.

USAAF United States Army Air Force.

Dai-Ichi Kaigun Kōkū Gijutsu-shō 1st Naval Air Technical Arsenal housed at Yokosuka, Japan. This group was responsible for aircraft design for the IJN.

Dai-Ichi Kaigun Kokusho 1st Naval Air Arsenal located at Kasumigaura.

Dai-Juichi Kaigun Kokusho This was the 11th Naval Air Arsenal located at the Hiro Naval Arsenal in Kure, Hiroshima, where seaplanes, flying boats and engines for the IJN were produced.

Hei Literally 'grade C'. Hei is most often used in the book to describe the third specification, such as 18-shi Hei.

Hikōki Aeroplane in Japanese.

Jidōsha Japanese for car/automobile.

Kai From time to time, Japanese aircraft would have *Kai* appended to their designation when the design was heavily modified but not to a point it required a new designation. Kai meant 'improved'. An example would be the Nakajima Ki-84-II Hayate Kai.

Kaigun Koku Hombu Imperial Japanese Navy Aviation Bureau of the Ministry of the Navy of Japan. Among a number of duties of this bureau, the pertinent one for this book was the Technical Department that oversaw the design of new aircraft and equipment.

Ko Literally 'grade A'. Ko is most often used in the book to describe the first model of a plane such as the Ki-115 Ko or the first specification, such as 18-shi Ko.

Koku Hombu Army Air Headquarters. This division of the Imperial Japanese Army was responsible for research and development of aircraft, aircraft engines and other aviation equipment. As such, specifications for aircraft would be issued from this division.

Kokuki Aircraft in Japanese.

Kūgishō Aircraft designed by the Dai-Ichi Kaigun Kōkū Gijutsu-shō were given the Kūgishō designation, a contraction of Kōkū Gijutsu-shō. One may see Kūgishō aircraft called by the Yokosuka designation but this would be incorrect.

Mitsubishi Jūkōgyō Kabushiki Kaisha The full name for Mitsubishi Heavy Industries Co Ltd.

Ōtsu Literally 'grade B'. Ōtsu is most often used in the book to describe the second model of a plane such as the Ki-93 Ōtsu or the second specification, such as 18-shi Ōtsu.

Park Ridge This was the location of No. 803 Special Depot in Park Ridge, Illinois. Captured aircraft selected for inclusion in the NASM museum were stored here until the collection was culled during the Korean War as the US Air Force needed the space.

Paul. E. Garber Preservation, Restoration, and Storage Facility Aircraft that survived the culling at Park Ridge were moved to this NASM facility located in Suitland-Silver Hill, Maryland.

Rikugun Kokugijutsu Kenkyūjo Air Technical Research Institute. This unit conducted research, design and development for the IJA. The facilities were located at Tachikawa.

Shi Beginning in 1931, when the IJN issued a specification for an aircraft, a shi number was assigned to it, based on the year of the Showa Japanese calendar. For example, the Mitsubishi G7M Taizan was designed to meet the 16-Shi Attack Bomber specification. 16 stood for Showa 16 or 1941.

Shimpū The word is an alternate reading of the Japanese *kanji* for 'divine wind' and is used in this text to describe those aircraft for use by and for suicide unit missions. Shimpū Tokubetsu Kōgekitai is the IJN designation for suicide units, meaning Divine Wind Special Attack Force. The IJA would use Shimbu Tokubetsu Kōgekitai, shimbu meaning 'band of heroic warriors' or 'brandishing a sword'. Kamikaze is not used by the Japanese as a description for suicide units but the word is popular in the West.

Tachikawa Dai-Ichi Rikugun Kokusho First Army Air Arsenal. IJA air depot that repaired, modified and distributed aircraft to IJA air units. It also produced the Ki-30, Ki-43 and Ki-51 in addition to being one venue for experimental aircraft development.

Tail Number For the purposes of this book, this refers to the US Navy method of marking captured aircraft. It is considered that the number applied corresponded to shipping allocation numbers for the aircraft when they were prepared for transport to the US.

Imperial Japanese Army

MUNEO HOSAKA

Kawasaki Ki-64

Designers at times relish the freedom to let their visions develop and flow from the drafting board to the tarmac, ready to take to the skies. Takeo Doi, working for Kawasaki, was just such a designer. Despite the very real work developing, testing and producing combat aircraft for the IJA, Doi had a concept that he, on his own, brought to the fore. Initially, the IJA would not hear of the design but later, when the Ki-64 took shape, their mind would change.

In 1939, Doi was involved with two Kawasaki programs: the Ki-45 Toryu and the Ki-60/Ki-61 Hein. The Ki-45 was proving to be a horribly troublesome aircraft. Problems with the landing gear, concerns with drag, engine difficulties and more were proving a thorn in Kawasaki's side. It was Doi who stepped in to solve the issues plaguing the initial Ki-45 design. In addition to working to fix the floundering Ki-45, by 1940, Doi was involved with the preliminary development of the Ki-60 heavy fighter and the Ki-61 Hein.

Even with such responsibilities, Doi had a design of his own for a high-speed fighter. His concept incorporated a number of novel features which were perceived as rather unorthodox in comparison to other more conventional types. Since Koi's aircraft was purely his own and not created to meet any sort of specification, Koi would be disappointed when the IJA forbade Kawasaki giving any further time to the design.

Doi's disappointment then turned to joy when, in October 1940, the IJA authorised Kawasaki to proceed with developing the Ki-64 to meet a requirement for a fighter capable of a maximum speed of 700km/h at 5,000m (435mph at 16,405ft) and a 5 minute climb to that height.

MUNEO HOSAKA

To power the Ki-64, Doi would enlist the help of fellow engineers employed by the Akashi engine plant. The decision was made to use the Kawasaki Ha-201 ([Ha-72] 11) engine. This was actually a combination of two Ha-40 engines, the Ha-40 being the licence-built version of the Daimler-Benz DB 601A. Each Ha-40 was a 12-cylinder, liquid-cooled powerplant and the Ha-201 was formed through having one engine in front of the cockpit and the second behind it. The rear engine drove the first of the contra-rotating propellers and it had a variable pitch. The front engine drove the second propeller, which was of a fixed pitch. Both propellers were three-bladed. All told, the Ha-201 was expected to produce 2,350hp.

The use of the Ha-201 was not the most novel feature of the Ki-64. It was the means of cooling the engine that was notable. The Ha-201 was to be cooled by a steam condensing system. A tank of 15.4 gallons of water was fitted into each wing and the outer wings and flaps served as the cooling surface, totalling 23.99m² (258.3ft²). The port wing serviced the front engine while the starboard wing provided coolant to the rear engine. As the water coolant turned to steam, it was pumped out into the wings where the steam would condense back into water which in turn was pumped back into the engine. The main benefit of this system was lower drag on the airframe as the need for air inlets was removed or minimised. Each laminar flow wing housed the fuel tanks and one 20mm Ho-5 cannon while two more were fitted in the fuselage deck. One drawback to the wings being packed with the cooling system apparatus was that it left little room for the fuel tanks and consequently the Ki-64's operational range suffered. The majority of the fuel was carried in the fuselage, the tanks being placed in and around the space left available by the Ha-201 engine. The main fuel tank was situated in front of the cockpit, holding 306.7 litres (81 gallons). Under it was the oil reservoir, holding 79.5 litres (21 gallons) of oil for the engines. Behind the cockpit were two coolant tanks holding 83.3 litres (22 gallons) and 117.4 litres (31 gallons) respectively. The smaller serviced the front engine, the larger the rear engine.

Doi tested the Ha-201 and the cooling system to a considerable degree. In 1942, one of the Ki-61 Hein fighters was specially modified to test the cooling method and its trial flights began in October 1942 and ran through to the end of 1943. Because of this thorough testing, the construction of the Ki-64 was delayed and so did not reach completion until December 1943. Nevertheless, Doi was satisfied that the cooling system would grant an additional 41km/h (25mph) to the Ki-64 and battle damage would not significantly reduce the effectiveness of it and as such the exhaustive testing was worth the effort.

With the Ki-64 complete, flight testing commenced in December 1943. Four test flights were successfully made without mishap. However, on the fifth, the rear engine caught fire. The test pilot was able to land the aircraft and the fire was quenched. Mechanics stripped the engine out of the Ki-64 and returned it to the Akashi plant for a full repair. The Ki-64 itself was returned to the city of Gifu which, at the time of World War 2, was a major industrial centre.

Plans were made to improve the Ki-64 by replacing the 2,350hp Ha-201 with an enhanced model that could generate up to 2,800hp. The propellers would be replaced with two, constant-speed contra-rotating propellers that were electrically operated. It was envisioned that with these modifications, the Ki-64 Kai would be able to attain a top speed of 800km/h (497mph).

Unfortunately for the Ki-64, repair work languished, especially in the face of more pressing needs for the Japanese arms industry and the production of more conventional aircraft. As a result, both the Ki-64 and the Ki-64 Kai were cancelled. After Japan's surrender, the Ha-201 was still at Akashi, its repairs incomplete. When US forces arrived in Gifu, the Ki-64 was found and technical teams gutted the airplane of its cooling system. The system was then crated and shipped to the United States for study at Wright Field in Dayton, Ohio.

Given the relatively long development time of the Ki-64, US intelligence had already become aware of the design. Thus, expecting the Ki-64 would see service, the airplane was assigned the codename *Rob*.

Kawasaki Ki-64 – data

Contemporaries
Republic XP-69 (US), Heinkel P.1076 (Germany), Caproni CA.183bis (Italy)

Type	Fighter
Crew	One

Powerplant
One Kawasaki Ha-201 ([Ha-72] 11), 24-cylinder, inverted-V, liquid-cooled engine developing 2,350hp at take-off, 2,200hp at 12,795ft, driving two, metal, 3-bladed contra-rotating propellers

Dimensions		
Span	13.48m	44.2ft
Length	11.00m	36.1ft
Height	4.24m	13.9ft
Wing area	28m²	301.3ft²
Wing loading	3.47 lb/m²	37.3 lb/ft²
Power loading	2.17kg/hp	4.8 lb/hp

Weights		
Empty	4,050kg	8,929 lb
Loaded	5,100kg	11,244 lb

Performance		
Max speed	690.3km/h at 5,000m	429mph at 16,405ft
Range	1,000km	621 miles
Climb	5 min 30 sec to 5,000m (16,405ft)	
Ceiling	12,000m	39,370ft
Fuel capacity	618 litres	136 gallons

Armament
Two 20mm Ho-5 cannons in the fuselage deck, one 20mm Ho-5 cannon in each wing

Deployment
None. Only one Ki-64 was completed and flown before the end of the war.

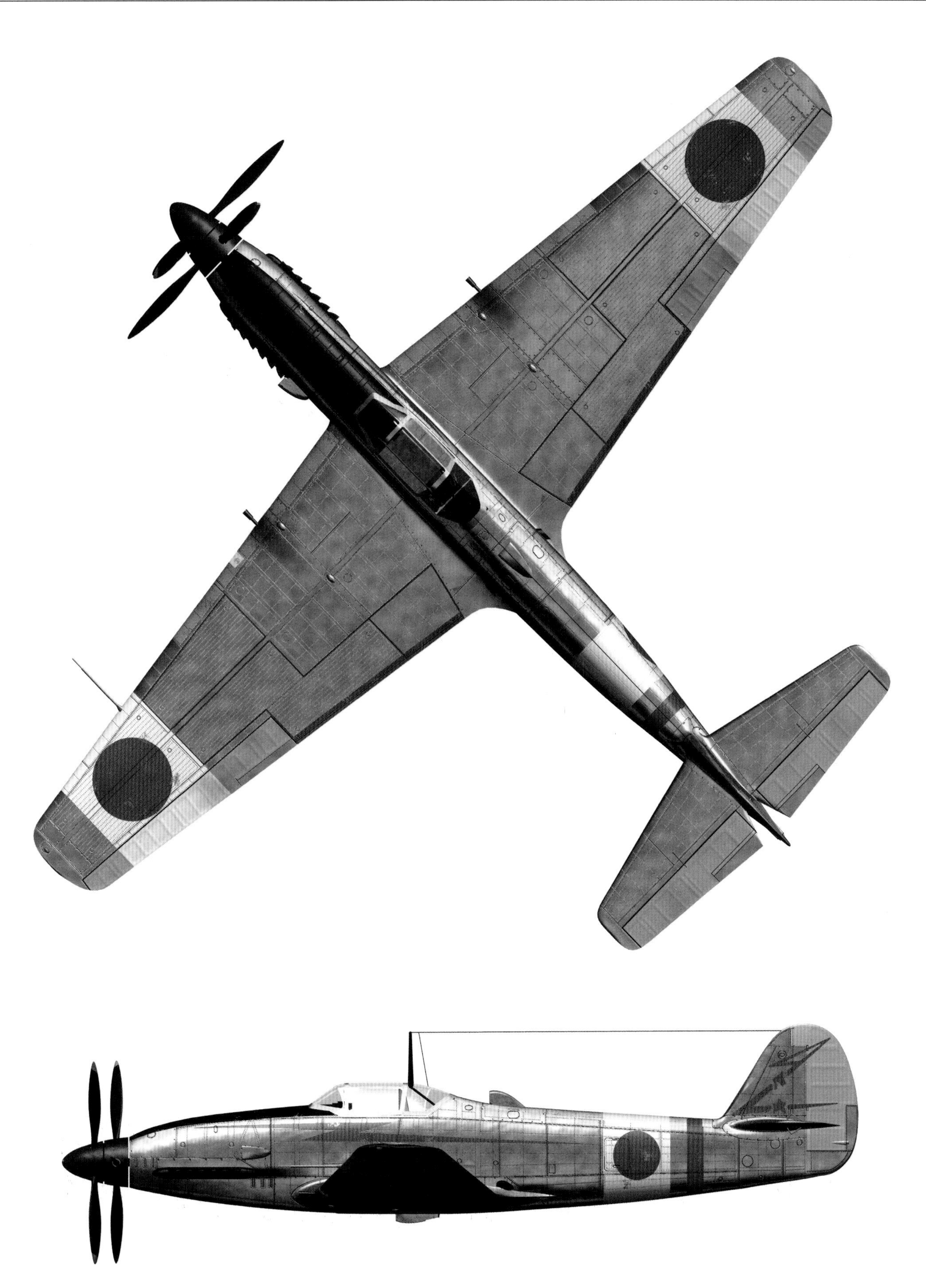

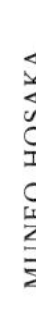
MUNEO HOSAKA

Kawasaki Ki-88

MUNEO HOSAKA

In August of 1942, the IJA saw a need for a aircraft that, in its primary role, would serve as an interceptor flying sorties to defend installations, airfields and other assets that were considered important and therefore subject to enemy attack. Design specifications were drafted by the IJA for the aircraft and it was Kawasaki who put forth what they felt was the answer: the Ki-88.

Prior to drafting their design specifications, the IJA had sifted through a number of ideas before settling on a plane that had to have a heavy armament to ensure it could inflict significant damage to enemy aircraft, especially bombers, and also good handling characteristics to make it not only a stable gun platform, but also to avoid a steep learning curve for new pilots.

To this end, Tsuchii Takeo, a designer for Kawasaki, began work on what would become the Ki-88. Takeo selected a 37mm cannon as the primary weapon, supported by two 20mm cannons. It is probable that the 37mm Ho-203 cannon and two Ho-5 20mm cannons would serve as the armament fit with all three weapons fitted in the nose. Given the size of the Ho-203 (which was a little over 1.53m (5ft) in length, weighing 88.9kg (196 lb)), this presented a problem in squeezing them, along with the engine, into the nose. To get around this, Takeo placed the 1,500hp Ha-140 liquid-cooled, turbo- (or super-) charged engine in the fuselage, behind the cockpit. The three-bladed propeller was driven using an extension shaft that ran from the engine to a gearbox connected to the propeller. In essence, Takeo built the aircraft around the Ho-203.

The main advantage of placing the engine in the fuselage was that it allowed the cannon to fire through the propeller hub, producing a more stable firing platform that resulted in improved accuracy. Another advantage was that it allowed a skilful designer to make the nose more streamlined, enhancing speed performance.

A good number of references infer that Takeo's design was inspired by the Bell P-39 Airacobra. While there is no evidence that specifically states that Takeo simply copied the American fighter, the P-39 was in limited operational use by the time design work began on the Ki-88 in 1942, notably seeing action in the Battle of Guadalcanal. Thus, the Japanese were aware of the design. Whether an example was ever captured for analysis is unknown but certainly intelligence was available on the plane. Or, it may be that Takeo arrived at the same conclusion as did H.M. Poyer, designer of the P-39, when looking at how best to accommodate a large calibre cannon in a single engine aircraft.

In June of 1943, Takeo finalised his design for the Ki-88. Apart from the use of a 37mm cannon and the engine placement, the Ki-88 bore no further resemblance to the P-39. The Ki-88 had a deep fuselage to accommodate the Ha-140 engine that was situated below and to the rear of the cockpit. The air scoop for the Ha-140's radiator was mounted on the bottom of the fuselage, just forward of the wing roots. The radiator itself was positioned back from the scoop on the bottom interior of the fuselage, almost directly underneath the pilot's seat. Jutting out on the left side of the fuselage, just above the trailing edge of the wing, was the scoop to provide air to the turbo- or super-charger of the Ha-140. The landing gear was conventional and the main gear retracted into the wings, while the tail wheel was fixed. A fuel tank was provided in each wing, mounted behind the wheel wells. On either side and to the bottom of the Ho-203 cannon were the Ho-5 cannons.

With the final design complete, work began on a full scale mock-up of the Ki-88 and this was completed sometime in 1943. In addition, work had already begun on construction of the fuselage and wings for a prototype and it was expected that by October

1943 the Ki-88 would be nearing completion. The IJA, however, had other plans for the Ki-88. After inspecting the mock-up and in reviewing the projected performance data of the plane, it was seen that it offered no real advantage over other designs then in operational use, notably the Kawasaki Ki-61 Hien. Thus, Kawasaki was ordered to terminate all work on the Ki-88.

Kawasaki Ki-88 – data

Contemporaries

Bell P-39 Airacobra (US), Bell XFL-1 Airabonita (US), Bell P-63 King Cobra (NATO codename *Fred* in Russian service) (US), Gudkov Gu-1 (Russia)

Type Interceptor
Crew One

Powerplant

One Kawasaki Ha-140, liquid-cooled, turbo- or supercharged engine developing 1,500hp driving a three-bladed propeller

Dimensions

Span	12.37m	40.6ft
Length	10.18m	33.4ft
Height	4.14m	13.6ft
Wing area	27.49m²	269ft²

Weights

Empty	2,949kg	6,503 lb
Loaded	3,899kg	8,598 lb

Performance (specifications are estimations by Kawasaki)

Max speed at 19,685ft	600km/h	373mph
Range	1,198km	745 miles
Climb	6 min 30 sec to 5,000m (16,404ft)	
Ceiling	11,000m	36,089ft

Armament

One 37mm Ho-203 cannon and two 20mm Ho-5 cannons

Deployment

None. The Ki-88 did not progress past a mock-up and partially completed prototype.

MUNEO HOSAKA

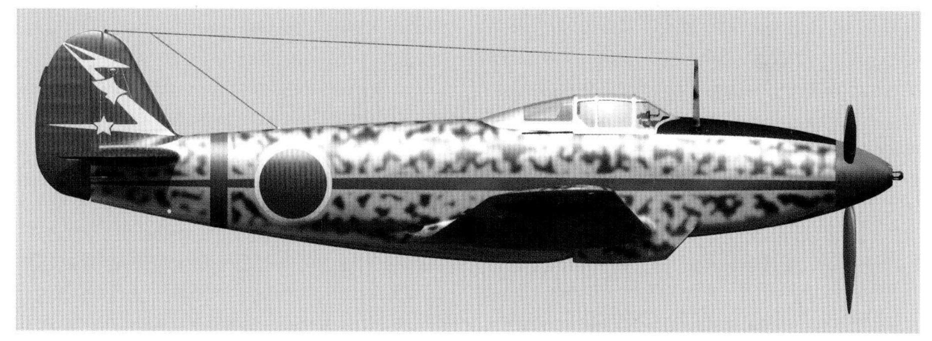

Kawasaki Ki-91

MUNEO HOSAKA

This story centres on the failure of a bomber that inspired the development of another new type. The Nakajima Ki-68 and the Kawanishi Ki-85, both four-engine, long-range bomber designs, hinged on the success of the IJN's Nakajima G5N Shinzan (Mountain Recess). The G5N would prove to be a failure and in turn led to the termination of the Ki-68 and Ki-85 programs; therefore the IJA was left without a long-range bomber project. It was Kawasaki who stepped in to fill the gap with their own design.

In 1938, the IJN was enamoured with the idea of a bomber that was capable of operating up to 6,486km (4,030 miles) from its base. In part, this was due to the initial desire to strike targets deep in Russia from Manchurian bases. Later, when Japan went to war with the United States, a need to attack the US mainland was identified and it was recognised that a two-engine design would not suffice – four engines would be required. On the understanding that the Japanese aircraft industry had very little experience in building such aircraft, the IJN used the Mitsui Trading Company as a cover to acquire a Douglas DC-4E four-engine airliner, ostensibly for use by Japan Air Lines. The development of the DC-4E four-engine passenger aircraft was funded by five airlines and Douglas with United Airlines building and testing the one prototype. While the DC-4E was impressive, in terms of its operating costs it did not add up. The aircraft was complex and this resulted in maintenance issues, which increased the cost of using the plane. Support for the DC-4E was withdrawn and Douglas was asked to simplify the design. As a consequence, the DC-4 saw operational use with the US Army as the Douglas C-54 Skymaster.

In early 1939, the sale of the DC-4E was completed and arrived in Japan to be reassembled. By this time, the IJN had informed Nakajima to be ready to study the DC-4E to produce a suitable bomber development from it. After having been flown several times, the DC-4E was then reported as having 'gone down in Tōkyō Bay', but in reality had been handed over to Nakajima whose engineers took it apart. Within a year, Nakajima had built the prototype G5N1 which first flew on 10 April 1941. The G5N1 used only the landing gear layout, wing design and radial engine fittings from the DC-4E coupled to a new fuselage, tail design and a bomb bay. The IJA planned to produce the G5N1 and Nakajima submitted the Ki-68 version using either the Mitsubishi Ha-101 or Nakajima Ha-103 engines in place of the Nakajima NK7A Mamoru 11 units on the G5N1. Kawanishi also submitted their Ki-85 which was to use the Mitsubishi Ha-111M engines.

As it was, the G5N1 proved to be a dismal failure. The NK7A engines were problematic and underpowered and the aircraft was too heavy and complex. These difficulties contributed to the overall poor performance of the G5N1. Despite the problems, three more G5N1 aircraft were built followed by a further two aircraft that replaced the NK7A engines for four Mitsubishi Kasei 12 engines. The two additional aircraft were designated G5N2, but even the Kasei 12 engines could not resuscitate the design and the problems remained. Due to its complications, the G5N1 was never used as a bomber. Two G5N1 (using Kasei 12s) and two G5N2 aircraft were converted to transports and served in this role until the end of the war. The Allies gave the G5N the codename *Liz*.

By May 1943, the cancellation of the G5N had also brought the demise of both the Ki-68 and the Ki-85 (of which Kawanishi had a mock-up constructed by November 1942), leaving the IJA with no active four-engine

MUNEO HOSAKA

Kawasaki Ki-91 – data

Contemporaries
Focke-Wulf TO 'Transozean' Projekt B (Germany), Focke-Wulf Fw 191C (Germany), Focke-Wulf Fw 300 (Germany)

Type	High-Altitude, Long-Range Bomber
Crew	Eight

Powerplant
Four Mitsubishi Ha-214 Ru, 18-cylinder, supercharged radial engines developing a maximum of 2,500hp; each engine to drive a four-bladed propeller

Dimensions		
Span	47.9m	157.4ft
Length	32.97m	108.2ft
Height	9.99m	32.8ft
Wing area	223.99m²	2,411.11ft²

Weights		
Empty	33,999kg	74,955 lb
Loaded	57,999kg	127,865 lb

Speed		
Max speed	580km/h at 9,808m	360mph at 32,180ft
Range	9,000 to 10,000km	5,592 to 6,213 miles
Climb	20 min 30 sec to 8,000m (26,246ft)	
Ceiling	13,500m	44,291ft

Armament
Twelve 20mm cannons, two cannons each in one of four turrets located in the nose, underside of the forward fuselage and top and bottom of the aft fuselage respectively. A fifth turret mounted the remaining four cannons. Standard bomb load 4,000kg (8,816 lb) (perhaps up to 8,000kg (17,636 lb) for shorter ranged missions)

Deployment
None. Prototype 60 per cent complete by the end of the war.

bomber designs on the table. Kawasaki, seeing the opportunity, immediately got to work on designing a new bomber. The man behind the Ki-91 was Takeo Doi, an engineer employed by Kawasaki. It was his goal to see the development of a successful four-engine bomber and engineer Jun Kitano would work with Doi to help turn the aircraft into reality. In June 1943, Doi and Kitano began their initial research and by October, work on the first design concept for the Ki-91 was underway.

The Ki-91 was slightly larger than the Boeing B-29 Superfortress which was to be mass produced in late 1943. Four Mitsubishi Ha-214 18-cylinder radial engines were chosen to power the Ki-91. As the plane was expected to operate at high-altitude, provisions were made to utilise superchargers with the engines and the projected maximum speed was 580km/h (360mph). To provide for the anticipated 10,001km (6,214 mile) range, each wing carried eight fuel tanks with a further two mounted in the fuselage above the bomb bay. For weapons, the Ki-91 was to carry a heavy armament of twelve 20mm cannons. Five power-operated turrets were to be used; one in the nose, one on the underside of the forward fuselage, one above and below the aft portion of the fuselage, and the last in the tail. The bottom turrets were remotely controlled while the remainder were manned. The tail turret was to mount four cannons while the rest had two cannons each. As far as bombs, a total payload of 4,000kg (8,818 lb) was envisioned and the Ki-91 was to have a tricycle landing gear with the nose gear using a single tyre and the main landing gear using dual tyres. A semi-recessed tail wheel was also installed.

Another feature of the Ki-91 was to be the use of a pressure cabin for the eight man crew. But the development of such a large pressurised cabin for the Ki-91 was expected to take some time to implement, even using knowledge from another of Doi's designs, the Kawasaki Ki-108, a twin-engine high-altitude fighter fitted with a pressure cabin for the pilot. Therefore, it was decided that the initial Ki-91 prototype would be built without pressurisation so as to avoid holding up development and allow its flight characteristics to be measured. Once the pressurised crew cabin for the Ki-91 was ready, subsequent aircraft were to have it installed.

In April 1944, a full-scale wooden mock-up was completed and Kawasaki invited IJA officials to come and review the Ki-91. Up until this time, the project was a private venture by Kawasaki to which considerable company resources has been allocated. If the IJA did not find the bomber to their liking, it would have been a waste of time, effort and money. Fortunately, the IJA saw potential in the Ki-91 and work continued. In May, the IJA inspected the Ki-91 mock-up and immediately ordered production of the first prototype. Kawasaki planned to construct the Ki-91 at a new plant in Miyakonojō in Miyazaki Prefecture. However, the IJA did not want to wait for the construction of a new plant and directed Kawasaki to use their established factory in Gifu Prefecture. By June 1944, the construction of the prototype Ki-91 had begun at the Gifu factory, together with the necessary tools and jigs to produce further aircraft.

However, June would see the first B-29 raids over Japan, but as the attacks were few and far between, work on the Ki-91 continued despite the worsening situation for the country. This would change by the close of 1944 when B-29s began to operate from the Mariana Islands and by 1945 bombing raids were far more frequent. In February 1945, a raid heavily damaged the factory in which the Ki-91 prototype was being constructed. The damage was extensive, ruining the tools and jigs. With the loss of equipment needed for future production coupled with dwindling supplies of aluminium, the IJA decided that fighters to combat the marauding B-29s had become a higher priority than bombers. Any hope of utilising such bombers was at best slim. With the Ki-91 at 60 per cent completion, Kawasaki stopped further work on the bomber and the project was officially cancelled in February 1945.

Had the Ki-91 achieved service, plans to attack the US mainland were in place to operate the bomber from the Kurile Islands using temporary bases, while another plan to strike Hawaii was formulated using bases in the Marshall Islands. The second plan was rendered obsolete when the Japanese lost the Marshall Islands to the Allies in February 1944. As a note, contemporary images sometimes show the Ki-91 as having a bomb bay battery of downward firing cannons for a ground-attack role. While the Japanese were interested in such concepts, there is no evidence that Kawasaki envisioned such a task for the Ki-91.

MUNEO HOSAKA

Kayaba Katsuodori

RONNIE OLSTHOORN

The Katsuodori depicted here is shown in the colours and markings of the 71st Sentai. It is intercepting Tōkyō-bound Northrop B-35 bombers of the 44th Bomb Squadron, 40th Bomb Group operating from Tinian.

Kayaba envisioned that his design for a fast, point defence interceptor would sweep through the Allied bombers like the katsuodori bird hunts for fish. Impressed with the prowess of the katsuodori, Kayaba named his design after the bird. But as we will see, his vision was to meet with a harsh reality.

The genesis of the Kayaba Katsuodori began as far back as 1937 with the Kayaba Ramjet Study Group, a collection of engineers and scientists who sought to investigate ramjet propulsion in Japan. The concept of the ramjet was actually patented in 1908 by French engineer René Lorin, but it was the Russian I. A. Merkulov who first built and tested one, the GIRD-04 in 1933. A ramjet is a very basic engine with few moving parts. In simple terms, it uses the high pressure air generated by the aircraft's forward motion and forces it through the inlet. The air is then mixed with combusted fuel – this heats the air and is forced out of the rear of the engine, providing forward propulsion. Unlike pulsejets (which were to be used on the Kawanishi Baika, see Page 61), the fuel flow is continuous. Without getting into the specifics of a ramjet, adjustments in the design of the inlet (to maximise the intake of air), combustor (to ensure effective operation during flight movements) and the outlet nozzle (to effect acceleration increases) all come into play on designing such an engine. The main drawback with a ramjet engine is that at subsonic speeds its performance is poor. Below 612km/h (380mph), a ramjet suffers significant loss in speed and becomes highly inefficient in terms of fuel consumption. The ramjet typically requires another power source to bring the aircraft up to the speed at which the ramjet can operate efficiently. Typically, this speed is at least 966km/h (600mph). Once the ramjet reaches that speed the engine is self-sufficient and, without fuel injection moderation, would propel the plane to speeds far in excess of the design's ability to handle the high temperatures and Mach number.

The Kayaba Ramjet Study Group saw the benefits of high speed with a relatively easy to manufacture engine. The group produced two test models before the final product, the Kayaba Model 1 ramjet, was realised. The Model 1 was projected to be able to offer speeds of 900km/h (559mph). With the engine complete, all that was needed was the aircraft to fit it into.

The airframe design began with Kumazō Hino. Hino was an officer in the IJA and had been the first Japanese to unofficially make a flight on 14 December 1910 when he accidentally took to the air in a Hans Grade monoplane while he was taxiing. This aircraft had been purchased from Germany. His interest in aviation saw him produce four aircraft designs: the Hino No. 1, No. 2 and the No. 3 and No. 4 Kamikaze-go airplanes. However, each of these designs was a failure. Pressure from his military superiors saw Hino give up on aviation by 1912.

However, in 1937, Hino was inspired to create a tailless glider. The project was taken over by the Kayaba Seisakusho (Kayaba Manufacturing Works) and then by Dr. Hidemasa Kimura who worked for the Aeronautical Research Institute of the Tōkyō Imperial University under Dr. Taichiro Ogawa. The result was the HK-1. The HK-1 (standing for Hino Kumazō) was built by the Itō Hikōki K.K. and was completed in February 1938. It was purely a research glider to test the tailless concept. Testing commenced in December 1938 with ground towing at Kashima in Ibaraki Prefecture and the first air released flights began in September 1939 at Tsudanuma in Chiba Prefecture. Because it showed positive results, the IJA took an interest in the concept. The HK-1 was purchased by the Rikugun Kokugijutsu Kenkyūjo in April

1940 for continued testing. However, a subsequent test flight on 16 April by an IJA officer pilot resulted in a hard landing that damaged the HK-1 beyond repair. In all, 182 flights had been made in the HK-1.

With the IJA still interested, the Rikugun Kokugijutsu Kenkyūjo set aside 200,000 yen to continue the project. Kimura, along with Kayaba's chief development designer Dr. Shigeki Naitō, set about the task of producing a new tailless aircraft, this time with a possible military application. The result was the Ku-2. The Ku-2 had no tail but rudders were fixed to the wing tips and the design was tested extensively from November 1940 through to May 1941 making 270 flights in all before it was damaged in a crash on 10 May. To further test the concept, Kimura (with the aid of Jōji Washimi) produced the Ku-3 which had no vertical control surfaces at all and featured a cranked delta wing form to test various angles of sweep. The only control came from the flaps arranged along the wings. 65 flights were carried out with the single Ku-3 before a crash in 1941 wrecked the glider.

The last design put forward by Kimura was the Ku-4. At the request of the Rikugun Kokugijutsu Kenkyūjo, the Ku-4 was to be powered and a rear mounted 120hp de Havilland Gipsy 4-cylinder, air-cooled, inline engine was selected, turning a two-bladed propeller. Unfortunately for Kimura, the IJA lost interest in the entire concept. With the loss of the Ku-2 and the Ku-3, the IJA cancelled the Ku-4 before it could be finished. With no backing, Kayaba could not afford the 100,000 yen to finish the Ku-4 alone. The IJA had paid Kimura and Kayaba 17,000 yen out of the 200,000 yen project money for costs associated with the Ku-2, Ku-3 and what was already paid into for the Ku-4. The remaining funding was not released. Shirō Kayaba, however, still had hopes that the concept could be a potent weapon and from this came the Katsuodori.

The roots of the Katsuodori come from the Ku-2. Unlike the Ku-2, the wings were moved higher on the fuselage and the wing form had a rearward sweep. The Katsuodori retained the vertical wingtip rudders used on the Ku-2. The ramjet filled most of the fuselage which meant there was no room for landing gear. Instead, a main skid was incorporated on the underside of the fuselage along with a small wheel mounted at the rear of the aircraft. Without integral landing gear, the Katsuodori was to be fitted with a simple, sprung set of landing gear that could be jettisoned when the aircraft took to the air. The pilot sat towards the front of the fuselage and was provided with a one piece canopy that offered respectable visibility to the front and sides.

In order to get the Katsuodori off the ground, Kayaba envisioned the use of four rocket booster units. Secured to each side of the fuselage under the wings were two rocket units and together all four could provide an estimated 7,200kg (15,873 lb) of thrust. The planned procedure for using the rockets was to have one on each side being fired first, and when these had burned out the next pair would be fired. Each rocket contained propellant for five seconds of thrust and, all told, the scheme would give the Katsuodori a total of ten seconds of thrust with which to get the plane off the ground and the ramjet functioning. Kayaba estimated that the Katsuodori would need to achieve 367km/h (228mph) before the ramjet would operate and certainly the speed provided by the rocket units would have been sufficient for this to happen. The rockets, once used, may or may not have been releasable but the latter is likely in order to minimise drag.

With the ramjet operating, the estimated performance of the Katsuodori was a speed of 900km/h (559mph) and a climb rate of three minutes to reach an altitude of 10,000 (32,808ft). Fuel load was 1,500kg (3,306 lb) and with a fuel consumption of 50kg (110 lb) per minute would grant a combat endurance of thirty minutes. Once the fuel was exhausted, the Katsuodori would use its gliding properties to return to base.

For weapons, Kayaba planned on mounting two 30mm cannons externally, one under each wing near the wing root. Kayaba did not wish to use existing 30mm cannon designs such as the Ho-155 preferring to produce a 30mm version of the 40mm Ho-301 cannon which his manufacturing facilities were constructing for use in the Ki-44-II Hei Shoki fighter. The Ho-301 used caseless ammunition with each round being, in effect, a rocket. The propellant cavity was partially lined with a thin aluminium cap. When the primer was struck, the propellant was ignited and the pressure would build up until the cap burst, the exhaust gas being vented out the back of the round to move the projectile forward. The main advantage of the weapon was its light weight for such a heavy calibre.

The design of the Katsuodori was nearly complete by 1943 and Kayaba anticipated that he could have had a flying prototype by 1944. By this time, however, the IJA was already involved with the rocket powered Ki-200 (the IJA version of the IJN's Mitsubishi J8M1 Syūsui – see Page 96) and so paid no attention to the Katsuodori. Kayaba, in trying to salvage the design, stated that he could adapt the Katsuodori to accept the Kūgishō Ne 20 turbojet or the KR10 rocket motor as used in the Ki-200. And since his design was nearly complete a prototype Katsuodori could be ready for testing before the Ki-200.

The advantages of the Katsuodori included a ramjet that was far less complex to construct than a turbojet. This would have been a critical asset in a Japanese war industry that was devastated by US bombing. It could also use standard aviation fuel, unlike the Ki-200 that required special fuels, and by extension, could operate from any airfield without the need of special fuelling apparatus and procedures. While the speed of the Katsuodori was on par with the Ki-200, the Katsuodori's combat endurance was far superior to the Ki-200 and the IJA's own planned rocket interceptor, the Rikugun Ki-202 Syūsui-Kai (see Page 40).

However, the Katsuodori had several drawbacks. The first was the use of the rocket boosters to get the plane up to speed. The Japanese did not have a successful track record for using such units. Improper placement of rocket boosters was the reason behind the aborted second flight of the Nakajima Kitsuka (Page 114), heavily damaging the aircraft. Attempts to use rocket boosters on the Mitsubishi Ki-109 to boost take-off and climb met with such poor results that the rockets were removed from the Ki-109 development all together. A misfire or variation in the thrust output might result in the plane careering out of control. Like the Ki-200, once fuel was exhausted the Katsuodori lost its speed advantage, and on the ground its recovery would take longer since the Katsuodori could not move on its own without means of wheeled apparatus. This made it vulnerable to intruder aircraft dedicated to airfield interdiction missions. Kayaba's election to use a 30mm version of the Ho-301 cannon would have been a recipe for disaster. The 40mm version, as used in combat by the Japanese, had an incredibly short range – only 149.5m (490ft) since it had a muzzle velocity of 241m/sec (790ft/sec). Coupling the very short range of such a weapon with a high closure rate due to the speed of the Katsuodori against a slow bomber, the pilot would have had mere seconds or less to line up the target, fire, and then bank to avoid collision. Since Kayaba did not proceed with a 30mm variant of the Ho-301, the muzzle velocity for the round is unknown but it cannot have been substantially more than the Ho-301.

Despite the potential advantages over the Ki-200, the Katsuodori would never see life outside plans on Kayaba's design board. The IJA was looking to the Ki-200 and their own Ki-202 for their interceptor needs and thus ended Kayaba's dream of seeing his Katsuodori taking to the skies to defend Japan.

PETER ALLEN

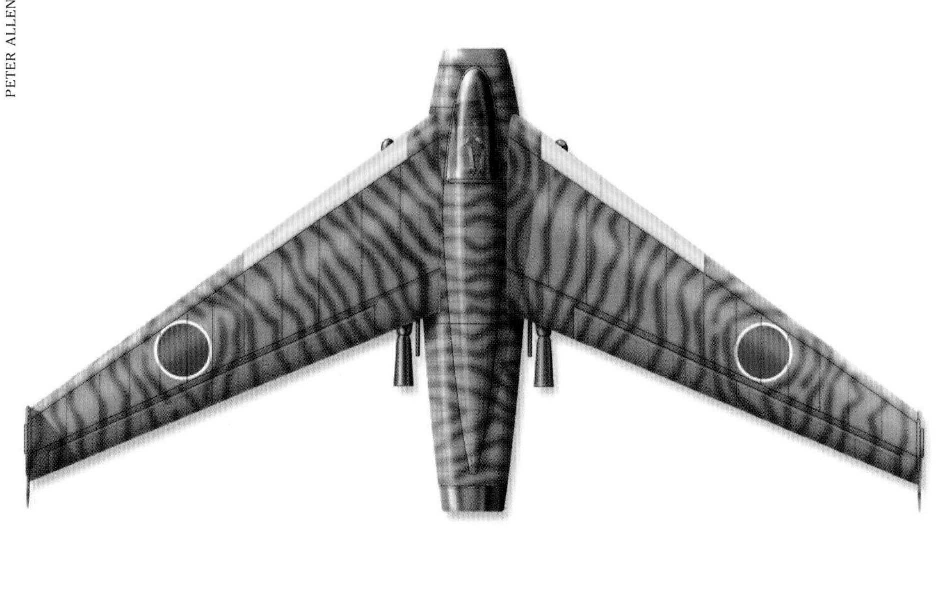

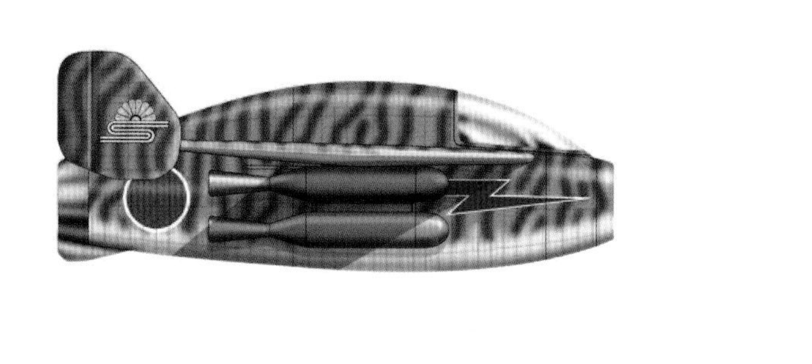

Kayaba Katsuodori – data

Contemporaries

Handley Page H.P.75 Manx (UK), BOK-5 (Russia), Blohm und Voss P.210/P.215 (Germany), Heinkel P.1078 (Germany), Northrop XP-56 Black Bullet (US), Northrop XP-79 Flying Ram (US), Skoda-Kauba SK P.14.01 (Germany), Lippisch Li P.13a (Germany), Messerschmitt Me P.1101L (Germany), Heinkel He P.1080 (Germany), Stöckel Rammschussjäger (Germany), Leduc Model 010 (France), Kostikov 302 (Russia)

Type	Point Interceptor
Crew	One

Powerplant

One Kayaba Model 1 (or possibly later) ramjet producing 300kg (661 lb) of thrust at 367km/h (228mph), 420kg (925 lb) of thrust at 490km/h (304mph), 550kg (1,212 lb) of thrust at 612km/h (380mph) and 750kg (1,653 lb) of thrust at 734km/h through 1,103km/h (456mph through 685mph)

Dimensions		
Span	8.99m	29.5ft
Length	4.48m	14.7ft
Height	1.85m	6.1ft
Wing area	12.57m^2	135.4ft^2
Wing sweep	25.5°	

Weights		
Empty	850kg	1,873 lb
Loaded	3,000kg	6,613 lb

Performance		
Max speed	900km/h	559mph
Landing speed	100km/h	62mph
Range	400km	248 miles
Climb	3 min to 10,000m (32,808ft)	
Ceiling	15,000m	49,212ft

Armament

Two 30mm cannon

Deployment

None. The Katsuodori did not advance beyond the drawing board.

Kokusai Ta-Go

RONNIE OLSTHOORN

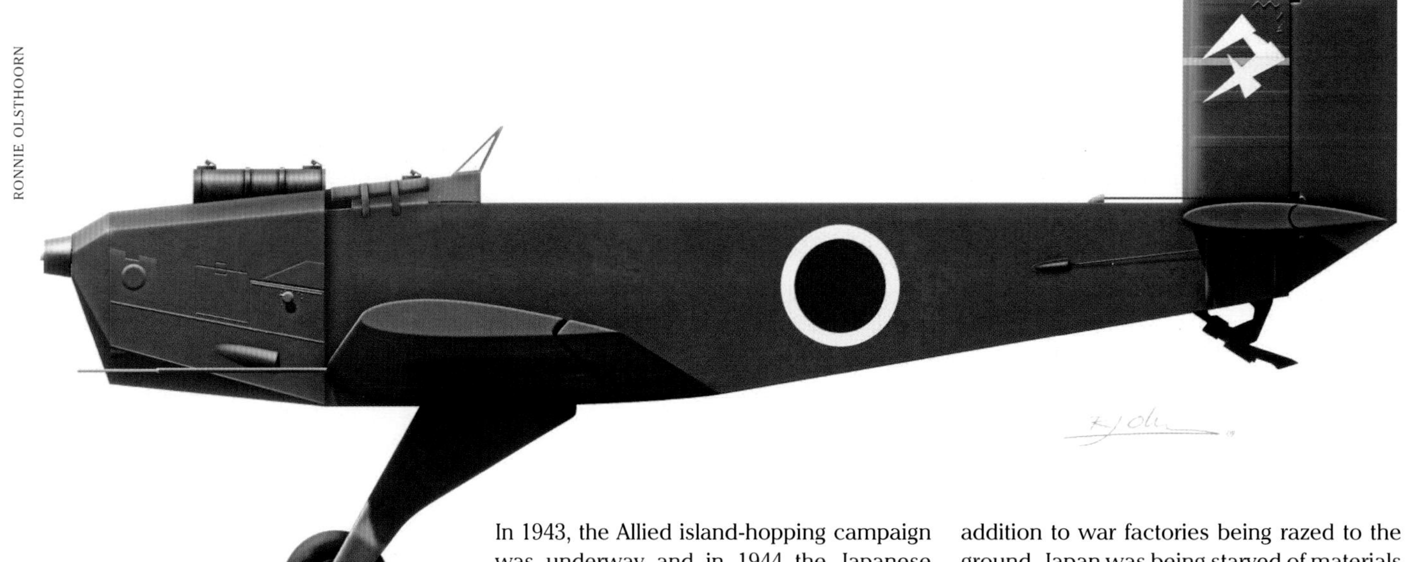

The profile depicts the Kokusai Ta-Go prototype in the colours it actually sported.

In 1943, the Allied island-hopping campaign was underway and in 1944 the Japanese would see their island outposts, bases and strongholds destroyed and lost to them forever. In 1945, the Japanese lost their holdings in Burma, Borneo, Iwo Jima and Okinawa. Japanese military planners had no doubts that the Allies would continue their progress and land forces on the main islands of Japan. The Allies did indeed have such a plan known as Operation Downfall. The Japanese, to defend against the invasion they felt was coming, put into motion Ketsugō Sakusen or Operation Decision.

Operation Decision's main component was the use of shimpū and shimbu missions targeting the Allied naval force, specifically landing craft, troop ships and support ships. To repel the invaders, all manner of craft were assembled for the Japanese defender of kokutai, the national polity of self sacrifice. Midget submarines such as the Kairyū, Koryū and the crude U-Kanamono, the Kaiten human torpedo, small explosive laden powerboats like the Maru-Ni (IJA) and Shinyo (IJN), and even frogmen (the Fukuryu) were prepared for the final showdown. Even the best tanks, the Type 3 Chi-Nu and Type 4 Chi-To, were held in Japan to counter Allied armour. Aircraft would also play a significant role in the defence of Japan. It was estimated that 10,000 aircraft of every type would be available to throw at the Allied invasion fleet. It was thought that the mass wave tactics would result in a tremendous loss of aircraft which the Japanese industry in 1945 would be unable to keep pace with unless steps were taken to remedy such a situation. The Ta-Go was one such remedy.

By 1945, Japanese industries were under regular bombardment from US airpower. In addition to war factories being razed to the ground, Japan was being starved of materials needed to sustain weapon production. Aluminium was a key material in aircraft production and it was estimated that by December 1945, even with strict control, the supply of this metal would be exhausted. Consequently, wood was to become the main material for aircraft construction, regardless of the type of aircraft concerned. Examples included the Tachikawa Ki-106 (a wooden version of the Nakajima Ki-84 Hayate) and the Kūgishō D3Y Myōjō (which was the wood derivative of the Aichi D3A *Val*). With the loss of heavy industrial machinery, it fell more and more to smaller workshops to produce components and sub-assemblies for aircraft. Often the labour force was not as skilled as before and working with wood was easier as it did not require the sophisticated tools and jigs necessary for construction of more conventional aircraft using metal components.

Captain Yoshiyuka Mizuyama, an officer in the IJA's aviation equipment section, was the man behind the Ta-Go (Ta being short for take-yari, or bamboo spear). It was his desire to design and build a plane that was simple in construction, used the bare minimum of war critical materials and could be produced rapidly. By doing so, the Ta-Go could quickly populate the aircraft pool available to units destined for shimbu missions and also replenish losses in short order. He hoped that the Ta-Go could be used to defend the seaside cities of Ōsaka and Kōbe. In an effort to help realise the Ta-Go, Mizuyama approached the Tachikawa Hikōki K.K. with his concept. Despite Mizuyama being an IJA officer, Tachikawa refused to assist him as his plan had no official sanction and was not approved by the Koku Hombu. As such, Tachikawa could not spare the capacity to develop the aircraft.

Undeterred, Mizuyama discovered a small shop in the city of Tachikawa within which he and his fellow men went about the task of designing and constructing the first prototype. Once the concept was completed, work began on building the Ta-Go. Using wood lathes to construct the fuselage and other components, the aircraft was made from plywood while fabric was used for some of the skinning and coverings for the control surfaces. The pilot was given a simple acrylic glass canopy. Instrumentation was kept to the bare minimum. The landing gear was fixed. For a motor, a Hitachi Ha-13 Ko 9-cylinder, air-cooled radial engine developing 450hp was selected, the cowling for it being made from plain sheet steel. The only armament was a single 500kg (1,102 lb) bomb. In February 1945, the Ta-Go prototype was nearly complete when Tachikawa was subjected to a bombing raid. In the ensuing attack, the shop was burnt to the ground and the Ta-Go inside destroyed.

Despite the setback Mizuyama forged ahead, going to Nippon Kokusai Kogyo K.K. (Japan International Air Industries Co. Ltd.) to pitch his Ta-Go. In the end the project was accepted and in part this may have been due to Kokusai's experience with light aircraft such as the Ki-76 (known as *Stella* by the Allies) and the Ki-86 Ko (codenamed *Cypress*), the latter of which Kokusai had built as the prototype all-wood Ki-86 Ōtsu. Of course, Kokusai was not as heavily taxed by wartime demands from either the IJA or the IJN and could thus allocate some assets to the development of the Ta-Go. Despite Kokusai taking on the Ta-Go project, it still remained an unofficial design and thus bore no Ki number.

Mizuyama's design for Kokusai differed from the one he proposed to Tachikawa because the new version was significantly scaled down and much smaller. In so doing, this reduced the amount of assemblies needed to produce the aircraft which, by extension, lowered the man-hours required to build it. Fewer assemblies meant less use of construction materials. With the resizing, the Ha-13 radial became too large for the proposed airframe and so the Hitachi [Ha-47] 11 inline engine, rated at 110hp, was selected as a replacement. This same engine was used in the Tōkyō Koku Ki-107 all-wood two-seat trainer which was to be the replacement for the Ki-86 had the former made it into service.

In addition to the size reduction, steps were taken to simplify the Ta-Go even more. Gone was the canopy and the pilot sat in a open cockpit with only a small acrylic glass windscreen as protection from the elements. For instrumentation, only the absolute basics were used consisting of a speedometer, altimeter, compass and the essential engine related gauges such as fuel and oil. The fuselage was slab sided and box shaped. While this granted easier construction, it was not the most aerodynamic design. Much of the fuselage used wood sparring and structure while the skinning was of plywood. The wings were low mounted with squared wing tips and they were hinged just outside of the landing gear to enable them to fold upwards to allow the aircraft to be hidden in caves as well as facilitate their construction within the confines of caves or small manufacturing lines. Both the vertical stabiliser and the horizontal stabilisers were rectangular in shape.

The landing gear was fixed, being made of steel tubing and fitted with rubber wheels, each gear supported by a single strut. To provide a modicum of streamlining the tubing that made up the landing gear was faired over using aluminium. The only measure of shock absorption came from the tyres and the tail skid, the latter also being built from steel tubing with a portion rubberised.

The [Ha-47] 11 engine was fitted with an angular plywood cowling, the engine driving a fixed-pitch, two-bladed wooden propeller. A metal engine mount was used while the fuel tank was situated on top of the engine and used a gravity feed system. Behind the tank and in front of the windscreen was a simple oil cooler, mounted flush in the fuselage. Given the much smaller dimensions of the revised Ta-Go, it was no longer able to carry the 500kg (1,102 lb) bomb Mizuyama's original version was designed for. Instead, it could only carry a 100kg (220 lb) bomb. The bomb was fitted to the underside of the fuselage and once in place could not be released by the pilot.

Mizuyama, with the assistance of his own men and Kokusai, had completed the first prototype of the new Ta-Go by the middle of June 1945 and it was made ready for flight. On 25 June, the Ta-Go took to the air for the first time with a Kokusai test pilot at the controls. Not surprisingly, the pilot reported handling concerns. After a number of additional test flights, revisions were made to the design. Once complete, Kokusai created a complete set of working blueprints for the production version. However, with the cessation of hostilities in August 1945, the Kokusai Ta-Go never entered production. The close of the war also saw the end of two Kokusai developments of the Ta-Go, known as the Gi-Go and Tsu-Go. Both remain shrouded in mystery because no information on them has surfaced to date.

Ironically, Tachikawa would return to the Ta-Go when the Gunjushō (Ministry of Munitions) authorised development of Mizuyama's initial design following the completion of the Kokusai Ta-Go prototype. The end of the war would find the Tachikawa Ta-Go prototype incomplete. As a note, with the acceptance of the Ta-Go by the Koku Hombu, a project number (meaning a Ki number) was assigned to the Ta-Go – Ki-128. It has not yet been confirmed whether this Ki number applied to the Kokusai Ta-Go, the Tachikawa Ta-Go or both.

Ta-Go – data

Contemporaries
Messerschmitt P.1104 Sprengstoffträger (Germany)

Specifications are for the Kokusai Ta-Go.

Type	Special Attack Aircraft
Crew	One

Powerplant
One Hitachi [Ha-47] 11, 4-cylinder, air-cooled inline engine developing 110hp for take-off driving a wooden, two-bladed propeller 7.1ft in diameter

Dimensions		
Span	8.90m	29.2ft
Length	7.40m	24.3ft
Height	3.87m	12.7ft
Wing area	5.10m²	54.9ft²
Wing loading	34.66kg/m²	7.1 lb/ft²

Weights		
Empty	345.5kg	761 lb
Loaded	585.5kg	1,290 lb

Performance		
Max speed	195km/h	121mph
Cruise speed	179km/h	111mph
Range	150km	93 miles
Ceiling	4,600m	15,091ft

Armament
One 100kg (220 lb) bomb

Deployment
None. A total of three Ta-Go aircraft were constructed: Mizuyama's own prototype aircraft that was destroyed by fire prior to flight, the one built and flown at Kokusai, and the Tachikawa Ta-Go which remained incomplete at the end of the war.

Maeda Ku-6

Interest in airborne forces can be traced as far back as 1917 because they can provide several tactical advantages. Being air dropped, parachute troops can be deployed into areas not easily accessible by ground forces as well as bypassing defences meant to hinder or repel attacks from specific avenues of approach. Also, the ability to place troops anywhere on the battlefield requires the enemy to use assets to protect against such operations, thereby spreading defending forces thinner. Such advantages come at a cost, however. Airborne forces typically do not have the firepower of comparable ground forces nor the ability to remain independent for long before outside support must be obtained.

Airborne troops were used by all of the major warring powers in World War 2 and special equipment and weapons were created for use by these units in an attempt to provide them with heavier firepower. Artillery such as the US Army M1A1 75mm pack howitzer and the German 7.5cm LG 40 recoilless gun were air-droppable and the troops used modified or special small arms such as the US M1A1 .30cal carbine and the Japanese Type 2 Paratroop rifle. Despite such weapons, airborne forces were deficient in one critical area: armoured vehicles. The ability to provide airborne troops with armoured support such as tanks was one sought by all the warring powers and tank designs did emerge. The key problem was how to send in the tanks with the troops during an operation. One of the first solutions was the glider tank.

The Japanese would create and utilise airborne forces during World War 2. The IJA called their forces the Teishin Dan (Raiding Brigades) while the IJN had the Rikusentai. Both would be used first in 1942 during the fighting in the Dutch East Indies. Unlike the Germans, British and Americans, the Japanese did not provide their paratroopers with a significant amount of specialised heavy weapons. In part, this may have been due to the fact that the Japanese parachute forces would rarely be used in their designated role. Instead, much of their fighting would be done as light infantry (much like the German Fallschirmjägers). Nevertheless, the IJA and IJN were considering ways to improve the striking power of their paratroopers and one such plan was a tank borne into battle on wings.

In 1943, the IJA set the wheels in motion to investigate a flying tank. The Army Head Aviation Office in league with the Fourth Army Research Department drafted the initial concept for the weapon. The aviation research section of Maeda was tasked with producing the wings that would form the glider portion of the weapon and the Army Head Aviation Office assigned the designation Ku-6 to the glider. The tank was to be designed and built by Mitsubishi and called the So-Ra (or Sora-Sha, literally 'sky tank'). To ensure there was no confusion, the Army Head Aviation Office called the entire combination the Kuro-Sha (taking the 'Ku' from Ku-6 with 'ro' meaning 6 and the 'Sha' for tank).

Mitsubishi's So-Ra was, due to the purpose for which it was intended, a tankette design. With a crew of two (driver/pilot and the commander/gunner), the So-Ra was to weigh 2,812kg (3.1 tons). The turret was set behind the driver/pilot compartment and was provided with three large, hinged ports to allow

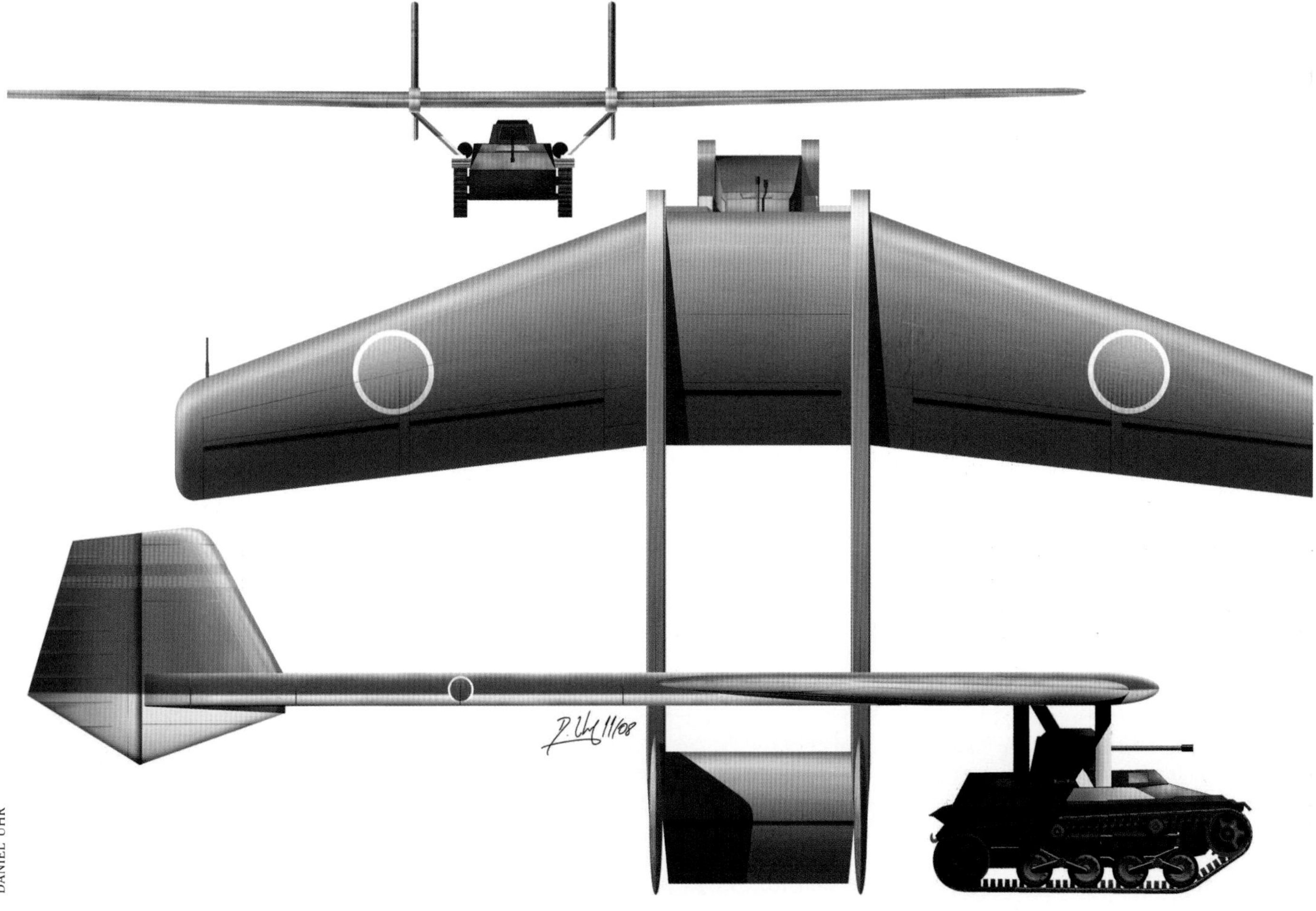

DANIEL UHR

some measure of vision for landing. Armour was likely very light and was certainly less than the 6mm-12mm armour protection of the Type 95 Ha-Go light tank then being used by Japanese airborne forces. Three weapon fits were proposed for the So-Ra. The first was a 37mm cannon (such as the 37mm Type 94 used in the Ha-Go), the second consisted of a machine gun armament (either a light weapon like the 7.7mm Type 97 machine gun or a heavier calibre) and the third was a flamethrower. Power was to come from an air-cooled engine producing 50hp that was estimated to give the So-Ra a maximum road speed of 42km/h (26mph).

The glider portion, the Maeda Ku-6, has been interpreted in at least two ways since the original design is not known, the documents either having not survived the war or have yet to be discovered. One version shows the wings secured to the So-Ra at the hull, on either side of the turret, with a tail boom fitted to the rear of the tank. A horizontal stabiliser sat on top of the vertical stabiliser. The driver/pilot moved the control surfaces via wires that ran into the tank. On the hull front was the tow cable attachment point. The second version has the So-Ra fitted with struts on the hull sides. Atop the struts was the main wing to which twin tail booms were fitted with a low mounted horizontal stabiliser connecting the vertical stabilisers. In essence, the So-Ra would hang below the wing. On landing, the tank would shed the wings and move into action with the paratroopers.

By 1945, the Ku-6 had been completed and Mitsubishi had produced a full scale mock-up of the So-Ra. Flight testing was conducted for a brief period and it is likely that the mock-up was used, suitably weighted to simulate the 2,812kg (3.1 tons) of an operational So-Ra. The So-Ra was to be towed by a Mitsubishi Ki-21 bomber. Tests soon showed the difficulty of the concept. The Kuro-Sha suffered from in-flight control problems, the driver/pilot had poor vision and landing was extremely difficult. Another concern was that the So-Ra could not stand up to heavier and more powerful tanks. Any usefulness the Ku-6 may have possessed was minimised with the advent of the Kokusai Ku-7 Manazuru (meaning 'Crane') glider that began development in 1942. First flown in August 1944, the Ku-7 was able to carry a 7,257kg (8 ton) tank within its fuselage which was more than enough to hold the 6,713kg (7.4 tons) of the Ha-Go light tank. With the Kuro-Sha's problems evident, the IJA terminated any further work on the Kuro-Sha favouring the Ku-7.

Maeda Ku-6 – data

Contemporaries

Antonov A-40 (or KT for Kryl'ya Tanka, flying tank) (Russia), Raoul Hafner's Rotabuggy and Rotatank (UK), Baynes Bat (UK), John Walter Christie's M1932 (US)

Specifications are based on the second variation of the Kuro-Sha, with the So-Ra beneath the wing.

Type	Glider (Ku-6)		
Powerplant	None		
Dimensions			
Span		21.97m	72.1ft
Length		14.96m	41.9ft
Height		2.98m	9.8ft
Wing area		59.99m^2	645.83ft^2
Weights			
Loaded (with the So-Ra)		4,200kg	9,259lb
Performance			
Max glide speed		174km/h	108mph
Armament		None	

Type	Tankette (So-Ra)		
Crew	Two		
Powerplant			
One 4-cylinder, air-cooled, gasoline engine developing 50hp at 2,400rp			
Dimensions			
Width		1.43m	4.7ft
Length		4.05m	13.3ft
Height		1.88m	6.2ft
Weights			
Loaded		2,900kg	6,393lb
Performance			
Max speed		42km/h	26mph
Armament			
One 37mm cannon, machine gun or flamethrower			
Armour	Unknown		
Deployment			
None. Only one prototype built and flown.			

Manshū Ki-98

DANIEL UHR

In late 1942, the Koku Hombu was looking for a number of new aircraft types as improvements on those in service. These included a heavy fighter capable of conducting ground attack operations and a high-altitude fighter. Nakajima and Tachikawa were tasked with the latter, coming up with designs that would later result in the Ki-87 and Ki-94 respectively (see Pages 28 and 53). For the former, Kawasaki attracted the interest of the Koku Hombu with their multi-role Ki-102. However, Kawasaki's design was not to go uncontested and the competition would come from a relatively small aviation company.

Manshūkoku Hikōki Seizo K.K. – the Manchurian Aeroplane Manufacturing Company Ltd., and better known as Manshū, a contraction of the kanji 'Man' in Manshūkoku and 'Hi' in Hikōki – was founded in 1938. Manshū was a subsidiary of Nakajima Hikōki K.K. and produced the Nakajima Ki-27 (codenamed *Nate* by the Allies) and the Nakajima Ki-84 (*Frank*) for the company. Manshū would produce few of their own designs and only one ever saw service, the Ki-79 advanced trainer. Manshū's main plant was located in Harbin in the Japanese puppet state of Mǎnzhōuguó. On learning of the Koku Hombu's desire for new aircraft, Manshū sought to put together a proposal to meet the fighter requirement. The company assigned their two best men to the project, engineers Noda and Hayashi, and what resulted was an aircraft that was far from the conventional types Manshū had worked on in the past.

The aircraft was a single-engine fighter with a pusher, twin-boom configuration. The heart of the plane was to be a Mitsubishi Ha-211-III 18-cylinder, air-cooled radial engine fitted within the fuselage and behind the cockpit. The four-bladed propeller, situated at the very rear of the fuselage, was driven by a 2m (6.5ft) long extension shaft. In order to maintain a well streamlined airframe no air scoops were used; instead, flush inlets were fitted along the top of the fuselage behind the canopy. To increase the flow of air to the engine, a fan driven by the engine was installed. Flush outlets forward of the propeller completed the air circuit across the engine. The thin wings were mounted low and on each wing was a boom that ended in an ovoid vertical stabiliser. A single, high mounted horizontal stabiliser connected the two tails.

A tricycle landing gear system was used, the nose gear retracting backwards into a wheel well that ran underneath the cockpit. Each of the two main wheels retracted into their respective tail booms. As the aircraft sat very high off the ground, the pilot had to access the cockpit via a hatch in the nose wheel well. If the pilot had to bail out, he had two choices. He could leave in a conventional fashion, but had to contend with both the twin tails and horizontal stabiliser along with the propeller. Manshū recommended that the pilot egress through the hatch out of the bottom of the aircraft. This method allowed the pilot to avoid being dashed on the tail but still had to contend with the propeller. Nevertheless, the chances of lowering the nose gear, sliding down and out through the hatch in a stricken plane were slim and Manshū were aware of this flaw in the design. The canopy was a bubble type that afforded an excellent field of view. For weapons, two Ho-5 20mm cannons and one Ho-204 37mm cannon were installed in the nose. Due to the short length of the fuselage, the barrels for the cannons, especially the Ho-204, protruded out from the nose.

Once the preliminary design for the fighter had been completed, Manshū submitted it to the Koku Hombu. Despite the unorthodox approach, it was accepted as the Ki-98 and work was allowed to proceed. Interestingly, the Koku Hombu rejected Tachikawa's Ki-94-I that was similar in concept to the Ki-98. With approval in hand, the draft for the Ki-98 was finalised by July 1943. Work then commenced on a wooden mock-up that was completed in December. Design work continued into the beginning of 1944 further refining the Ki-98. A scale model of the aircraft were constructed and sent to Japan for wind tunnel testing at Rikugun Kokugijutsu Kenkyūjo. Unfortunately for Manshū, the worsening war situation saw some of their personnel called into service or shifted to other departments and this, coupled with a plethora of design revisions, saw work on the Ki-98 slow down. Nevertheless, wind tunnel tests showed excellent results and Manshū began to make the preparations to construct the first prototype.

In the spring of 1944, the Koku Hombu instructed Rikugun Kokugijutsu Kenkyūjo to tell Manshū that the Ki-98 should be adapted to serve as a high-altitude fighter. This they did, sending Manshū suggestions for design changes to the Ki-98 to make it suitable for the new role. On receiving the news Manshū had to substantially alter its initial design to meet the new demands. With strained manpower and resources, the mandated changes set the Ki-98 program further back and scuppered plans to build the prototype.

One of the most important changes was the need to fit an engine with a turbosupercharger resulting with the Ha-211-III being replaced by the Mitsubishi Ha-211 Ru which incorporated this feature. As the turbosupercharger was exhaust driven it required the appropriate additional piping, which, of course, was not originally included. The new engine was therefore larger than the original and this made it necessary for the fuselage to be lengthened and slightly widened. As the new propeller had a larger diameter, the twin booms had to be moved further apart to accommodate the blades and, by extension, the wings had to be reworked as well. Finally, the airframe had to be strengthened to support the heavier weight. Another alteration was to offer the pilot a more suitable way to bail out of the aircraft. Given the extreme difficulty in having to drop the nose wheel to gain access to the well hatch, the revised Ki-98 incorporated explosive bolts that shed the tail unit to allow the pilot to exit more conventionally. The weapon fit remained unchanged.

With the new specifications in hand, the Ki-98 design was reworked and redrafted but it would not be until October 1944 that the redesign was completed to be followed by a mock-up of its revised fuselage. Manshū expected to have the first prototype finished and ready for flight testing by early 1945. These plans were dashed following a US bombing raid on Manshū's Harbin factory on 7 December 1944. It was not until January 1945 when work commenced on the Ki-98. Despite Manshū attempts to increase the pace of construction work, progress still lagged.

At the start of August 1945, the fuselage, wings and the tail booms were completed and were ready to be assembled. However, on 8 August 1945, the Soviet Union declared war on Japan and initiated its invasion of Mǎnzhōuguó the next day. With the Mǎnzhōuguó Imperial Army and the Japanese Kwantung Army unable to stem the tide of Soviet forces, Manshū ordered all relevant documentation including models, mock-ups, jigs, tools and the incomplete Ki-98 to be destroyed to prevent the aircraft and information on it being captured by the Soviets.

Manshū Ki-98 – data

Contemporaries
Arkhangelskiy BSh (Russia), Saab 21 (Sweden), Vultee V.78 (US), Bell XP-52 (US)

Performance specifications are estimates based on Manshū's projections.

Type	High Altitude Fighter
Crew	One

Powerplant
One Mitsubishi Ha-211 Ru 18-cylinder, air-cooled radial engine with a turbosupercharger developing 2,200hp for take-off, 1,960hp at 2,000m/6,561ft and 1,750hp at 8,500m/27,887ft driving a four-bladed, metal, 3.6m/11.8ft diameter propeller

Dimensions		
Span	11.24m	36.9ft
Length (total)	11.39m	37.4ft
Boom length	8.26m	27.1ft
Height	4.29m	14.1ft
Wing area	23.99m	258.3ft²
Wing loading	187.48kg/m²	38.4 lb/ft²
Power loading	2.72kg/hp	6 lb/hp

Weights		
Empty	3,500kg	7,716 lb
Loaded	4,500kg	9,920 lb

Performance		
Max speed	731km/h at 10,000m	454mph at 32,810ft
Climb	5 min 30 sec to 5,000m (16,404ft)	
Range	1,249km	776 miles
Endurance	2 hours 15 min at 499km/h (310mph)	
Ceiling	10,000m	32,808ft

Armament
One Ho-204 37mm cannon and two Ho-5 20mm cannons

Deployment
None. The only prototype was never completed and was destroyed to prevent capture.

RONNIE OLSTHOORN

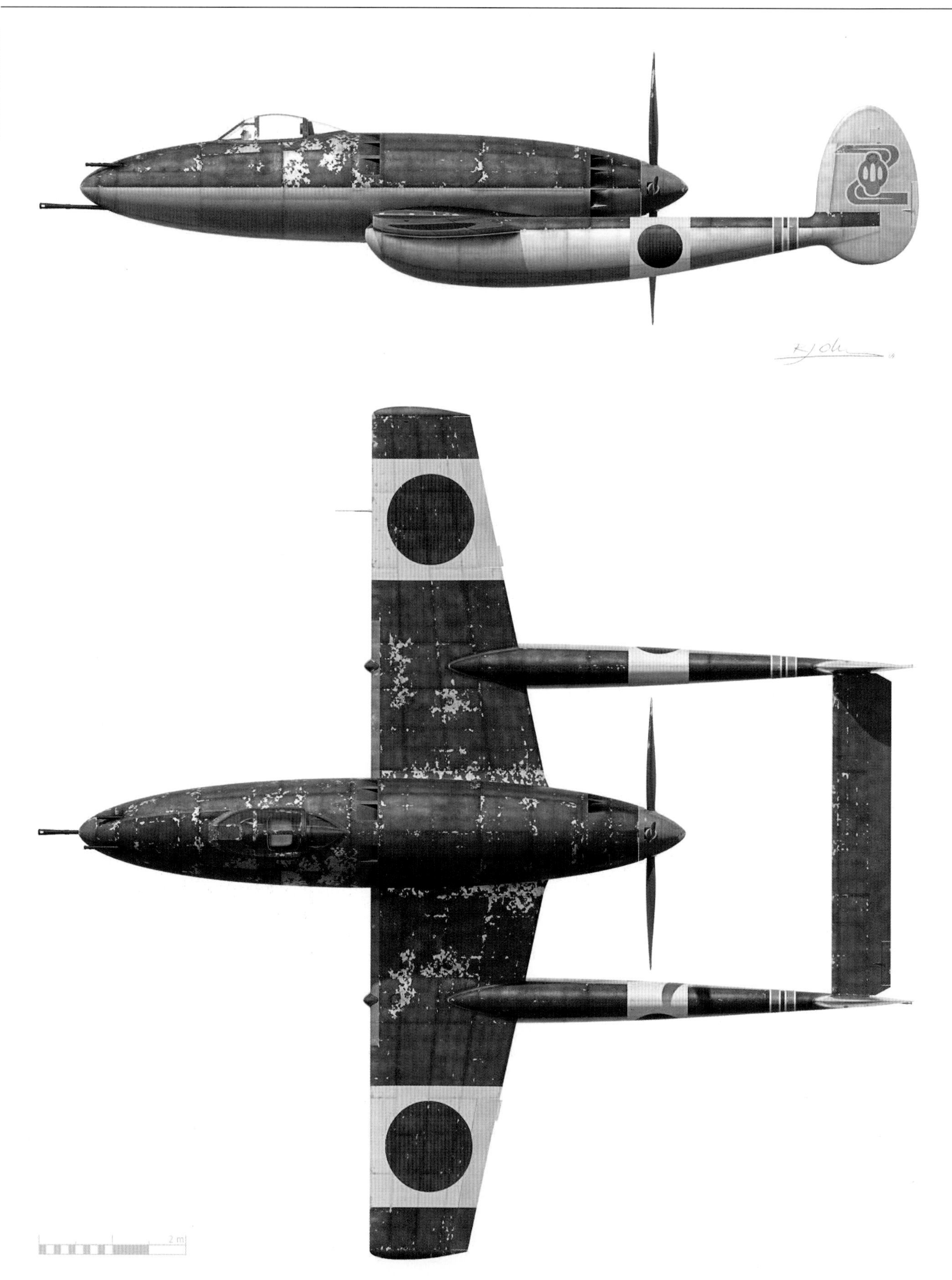

Mitsubishi Ki-73

In 1943, the Koku Hombu issued a specification for a fighter capable of operating for long distances in order to act as an escort for bomber formations. Despite the defensive weapons Japanese bombers carried, they were still vulnerable to interception. If a fighter had the extended range, it would be able to protect the bomber formations by being able to engage enemy interceptors and allow as many bombers as possible to survive and deliver their bomb loads. It was this desire that fuelled the Koku Hombu to issue their specification and from which Mitsubishi would build the aircraft to meet it.

Mitsubishi's Tomio Kubo, along with engineers Kato, Sugiyama and Mizuno, began the investigation on how best to meet the specifications. They settled on using a single engine design and the heart of it would be the Mitsubishi Ha-203-II engine. This was a 24-cylinder, horizontal-H, liquid-cooled engine that was projected to generate 2,600hp. The Ha-203-II was chosen due to its horizontal-H configuration – in essence, two flat engines placed one on top of the other and geared together (a flat engine is one in which the pistons move horizontally). Each flat engine had its own crankshaft. Although horizontal-H engines have a poor power-to-weight ratio, they offer the advantage of being more compact, which made the Ha-203-II the ideal choice for the aircraft, now designated the Ki-73.

Unfortunately, Mitsubishi was having a very difficult time with the Ha-203-II. In fact, because of the relative complexity of the horizontal-H design the engine experienced near constant problems during its development. Ultimately Mitsubishi was unable to overcome these difficulties and abandoned the Ha-203-II. Due to the delays and eventual cancellation of the engine, Kubo's Ki-73 design was abandoned even before he and his team could produce a mock-up, let alone a prototype. Even though the Ki-73 went nowhere, Allied intelligence was aware of this new project. Information obtained from various sources, including captured documents, led intelligence officers to conclude that the Ki-73 would see service. As such, in 1944, the Ki-73 was assigned the codename *Steve*. As it was, no Allied pilot would ever encounter the Ki-73 in any form.

What Allied pilots might have encountered had the war gone on would have been the Mitsubishi Ki-83. Not discouraged by the Ki-73's demise, Kubo would go on to design the twin-engine Ki-83 to meet Koku Hombu's specification. The result was a highly capable aircraft that would have provided a challenge to Allied air power. However, only four Ki-83 prototypes were built before the end of the war.

Very little is known to show what the Ki-73 looked like. The artwork depicted for the Ki-73 in this book is based on an interpretation of the Ki-73 printed in Richard Bueschel's 1966 book *Japanese Code Names*. The illustration was based on the Ki-83 on the assumption that Tomio Kubo would have used aspects of the Ki-73 in the Ki-83. *Steve* is shown here in the markings and colours of the 101st Sentai.

Mitsubishi Ki-73 – data

Contemporaries
Consolidated Vultee XP-81 'Silver Bullet' (US), North American P-51D 'Mustang' (US), Lavochkin La-11 (NATO codename *Fang*) (Russia), Westland Wyvern (UK)

Specifications
Outside of the intended engine and the aircraft's role, specifications on the Ki-73 are unknown

Deployment
None. The Ki-73 never advanced past the concept stage.

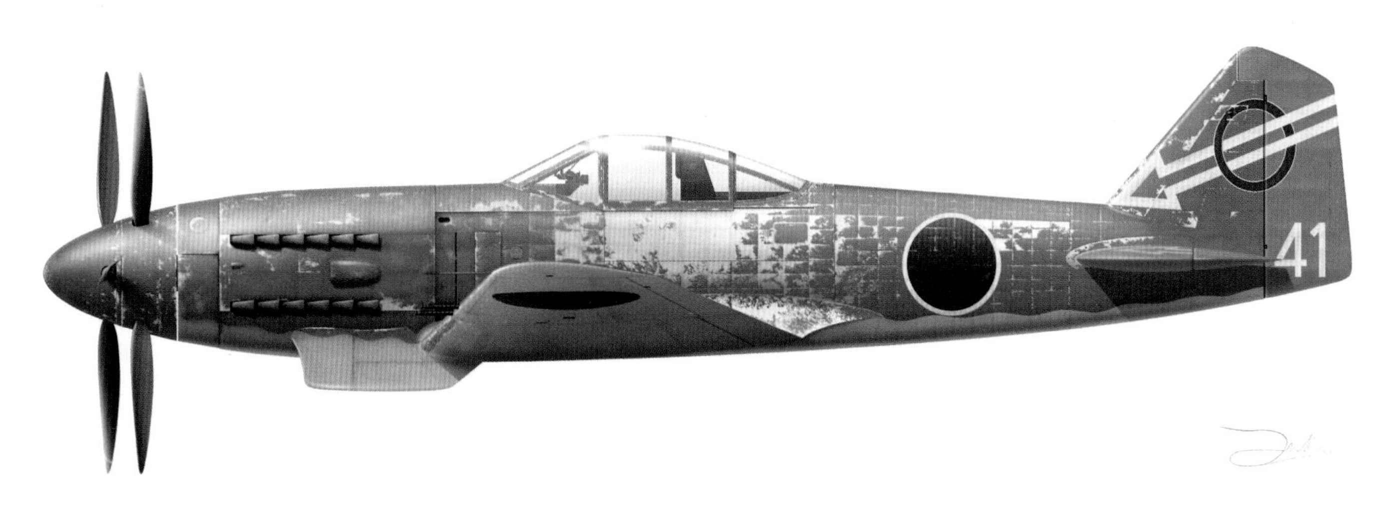

KELCEY FAULKNER

Nakajima Ki-87

MUNEO HOSAKA

Altitude is a major factor in an engine's performance and, by extension, the aircraft as a whole. Known as density altitude, the higher the altitude, the less dense the air. The effects of this manifest themsleves in lower wing lift, a reduction in propeller efficiency and reduced horsepower output from the engine. As such, a plane that was not designed to operate in such conditions suffers accordingly. The Koku Hombu sought an answer to the problem and Nakajima looked to provide the solution. The result was the Ki-87.

In mid-1942, the Koku Hombu drew up a set of specifications for a high-altitude fighter. These called for a plane capable of operating at high altitude, heavily armed with a maximum range of 3,000km (1,864 miles) and capable of 800km/h (497mph). Examination of the specifications called into question the viability of meeting such performance expectations. After deliberation, they were revised. The role remained the same but the speed requirement was dropped entirely to the point that no mention was made at all for a minimum or maximum speed. The range requirement was adjusted to one hour of loiter flight time in addition to a half hour of combat flight time up to 800km/h (497 miles) from the airfield that the aircraft operated from. Finally, a heavy armament requirement called for two 30mm cannons and two 20mm cannons.

With these new specifications, Nakajima was contracted in November 1942 to produce three prototypes and seven pre-production aircraft for the IJA. The prototypes were to be completed between November 1944 and January 1945 with the pre-production planes finished between February and April 1945. The design of the Ki-87 was headed by Kunihiro Aoki.

Nakajima initially selected the Nakajima [Ha-44] 11 18-cylinder radial engine as the heart of the Ki-87. The [Ha-44] 21 (known also as the Ha-219 Ru) was also considered but the [Ha-44] 11 would be the engine used in the first prototype. Both engines were rated at 2,400hp and each used a turbosupercharger that would maintain and enhance the engine's power output at altitude. A turbosupercharger is an air compressor used to force air induction to the engine. It does this by having a turbine and a compressor linked together via a shared axle. Engine exhaust spins the turbine which in turn spins the compressor which draws in outside air, compresses it and then directs the air to the intake manifold of the engine. This compressed air, delivered at high pressure, results in more air reaching the cylinders for combustion. The net effect of this is that at higher altitudes where the air is thinner, the turbosupercharger allows the engine to function as if it was at a lower altitude where the air is heavier and thus engine performance is not adversely affected. A benefit of this is that because the air is thinner at higher altitudes, there is less drag on the aircraft and since the turbosupercharger preserves the horsepower of the engine, overall speed is improved.

A sizable portion of the aircraft's forward fuselage was taken up by the [Ha-44] 11 engine assembly and the large turbosupercharger was fitted to the starboard side of the fuselage, just ahead of the cockpit. To cool the engine, a sixteen-bladed fan was mated to the four-bladed, constant speed propeller, turning at 150 per cent of the propeller speed.

The engine reduction gear ratio was set at 0.578. As the Ki-87 was designed for high altitude operation, the pilot was to be provided with a pressurised cockpit (though the prototype was not equipped with one).

For weapons, Nakajima kept to the specifications mounting a 20mm Ho-5 cannon in each wing root, synchronised to fire through the propeller, and a 30mm Ho-155 cannon in each wing to the outside of the main landing gear wheel wells. Ammunition was stored in the inner wing near the fuselage. Hydraulic pressure was used to load the cannons and they were fired by electrical triggers. If required, provision was made to carry a 250kg (551 lb) bomb or a drop tank along the centreline. Because of the heavy weapon fit and to ensure enough room for the self-sealing wing fuel tanks, Nakajima designed a landing gear arrangement that was rare in Japanese aircraft development – the main landing gear struts would retract backwards and the wheels would rotate 90° to fit flush into the wheel wells.

Given the task the Ki-87 had to perform, Nakajima provided a degree of protection for the pilot in the form of 66mm thick, bullet proof glass in the front of the canopy and back protection via armour plate 16mm thick. To extend the range of the Ki-87, two 300 litre (79 gallon) drop tanks could be fitted under each wing beside the landing gear wells. The pilot could jettison them via electrically controlled releases and these could be used in conjunction with centreline payloads.

As work progressed on the Ki-87, the IJA saw fit to change the design by insisting that the turbosupercharger be placed in the rear of the fuselage beginning with the third preproduction Ki-87. Nakajima protested against

MUNEO HOSAKA

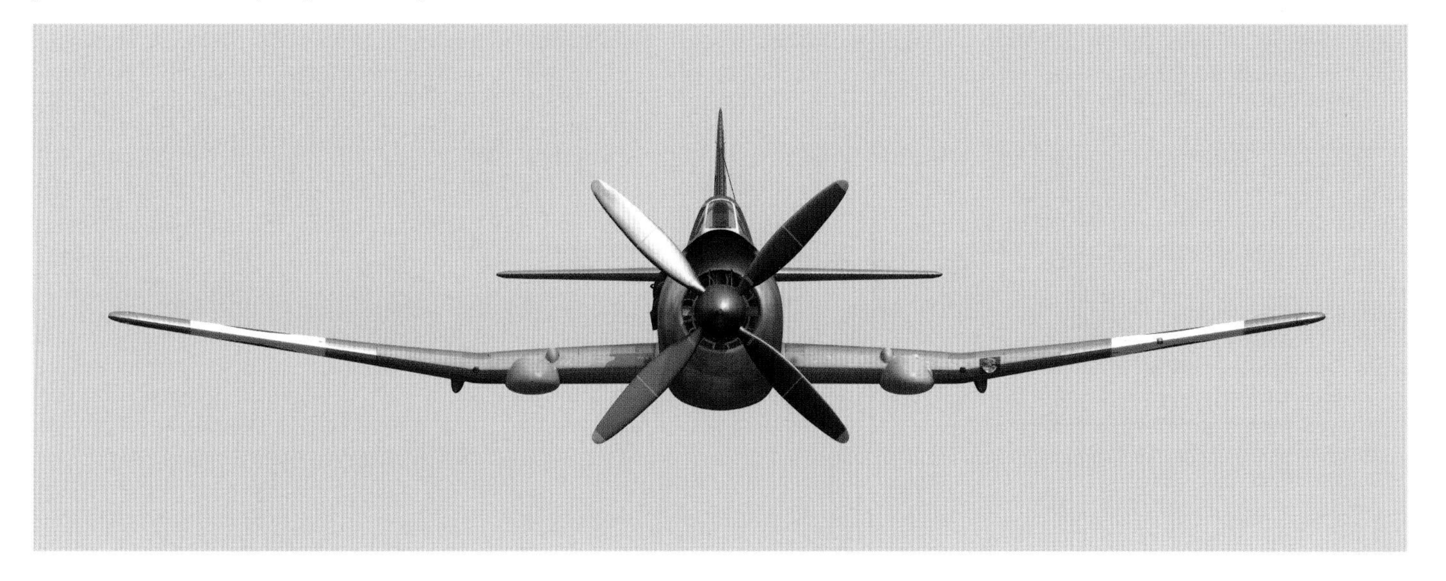

Nakajima Ki-87 – data

Contemporaries Sukhoi Su-1 (Russia)

Because the Ki-87 was not flown to its full ability, the performance statistics are estimates made by Nakajima.

Type High-Altitude Interceptor
Crew One

Powerplant One Nakajima [Ha-44] 11, 18-cylinder, air-cooled radial developing 2,400hp for take-off, 2,200hp at 1,500m/4,920ft, 2,050hp at 6,000m/19,685ft and 1,850hp at 10,500m/34,450ft and driving a constant speed, 4-bladed propeller

Dimensions

Span	13.41m	44.0ft
Length	11.79m	38.7ft
Height	4.48m	14.7ft
Wing area	25.99m²	279.8ft²
Wing loading	216.29kg/m²	44.3 lb/ft²
Power loading	2.35kg/hp	5.2 lb/hp

Weights

Empty	4,387kg	9,672 lb
Loaded	5,632kg	12,416 lb
Maximum	6,100kg	13,448 lb

Performance

Max speed	707km/h at 11,000m	439mph at 36,090ft
Endurance	2 hours	
Climb	14 min 12 sec to 10,000m (32,810ft)	
Ceiling	12,855m	42,175ft

Armament
Two 30mm Ho-155 cannons, Two 20mm Ho-5 cannons and provision for one 551 lb bomb

Deployment
None. Only one Ki-87 was completed and test flown with two others incomplete before the war ended.

Survivors
Nakajima Ki-87 (FE-153)
This was the only Ki-87 to fly, having the serial 8701. Captured at the IJA air base at Chofu, the Ki-87 (nicknamed 'Big Boy' by the men who saw the large aircraft) was crated and shipped to the US, appearing on 10 March 1946 at MAMA. Under restoration for the museum, the Ki-87 was soon moved to Park Ridge. However, after 1 May 1949 (the last written report documenting the aircraft) all trace of the Ki-87 disappeared, a likely victim of the cutter's torch.

Nakajima Ki-87 (FE-155)
It has been surmised that FE-155 was, in fact, a typographical error made on a later report concerning FE-157 (see below). On the flip side, it may be that the FE-155 entry was a correction and that FE-157 as listed on the earlier report was designated in error. In either case, only two of the Ki-87 aircraft reached the US.

Nakajima Ki-87 (FE-157)
FE-157 was, most likely, the second of the two remaining Ki-87 prototypes found incomplete when the war ended. Listed as FE-157 on 10 March 1946 at MAMA, the plane would later reappear on a 1 August 1946 report as FE-155 and was located at the AOAMC in Newark, New Jersey.
No further trace of this Ki-87 exists after the August report and the aircraft was most probably scrapped.

the change but could do little to sway the IJA on the matter. In addition, the third prototype Ki-87 would have a reduction gear ratio set at 0.431 and the seventh pre-production Ki-87 was to feature a cooling fan that spun faster to facilitate enhanced engine cooling.

Despite the worsening war situation, Nakajima was able to complete the first prototype, c/n 8701, by February 1945 rolling it out from their Ōta Plant. Problems with the electrical system that operated the landing gear and difficulties with the turbosupercharger delayed flight testing. It was not until April 1945 that the Ki-87 was able to take to the air. Due to the issues with the landing gear, Nakajima forbade the test pilot from retracting the main gear lest it fail in the up position, thereby damaging or destroying the Ki-87 with the resultant belly landing. This, however, prevented any chance of a thorough evaluation of the Ki-87's top speed and full manoeuvrability. Consequently, there was no attempt to monitor and collect performance data. During the five flights the prototype did make, the pilot reported good handling characteristics and it was thought that the Ki-87 was superior in comparison to the Nakajima Ki-84 Hayate (*Gale*).

Even as testing of the Ki-87 was underway with work continuing to meet the IJA turbosupercharger position requirement, Nakajima designers developed the Ki-87-II. Replacing the [Ha-44] 11 would be the Nakajima [Ha-46] 11 (known also as the Ha-219) that could provide 3,000hp. The turbosupercharger was situated in the belly of the fuselage as demanded by the IJA. Performance estimates showed a 4 per cent increase in speed compared to the Ki-87.

Ultimately, the Ki-87's design team failed to overcome the problems with its engine. Because they were unable to solve difficulties with both the turbosupercharger and the [Ha-44] 11 as well as the temperamental landing gear system, the Ki-87 would make no more test flights. When hostilities ceased the other two prototypes remained incomplete and the Ki-87-II was still on the drawing board.

MUNEO HOSAKA

Nakajima Ki-115 Tsurugi

KELCEY FAULKNER

By 1945, Japan was reeling from one defeat after another in the face of the Allied advance. With the possibility of an Allied invasion looming in the minds of Japanese military leaders and planners, several means to repel the invaders were considered, investigated, and in some cases, allowed to proceed towards a finalisation. One of the ideas developed was to use aircraft for shimbu (suicide) missions against the invasion fleet. Airworthy aircraft of any type were to be thrown against Allied shipping. In order for the missions to succeed, wave attacks were envisioned, involving scores of aircraft. Sheer numbers would ensure successful hits on naval ships and landing craft even in the face of heavy anti-aircraft fire and combat air patrols. Even one aircraft that struck a ship had the potential to cause significant damage. Such mass attacks, however, led to the conclusion that the available pool of aircraft would quickly be depleted. Thus, it was clear that an airplane had to be designed that could be built rapidly to swell the number of aircraft available for these shimpū missions. It was Nakajima that would provide one answer.

On 20 January 1945, the IJA issued specifications for an aircraft that could be built by semi-skilled labour, would use very few war critical materials, had the ability to accept any radial engine with a 800hp to 1,300hp rating, was easy to maintain in the field, was able to carry at least one bomb and had a maximum speed of at least 340km/h (211mph) with landing gear and 515km/h (320mph) without landing gear. Nakajima was tasked with making the specifications a reality and engineer Aori Kunihiro was assigned the project. Kunihiro would have assistance from the Mitaka Kenkyūjo (Mitaka Research Institute) and Ōta Seisakusho K.K. (Ōta Manufacturing Co Ltd).

Because semi-skilled workers would be used to build Kunihiro's aircraft, the Ki-115 Ko was simplicity itself. The fuselage used a steel structure with steel panelling and centre sections with tin used for the engine cowling. The tail was made of wood with fabric covering while the slightly swept wings were of metal with stressed skinning on the outer wing surfaces. The Ki-115 Ko could accept a variety of radial engines and to simplify the installation only four bolts were used to secure the engine to the fuselage. The Nakajima [Ha-35] 23 (Ha-25) radial engine was used on the prototype Ki-115 Ko and would be found on the subsequent production aircraft. The pilot was provided with an open cockpit with simple instruments and controls. A crude aiming sight was provided as well. The landing gear could be jettisoned after take-off, had no suspension outside of the balloon tyres and was made out of pipes. For weapons, the Ki-115 Ko carried only a single bomb and this was held in a recess under the fuselage between the wings. The heaviest bomb that could be carried weighed 800kg (1,764 lb) and the bomb had no provision for release from the cockpit.

In March 1945, the prototype of the Ki-115 Ko, called the Tsurugi (which means 'sword' or 'sabre'), was rolled out and flight testing commenced. As soon as the trials had started problems began to surface. The landing gear contributed to poor ground handling and this was compounded by the poor view afforded the pilot. Once in the air, the flight characteristics of the Ki-115 Ko were anything but stellar and even skilled test pilots had some difficulty in flying the aircraft, let alone a pilot with minimal training. Nevertheless, given the mission of the Ki-115, flight trials continued while modifications were investigated to improve the aircraft. By June 1945, the initial flight testing was completed. Two further changes were made to the Ki-115 Ko and this involved adding suspension to the landing gear and including auxiliary flaps to the inboard trailing edge of the wings. Production models of the Ki-115 were to be fitted with two solid-fuel rockets, one under each wing. The purpose of the rockets was to boost the speed of the aircraft during the final, terminal dive on the target. With the Ki-115 Ko deemed acceptable, Nakajima began production of the Tsurugi at both their Iwate and Ōta plants. The IJA anticipated that 8,000 aircraft per month would be assembled from production lines scattered throughout Japan.

Even with production underway, steps were being taken to further simplify the Ki-115. To save on precious metals, the wings of the Ki-115 Ko would be replaced with wooden versions and the wing area increased. To better address pilot vision, the cockpit would be moved forwards. The version of the Tsurugi was to be designated the Ki-115 Ōtsu. A variation of the Ki-115 Ko was the Ki-115-III (also known as the Ki-115 Hei). The only two modifications was the provision of a bomb release and cockpit being moved even further forwards. But even these models would not be the end because the Ki-230, a further development of the Ki-115, was also investigated.

The IJN, having learned of the new plane, became interested in the Ki-115 and sought to produce it for themselves. To facilitate this, Nakajima provided Showa Hikōki K.K. (Showa Aeroplane Co Ltd) with two Ki-115 Ko aircraft. In IJN service, the aircraft was to be called the Toka, meaning Wisteria. Showa was to adapt the design to accept any number of IJN radial engines from older, refurbished motors to ones then in current service.

By the time the war ended, Nakajima had only been able to produce 104 of the Ki-115 Ko (22 from the Iwate plant and 82 from the Ōta plant) and none would be used in anger. Neither the Ki-115 Ōtsu, Ki-115-III or the Ki-230 would be constructed, remaining forever as design board projects. Likewise, Showa had no time to produce the Toka.

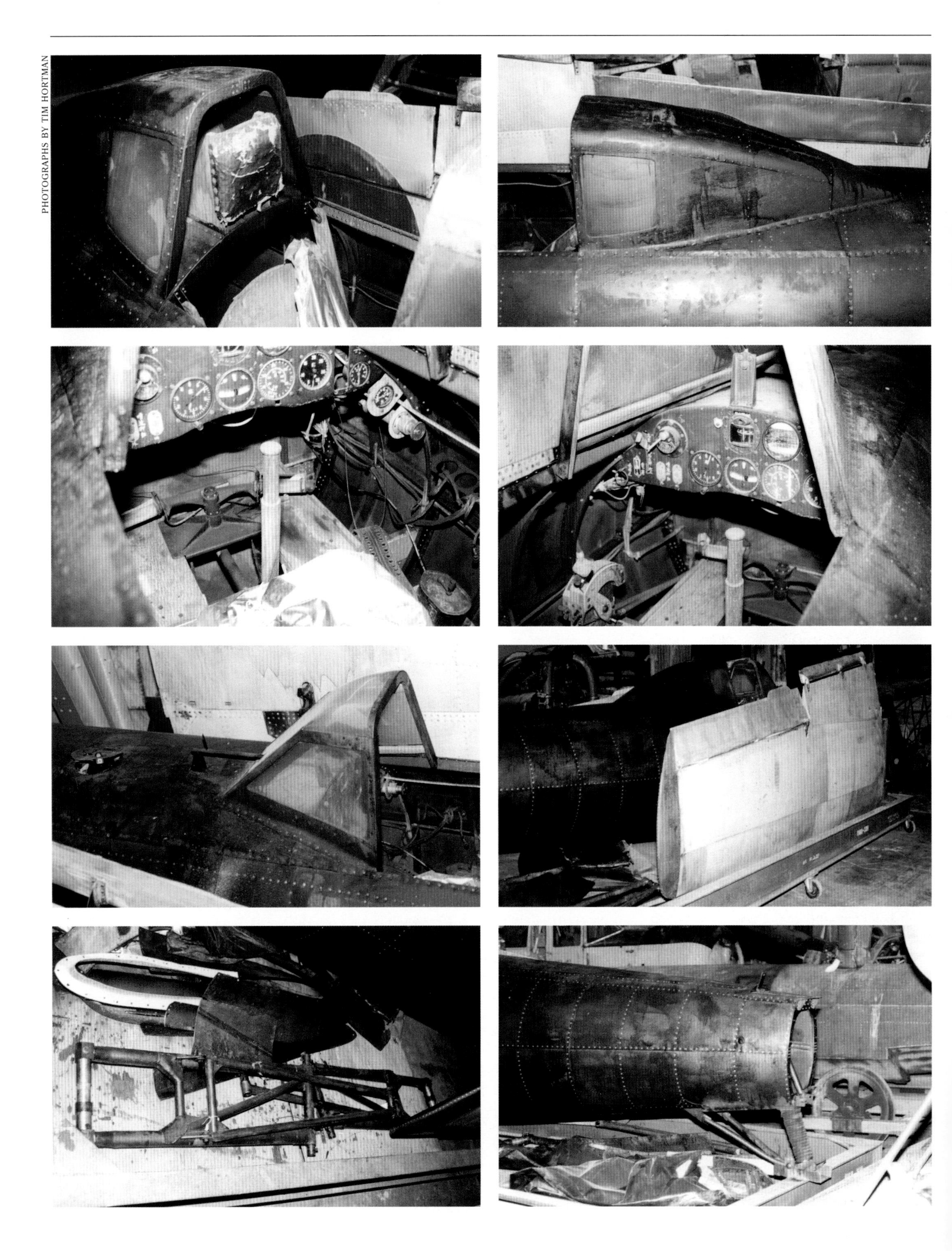

PHOTOGRAPHS BY TIM HORTMAN

PHOTOGRAPHS BY TIM HORTMAN

Nakajima Ki-115 Tsurugi – data

Contemporaries
Bell XP-77 (US), Blohm und Voss BV 40 (Germany), Zeppelin 'Fliegende Panzerfaust' (Germany), Messerschmitt Me 328 (Germany), Messerschmitt P 1104 (Germany)

Specifications in parentheses are for the Ki-115 Ōtsu/Ki-115-III and are estimates only. The Toka would have had similar dimensions though the weights and speed would have varied depending on the engine used.

Type	Special Attack Aircraft
Crew	One

Powerplant One Nakajima [Ha-35] 23, 14-cylinder, air-cooled radial engine developing 1,130hp for take-off and 980hp at 6,000m/19,685ft (same engine was to be used in the Ki-115 Ōtsu/Ki-115-III

Dimensions

Span		8.59m	28.2ft
	(Ōtsu/III)	9.69m	31.8ft
Length		8.53m	28.0ft
	(Ōtsu/III)	8.53m	28.0ft
Height		3.29m	10.8ft
	(Ōtsu/III)	3.29m	10.8ft
Wing area		12.39m²	133.4ft²
	(Ōtsu/III)	14.49m²	156.0ft²
Wing loading		207.99kg/m²	42.6 lb/ft²
	(Ōtsu/III)	181.13kg/m²	37.1 lb/ft²
Power loading		2.31kg/hp	5.1 lb/hp
	(Ōtsu/III)	2.31kg/hp	5.1 lb/hp

Weights

Empty		1,640kg	3,615 lb
	(Ōtsu/III)	1,690kg	3,725 lb
Loaded		2,580kg	5,688 lb
	(Ōtsu/III)	2,630kg	5,798 lb
Maximum		2,880kg	6,349 lb

Performance

Max speed		551km/h	342mph
		at 2,800m	at 9,186ft
		620km/h	385mph
	(Ōtsu/III)	at 5,800m	at 19,028ft
Cruise speed		300km/h	186mph
Range		1,199km	745 miles
	(Ōtsu/III)	1,199km	745 miles
Ceiling		6,500m	21,325ft
	(Ōtsu/III)	6,500m	21,325ft

Armament One 250kg (551 lb), 500kg (1,102 lb) or 800kg (1,764 lb) bomb (same for the Ki-115 Ōtsu/Ki-115-III)

Survivors
Nakajima Ki-115 Ko Tsurugi (FE-156)
One of four captured at Nakajima's No.1 plant in Ōta, Gunma Prefecture, this Ki-115 Ko (serial 1002) was listed on the MAMA 1 August 1946 report as being in storage and was moved to Park Ridge in September 1949. Lucky enough to survive the scrap heap, the Ki-115 Ko is currently in storage, unrestored and in poor condition at the Paul. E. Garber facility in Suitland-Silver Hill, Maryland (pictured left).

Nakajima Ki-115 Ko
Apparently another surviving Ki-115 Ko is being restored in Japan but there are few, if any details, on who is restoring the aircraft nor the history of the Ki-115 involved.

In 1991, two other Ki-115 aircraft were reported to be found in Japan, one in Kanda and the other in Koganei. Who has them and in what condition is neither known nor confirmed.

Nakajima Ki-230 – data (estimated)

Type	Suicide Attack Aircraft
Crew	One

Powerplant
One 14-cylinder, air-cooled radial engine developing at least 1,100hp.

Dimensions

Span	39.69m	1.8ft
Length	8.47m	27.8ft
Height	3.29m	10.8ft
Wing area	13.09m²	141.0ft²

Weights

Empty	1,700kg	3,747 lb
Loaded	2,400kg	5,291 lb

Performance

Max speed	557km/h	346mph
	at 2,800m	at 9,185ft
Range	1,199km	745 miles
Ceiling	6,500m	21,325ft

Armament
One 250kg (551 lb) or 500kg (1,102 lb) bomb

Deployment
None. A total of 105 Ki-115 Ko aircraft were built but none saw combat. No Ki-115 Ōtsu, Ki-115-III, Ki-230 or Toka aircraft were constructed.

Nakajima Ki-201 Karyū

DANIEL UHR

The Ki-201 depicted here sports the colours of the 244th Sentai, one of the more successful Japanese home defence air units.

As a result of the development of the Nakajima Kitsuka for the IJN, Japan's first turbojet-powered aircraft to fly (see Page 114), Nakajima was in the position of being the leader in the fledgling jet aircraft field. Seeking to expand on that position, Nakajima took it upon themselves to offer a jet that would be superior to the Kitsuka. This was to make the most of what little data was received from Germany on the Messerschmitt Me 262. With the Kitsuka under development for the IJN, Nakajima provided the IJA with their proposal for what was to be the definitive Japanese version of the Me 262, the Ki-201 Karyū, the Fire Dragon.

Depending on the source, the IJA was or was not interested in developing its own jet aircraft. However, evidence supports the fact that the IJA wished to have its own jet-powered fighter or was looking to have an option should the Ki-202 and fighter variant of the Kitsuka not meet their expectations. In October 1944, the Japanese embassy informed the Germans that the IJA would be the producer of the Me 262 and requested reports and projections for the production of 100 and 500 aircraft a month. It was known that the wartime manufacturing capability of Japan could not produce an exact copy of the Me 262 and adaptations would have to be made to accommodate Japanese capabilities. Nakajima sought to provide that answer.

The genesis of the Ki-201 took place on 12 January 1945 with the formation of the design team led by Nakajima engineer Iwao Shibuya. Unlike the Kitsuka project, from the outset Shibuya designed the Karyū as a fighter. In addition, Shibuya realised that the aerodynamics of the Me 262 had been tested and felt assured that by applying as much of the design of the Me 262 into the Karyū as was possible would result in an aircraft that would need minimal testing before production was started. This idea was shown to good effect in the development of the Mitsubishi J8M Syūsui.

Shibuya had the same access to the Me 262 information as the IJN. It consisted of sketches

DANIEL UHR

Nakajima Ki-201 Karyū – data

Contemporaries Messerschmitt Me 262A-1a (Germany), Avia S-92 Turbina (Czechoslovakia)

Type	Fighter
Crew	One

Powerplant
Two Ne 230 axial-flow turbojets rated at 885kg (1,951 lb) of static thrust each; later, two Ne 130 axial-flow turbojets rated at 908kg (2,002 lb) of static thrust each

Dimensions			
Span		13.68m	44.9ft
Length		11.49m	37.7ft
Height		4.05m	13.3ft
Wing area		23.96m²	258ft²
Weights			
Empty		4,495kg	9,910 lb
Loaded		7,021kg	15,478 lb
Overload		8,492kg	18,722 lb
Performance			
Max speed		812km/h	504mph
	(Ne 230)	at 10,000m	at 32,808ft
		845km/h	525mph
	(Ne 130)	at 10,000m	at 32,808ft
Landing speed		161km/h	100mph
Max dive speed		1,006km/h	625mph
Take-off distance		945m	3,100ft loaded
		1,588m	5,209ft in overload
Range at 60% thrust		987km	613 miles
		at 7,995m	at 26,230ft
Fuel capacity		2,200 to 2,590 litres	560 to 684 gallons
Climb	(Ne 230)	6 min 54 sec to 6,000m (19,685ft)	
	(Ne 130)	6 min 17 sec to 6,000m (19,685ft)	
	(Ne 230)	14 min 56 sec to 10,000m (32,808ft)	
	(Ne 130)	13 min 15 sec to 10,000m (32,808ft)	
Ceiling		12,000m	39,370ft

Armament
Two Ho-155-II 30mm cannons and two Ho-5 20mm cannons; one 1,763 lb bomb or one 1,102 lb bomb; proposed Navy version to be fitted with two Type 5 30mm cannons and two Type 99 20mm cannons

Deployment
None. The prototype Ki-201 was incomplete by the close of the war.

and drawings of the Me 262A-1 and little else. Whereas the Kitsuka only bore a superficial resemblance to the Me 262, Shibuya's design would seek to match the Me 262 as much as possible. Shibuya and his team may have had little, if any, contact with the Kitsuka developers despite being in the same company. The first draft of the Karyū nearly matched the dimensions of the Me 262. However, it featured a straight wing as opposed to the swept wing of the German jet. This was quickly changed and the revised Karyū was larger and heavier than the Me 262, but replaced the straight wing with a gently swept wing.

Initial design work, including wind tunnel testing, was completed in June 1945. For all intents and purposes, the Ki-201 was a larger derivative of the Me 262. That it was bigger and heavier than the German jet may point to adaptations the Japanese had to make in order to produce the Karyū. For example, the Japanese did not have the experienced fabricators to make the thin, sheet steel used in the nose of the Me 262. The result was that the Karyū's nose had to make do with duralumin which was heavier. In addition, it is certain that the Karyū incorporated simplifications to accommodate production by semi-skilled labour and construction using less critical war materials. The latter was borne out by the intense interest by the Japanese in obtaining the German process for making plywood (and likely the bonding glues as well) which the Germans used in their aviation industry because, although Japan was lacking in aviation metals by the close of the war, they had ample access to wood.

The Karyū was initially slated to be fitted with Ne 230 axial-flow turbojet engines each rated at 85kg (1,951 lb) thrust. These were calculated to push the Karyū at a maximum speed of 812km/h (504mph). However, it was also planned that once they became available, the Ne 230 engines would be switched for the improved Ne 130 axial-flow turbojets. Projected to produce 908kg (2,001 lb) of thrust each, the calculated speed of the Karyū with the Ne 130s was a maximum 852km/h (529mph).

For armament, the Karyū was fitted with two Ho-155-II 30mm cannons and two Ho-5 20mm cannons. On the chance that the IJN might acquire the Ki-201, provision was also made to use two Type 5 30mm cannons and two Type 99 20mm cannons. More notable was that the Karyū was slated to be equipped with the Ta-Ki 15 airborne intercept radar. Used in conjunction with the Ta-Chi 13 ground control radar, the Karyū could be guided to its targets by ground controllers with a 153km (95 mile) radius. Such a system would have been a benefit in low-light, night or poor flying weather interceptions. In addition to the cannon fits, the Karyū was to be capable of carrying a 800kg (1,763 lb) or 500kg (1,102 lb) bomb.

With the initial progress of the IJN's J8M Syūsui program, which would provide the IJA with the Ki-200 and the subsequent IJA Ki-202 Syūsui-kai project, IJA interest in the Ki-201 looked to have waned. The result was delays in further developing the Karyū. Nakajima wanted to have the final design of the Ki-201 completed by July 1945 with more advanced testing underway by August. The first prototype of the Karyū was to be completed and ready for flight trails by December 1945, and in addition, a further 18 examples of the Ki-201 were to be built and delivered by March 1946.

Despite the delays, work commenced on the prototype. Nakajima's Mitaka plant, which was located on the western edge of Tōkyō, was the facility for the prototype Ki-201's construction. Regular production of the Ki-201 was intended to be carried out at the Kurosawajiri Research Works No.21 situated near Kitakami, in Iwate Prefecture, in Honshū. The fuselage for the Karyū was nearly complete when Japan surrendered on 15 August 1945. With the surrender, work on the Ki-201 ceased. It would be nearly 30 years before the next Japanese designed and built jet fighter would fly, this being the Mitsubishi F-1 which first flew on 3 June 1975.

Rikugun Ki-93

MUNEO HOSAKA

At the time the Ki-93 was conceived the war situation for Japan was dire. The mainland was suffering from near daily B-29 raids and looming on the horizon was the anticipated US invasion of Japan. A means to counter the B-29s as well as to attack Allied invasion ships was needed. The resulting Ki-93 would be a first and a last for Rikugun and Japan.

When Rikugun Kokugijutsu Kenkyūjo began the design research for the Ki-93, the goal was to provide an aircraft that could provide a platform for anti-bomber operations and anti-shipping missions. In both cases the aircraft had to be able to absorb damage when flying in the face of interceptors, the defensive machine guns of the bombers, and the anti-aircraft weapons of ships.

Two versions of the all-metal Ki-93 were to be constructed. The first, the Ki-93-I Ko, was the heavy fighter that would combat bombers. The second was the Ki-93-I Ōtsu and this was the anti-shipping model. The Mitsubishi Ha-211 radial engine was considered at first to power the Ki-93 but both models were ultimately powered by two Mitsubishi Ha-214 18-cylinder, air-cooled radial engines, each providing a maximum of 2,400hp. In order to give the aircraft a measure of survivability in the face of enemy fire, armour plating was used. The pilot was provided with five armour plates, each 12mm thick. Two plates were placed just forward of the cockpit in the nose, one on each side of the pilot and the fifth would protect his back. The front glazing was composed of 70mm thick bullet proof glass. The rear gunner was also protected by a 12mm armour plate, offering defence from rounds being fired at the Ki-93 from behind. Likewise, the fuselage fuel tanks were given a measure of protection from incoming fire via an 8mm thick armour plate. Each engine was also provided with armour plating in the nacelles. Should the armour protecting the fuel tanks be penetrated, each tank was self-sealing and, to prevent fuel fires, had an automatic fire

MUNEO HOSAKA

Rikugun Ki-93 – data

Contemporaries
Henschel Hs 129B-3/Wa (Germany), Messerschmitt Me 410A-1/U4 (Germany), Tupolev ANT-46 (Russia), North American B-25G Mitchell (US), Bell YFM-1 Airacuda (US), Curtiss XP-71 (US), de Havilland Mosquito FB Mk.XVIII (UK)

Type	Heavy Fighter (Ki-93-I Ko) and Ground Attack Aircraft (Ki-93-I Ōtsu)
Crew	Two

Powerplant
Two Mitsubishi Ha-214, 18-cylinder, air-cooled radials, developing 2,400hp for take-off, 1,970hp at 1,500m/4,920ft and 1,730hp at 8,452m/27,729ft; each engine drove a 6-bladed, metal propeller

Dimensions

Span	18.98m	62.3ft
Length	14.20m	46.6ft
Height	4.84m	15.9ft
Wing area	54.74m²	589.3ft²
Wing loading	184.80kg/m²	39.9 lb/ft²
Power loading	2.22kg/hp	4.9 lb/hp

Weights

Empty	7,686kg	16,945 lb
Loaded	10,660kg	23,501 lb

Performance

Max speed	625km/h at 8,300m	388mph at 27,230ft
Cruise speed	350km/h	217mph
Range	3,000km	1,864 miles
Endurance	6 hours	
Climb	4 min 18 sec to 3,000m (9,840ft) 9 min 3 sec to 6,000m (19,685ft)	
Ceiling	12,049m	39,530ft

Armament
One 57mm Ho-401 cannon with 20 rounds of ammunition, two 20mm Ho-5 cannons with 300 rounds of ammunition per gun and one 12.7mm Ho-103 machine gun with 400 rounds of ammunition (Ki-93-I Ko); One 75mm Type 88 cannon, one 12.7mm Ho-103 machine gun and two 250kg (551 lb) bombs (Ki-93-I Ōtsu)

Deployment
None. Two Ki-93 prototypes (one of each version) were produced but did not enter production before the end of the war.

Survivors
Rikugun Ki-93-I Ōtsu (FE-152)
The second prototype that had not flown by the end of the war was taken at what is present day Takahagi in Ibaraki Prefecture. The aircraft was crated and arrived at MAMA being listed on 10 March 1946. It was to be restored for display and this began on September 1946. Moved to Park Ridge on 18 September 1946. All traces of the Ki-93-I Ōtsu stopped at Park Ridge in 1949.

extinguishing system. Finally, a defensive armament, consisting of a single 12.7mm Ho-103 machine gun was fitted in a rear firing position to be operated by the second crewman.

The difference in the two versions was in the offensive weapon fits, both mounted in ventral gondolas. The Ki-93-I Ko was equipped with a powerful 57mm Ho-401 cannon and this was backed up by two 20mm Ho-5 cannons (although one initial design did away with the two Ho-5 cannons and used a single 37mm cannon with 40 rounds of ammunition). It was anticipated that the Ho-401 cannon would inflict enough damage with a single hit to cripple or shoot down a B-29. The Ho-401 could fire 90 rounds per minute with a muzzle velocity of 518.2m/sec (1,700ft/sec). For the Ki-93-I Ōtsu, the large 75mm Type 88 cannon was fitted. The weapon was an adaptation of the Type 88 anti-aircraft gun that had been modified for use on aircraft. Besides the Ki-93, this weapon was also used operationally in the Mitsubishi Ki-109 (flown by the 107th Sentai). The Type 88 had to be hand loaded by the second crewman. In addition to the cannon the Ki-93-I Ōtsu would carry two 250kg (551 lb) bombs.

Rikugun had Dai-Ichi Rikugun Kokusho, located in Tachikawa (which is about 24 miles from the centre of Tōkyō), construct the Ki-93. The first prototype in the Ki-93-I Ko configuration was completed by April 1945. In the same month the aircraft successfully took to the air making it the first Rikugun aircraft to be built and flown. However, further flight testing was hampered by the war situation, so much so that the test program was never completed. Despite the worsening conditions in Japan and delays with the flights of the first prototype the second aircraft in the Ki-93-I Ōtsu configuration was completed. However, it would never fly.

With the surrender of Japan, the Ki-93 would become the last heavy fighter and ground attack aircraft to be built during the war.

MUNEO HOSAKA

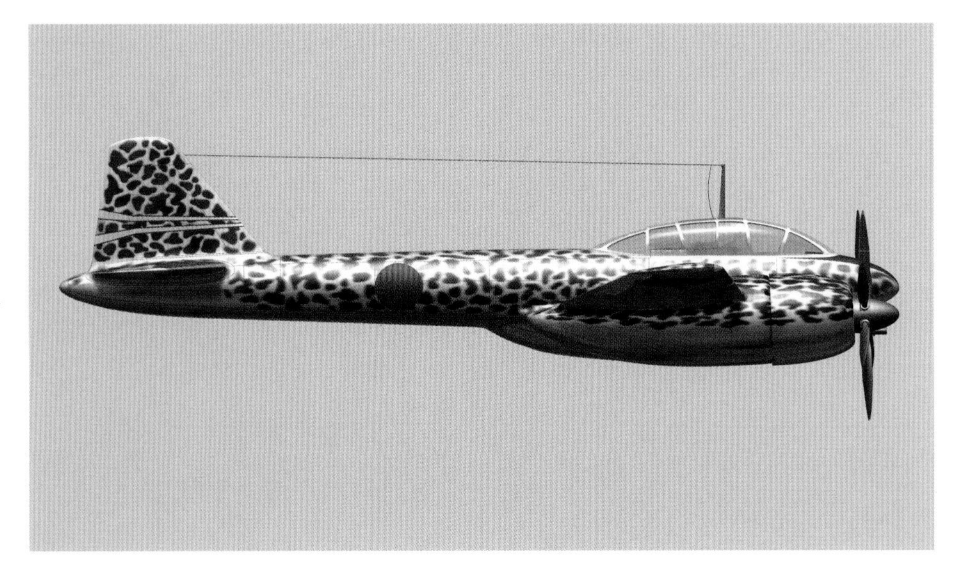

Rikugun Ki-202 Syūsui-Kai

DANIEL UHR

The IJA was not satisfied with the Ki-200 (the IJA designation for the Mitsubishi J8M1 Syūsui – See Page 96). They felt that the IJN's plans to adopt and adapt the Messerschmitt Me 163B as the J8M1 would amount to the same, if not more, effort and development compared to creating a new design based on, but not a direct adaptation of, the Me 163B. Although the IJA attempted to make the IJN see their point-of-view, the IJN pushed aside such plans, forging ahead with their J8M program. Thus, the IJA took it upon themselves to design the better aircraft they had wanted from the outset.

The IJA saw a main flaw in the Ki-200 that resulted in aspects of the plane's performance that they found unacceptable: the limited fuel capacity. Because of this, combat endurance was reduced and fuel was rapidly consumed by the KR10 (Toku-Ro 2) engine. Even with the IJN's proposed J8M2, which removed a Type 5 30mm cannon to make way for more fuel, the IJA felt that the endurance was still insufficient. Starting in 1945, Rikugun Kokugijitsu Kenkyujo began the process of developing the IJA's own rocket aircraft using the Me 163B as a template. This development was in secret and the designation given to the aircraft was the Ki-202 Syūsui-Kai which meant 'Autumn Water – Improved'.

The IJA took the obvious route and increased the fuel capacity by stretching the fuselage to make room for larger fuel tanks. They also planned to use an improved motor, but exactly what power plant depends on which source is referred to. Two main options appear. One was the KR10 as used in the Ki-200 that developed 1,500kg (3,306 lb) of thrust, but with a secondary rocket added providing a further 400kg (881 lb) of thrust. The other motor was the KR20, which may also be known as the Mitsubishi Toku-Ro.3. The KR20 promised 2,000kg (4,409 lb) of total thrust and may have been fitted with a cruise chamber. This is a secondary combustion chamber which was typically mounted above or below the main combustion chamber. The purpose of having two such chambers is that the main one (or both if necessary) can be used for full power needs such as take-off and rapid ascent, while the cruise chamber has a lower thrust output and can be employed for normal cruise speeds once the plane is aloft and the main chamber shut off. The benefit of this is the conservation of fuel, allowing the plane to remain airborne and in action longer. Wartime Allied intelligence reports stated that the Germans had provided data to the Japanese on the Walther HWK 509C rocket motor which used a cruise chamber. If this was so, then the KR20 was most likely the Japanese development of the HWK 509C motor and the answer the IJA was looking for in extending the range of the Ki-202. Contemporary illustrations of the Ki-202 clearly show some form of a secondary means of thrust. As a stop-gap measure, the Ki-202 could have accepted the KR10 motor if problems arose with the development and production of the KR20 and thus any delays in flight testing could have been avoided.

Although the Ki-202 was larger than the Ki-200, no attempt was made to include a landing gear system. Like the Ki-200, the Ki-202 retained a central landing skid, tail wheel and would use the jettisonable wheeled dolly for take-off and ground handling. No provision for catapult launching is known to have been considered as a means to conserve fuel that would have been consumed during normal take-off procedures.

For weapons, the Ki-202 was slated to use two Ho-155 30mm cannons, one mounted in the each wing root, the same as the Ki-200.

Insofar as the larger size and motor, the Ki-202 was estimated to have an endurance of 10 minutes and 28 seconds, whereby the Ki-202 was calculated to achieve 5 minutes and 30 seconds. With a near doubling of the endurance time, this would have allowed the Ki-202 to remain in combat for a longer period or, at the least, extend its operational radius. It was projected that the final design of the Ki-202 would be completed by February 1945 with construction of the first prototype commencing shortly afterwards. The first test flight was scheduled for August 1945.

As it was, the Ki-202 design would remain just that, a design. When the war ended, no metal had been cut on the Ki-202 prototype nor was a mock-up even constructed. In part, the Ki-202 program may have hinged on the success or failure of the J8M1. The technical issues in producing the KR10 in a reliable form most likely stymied work on the KR20, which was to be the main powerplant for the Ki-202. The problems with the KR10 delayed flight testing of the J8M1 until July 1945 and even then, a fuel system failure caused the crash of the Syūsui during its maiden flight. This set back the J8M1 further still and although the fuel system problem was corrected, the war ended before any further flights could be made. Had the J8M1 succeeded and the IJA version, the Ki-200, entered service, it is likely development of the Ki-202 would have rapidly proceeded and had it succeeded, the IJA would have offered it to the IJN. If accepted, the designation would have been the J8M3.

Rikugun Ki-202 Syūsui-Kai – data

Contemporaries
Messerschmitt Me 163C-1a (Germany)

Type	Interceptor/Fighter
Crew	One

Powerplant (planned)
One Toku-Ro.3 (KR20) bi-fuel rocket motor producing 2,000kg (4,409 lb) of thrust with supplementary rocket or cruise chamber producing 400kg (880 lb) of thrust

Dimensions		
Span	9.72m	31.9ft
Length	7.68m	25.2ft
Height	2.74m	9ft
Wing area	18.39m²	198ft²
Wing loading	272.43kg/m²	55.8 lb/ft²

Weights		
Empty	1,619kg	3,569 lb
Loaded	3,384kg	7,460 lb
Maximum loaded	5,015kg	11,057 lb

Performance (estimated by Rikugun)		
Max speed	900km/h	559mph
	at 10,000m	at 32,808ft
Landing speed	132km/h	82mph
Range	10 min 28 sec of endurance	
Climb	1 min 21 sec to 2,000m (6,561ft)	
	2 min 0 sec to 4,000m (13,123ft)	
	2 min 34 sec to 6,000m (19,685ft)	
	3 min 2 sec to 8,000m (26,246ft)	
	3 min 26 sec to 10,000m (32,808ft)	
Ceiling	12,000m	39,370ft

Armament
Two Ho-155 30mm cannon

Deployment
None. The Ki-202 did not advance beyond the design board.

DANIEL UHR

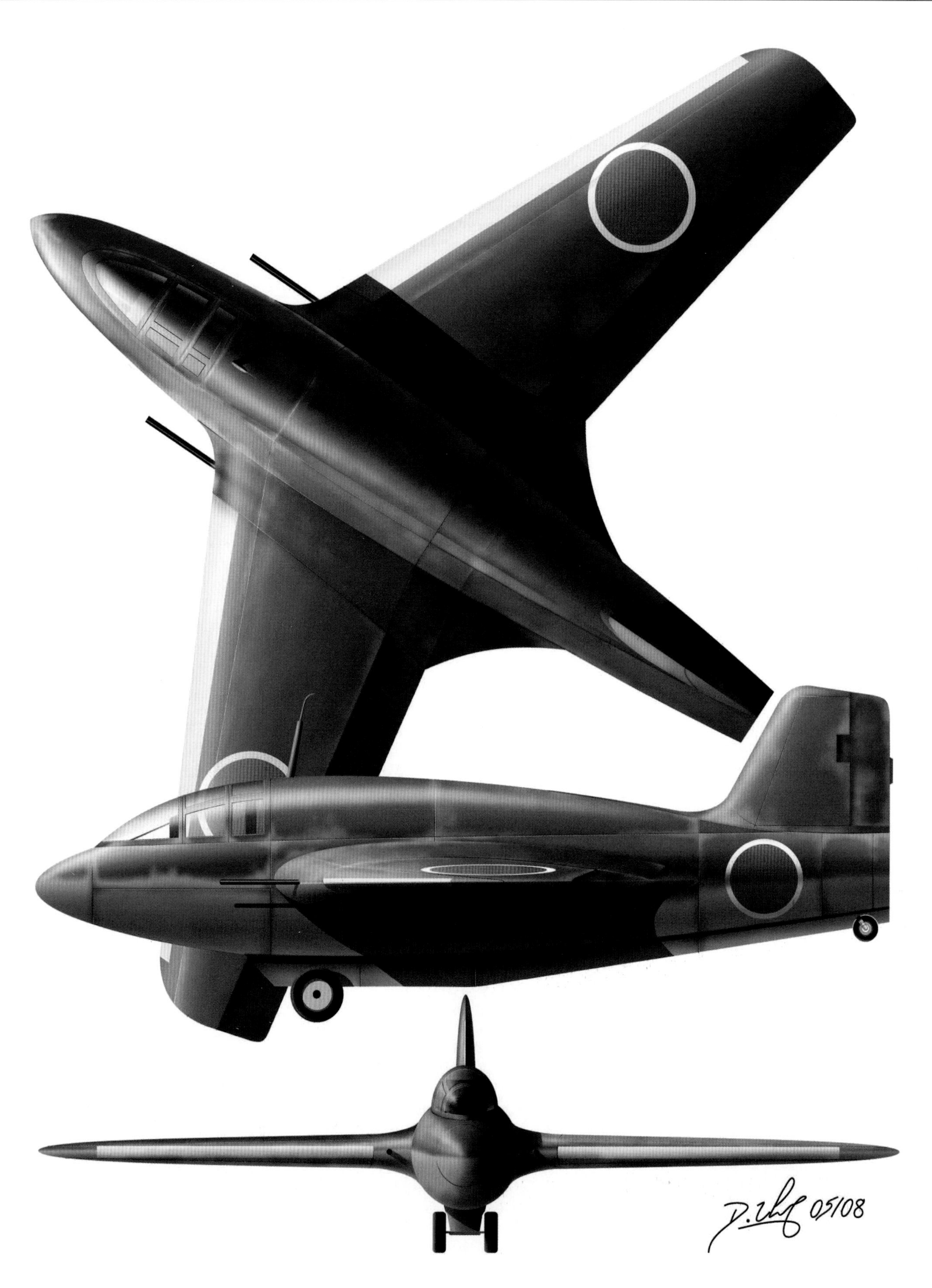

Rikugun Kogiken Series

Kogiken Plan I – data (estimated)

Contemporaries Arado P.530 light bomber (Germany), Bell P-39 Airacobra fighter (US), Caudron C.670 light bomber (France), Farman N.C.223 heavy bomber (France), Messerschmitt Me 210 and 410 heavy fighter (Germany), Piaggio P.119 fighter (Italy), Potez 63 heavy fighter (France), Yakovlev Yak-2 light bomber (Russia).

Type Type A Heavy Fighter
Crew One

Powerplant One Nakajima Ha-45 18-cylinder, air-cooled radial engine developing 1,480hp for take-off and 1,460hp at 5,800m (19,028ft), driving a four-bladed metal propeller

Dimensions		
Span	9.32m	30.6ft
Length	8.71m	28.6ft
Height	3.29m	10.8ft
Wing area	14.59m²	157.1ft²

Weights		
Empty	2,291kg	5,050lb
Loaded	3,140kg	6,922lb

Performance		
Max speed	699km/h at 5,800m	434mph at 19,028ft
Max range	599km	372 miles plus 1 hour

Armament
One 37mm Ho-203 cannon or one 20mm Ho-5 cannon and four 12.7mm Ho-103 machine guns

Kogiken Plan I – data

Type Type B Heavy Fighter
Crew One

Powerplant One Nakajima Ha-45 18-cylinder, air-cooled radial engine developing 1,480hp for take-off and 1,460hp at 5,800m/19,028ft, driving a four-bladed metal propeller

Dimensions		
Span	9.32m	30.6ft
Length	8.86m	29.1ft
Height	3.68m	12.1ft
Wing area	14.59m²	157.1ft²

Weights		
Empty	2,295km/h	5,059lb
Loaded	3,205kg	7,065lb

Performance		
Max speed	699km/h at 5,800m	434mph at 19,028ft
Max range	599km	372 miles plus 1 hour

Armament
One 20mm Ho-5 cannon, four 12.7mm Ho-103 machine guns and two 7.7mm Type 89 Model 2 machine guns

Without doubt, war often provides for rapid advancements in military technology. The key driver of this is the need for a weapon that is superior to those used by the opposition. In the majority of cases, improvements in weapons come about because one participant fields a weapon that the other participants have no answer for or cannot adequately counter with currently available weapons. This, then, spurs development of an equal or better weapon and the cycle repeats – an arms race! In some cases, development of a weapon does not result from actually encountering new developments on the battlefield. Instead, study of what could be encountered in the future, coupled with what can reasonably be advanced in terms of technology, provides the required emphasis for development – in essence, an attempt to second-guess likely developments so that if and when they manifest themselves the answer will already be in place. It was the latter that prompted the IJA's Rikugun Kokugijutsu Kenkyūjo to initiate a series of studies and plans for a host of aircraft suitable to meet different roles.

In the summer of 1941, Kogiken (a contraction of Kokugijutsu Kenkyūjo) formed a group headed by aeronautical engineer Lieutenant Commander Ando Sheigo. The task put to Sheigo and his group of engineers was to study Japanese aviation technology in terms of what was possible at present and in the near future. In addition, some effort was to be spent on reviewing the aircraft technology of other countries. From the results of these studies, the group was to assemble and draft proposals for aircraft to fill various roles that could take advantage of future innovation. In all there were four roles or classes of aircraft the Kogiken group had to produce designs for: heavy fighter, light bomber, heavy bomber and reconnaissance. There was a fifth class, that of high speed, but methods to achieve high speed aircraft were often incorporated into designs in the other four classes. In addition to Kogiken, the IJA's two biggest aircraft providers, Tachikawa and Kawasaki, were also invited to participate in some of the studies and tender their own designs.

A central theme in all of the Kogiken aircraft was the use of only a select group of engines. The two most prominent were the Nakajima Ha-45 and the Mitsubishi Ha-211-II, both of which were 18-cylinder, air-cooled radial engines. At the time of the Kogiken study, these engines were still in development but were expected to be operational in the very near future. Another factor concerning the engines was that, in some cases, the designs were built around the ability to replace the radial power unit with an inline engine without significant modifications. The primary inline engines were the Daimler-Benz DB601 and DB605. The former was licence built in Japan as the Kawasaki Ha-40.

By the close of September the designs were nearing completion. Since there were no performance requirements or specifications applied to any of the classes of aircraft, this essentially left the engineers and designers with free rein to come up with aircraft they thought would be suitable for the roles. In many cases this led to aircraft concepts that featured, at least for the Japanese, unconventional mechanisms and approaches. Each aircraft was designated as a plan with each plan grouped by their respective class.

The first class, the heavy fighter, had four main designs, all Kogiken creations. Two were for a single-engine aircraft while the other two were twin-engine concepts. The first was the Kogiken Plan I Type A heavy fighter. Outwardly it was a fairly conventional aircraft. It used low mounted, thin laminar flow wings but in order to reduce drag the Ha-45 engine was placed within the fuselage, along the aircraft's centre of gravity. This, in

Kogiken Plan I Type A heavy fighter (in the colours of the 2nd Chutai, 48th Sentai)

KELCEY FAULKNER

Kogiken Plan I – data

Type:	Type A Long Range Heavy Fighter	
Crew:	Two	

Powerplant: Two Mitsubishi Ha-211-II 18-cylinder, air-cooled radial engines developing 2,100hp for take-off, each driving a four-bladed metal propeller

Dimensions		
Span:	15.97m	52.4ft
Length:	11.97m	39.3ft
Height:	N/A	
Wing Area:	44.99m²	484.3ft²

Weights		
Empty:	N/A	
Loaded:	9,400kg	20,723 lb

Performance		
Max Speed:	699km/h	434mph
Max Range:	4,000km	2,485 miles
Climb:	8 min to 6,000m (19,685ft)	
Ceiling:	11,500m	37,729ft

Armament
One 20mm Ho-5 cannon and three 12.7mm Ho-103 machine guns

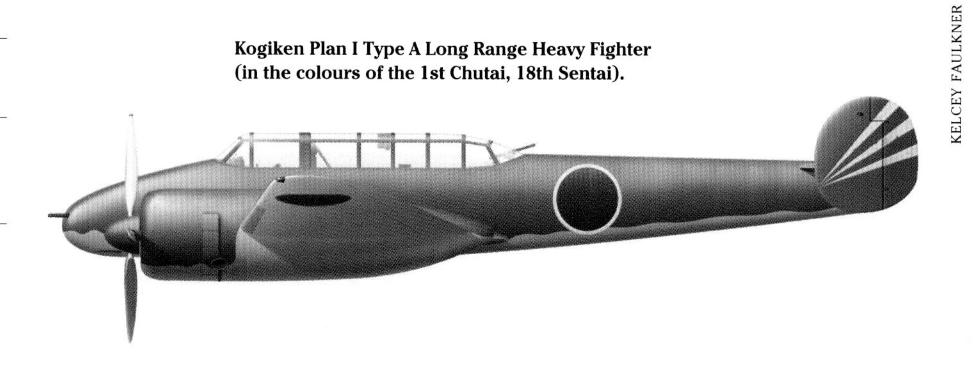

Kogiken Plan I Type A Long Range Heavy Fighter (in the colours of the 1st Chutai, 18th Sentai).

essence, put the motor approximately in the middle of the aircraft. The cockpit was situated ahead of the engine, the four-bladed propeller being driven via a 2.5m (8.2ft) long extension shaft. For weapons, either a 37mm Ho-203 cannon or a 20mm Ho-5 cannon was to be fitted, firing through the propeller hub with two 12.7mm Ho-103 machine guns in the nose and one in each wing. Perhaps as an oversight, the design of the fighter made no provision for cooling the internal engine. Mention was made that the fighter would have been equipped with a Type 3 radio system and provision was made to use the anticipated Nakajima 2,000hp Ha-145 18-cylinder radial engine. Finally, the aircraft was to use a retractable tricycle landing gear.

The Kogiken Plan I Type B Heavy Fighter plan used the same fuselage shape and wings as the Type A but this time the Ha-45 engine was moved towards the nose, needing only a 1.45m (4.7ft) extension shaft, and the cockpit was moved to the back behind the wings. Gone was the tricycle landing gear, replaced with a more conventional retractable main gear and tail wheel arrangement. The heavy armament of the Type A was modified for the Type B with one Ho-5 cannon firing through the hub, four Ho-103 machine guns (two in the nose on either side of the engine, one in each wing) and two 7.7mm Type 89 Model 2 machine guns situated just forward of the cockpit. A Type 3 radio was also to be included for the pilot.

The second pair of plans fell into the role of long range heavy fighters. In both cases, the aircraft bore a striking resemblance to the German Messerschmitt Bf 110 although the influence may have come from closer to home in the civilian Mitsubishi Ōtori (Phoenix) long range communication aircraft built in 1936 for the Asahi Shimbun newspa-

Kogiken Plan II – data

Type	Light Bomber	
Crew	Three	

Powerplant Two Nakajima Ha-39 18-cylinder, water-cooled radial engines, each developing 1,760hp at 3,000m/9,842ft driving a four-bladed metal propeller

Dimensions		
Span	14.59m	47.9ft
Length	10.69m	35.1ft
Height	3.77m	12.4ft
Wing area	31.99m²	344.4ft²

Weights		
Empty	5,303kg	11,691 lb
Loaded	7,510kg	16,556 lb

Performance		
Max speed	649km/h	403mph
	at 3,000m	at 9,842ft
Max range	1,400km	869 miles plus 1 hour

Armament
Two 7.7mm Type 89 machine guns; normal bomb load of 300kg (661 lb) to a maximum of 400kg (881 lb)

Kogiken Plan III – data

Type	Light Bomber	
Crew	Three	

Powerplant Two Nakajima Ha-45 18-cylinder, air-cooled radial engines, each developing 1,460hp at 5,800m/19,028ft driving a four-bladed metal propeller

Dimensions		
Span	14.14m	46.4ft
Length	10.85m	35.6ft
Height	3.77m	12.4ft
Wing area	26.59m²	286.3ft²

Weights		
Empty	4,610kg	10,163 lb
Loaded	6,610kg	14,572 lb

Speed		
Max speed	710km/h	441mph
	at 5,800m	at 19,028ft
Max range	1,400km	869 miles plus 1.5 hours

Armament
Two 7.7mm Type 89 machine guns; normal bomb load of 300kg (661 lb) to a maximum of 400kg (881 lb)

Kogiken Plan III – data

Type	Revised Light Bomber	
Crew	Three	

Powerplant
Two Nakajima Ha-45 18-cylinder, air-cooled radial engines, each developing 1,480hp driving a four-bladed metal propeller

Dimensions		
Span	14.14m	46.4ft
Length	9.96m	32.7ft
Height	3.77m	12.4ft
Wing area	26.59m²	286.3ft²

Weights		
Empty	4,480kg	9,876 lb
Loaded	6,480kg	14,285 lb

Speed		
Max speed	710km/h	441mph
	at 5,800m	at 19,028ft
Max range	1,400km	869 miles plus 1.5 hours

Armament
Two 7.7mm Type 89 machine guns; normal bomb load of 300kg (661 lb) to a maximum of 400kg (881 lb)

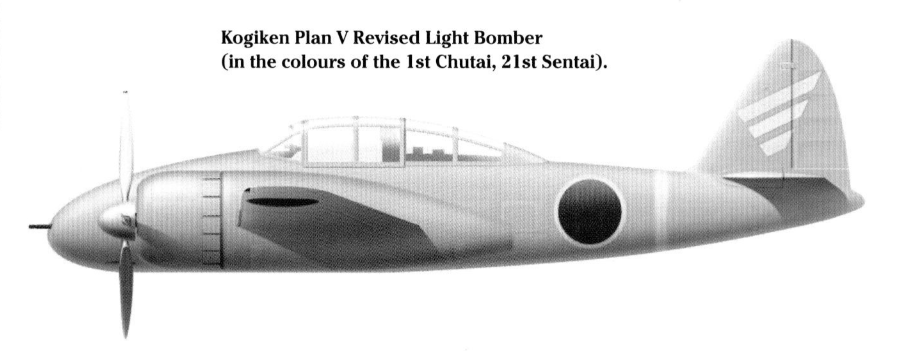

Kogiken Plan V Revised Light Bomber (in the colours of the 1st Chutai, 21st Sentai).

KELCEY FAULKNER

per. Both were twin-engine designs and fitted with the Ha-211-II radial although the Ha-145 and the Kawasaki Ha-140 12-cylinder, liquid cooled inline engine were also considered. At this time, the latter was a projected development of the Ha-40 engine, which as noted was a licence-built version of the German Daimler-Benz DB601A. They each carried a crew of two. The Kogiken Plan I Type A Long Range Heavy Fighter carried an armament of one 20mm Ho-5 cannon and two 12.7mm Ho-103 machine guns in the nose with a rear firing Ho-103 for the second crewman. The Kogiken Plan I Type B Long Range Heavy Fighter was identical to the Type A but featured a slightly different weapon fit. It retained the two forward firing Ho-103 machine guns but would either add a second Ho-5 in the nose or swap both Ho-5 weapons for two 30mm cannons, perhaps based on the 30mm Ho-155 that would eventually evolve from the Ho-5. A variation of the Type B, the Plan II Long Range Fighter, had a slightly redesigned wing that reduced the wing area from 44.99m^2 (484.3ft^2) down to 41.99m^2 (452ft^2). A final variation, the Plan III Long Range Fighter, reduced the crew glazing and fitted a remote controlled Ho-103 machine gun in the tail.

The light bomber plans would feature an approach that would not be repeated in subsequent Japanese designs. The Kogiken Plan II Light Bomber used two airframes connected by a wing centre section. The vertical stabilisers were connected by a single horizontal stabiliser. The pilot and crewman sat in a cockpit on the left airframe while a third crewman had a station in the right. The main landing gear retracted outwards into the outer wing panels. Buried in each airframe was a Nakajima Ha-39, 18-cylinder, water cooled radial engine that developed 1,760hp

Kogiken Plan VI – data

Type	Heavy Bomber	
Crew	Four	

Powerplant
Four Mitsubishi Ha-211-II 18-cylinder, air-cooled radial engines, each developing 2,100hp driving a four-bladed metal propeller

Dimensions		
Span	22.09m	72.5ft
Length	17.09m	56.1ft
Height	5.12m	16.8ft
Wing area	61.00m^2	656.5ft^2

Weights		
Empty	9,053kg	19,958 lb
Loaded	15,198kg	33,505 lb

Performance		
Max speed	720km/h	447mph
	at 6,000m	at 19,685ft
Max range	3,000km	1,864 miles plus 2 hours

Armament
One 7.7mm Type 89 machine gun, one 12.7mm Ho-103 machine gun and fourteen 50kg (110 lb) bombs, eight 100kg (220 lb) bombs, two 250kg (551 lb) bombs or one 500kg (1,102 lb) bomb

Kogiken Plan I Type A – data

Type	High Speed Heavy Bomber	
Crew	Four	

Powerplant
Four Mitsubishi Ha-211-II 18-cylinder, air-cooled radial engines, each developing 2,100hp driving a four-bladed metal propeller

Dimensions		
Span	826.33m	6.4ft
Length	19.78m	64.9ft
Height	5.09m	16.7ft
Wing area	88.00m^2	947.2ft^2
Wing loading	219.7kg/m^2	45 lb/ft^2
Power loading	2.76kg/hp	6.1 lb/hp

Weights		
Empty	12,540kg	27,645 lb
Loaded	19,340kg	42,637 lb
Useful load	6,800kg	14,991 lb

Performance		
Max speed	684km/h	425mph
	at 8,500m	at 27,887ft
Cruise speed	515km/h	320mph
	at 8,500m	at 27,887ft
Climb	3 min 9 sec to 3,500m (11,482ft)	
	6 min 3 sec to 5,000m (16,404ft)	
Max range	3,000km/1,864 miles	

Armament
Two 7.7mm Type 89 machine guns, one 12.7mm Ho-103 machine gun and up to 1,500kg (3,306 lb) of bombs

Kogiken Plan V – data

Type	Light Bomber	
Crew	Three	

Powerplant
Two Nakajima Ha-45 18-cylinder, air-cooled radial engines, each developing 1,480hp driving a four-bladed metal propeller

Dimensions		
Span	14.14m	46.4ft
Length	10.48m	34.4ft
Height	3.77m	12.4ft
Wing area	26.59m^2	286.3ft^2

Weights		
Empty	4,480m	9,876 lb
Loaded	6,480kg	14,285 lb

Performance		
Max speed	710km/h	441mph
	at 6,000m	at 19,685ft
Max range	1,400km	869 miles plus 1.5 hours

Armament
Two 7.7mm Type 89 machine guns, 300kg (661 lb) in bombs

Kogiken Plan V – data

Type	Revised Light Bomber	
Crew	Two	

Powerplant
Two Mitsubishi Ha-211-II 18-cylinder, air-cooled radial engines, each developing 2,100hp driving a four-bladed metal propeller

Dimensions		
Span	14.23m	46.7ft
Length	10.63m	34.9ft
Height	3.71m	12.2ft
Wing area	26.59m^2	286.3ft^2

Weights		
Empty	4,438kg/9,784 lb	
Loaded	6,445kg/14,208 lb	

Performance		
Max speed	746km/h	463mph
	at 6,000m	at 19,685ft
Max range	1,400km	869 miles plus 1.5 hours

Armament
One 7.7mm Type 89 machine gun and 250kg (551 lb) in bombs

Kogiken Plan I Type B – data

Type	High Speed Heavy Bomber	
Crew	Four	

Powerplant Four Mitsubishi Ha-211-II 18-cylinder, air-cooled radial engines, each developing 2,100hp driving a four-bladed metal propeller

Dimensions		
Span	28.19m	92.5ft
Length	20.66m	67.8ft
Height	5.18m	17ft
Wing area	99.00m²	1,065.6ft²
Wing loading	221.66kg/m²	45.4 lb/ft²
Power loading	3.12kg/hp	6.9 lb/hp

Weights		
Empty	13,090kg	28,858 lb
Loaded	21,985kg	48,468 lb
Useful load	8,895kg	19,610 lb

Performance		
Max speed	660km/h	410mph
	at 8,500m	at 27,887ft
Cruise speed	495km/h	307mph
	at 8,500m	at 27,887ft
Climb	4 min 8 sec to 3,000m (9,842ft)	
	8 min 0 sec to 5,000m (16,404ft)	
Max range	4,000km	2,485 miles

Armament Two 7.7mm Type 89 machine guns, one 12.7mm Ho-103 machine gun and up to 1,500kg (3,306 lb) of bombs

Kogiken Plan II – data

Type	High Speed Heavy Bomber	
Crew	Five	

Powerplant Four Mitsubishi Ha-211-II 18-cylinder, air-cooled radial engines, each developing 2,100hp driving a four-bladed metal propeller

Dimensions		
Span	27.09m	88.9ft
Length	20.54m	67.4ft
Height	5.33m	17.5ft
Wing area	98.00m²	968.7ft²
Wing loading	219.70kg/m²	45 lb/ft²
Power loading	2.81kg/hp	6.2 lb/hp

Weights		
Empty	12,805kg	28,230 lb
Loaded	21,985kg	48,468 lb
Useful load	6,975kg	15,377 lb

Speed		
Max speed	680km/h	422mph
	at 8,500m	at 27,887ft
Cruise speed	509km/h	316mph
	at 8,500m	at 27,887ft
Climb	4 min 0 sec to 3,000m (9,842ft)	
	6 min 4 sec to 5,000m (16,404ft)	
Max range	3,000km	1,864 miles

Armament One 7.7mm Type 89 machine gun, three 12.7mm Ho-103 machine guns and up to 1,500kg (3,306 lb) of bombs

and drove a four-bladed propeller via an extension shaft. It was proposed that a surface evaporation cooling system be used which consisted of a network of piping that would take the steam produced by the engines as the water circulated through them out into the wings where the cooler air would condense the steam back into water that was then recycled through the engines. The main benefit from this method of cooling was that it allowed for a more streamlined fuselage which increased air speed. Typical of early war Japanese light bombers, the armament was light consisting of two 7.7mm Type 89 machine guns. For bombs, a regular payload of 300kg (661 lb) could be carried with a maximum of 400kg (881 lb).

The Kogiken Plan III Light Bomber was basically identical to Plan II. The main change was the replacement of the Ha-39 engines with the Ha-45 and the latter were situated deeper into the fuselages requiring a .83m (2.7ft) long extension shaft. Without the complex cooling system of Plan II, Plan III was

Kogiken Plan III Revised Light Bomber.

KELCEY FAULKNER

smaller, lighter and faster. In addition, the canopy for the third crewman was made flush with the fuselage and was provided with a ventral fairing to facilitate bombing or reconnaissance duties. The propellers were fitted with ducted spinners to help cool the engines. The Kogiken Plan III Revised Light Bomber was a version of the Plan III but with the Ha-45 radials placed in a conventional fashion in the nose – the ducted spinners were left out. Another light bomber, the Kogiken Plan V Light Bomber, shared a similarity to the Plan III Revised but whereas the twin airframes were of the same length, the Plan V had the right airframe shorter to the point that the propeller spun behind the one on the left airframe. The canopy for the pilot and second crewman was also lengthened. The Kogiken Plan V Revised Light Bomber broke away from the previous designs. The twin airframe scheme was dropped and an engine was placed in a large nacelle in each wing. The Ha-211-II engine was specified but the Ha-45 could also be used. The crew was reduced to two and the armament was dropped to a single 7.7mm Type 89 machine gun while the bomb payload was lowered to 250kg (551 lb).

In the heavy bomber class, only one standard heavy bomber design was completed by Kogiken and this was the Kogiken Plan VI Heavy Bomber. The fuselage was conventional and was reminiscent of the solid nosed Junkers Ju 88 bombers although the Plan VI had longer glazing over the compartment for the crew of four. The similarities ended there. Set into each wing was a nacelle that housed two engines driving two propellers in a push-pull configuration. Originally Ha-45 radial engines were planned but the Ha-211-II was the engine of choice. The design could have been adapted to take the forthcoming Mitsubishi Ha-214 18-cylinder air cooled radial or the Kawasaki Ha-201 which was made from two Ha-40 12-cylinder inline engines mounted in tandem and was under development at the time. Defensive armament was light consisting of a single 7.7mm Type 89 machine gun and a 12.7mm Ho-103 machine gun. A variable bomb load could be carried depending on the mission. A slight variation of the Plan VI increased the wing area to 69.99m² (753.4ft²).

There was far more activity in the high speed heavy bomber category. Here, Tachikawa and Kawasaki made proposals as well as Kogiken. The Kogiken Plan I Type A High Speed Heavy Bomber was similar to the Plan IV Heavy Bomber but was larger. Instead of a conventional empennage, the Plan I Type A used a horizontal stabiliser ending in rounded vertical stabilisers. The glazing for the four man crew was longer and the fuselage was more streamlined. The same engine and engine arrangement was used but the nacelles had a slightly improved shape. For defence, two 7.7mm Type 89 machine guns and one 12.7mm Ho-103 machine gun were fitted and a maximum bomb load of 1,500kg (3,306 lb) could be carried. The Kogiken Plan I Type B High Speed Heavy Bomber was basically identical save it was larger and had a longer range. The final design from Kogiken, the Plan II High Speed Heavy Bomber, was slightly smaller and lighter than the Type B but added a fifth crew member and beefed up the defensive armament to three Ho-103 machine guns and one Type 89 machine gun.

The Kawasaki High Speed Heavy Bomber was the smallest of all the designs in the class. Consequently, its performance was less and carried a lighter bomb load and defensive armament. Instead of the Ha-211-II engines it used two Ha-140 24-cylinder, inverted V inline engines, which again were two Ha-40 engines placed in tandem. It was also unique in using the 7.92mm Type 98 machine gun in its defensive armament fit. Tachikawa's designs, the Plan I, Plan II and Plan III High Speed Heavy Bombers, were all variations on the same theme with minor differences

Kawasaki – data

Type	High Speed Heavy Bomber	
Crew	Four to Five	
Powerplant	Two Kawasaki Ha-140 24-cylinder, liquid-cooled inverted V engines, each developing 1,350hp driving a four-bladed metal propeller	
Dimensions		
Span	19.17m	62.9ft
Length	14.87m	48.8ft
Height	N/A	
Wing area	48.00m²	516.6ft²
Wing loading	199.69kg/m²	40.9 lb/ft²
Power loading	3.40kg/hp	7.5 lb/hp
Weights		
Empty	6,170kg	13,602 lb
Loaded	9,590kg	21,142 lb
Useful load	3,420kg	7,539 lb
Performance		
Max speed	580km/h	360mph
	at 6,000m	at 19,685ft
	610km/h	379mph
	at 7,500m	at 24,606ft
Cruise speed	400km/h	248mph
	at 7,500m	at 24,606ft
Climb	N/A	
Max range	3,000m	1,864 miles
Armament	Two 7.92mm Type 98 machine guns, one 12.7mm Ho-103 machine gun and up to 1,000kg (2,204 lb) of bombs	

Tachikawa Plan I – data

Type	High Speed Heavy Bomber	
Crew	Six	
Powerplant	Four Nakajima Ha-145 18-cylinder, air-cooled radial engines, each developing 2,000hp driving a four-bladed metal propeller	
Dimensions		
Span	24.47m	80.3ft
Length	17.67m	58ft
Height	4.45m	14.6ft
Wing area	85.00m²	914.9ft²
Wing loading	223.61kg/m²	45.8 lb/ft²
Power loading	3.49kg/hp	7.7 lb/hp
Weights		
Empty	9,540kg	21,032 lb
Loaded	19,000kg	41,887 lb
Useful load	9,460kg	20,855 lb
Performance		
Max speed	684km/h	425mph
	at 9,300m	at 30,511ft
Cruise speed	480km/h	298mph
	at 9,300m	at 30,511ft
Climb	N/A	
Max range	4,899km	3,044 miles
Armament	Two 7.7mm Type 89 machine guns, one 20mm Ho-5 cannon and up to 1,500kg (3,306 lb) of bombs	

Tachikawa Plan II – data

Type	High Speed Heavy Bomber	
Crew	N/A	
Powerplant	Four Nakajima Ha-145 18-cylinder, air-cooled radial engines, each developing 2,000hp driving a four-bladed metal propeller	
Dimensions		
Span	28.49m	93.5ft
Length	N/A	
Height	N/A	
Wing area	80.00m²	861.1ft²
Wing loading	223.61kg/m²	45.8 lb/ft²
Power loading	3.31kg/hp	7.3 lb/hp
Weights		
Empty	N/A	
Loaded	17,900kg	39,462 lb
Useful load	N/A	
Performance		
Max speed	694km/h	431mph
	at 9,300m	at 30,511ft
Cruise speed	490km/h	304mph
	at 9,300m	at 30,511ft
Climb	N/A	
Max range	5,049km	3,137 miles
Armament	Up to 1,000kg (2,204 lb) of bombs	

Kogiken Plan IV – data

Type	Reconnaissance Plane	
Crew	Two	

Powerplant Two Nakajima Ha-45 18-cylinder, air-cooled radial engines, each developing 1,480hp driving a four-bladed metal propeller

Dimensions		
Span	14.47m	47.5ft
Length	10.33m	33.9ft
Height	3.74m	12.3ft
Wing area	30.00m²	301.3ft²
Wing loading	N/A	
Power loading	N/A	

Weights		
Empty	4,591kg	10,121 lb
Loaded	7,367kg	16,241 lb
Useful load	N/A	

Performance		
Max speed	705km/h	438mph
	at 6,000m	at 19,685ft
Cruise speed	N/A	
Climb	N/A	
Max range	3,000km	1,864 miles plus 2 hours

Armament One 7.7mm Type 89 machine gun

Kogiken Plan IV Revised – data

Type	Reconnaissance Plane	
Crew	Two	

Powerplant Two Nakajima Ha-45 18-cylinder, air-cooled radial engines, each developing 1,480hp driving a four-bladed metal propeller

Dimensions		
Span	14.47m	47.5ft
Length	10.69m	35.1ft
Height	3.59m	11.8ft
Wing area	30.00m²	301.3ft²
Wing loading	N/A	
Power loading	N/A	

Weights		
Empty	4,426kg	9,757 lb
Loaded	7,202kg	15,877 lb
Useful load	N/A	

Performance		
Max speed	715km/h	444mph
	at 6,000m	at 19,685ft
Cruise speed	N/A	
Climb	N/A	
Max range	3,000km	1,864 miles plus 2 hours

Armament One 7.7mm Type 89 machine gun

between them. The key changes from the Kogiken plans were the engines used. The Plan I and Plan II bombers used four Ha-145 radials while the Plan III used only two of the Mitsubishi Ha-211MB 18-cylinder, air-cooled radial engines. Of all the designs, the Tachikawa Plan I had the largest crew compliment at six men.

In the reconnaissance class, three primary designs emerged, all by Kogiken. Each of them simply followed trends set in the fighter and bomber classes. The Kogiken Plan IV Reconnaissance Plane was essentially the Kogiken Plan III Revised Light Bomber adapted for the reconnaissance role. Not surprisingly, the Kogiken Plan IV Revised Reconnaissance Plane was derived from the Kogiken Plan V Revised Light Bomber. The Kogiken Plan VIII High Speed Reconnaissance Plane was based on the Kogiken Plan VI Heavy Bomber but had a highly streamlined fuselage with nearly flush glazing over the crew compartment. As was typical of early Japanese reconnaissance aircraft the

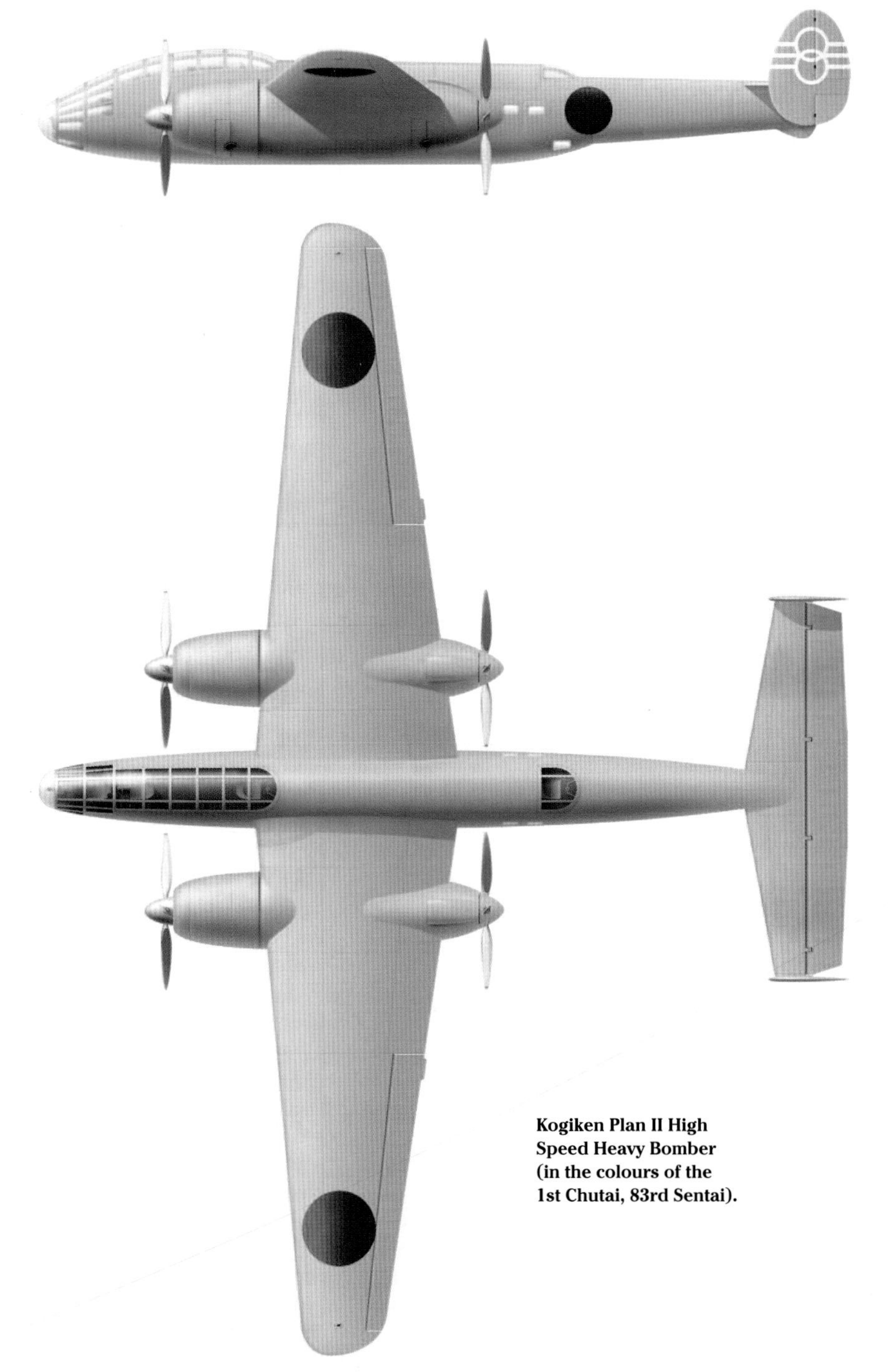

Kogiken Plan II High Speed Heavy Bomber (in the colours of the 1st Chutai, 83rd Sentai).

KELCEY FAULKNER

defensive armament was extremely light for all of these planes.

None of the Kogiken aircraft would be constructed. In part, this was due to the designs using technology that was either in development or not yet available. Another factor was the unorthodox nature of many of the aircraft drafted – one might liken the Kogiken aircraft to the results of a brainstorming with minimal restrictions on what might be deemed possible. Nevertheless, the study was not a wasted effort and it is certainly reasonable to presume that the information provided valuable data and worthwhile methods for subsequent IJA aircraft. For example, the Kawasaki Ki-64 would use the Ha-201 coupled engine with a surface evaporation cooling system. Another example was the Kawasaki Ki-88 which was to use a fuselage-buried Ha-140 engine that drove the propeller via an extension shaft. The Mitsubishi Ki-46-III (codenamed *Dinah* by the Allies) may have also benefitted from some of the aerodynamic streamlining studies done by Kogiken.

KELCEY FAULKNER

Kogiken Plan VIII High Speed Reconnaissance Plane (in the colours of the 2nd Chutai, 81st Sentai).

Tachikawa Plan III – data

Type High Speed Heavy Bomber
Crew Four

Powerplant
Two Mitsubishi Ha-211MB 18-cylinder, air-cooled radial engines, each developing 2,200hp driving a four-bladed metal propeller

Dimensions		
Span	24.38m	80ft
Length	17.58m	57.7ft
Height	4.81m	15.8ft
Wing area	66.00m²	710.4ft²
Wing loading	219.70kg/m²	45lb/ft²
Power loading	4.12kg/hp	9.1lb/hp

Weights		
Empty	8,075kg	17,802lb
Loaded	14,500kg	31,967lb
Useful load	6,234kg	13,743lb

Performance		
Max speed	641km/h	398mph
	at 8,500m	at 27,887ft
Cruise speed	499km/h	310mph
	at 8,500m	at 27,887ft
Climb	N/A	
Max range	4,999km	3,106 miles

Armament Two 7.7mm Type 89 machine guns, one 12.7mm Ho-103 machine gun and up to 1,500kg (3,306lb) of bombs

Kogiken Plan IV Revised – data

Type Reconnaissance Plane
Crew Two

Powerplant
Four Mitsubishi Ha-211-II 18-cylinder, air-cooled radial engines, each developing 2,100hp driving a four-bladed metal propeller

Dimensions		
Span	17.67m	58ft
Length	13.10m	43ft
Height	3.56m	11.7ft
Wing area	61.00m²	656.5ft²
Wing loading	N/A	
Power loading	N/A	

Weights		
Empty	7,420kg	16,358lb
Loaded	9,910kg	21,847lb
Useful load	N/A	

Performance		
Max speed	775km/h	481mph
	at 6,000m	at 19,685ft
Cruise speed	N/A	
Climb	N/A	
Max range	3,000km	1,864 miles plus 2 hours

Armament None

Deployment None of the Rikugun Kogiken plans progressed beyond the planning stage.

Tachikawa Ki-74

MUNEO HOSAKA

In 1939, a specification was drawn up that called for an aircraft capable of conducting long range reconnaissance and it was Tachikawa that answered the call to provide such a plane. However, the resulting Ki-74 would find itself both a victim of development delays and the changing fortunes of war.

In the spring of 1939, the Koku Hombu issued a specification for a long range reconnaissance aircraft that could muster a range of 5,000km (3,107 miles) and a cruise speed of at least 280mph. The reason for this request was to provide a plane capable of operating from bases in Manchuria and flying to the west of Lake Baikal. The lake, the deepest in the world, is located north of Mongolia, near the southern Siberian city of Irkutsk. Certainly the intent was to monitor Russian and their allied Mongolian forces, especially in the face of Japanese defeats at the Battle of Lake Khasan in 1938 and the Battle of Khalkhin Gol in 1939, both at the hands of the Soviets.

Tachikawa submitted a proposal to meet the Koku Hombu's specifications, drawn up by the design team led by Dr. H. Kimura. The initial design for the Ki-74 was drafted in 1939. To achieve the required performance, Kimura selected two Mitsubishi Ha-214M radial engines. Each engine developed 2,400hp and would drive a six-bladed propeller. It was the pressure cabin for the Ki-74 that would be the stumbling block to finalising the design.

Even before the Ki-74 was conceived, work on developing a pressure cabin for use in high-altitude aircraft was being conducted by Tachikawa. The purpose of such a cabin was to maintain air pressure for the crew when operating at altitudes in which the outside air pressure is much lower and the air thinner. Cabin pressurisation is desired for aircraft flying higher than 3,048m (10,000ft) and doing so provided the crew with a much more comfortable working environment that did not require the use of oxygen and flight gear to protect against the cold. It also prevented conditions like hypoxia, barotrauma and altitude/decompression sickness. Two designs were built that would test pressure cabin concepts. The first was the Tachikawa Ki-77. Conceived as a plane to make a non-stop flight from Tōkyō to New York, work on the Ki-77 began in 1940. For the Ki-77, Dr. Kimura utilised a sealed crew cabin but one which was not pressurised. The belief was that the cabin would keep in the oxygen but in testing it failed to meet expectations and the crew had to wear their oxygen masks constantly. With the poor showing of the Ki-77 cabin, Tachikawa tested a fully pressurised cabin in the Tachikawa SS-1. The SS-1 was a modification of the Army Type LO transport which itself was a licence built version of the Lockheed Model 14 Super Electra (codenamed *Thelma* by the Allies). Work on the SS-1 also began in 1940 and the one and only example was completed in May 1943 with subsequent testing providing excellent data on pressurised crew cabins.

MUNEO HOSAKA

The research into pressure cabins and the construction of the Ki-77 and SS-1 delayed the Ki-74 project so badly that work on it was halted; once it became obvious that the cabin for the new plane would not be ready the entire project was shelved. No prototype was produced.

However, towards the close of 1941, the Ki-74 project was resurrected in order to investigate the possibility of adapting the design to suit the role of a long range, high altitude bomber and reconnaissance platform. One such bombing mission envisioned was against the United States. To meet such a requirement, adjustments had to be made to the initial reconnaissance-only Ki-74 design. Armour was incorporated along with self-sealing fuel tanks. In addition, the appropriate apparatus for bombing was introduced. Finally, the initial Ha-214M radial engines were replaced by two Mitsubishi Ha-211-I radial engines, each producing 2,200hp. Once the redesign was completed it was presented to the Koku Hombu who approved it in September 1942 ordering three prototypes.

It was not until March 1944 that the first Ki-74 prototype was completed, but the other two aircraft were ready soon afterwards. The latter two aircraft differed from the first Ki-74 only in the fact that they used the Mitsubishi Ha-211-I Ru engines that incorporated turbo-superchargers. With the completion of the authorised batch of three aircraft, flight testing of the Ki-74 began. Handling was considered acceptable but the Ha-211-I and the Ha-211-I Ru engines were proving to be temperamental and prone to mechanical problems. A further thirteen pre-production aircraft were ordered, but due to the severe problems with the engines it was decided to replace them with Mitsubishi Ha-104 Ru radials. While the Ha-104 Ru was more reliable it also developed less horsepower, in fact only 2,000hp.

Tachikawa Ki-74 – data

Contemporaries Dornier Do 217P-0 (Germany), Dornier Do 317 (Germany), Focke-Wulf Fw 191 (Germany), Junkers Ju 86P and Ju 86R (Germany), Junkers Ju 388 Störtebeker (Germany), BOK-11 (Russia), De Havilland Mosquito B.Mk XVI (UK)

Type	High-Altitude, Long-Range Reconnaissance/Bomber
Crew	Five

Powerplant [First Prototype] Two Mitsubishi Ha-211-I, 18-cylinder, air-cooled radial engines rated at 2,200hp for take-off, 2,070hp at 1,000m/3,280ft and 1,930hp at 5,000m/16,405ft; [Second and Third Prototypes and Fourth Pre-production Ki-74] Two Mitsubishi Ha-211-I Ru 18-cylinder, air-cooled radial engines rated at 2,200hp for take-off, 2,070hp at 1,000m/3,280ft and 1,720hp at 9,500m/31,170ft; [Remaining aircraft] Two Mitsubishi Ha-104 Ru 18-cylinder, air-cooled radial engines rated at 2,000hp for take-off, 1,900hp at 2,000m/6,560ft and 1,750hp at 6,000m/19,685ft; all engines spun four-bladed propellers

Dimensions		
Span	26.97m	88.5ft
Length	17.64m	57.9ft
Height	5.09m	16.7ft
Wing area	80.00m²	861.11ft²
Wing loading	242.65kg/m²	49.7 lb/ft²
Power loading	4.39kg/hp	9.7 lb/hp

Weights		
Empty	10,200kg	22,487 lb
Loaded	19,400kg	42,770 lb

Performance		
Max speed	570km/h	354mph
	at 8,500m	at 27,890ft
Cruise speed	401km/h	249mph
	at 8,000m	at 26,245ft
Range	8,000km	4,971 miles
Climb	17 min to 8,000m (26,245ft)	
Ceiling	12,000m	39,370ft

Armament One remote-controlled 12.7mm Ho-103 machine gun in the tail; 1,000kg (2,205 lb) of bombs

Deployment Did not see service. 16 built (3 prototypes, 1 long-range transcontinental aircraft, 12 pre-production aircraft).

Survivors

Tachikawa Ki-74 (FE-2206)

This was one of four total Ki-74 bombers captured at the end of the war. Two were taken at Tachikawa's factory while the remainder were obtained from the IJA's test centre at Tama Airfield (now Yokota Air Base in Fussa, Japan). All four (see below) were listed on the 10 March 1946 report. FE-2206 was listed as being at AOAMC on 1 August 1946 but was later relegated for disposal.

Tachikawa Ki-74 (FE-2207)

This example was at MAMA in storage as listed on the 1 August 1946 manifest. It was later slated for transfer to the Park Ridge storage facility in September 1946 but no further trace of FE-2207 remains and was most likely scrapped.

Tachikawa Ki-74 (FE-2208)

Like FE-2206, this Ki-74 was housed at AOAMC on 1 August 1946 and met the same fate.

Tachikawa Ki-74 (FE-2209)

FE-2209 was the third Ki-74 kept at AOAMC and joined the previous two aircraft on the scrapheap.

The Ki-74 as built was a mid-wing monoplane. The pressure cabin made up the majority of the front of the aircraft with the bomb bay underneath. The use of the pressure cabin necessitated smaller window arrangements (as opposed to more conventional glazing) and the flight deck was offset to the port side of the fuselage. The aircraft had a crew of five which consisted of the bombardier, pilot, co-pilot, navigator/radio operator and gunner. All were housed within the cabin with the bombardier in the nose, the pilot and co-pilot on the flight deck and the navigator/radio operator and gunner in stations behind the flight deck. Because the Ki-74 was expected to operate at high-altitude where interception would be difficult, the plane carried a very minimal armament consisting of a tail mounted 12.7mm Ho-103 machine gun that was fired by the gunner via remote control. Although the Ki-74 was not a dedicated bomber, it carried a payload of 1,000kg (2,205 lb) of bombs which was comparable to IJA bombers then in service.

As construction commenced on the pre-production Ki-74s, plans were formulated to put them to use. When a number of Ki-74s had been built, they were to be assembled into shotai (a flight comprised of three aircraft) and massed to conduct bombing missions against the US airbases in Saipan from which B-29 Superfortresses operated.

While the bulk of the Ki-74s were constructed as bombers and reconnaissance platforms, another task was proposed. With much of the communication between Japan and Germany severed by the Allies, especially by sea, a plan was made to use a Ki-74 for non-stop flights to and from Germany. In 1944, the fourth pre-production Ki-74 was removed from the line and underwent modifications to allow it to accomplish such a feat. Higher powered Ha-211-I-Ru engines were utilised and fuel was carried to enable the aircraft to fly up to 12,000km (7,456 miles) – sufficient to fly from Tōkyō to Berlin. In addition, all non-essential equipment was removed and the flight deck was reallocated to the middle of the fuselage and lengthened. The modified Ki-74 would never make such a flight as Germany surrendered to the Allies before it could make the first attempt. The fifteen Ki-74s were never to see combat, in part because the flight testing of the twelve remaining pre-production aircraft was not completed before the end of Japan's part in World War 2.

Prior to the end of hostilities, two further variants of the Ki-74 were proposed. The first adapted the Ki-74 to a transport role but this was soon discarded. The second was the Ki-74-II which would have been a dedicated bombing platform. As such, the Ki-74-II was a redesign which showed some big differences to the Ki-74. The foremost alteration was the pressure cabin which was smaller and kept forward of the wings within the fuselage. This allowed for a deeper bomb bay that was needed to carry the planned 2,000kg (4,410 lb) bomb load. Due to the heavier weight, the operating range was estimated to be 7,144km (4,439 miles) (in comparison to the 8,000km/4,971 miles of the Ki-74). Because of the heavier bomb load, the Ki-74-II was to be supported on a twin tyred front landing gear. The wings for the Ki-74-II were to be more slender than the Ki-74 for high-altitude operation and instead of the single tail mounted machine gun, two machine guns or cannons were to be used. Two Mitsubishi Ha-104-Ru engines would power the bomber, but like the transport concept, the Ki-74-II was abandoned and did not advance beyond the design stage.

Thanks to its long development history the US was aware of the Ki-74. The main thing they did not know was the role. Thinking that the Ki-74 was a fighter it was assigned the codename *Pat*. It was not until May 1945 that the true role of the Ki-74 was discovered and so the codename was changed to *Patsy*.

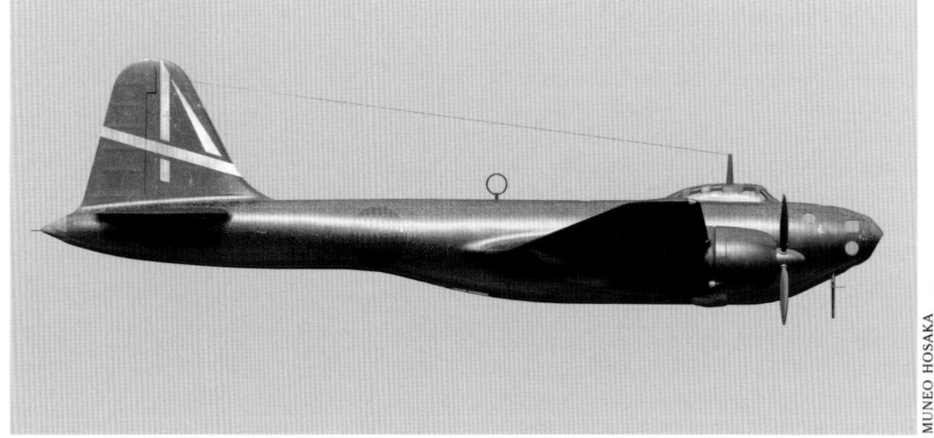

MUNEO HOSAKA

Tachikawa Ki-94-I

MUNEO HOSAKA

In the summer of 1942, the Koku Hombu was formulating specifications for a fighter that supported a heavy armament and could operate at high altitude. After settling on the specifications, the Koku Hombu approached Tachikawa and Nakajima and asked each firm to produce a design to meet these requirements.

The specifications for the fighter included a maximum speed of 800km/h (497mph) and a range of 3,000km (1,864 miles). The Koku Hombu knew the demands were high, perhaps even impossible to obtain, and so asked Tachikawa and Nakajima to put forward proposals to meet the demands. But they handicapped Tachikawa by allowing Nakajima to ignore the range requirement. As such, Nakajima could concern themselves with making their design fast without worrying about how far it could operate. Undeterred, Tachikawa's designers set about the task of coming up with a concept that would achieve what the Koku Hombu asked for. What resulted was a departure from the conventional.

It was decided that two Mitsubishi Ha-211 Ru (Ha-43 Ru), 18-cylinder, air-cooled radial engines should be used placed in the fuselage in a push-pull configuration. The key advantage this offered was a reduction in drag over a more conventional, wing mounted engine arrangement. Secondly, the centreline thrust symmetry of the aircraft would be maintained in case of engine failure which, in turn, allowed for nearly no loss of control. Each engine was to drive a four-bladed propeller. A twin-boom arrangement was mated to the low mounted wings. For weapons, a 30mm Ho-155 cannon was fitted into each wing while a 37mm Ho-2044 cannon was situated directly below the Ho-155, installed in the tail boom. If required, the Ki-94-I would be capable of carrying up to 500kg (1,102 lb) of bombs. The Ki-94-I was to use a pressurised cockpit for the pilot and featured a tricycle landing gear.

Once the Ki-94-I was finalised, construction began on a wooden mock-up to be completed in October 1943. Tachikawa then invited representatives from the Koku

MUNEO HOSAKA

Tachikawa Ki-94-I – data

Contemporaries
Junkers EF 112 (Germany), Tupolev ANT-23 (Russia)

Because the Ki-94-I was never built, the specifications are based on Tachikawa's final design plans and estimated performance.

Type	Heavy Fighter
Crew	One

Powerplant Two Mitsubishi Ha-211 Ru (Ha-43 Ru) 18-cylinder, air-cooled radial engines; rated at 2,700hp at 1,500m/4,921ft, 2,800hp at 2,800m/9,186ft and 1,750hp at 10,500m/34,448ft; each engine drove a four-bladed, VDM propeller, the front having a 3.3m (10.8) diameter, the rear a 3.4m (11.1ft) diameter

Dimensions		
Span	12.86m	42.2ft
Length	13.04m	42.8ft
Height	3.84m	12.6ft
Wing area	36.99m²	398.2ft²
Wing loading	237.77kg/m²	48.7 lb/ft²
Power loading	2.49kg/hp	5.5 lb/hp

Weights		
Empty	6,500kg	14,330 lb
Loaded	8,800kg	19,400 lb

Performance		
Max speed	781km/h	485mph
	at 10,000m	at 32,810ft
Range	1,520km	944 miles
Max range	2,519km	1,565 miles
Endurance	2.5 hours	
Max endurance	5 hours	
Climb	9 min 56 sec to 10,000m (32,808ft)	
Ceiling	14,000km	45,931ft

Armament
Two 57mm Ho-401 cannons, two 37mm Ho-204 cannons, two 30mm Ho-15 cannons and up to 500kg (1,102 lb) of bombs

Deployment
None. Did not advance past a mock-up.

MUNEO HOSAKA

Hombu to visit and inspect the Ki-94-I. On inspection and review, Tachikawa was to be disappointed when the design was rejected outright. The Koku Hombu inspectors found the Ki-94-I to be too unorthodox, too complex to build and that Tachikawa's performance estimates were optimistic.

Tachikawa, however, did not give up on the Ki-94-I and reworked the aircraft into a heavy fighter that was designated the Rikugun Kogiken Ki-104. To boost the armament, two 57mm Ho-401 cannons were added. Unfortunately, this design was also rejected. With the rejection of the high altitude fighter and the subsequent heavy fighter revision, Tachikawa finally abandoned the Ki-94-I. Tachikawa did not wish to let Nakajima's design against the high altitude fighter specifications, the Ki-87, go unchallenged. The result was the Ki-94-II.

MUNEO HOSAKA

Tachikawa Ki-94-II

MUNEO HOSAKA

Tachikawa Ki-94-II – data

Contemporaries
Focke-Wulf Fw 190 V18/U1 (Germany), Focke-Wulf Ta 152H (Germany), Mikoyan-Gurevich MiG-3D (Russia), Mikoyan-Gurevich I-220 and I-230 series (Russia),Yakovlev I-28 (Russia), Polikarpov ITP(M-2) (Russia), Yakovlev Yak-3PD and Yak-3TK (Russia)

Because the Ki-94-II was never flown, the specifications are based on Tachikawa's estimated performance.

Type	High-Altitude Fighter
Crew	One

Powerplant One Nakajima [Ha-44] 13 (Ha-219), 18-cylinder radial engine, developing 2,450hp for take-off, fitted with a Ru-204 turbosupercharger, driving a constant speed, four-bladed metal propeller

Dimensions		
Span	13.99m	45.9ft
Length	11.97m	39.3ft
Height	4.60m	15.1ft
Wing area	27.99m²	301.3ft²
Wing loading	230.45kg/m²	47.2 lb/ft²
Power loading	2.63kg/hp	5.8 lb/hp

Weights		
Empty	4,690kg	10,340 lb
Loaded	6,450kg	14,220 lb

Performance		
Max speed	720km/h	447mph
	at 10,000m	at 32,808ft
Range	2,200km	1,367 miles
Climb	17 min 38 sec to 10,000m (32,808ft)	
Service ceiling	14,250m	46,751ft

Armament
Two 30mm Ho-155 cannons, two 20mm Ho-5 cannons and either two 30kg (66 lb) air-to-air rockets or one 500kg (1,102 lb) bomb

Deployment
None. One prototype was completed with a second under construction when the war ended.

Survivors
Tachikawa Ki-94-II (FE-150)
This was the first prototype and was surrendered at Tachikawa's facility near Tōkyō. Delivered to MAMA for storage and eventual servicing, it was listed on a 10 March 1946 manifest of aircraft available for aviation industry evaluation. On 1 August 1946, the Ki-94-II was still at MAMA but no effort was made to restore it although it was designated for display at NASM. September 1946 saw the start of restoration work for display purposes and the project was to be completed by 18 September 1946. The last known whereabouts of the Ki-94-II was in Park Ridge in 1949.

In October 1943, the Koku Hombu rejected Tachikawa's radical, twin engine, twin-boom, push-pull fighter, the company's answer to the Koku Hombu's request for a high-altitude fighter. Tachikawa was told the Ki-94-I was unconventional, complex and its estimated performance specifications were optimistic. The rejection left Nakajima's Ki-87 the sole contender for the specification, something Tachikawa was not going to let happen.

Soon after the rejection Tachikawa utilised the same specifications given to Nakajima to plan a revised design. Whereas Tachikawa had to meet the Koku Hombu's 3,000m (1,864 mile) range requirement and a 800km/h (497mph) maximum speed, Nakajima only had to contend with meeting the speed maximum. Unbridled by the range issue, Tachikawa engineers went about the task of producing a design capable of matching and exceeding the Ki-87.

Knowing that the Koku Hombu would likely reject anything out of the ordinary in concept, a more conventional approach was taken. The man behind the revised aircraft was Tatsuo Hasegawa. Retained from the Ki-94-I was the pressurised cockpit for the pilot but everything else was redesigned. The new project used a standard configuration for a single-engine, all-metal fighter to ensure acceptance by the Koku Hombu. The powerplant selected for the plane was the Nakajima [Ha-44] 13 (Ha-219), 18-cylinder radial engine that was rated at 2,450hp. The engine was equipped with a fan cooled, exhaust driven Ru-204 turbosupercharger that was situated on the underside of the fuselage. Originally, it was planned that a six-bladed propeller should be used. However, testing showed that when in operation a blur was created by the spinning prop, obscuring the pilot's forward vision. Therefore, a four-bladed propeller was selected. For weapons the aircraft had a similar cannon armament as the Ki-94-I, but this was downgraded to two Ho-155 30mm cannons and two Ho-5 20mm cannons with one of each calibre cannon fitted into each wing. The wings were a typical laminar flow-type with the cockpit situated behind the trailing edges of the wings. As the dimensions show, the new design was fairly large by Japanese standards, even superseding Nakajima's Ki-87 in size.

With the drafts completed, Tachikawa presented them to the Koku Hombu. After review, the design was accepted as the Ki-94-II and Tachikawa received the order to produce a static test airframe, three prototypes and 18 pre-production aircraft. As soon as approval was received for the Ki-94-II, work began on the construction of the first two prototypes with the first to be completed by 20 July 1945. However, this date would not be met as delays in production caused the program to fall behind schedule which, in turn, delayed the final completion of the first Ki-94-II.

Tachikawa scheduled the first flight for 18 August 1945. However, on 15 August 1945, the war ended for Japan and the Ki-94-II was prevented from making any flights. The end of the war meant that the second prototype was never completed.

MUNEO HOSAKA

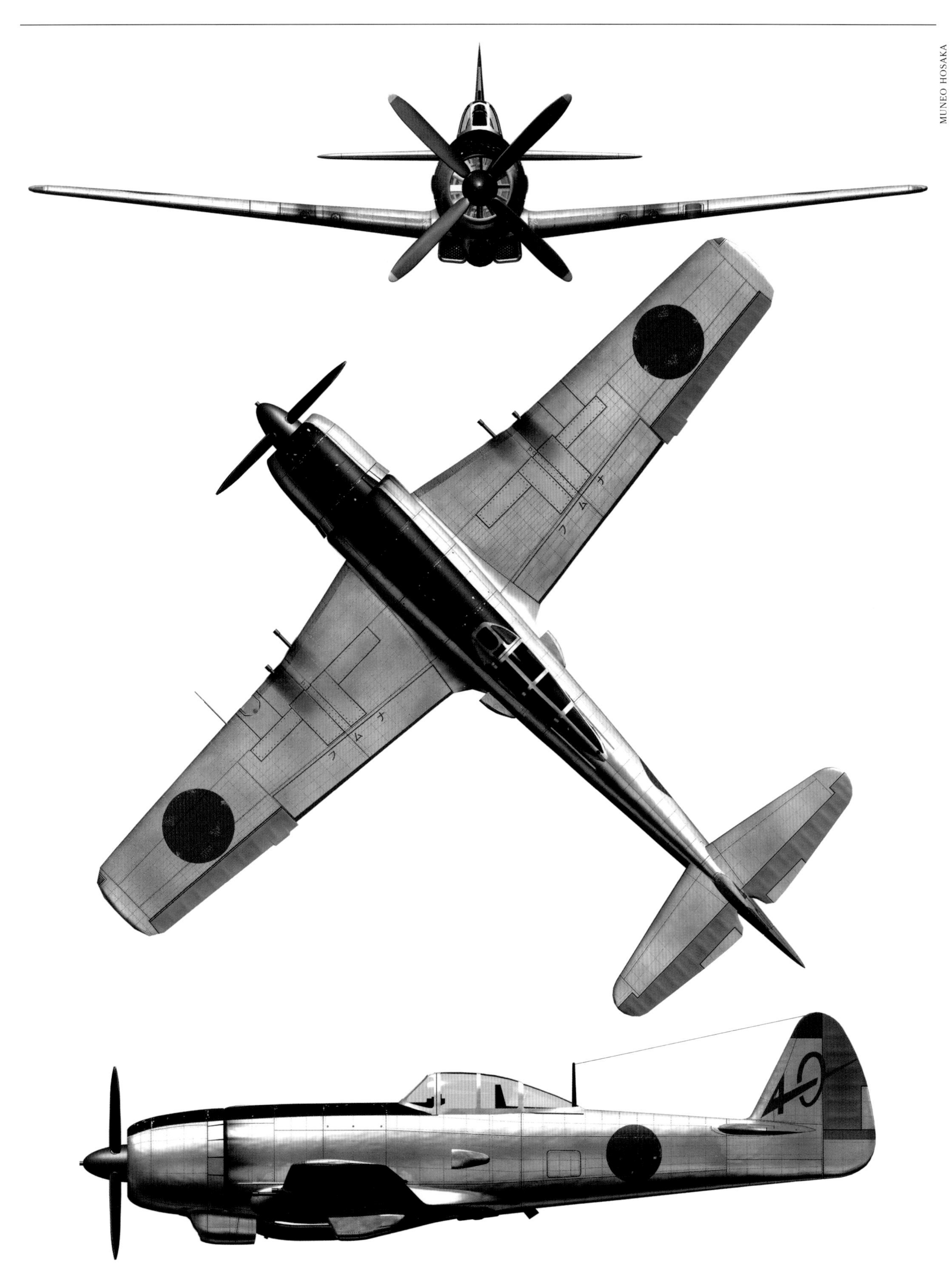

MUNEO HOSAKA

Tachikawa Ki-162 and Other IJA Jet Projects

It was only after January 1945 that the Japanese were given access to the very latest German jet technology. Prior to that, access came only after German equipment had achieved operational status. Thus, in the beginning of 1944, the Japanese were made aware of the Messerschmitt Me 262 jet fighter and Me 163 rocket-powered interceptor long after they were flying. Consequently, it was not long before official requests for data came from Japanese representatives in Berlin. In the subsequent negotiations the Germans were told that only the IJA would be building the Japanese version of the Me 262, the Nakajima Ki-201 Karyū, the development of which began in January 1945. But even before this, the IJA began to formulate jet designs of its own, spurred by the release of technical information by the Germans.

In late 1944, the IJA initiated a study for a single engine jet fighter and the task was given to the Tachikawa Dai-Ichi Rikugun Kokusho. The IJA's Captain Hayashi and Captain Yasuda assembled and led two teams to research the concept and begin design. The one restriction imposed was the requirememt for at least a half hour's endurance. At this time, only the Ne 12 series of turbojets was available. The Ne 12, a development of an earlier project called the Ne 10, was found to be too heavy. A lighter model, the Ne 12B, was produced in limited numbers until the Ne 20 turbojet was first tested in March 1945. This engine proved to be superior to the Ne 12B.

The problem facing both Hayashi and Yasuda was that performance and endurance on a par with a twin engine design had to be achieved using only a single power unit. With the Ne 12B unacceptable, both of these looked to the projected developments of the Ne 20. These included the Ishikawajima Ne 130, Nakajima Ne 230 and the Mitsubishi Ne 330 turbojets because they were expected to produce improved thrust over the Ne 20.

The depiction of the 'Tachikawa Ki-162' shown here is displayed in the colours of the 23rd Independent Chutai, operating in Okinawa, 1945.

DANIEL UHR

With at least the basic dimensions of the turbojet in mind, each team got to work drafting their designs for the jet fighter. Two concepts emerged from both teams towards the middle of 1945.

Hayashi's team took the turbojet and placed it inside the fuselage near the tail. The fuselage was to be fairly slender in shape with the cockpit forward of the low mounted wings which were to be placed about mid-fuselage. The aircraft was to have a nose intake with the turbojet's exhaust being vented out through the tailpipe or rear of the fuselage. Yasuda's group took the turbojet and placed it on top of the fuselage. As opposed to Hayashi's more slender aircraft, the Yasuda design had a shorter and wider fuselage. As a result of the engine being on top, this eliminated the possibility of a conventional tail stabiliser arrangement and thus each tailplane ended in a vertical stabiliser. Yasuda felt that with the engine outside the fuselage, the nose could then be used to carry armament allowing for improved and concentrated accuracy. Yasuda's design was very reminiscent of the Heinkel He 162 Volksjäger.

At this juncture, the Volksjäger will be discussed briefly. The He 162 was designed as a fighter that could be built quickly with semi-skilled or unskilled labour, using few war critical materials and only a single turbojet. This enabled the He 162 to be turned out more quickly than the more complex Me 262 then in service. The He 162 began with the Volksjäger competition, but as Heinkel had the inside track with Deputy of the Reich Ministry of Armament and War Production, Karl-Otto Saur, who also happened to be the managing director for Heinkel, the study for the He 162 was already underway. By the time the other competing designs were submitted for the competition, the mock-up of the He 162 was already under construction. Little surprise the contract for the Volksjäger went to Heinkel in September 1944. On 6 December 1944, the He 162 V1 flew for the first time.

The He 162 used a light metal monocoque fuselage with a moulded plywood nose. The high-mounted wing was one piece, made of wood and plywood skinning with metal wing tips. The two tailplanes sported vertical stabilisers on their ends. Only four bolts secured the wings to the fuselage. A single BMW 003A-1 Sturm turbojet sat atop the fuselage just behind the cockpit and to help him abandon the aircraft in an emergency, the pilot was provided with an ejection seat. For weapons, two MG 151 20mm cannons were fitted with 120 rounds per gun. The top speed of the He 162 was 905km/h (562mph) at 6,000m (19,690ft) with a 438km (272 mile) radius at full power.

In January 1945, Erprobungskommando 162 was created to field test the He 162 and on February 6 I/JG 1 was ordered to convert to the jet fighter. The He 162 was an unforgiving aircraft but in the hands of a skilled pilot it was an exceptional dogfighter. Pilots were told to avoid combat with Allied aircraft, however in late April and early May, I/JG 1 scored a handful of aerial victories. This was tempered by the loss of 13 aircraft and 10 pilots, mostly due to accidents. The only other unit activated, the 1.(Volkssturm)/JG 1 at Sagan-Kupper, never received their He 162 fighters and this was fortunate. The pilots of this unit were to only receive training in the He 162S, a glider version of the He 162 that had no engine, non-retractable landing gear and a rudimentary second cockpit for the instructor. After a few gliding flights, the untrained pilot was expected to fly the jet powered He 162 and the results would have been disastrous. A flyable two-seat He 162 known as the Doppelsitzer, fitted with a second cockpit for the instructor at the expense of the cannons and ammunition, oxygen system and fuel capacity, was not completed by the end of the war in Europe.

On 15 April 1945, the Oberkommando der Luftwaffe approved the release of specifications and production data for the He 162 to the Japanese. A delegation of IJN officials studied the He 162 and visited Heinkel's He 162 production line in Rostock, Germany. Impressed with the aircraft, the Japanese quickly requested technical data on the fighter. Of course, by this stage of the war for Germany there was no way that physical blueprints, production tools, jigs or a sample He 162 could be shipped to Japan. Instead, the only means available to rapidly send information on the jet was via wireless transmission – i.e., radio. To help facilitate the transmission of the data, Commander Yoshio Nagamori used a datum line (a fixed, measurable line, used as a reference from which angular or linear measurements are taken) to measure the He 162 and transmitted the resulting dimensions to Japan. Only a portion of the data Nagamori sent was received in Japan.

Even though parts of the measurements for the He 162 made it to the Japanese mainland, enough was received to begin making use of the information, filling in the gaps, revising the design to suit Japanese production capability and compiling the drafts needed to realise the aircraft. Even though the IJN was the branch that obtained the He 162 data, it appeared that it would be the IJA who would produce it. In addition to developing the aircraft from the data, plans were made to begin production.

Whether Captain Yasuda and his team used the He 162 as their influence or arrived at a similar design by coincidence may never be known. But the IJA would reject Yasuda's fighter and instead selected Captain Hayashi's design for continued work. Perhaps it was felt that with the acquisition of the He 162, Yasuda's design was redundant. With Hayashi's aircraft approved, he and his team moved forward with refining the design and constructing a prototype. However, by August 1945 when hostilities ceased, none of the IJA's jet programs were ready to fly. Neither Hayashi's jet nor the Japanese version of the He 162 would progress past the initial design stage. Only the Nakajima Ki-201 ever made it to the construction phase which, by the end of the war, amounted to a single incomplete fuselage.

As a note, 'Ki-162' has been used by some as the designation for the Japanese produced He 162. There is no historical evidence to support this although it is not without precedent, such as the case with the proposed Mitsubishi Ki-90 that was to be the Japanese version of the Junkers Ju 90. In addition, one may see the full name as the 'Tachikawa Ki-162'. It is not unreasonable to believe that Tachikawa may have played a part in assessing the He 162 data given that the IJA had the Tachikawa Dai-Ichi Rikugun Kokusho and the Rikagun Kokugijutsu Kenkyūjo (also at Tachikawa) at their disposal. Whether Tachikawa would have actually built the production Japanese He 162 is not known.

Tachikawa Ki-162 – data

Contemporaries

Blohm und Voss P.221/01 (Germany), Republic F-84 Thunderjet (US), Heinkel He 162 (Germany), Arado E.580 (Germany), BMW Strahljäger I (Germany), Heinkel P.1073 (Germany), Henschel Hs 132 (Germany), Antonov SKh (Russia)

Specifications

Very little is known of the jet designs created by Yasuda or Hayashi and thus no specification information has surfaced. Likewise, since there was little time to act on the He 162 data, there is no information on what the specifications would have been for the Japanese version though it would not be unreasonable to conclude the dimensions and performance would have been similar to the German jet.

Deployment

None. None of the jet fighters got past the design stage.

Imperial Japanese Navy

Kawanishi Baika

The invasion of the Japanese home islands was a genuine threat to Japanese military planners. Operation Downfall was the Allied plan to launch the final blow against Japan. This consisted of the capture of Kyūshū (Operation Olympic) that would provide the jump-off point for the invasion of Honshū, near Tōkyō (Operation Coronet). Given the geography of Japan, Japanese military leadership was able to narrow the likely avenues of attack. To that end, Operation Ketsugō was formulated. A critical component of the operation was special attack units and they needed aircraft in mass numbers to succeed in repelling the invasion. This provided the spark for the Kawanishi Baika.

On 2 July 1944, the Kaigun Koku Hombu issued a directive to Kawanishi Kokuki K.K. to produce a special attack aircraft. The design was to be a replacement for the Kūgishō Ōka Model 11 and Model 22 as well as the special attack version of the Nakajima Kitsuka. The new aircraft, called the Baika (meaning Plum Blossom), needed to be constructed from as much non-critical war materials as possible and be of simple design to allow for production by unskilled or semi-skilled labour in small, scattered workshops. These demands were a result of the relentless Allied bombing of Japanese industry and that Allied naval forces had a stranglehold on imports of raw materials needed to sustain the Japanese military. To meet this directive, Professors Ichirō Tani and Taichirō Ogawa, both of the Aeronautical Institute of the Tōkyō Imperial University, began to study a means to achieve the requirements of the task before them, supported by Kawanishi.

The engine for the Baika, the Maru Ka-10 pulsejet, was derived from the German Argus As 109-014 pulsejet, the technical plans for it having been delivered to Japan via submarine in 1944. The Aeronautical Institute of the Tōkyō Imperial University studied the design and in time developed the Ka-10. A pulsejet is a simplistic engine that operates by mixing air that is taken into the engine via a shuttered or valve intake with fuel that is then ignited in the combustion chamber. The force of the explosion closes the intake and thus the resulting gas can only be expelled through the exhaust and forward thrust is generated. This cycle, or pulse, is repeated over and over up to 45 times per second in the case of the Argus Ar 109-014.

A pulsejet has four main benefits. Firstly, due to the simple nature of the engine it can be easily built. Secondly, it can use low grade fuels. Third, pulsejets offer reduced maintenance. Finally, they have a lower cost per unit when compared to other engines. However, the pulsejet does have three major flaws – it is not fuel efficient and, due to the operating nature of the engine, it is noisy and generates significant vibration.

The choice in using the pulsejet for the Baika was clear. With the situation for Japan being what it was in late 1944 and into 1945, the Ka-10 offered a far less complex engine than a turbojet or piston engine. This meant it could be built in greater numbers by unskilled or semi-skilled labourers. Because it could use low grade gasoline it put less of a strain on the supply chain struggling to provide more refined aviation fuel. Tani and Ogawa did find that the Ka-10 suffered from having a short

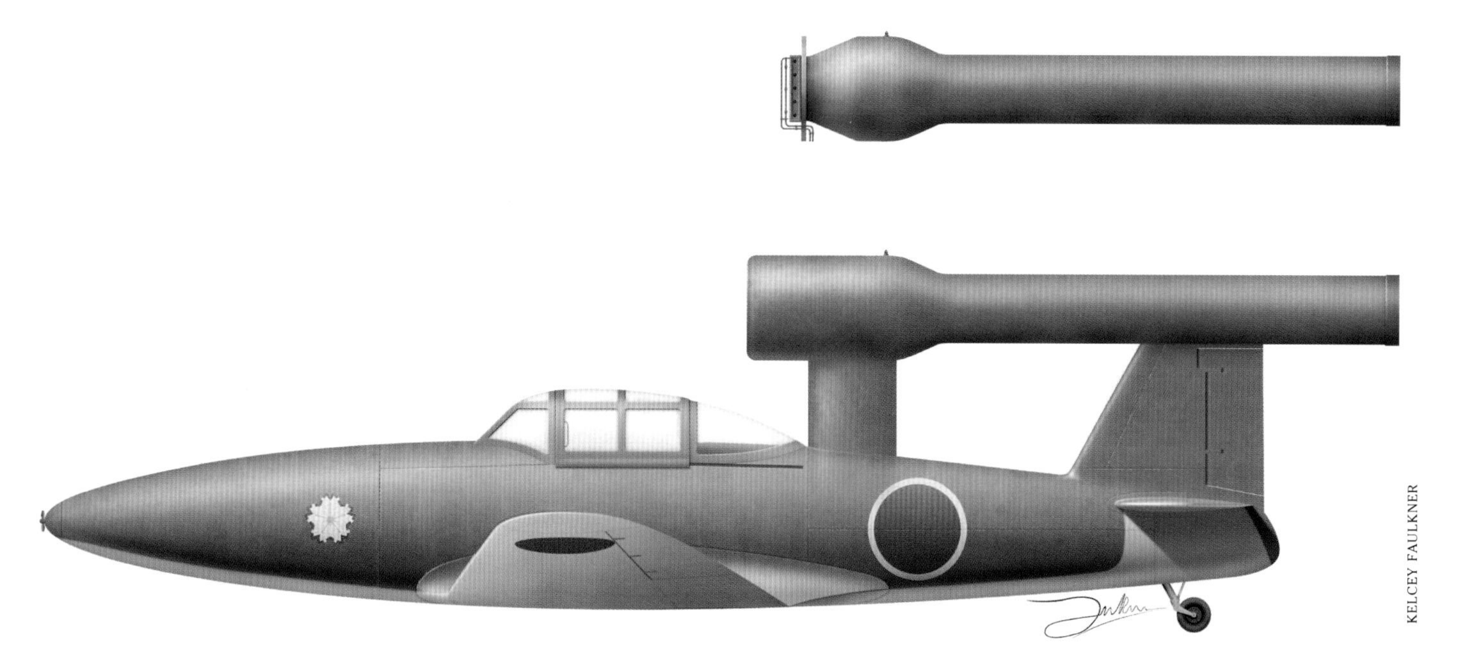

service life in regard to its fuel valve. They also had concerns that the high noise of the engine would provide enough advance warning that countermeasures could be set or sent up to combat the Baika. Finally, it was realised that the vibration caused by the engine would put a strain on the aircraft, perhaps causing failures in the aircraft's structure. The benefits, however, outweighed the disadvantages and work on the Baika design proceeded.

A meeting was called on 5 August 1945 to be held at the Aeronautical Institute of the Tōkyō Imperial University. It was attended by Admiral Wata and Admiral Katahira from the Kaigun Koku Hombu, professors Naganishi, Ogawa and Kihara of the Aeronautical Institute, and Chairman Katachiro of Kawanishi. In the discussions, the Baika was selected over the rival Kūgishō Ōka Model 43B, the latter being seen as too complex to build in numbers quickly, especially since it used the Ne 20 turbojet. Some revisions, specifically in simplifying the design, resulted in two versions of the Baika being discussed. As the Baika was to be used to defend the home island, launch rails were to be constructed that would use a solid fuel rocket to hurl the Baika into the air. The second version incorporated a simple landing gear and it was decided that the Baika with the landing gear would be used for training pilots before they converted to the rail launched Baika. After all, given the mission of shimpū attacks on Allied invasion ships, the pilot would not be returning and would have no need of landing gear. At the conclusion of the meeting, Kawanishi was given an order for one Baika prototype and ten two-seat trainers. The company was given a deadline of September to have the finalised design completed as well as a production plan finished. Mass production was to begin in October 1945.

Kawanishi was given the following specifications for the Baika:

- length of no more than 8.5m (27.8ft)
- height of no more than 4m (13.1ft)
- width, with folded wings, of no more than 3.6m (11.8ft)
- speed, with the Ka-10, must be at least 463km/h (287mph) at sea level
- a ceiling of 2,000m (6,561ft)
- range of at least 130km (80 miles)
- 100kg (220lb) explosive payload

As the Baika was developed, three versions of the aircraft emerged. Two were similar except for the cockpit placement. Despite the initial direction that the Baika would be rail launched, all versions used landing gear. The first version, or Type I, had the Ka-10 pulsejet directly above and behind the cockpit – this resulted in a fairing that enveloped a portion of the front support strut for the engine. The second version, the Type II, moved the Ka-10 further back, eliminating the need for the fairing. The final version, or Type III, placed the Ka-10 below the fuselage instead of above it. With the first two, the adjustment of the pulsejet may be due to maintain the centre of gravity on the aircraft. Facilitating pilot egress was likely not the reason for the move. The need for landing gear suggests that rail launching was not the only means to get the Baika airborne. Towing or using rocket boosters may have been considered or the use of the landing gear may have simply been for training use only. It is probable that the landing gear could be jettisoned to improve aerodynamics. The Type III, with the underslung engine, would suggest that it was to be carried by a parent aircraft much in the manner of the Ōka in addition to rail launching. It is unknown what the two-seat trainer version would have looked like. It is not unreasonable to assume that the warhead would have been removed and a second cockpit installed with ballast simulating the warhead, much like the Kūgishō Ōka Model 43 K-1 Kai, the two-seat trainer for the Ōka.

Initially, the Baika featured 8mm of armour protection for the pilot and although this only protected his back, it was a means to allow for some modicum of defence against interceptors firing from behind rather than ground fire. However, this was changed and the armour was removed, allowing for an increase in the warhead size up to 250kg (551lb). While this did result in a reduction of range, it was not seen as a detriment given that the likely engagement distances would be rather less than 130km (80 miles).

On 6 August 1945, another meeting on the Baika was called. Masayama Takeuchi of the Kaigun Koku Hombu had concerns in regard to its construction and sought to have the Baika built from as little war-critical material as possible, meaning that wood would be used wherever possible. The Baika also had to have passable handling characteristics in the air to give the pilot the best opportunity to strike his target. Beginning on 8 August 1945, a team of 60 men was assembled at Kawanishi to oversee development and production of the Baika to be led by engineer Tamenobu. It all came too late for on 15 August hostilities came to a close and the Baika project came to an end before it had left the drawing board.

As a note, some sources make the case that the German Fieseler Fi 103R Reichenberg, the manned version of the Fi 103 (V-1), was an influence for the Baika. There are US intelligence reports which indicate that the Japanese were well aware of the Fi 103 by October 1943 and that one was obtained in November 1944. These reports also suggest that the Japanese were very interested in the air launching techniques for the weapon. Another report indicates that the Japanese also knew of the Reichenberg project. A 1946 USAAF report shows the Baika as a copy of the Fi 103R. Finally, a manifest of cargo on the Japanese submarine I-29 (the same that carried data on the Messerschmitt Me 163B and Me 262; see the Mitsubishi J8M Syūsui chapter for more information) listed a single Fi 103 fuselage as being onboard. The contemporary illustrations of the Baika today (including the one here) are derived from the drawings of the aircraft made by Technical Commander Eiichi Iwaya in the 1953 Japanese book *Koku Gijutsu No Zenbo*. Whether the Baika was truly inspired by the Fi 103R or was simply an independent design may never be known for certain.

Kawanishi Baika – data

Contemporaries
Fieseler Fi 103R Reichenberg (Germany)

Type	Special Attack Aircraft	
Crew	One	
Powerplant		
One Maru Ka-10 pulse jet; rated at 360kg (794lb) of thrust		
Dimensions		
Span	6.58m	21.6ft
Length	6.97m	22.9ft
Height, unknown	up to 3.99m/13.1ft by requirements	
Wing area	7.58m²	81.6ft²
Weights		
Empty	750kg	1,653lb
Loaded	1,430kg	3,152lb
Armament	One 250kg (551lb) warhead	
Performance		
Max speed	648km/h at 2,000m	402mph at 6,561ft
Cruise speed	485km/h at 6,000m	301mph at 19,685ft
Range	278km	172 miles
Climb	3 min 55 sec to 2,000m/6,561ft	
Ceiling	2,000m	6,561ft
Fuel capacity	600 litres	158 gallons

Deployment
None. Did not advance past the drawing board.

Kawanishi H11K Soku

By 1944, Japan was hard pressed to fuel her war machine with the raw materials it desperately needed. Being an island, only two means were available for Japan to receive ore, fuel and other vital materials from what holdings Japan had left. The first was by sea and the second was by air. The sea route was fraught with risk due to the US Navy and Allied submarine and warship presence in the Pacific. Thus, delivering cargo by air, while also not without risk, appeared a better option, despite the lower tonnage capacity in comparison to sea-going freighters. Therefore, the Kaigun Koku Hombu asked Kawanishi to design what would be one of only a handful of dedicated transport seaplanes of the war.

The IJN knew full well the impact the US Navy's unrestricted submarine warfare doctrine was having, which made merchant ships the primary target. By the end of the war, 1,200 Japanese merchant ships had been sent to the bottom along with five million tons of cargo. In part this was due to poor convoy methods and protection by the IJN, but also because the US had broken the Japanese merchant marine cipher (the 'maru code'). Hence, moving cargo by sea would more often than not result in the shipping being located and sunk. In 1944, shipping losses were at their highest and by 1945, while they did decline, it was because fewer ships were moving on the open ocean.

The desperation for fuel and other war materials was illustrated by the IJA's Kokusai Ki-105 Ōtori (meaning Phoenix), the twin-engine version of the Kokusai Ku-7 Manazuru (Crane) transport glider. The IJA planned to use the Ki-105 as a fuel tanker which would fly from Japan to the Sumatra oil fields in Indonesia, load up with fuel and then return. However, to make the return trip the Ki-105 would consume some 80 per cent of the fuel by the time the aircraft returned to Japan. The IJN looked for a better solution with a large transport capable of carrying a significant cargo load. Because a large expanse of ocean had to be crossed in order to reach what few territories the Japanese still held, the IJN desired to have a seaplane to do the job. In January 1944, the IJN asked Kawanishi to develop such an aircraft.

Kawanishi was a leader in flying boat development and had gained most of its experience in designing large sea going aircraft. Two of their most successful designs were the Kawanishi H6K (codenamed *Mavis* by the Allies) and the H8K (*Emily*), with the latter arguably the best flying boat of World War 2. The company was also not lacking in cargo flying boat design having modified the H6K to serve as a transport as the H6K2-L and H6K4-L. Even the H8K was adapted as a transport, the H8K2-L Seikū (or Clear Sky). Kawanishi had also been working on the design of the K-60, a long-range transport flying boat. With these credentials, Kawanishi was able to capitalise on their knowledge to begin the design of the H11K Soku (Blue Sky) for the IJN.

Kawanishi was instructed by the IJN to use as much wood as possible in the construction of the Soku since a flying boat of such size would have consumed a large amount of precious alloys needed for other aircraft such as fighters. Within Kawanishi, the Soku was called the KX-8 and the initial design draft was processed rapidly. The aircraft drew heavily from the H8K being a high-wing, cantilever monoplane but overall, the Soku was much larger. The keel of the Soku was nearly identical to the H8K. To power the flying boat four Mitsubishi MK4Q Kasei 22 (Ha-32-22) radials, each developing 1,850hp, were selected with two per wing. As ordered by the IJN, both the fuselage/hull and the wings were to be built of wood and under each wing would be a non-retractable float. The Soku had two decks. The lower deck could accommodate up to eighty fully equipped soldiers including a number of vehicles or a comparable amount of cargo. A smaller, upper deck housed quarters for the crew of five. The main departure from the H8K transports was that the Soku utilised a split nose that was hinged to allow the two nose sections to be opened outward to each side of the fuselage, providing ready access to the lower deck. This facilitated easier loading and unloading increasing the speed and ease of these procedures. As a measure of protection the Soku was to be fitted with three 13mm Type 2 machine guns.

Kawanishi presented the KX-8 to the IJN and the design was accepted. Authorisation was given to construct a full scale wooden mock-up of the Soku now designated the H11K1 for inspection before Kawanishi could proceed with the actual prototype. Construction of the mock-up commenced at the port of Komatsujima in the city of Komatsushima on the island of Shikoku (the smallest of the four main islands making up Japan). This area was selected by Kawanishi because it had access to the Seto Inland Sea which, once the prototype was built, would be needed to undertake sea and flight trials. Unfortunately for the Soku, the deteriorating

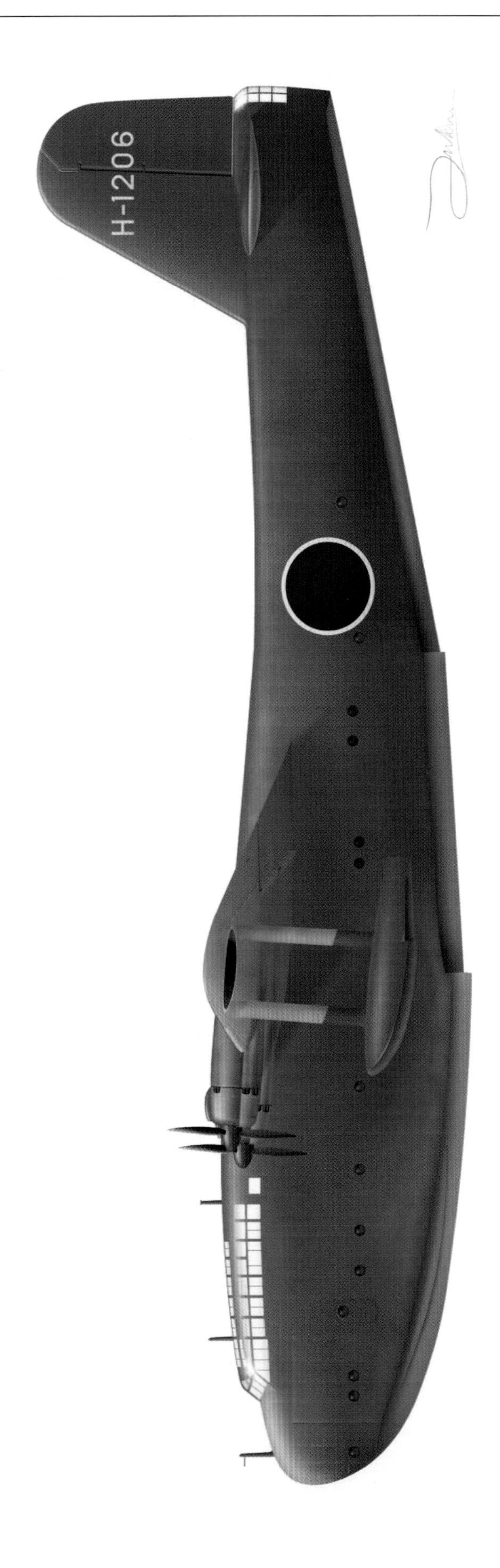

KELCEY FAULKNER

war picture saw delay after delay affect the construction of the mock-up. To add to the problem, Kawanishi was instructed by the IJN in 1945 to reduce production of the H8K and instead, concentrate on building the Kawanishi N1K2-J Shiden-Kai fighter. Together, these factors would see the mock-up approaching its completion in April 1945, well over a year after the design had been initiated.

On 1 April 1945, bombing raids conducted on targets along the Seto Inland Sea saw the nearly completed Soku mock-up destroyed. With this loss, all further work on the Soku design was shelved.

Kawanishi H11K Soku – data

Contemporaries

Blohm und Voss BV 222 Wiking (Germany), Blohm und Voss BV 238 (Germany), Dornier Do 214 (Germany), Boeing C-98/B-134 (US), Consolidated PB2Y-3R Coronado (US), Martin JRM-1 Mars (US), Martin PBM-3R Mariner (US), Sikorsky VS-44 Excalibur (US), Convair R3Y Tradewind (US), Short Sandringham (UK), Short Solent (UK)

Because the H11K1 was not built, the specifications given are estimates made by Kawanishi.

Type	Transport Flying Boat
Crew	Five

Powerplant

Four Mitsubishi MK4Q Kasei 22 (Ha-32-22) 14-cylinder, air-cooled radial engines developing 1,850hp for take-off, 1,680hp at 6,886ft and 1,550hp at 5,500m/18,044ft; each engine drove a 4.3m (14.1ft) diameter, four-bladed, alternating stroke propeller

Dimensions		
Span	47.97m	157.4ft
Length	37.70m	123.7ft
Height	12.55m	41.2ft
Wing area	289.95m²	3,121ft²
Wing loading	156.72kg/m²	32.1 lb/ft²
Power loading	6.12kg/hp	13.5 lb/hp

Weights		
Empty	26,405kg	58,213 lb
Loaded	45,550kg	100,420 lb
Useful load	19,095kg	42,097 lb

Performance		
Max speed	470km/h	292mph
	at 5,000m	at 16,404ft
Cruise speed	369km/h	229mph
Landing speed	144km/h	89mph
Range	3,890km	2,417 miles
Climb	11 min 30 sec to 3,000m (9,842ft)	
Ceiling	N/A	

Armament

Three 13mm Type 2 machine guns with 200 rounds of ammunition per gun

Deployment

None. The H11K1 Soku did not advance past the mock-up stage.

Kawanishi K-200

There are a few Japanese wartime aircraft such as the Kūgishō Tenga jet bomber that remain shrouded in mystery to this day. The Kawanishi K-200 most certainly falls into this category, a design that had it proceeded would have resulted in the first turbojet powered flying boat.

Very little is known of the genesis of the K-200. Kawanishi may have been approached by the IJN to initiate the project or Kawanishi may have undertaken the design themselves to see if a flying boat could be constructed using the new jet engines being designed following the success of the Ne 20 turbojet. Towards the close of the war, Kawanishi was developing two other large flying boats: the Kawanishi K-60 and the Kawanishi H11K Soku. Both of these were at the behest of the IJN so it may not be unreasonable to assume that the IJN also asked Kawanishi if they could add a jet powered flying boat to the mix. Exactly when Kawanishi began to study the prospect of the K-200 is not known though 1945 is the likely year.

Depending on the source, the K-200 was either to be the replacement for all IJN flying boats in service or the K-200 was to be a carrier for a Japanese atomic weapon. The former assumption would likely have depended on the performance of the K-200 had it been built. Certainly the prospect of the K-200 did not deter other flying boat projects such as the K-60 nor improvements of the H8K already in use. If the K-200 was to be such a replacement for operational flying boats and proved superior to them, it most likely would not have entered widespread service until 1946. As far as the latter, the K-200 would have needed capabilities that exceeded flying boat designs then in service in order to serve as a means to drop an atomic weapon on the US. It has been suggested that the Nakajima Fugaku was also devised to carry an atomic weapon but there is no support for this notion. The same may be said for the K-200. One can speculate as to whether the K-200 would have been any more successful in penetrating US coastal defences than a high flying bomber. As we shall see, the K-200 may have had a flaw that would have made any such use all but impossible.

What the definitive shape of the K-200 was to be is open to conjecture. Certainly Kawanishi would have utilised their successes with the H8K and to a lesser degree with the Kawanishi H6K (codenamed *Mavis*) as a foundation for the K-200. As such, it is likely that the hull design would have followed a similar pattern. One speculative illustration of the K-200 shows a hull not unlike the H6K but deeper, though not to the extent of the H8K. A conventional tail akin to the H8K was used but the horizontal stabilisers were mounted halfway up the vertical stabiliser. The wings appeared very similar to the H8K and were fitted to the hull in a like position, this being on the top of the hull and, at least for the K-200, nearly central mounted on the hull. Interestingly, the K-200 was illustrated with fixed wing floats, which contrasted with the retractable floats used by the H8K3 as a means to increase speed. Perhaps such a modification would have been considered for the K-200 as well.

The K-200 is shown as having an armament layout similar to the H8K1. If this was the case, a Type 99 20mm cannon was fitted in a tail turret and in the top mounted turret forward of the wings. On either side of the forward bow was a blister that would have been armed either with the Type 99 cannon or a Type 92 7.7mm machine gun. Finally, a Type 99 cannon would have been fitted in the bow. The K-200 was also probably able to carry a payload of bombs, depth charges or torpedoes.

As far as propulsion, the K-200 was to use six turbojets. They were to be mounted on top of the wings with each turbojet housed in a separate nacelle. Grouped in sets of three, the engines were fitted to each side of the hull on top of the wings. The reason for this was to minimise the amount of sea spray ingested by the engines during use. If the K-200 was of similar dimensions to the H8K, then the turbojet engines would have to move something in the region of 24,948kg/55,000 lb of weight when the K-200 was fully loaded. If the Ne 330 turbojet was the engine of choice, all six would produce a combined thrust of 7,800kg/17,196 lb. This may have been sufficient to give the K-200 a speed superior to the H8K2, which topped out at 467km/h (290mph).

Where the K-200 may have come up short is in terms of its range. Six turbojets would have required a significant amount of fuel in order to give the flying boat a useful operational radius. As an example, the Ne 20 turbojet consumed around 740kg (1,630 lb) of fuel per hour. The Nakajima Kitsuka, which used two Ne 20 engines, carried a maximum of 1,447kg (3,190 lb) of fuel (and without drop tanks only 723.5kg/1,595 lb) and therefore, at its cruise speed, could muster a 824km (512 mile) operational range. If the Ne 330 consumed approximately 2,535kg (5,588 lb) of fuel per hour at full thrust, then six would require at least 15,028kg (33,528 lb) of fuel for approximately one hour of operation at maximum speed. Flying at a cruise speed would, of course, extend the operating range. Options to attempt to save weight may have included removing any armour, stripping the defensive armament and/or constructing the aircraft from wood as was the plan for the H11K Soku. Even with such measures the K-200 would have been hard pressed to match, let alone exceed, the range of the H8K or more conventional piston engine flying boats.

It is not known how far Kawanishi studied the feasibility of the K-200, if at all. With resources allocated to the H8K, the H11K Soku and the K-60 among other projects, Kawanishi designers may have put the K-200 to one side pending availability of turbojets sufficient to warrant the effort in developing the flying boat. Aside from anything else, even a reliable turbojet such as the Ne 20 could only muster four to five hours of operation before it would suffer from problems. It may have been seen that preliminary performance estimates fell short of expectations and offered no significant advantage over designs currently in use or projected to enter service. Finally, a lack of materials necessary to construct the K-200 may have played a role in sidelining the design; the engine and construction material issue saw the K-60 ground to a halt and this may very well have extended to the K-200. Regardless of the reasons, the K-200 would never be anything more than a concept.

As a side note, following the war it was planned to construct a civilian version for use by Japan Airlines.

Kawanishi K-200 – data

Contemporaries
Beriev R-1 (Russia), Martin P6M Seamaster (US)

Specifications
There is no exact information available on the Kawanishi K-200.

Deployment
None. The K-200 existed only as a concept or paper design.

DANIEL UHR

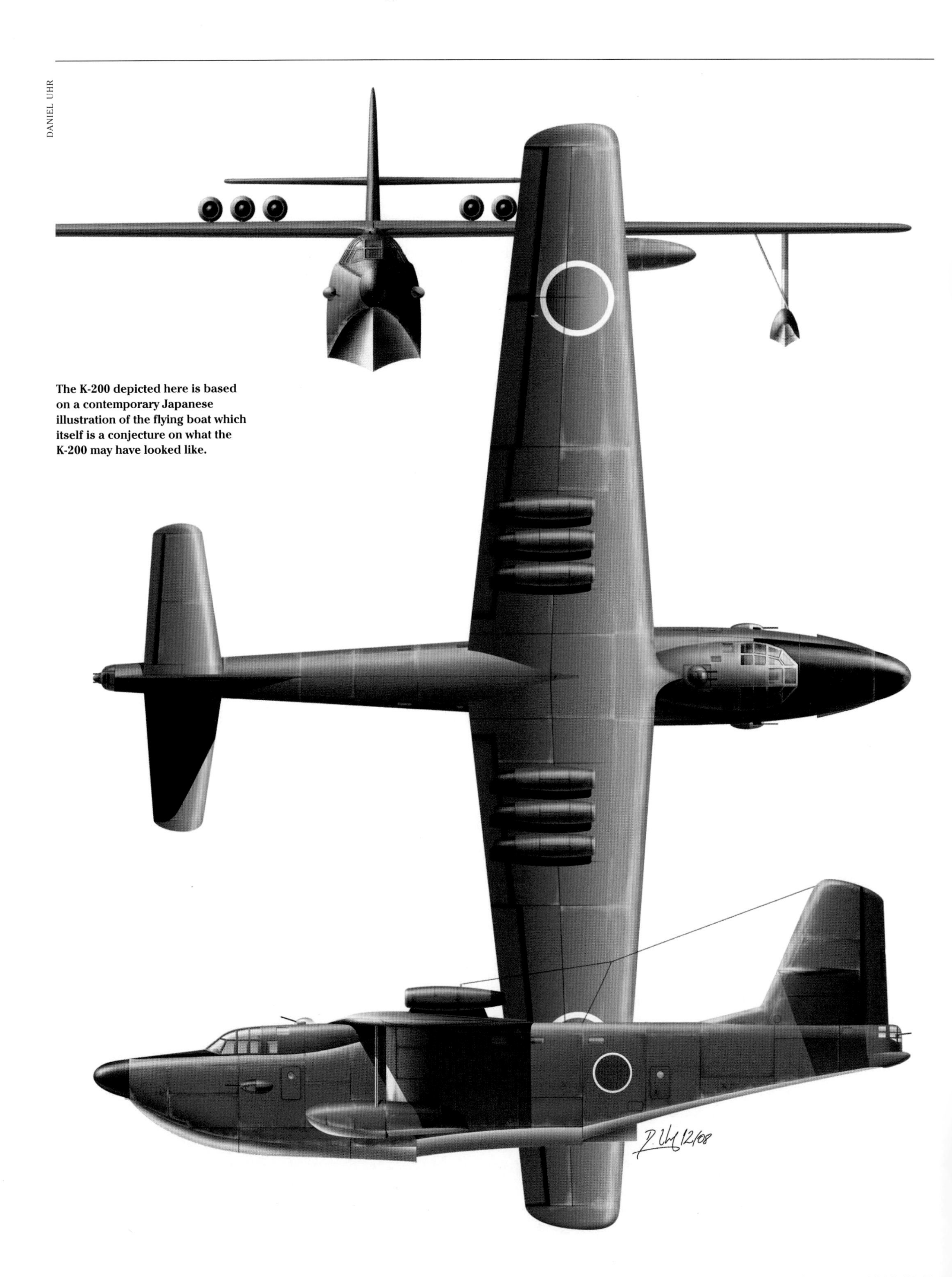

The K-200 depicted here is based on a contemporary Japanese illustration of the flying boat which itself is a conjecture on what the K-200 may have looked like.

Kūgishō High-Speed Projects

Every aircraft creator seeks to reduce drag in their designs. The definition of drag is the force that resists movement through a fluid, which, of course, includes air. The more drag, the slower the aircraft moves through the air due to the resistance. Drag cannot be completely removed from a design, but even in the early years of aviation various methods for minimising drag were investigated and many different solutions were tried. Not surprisingly, such applications were valued by those providing the military with aircraft and in Japan, prior to the outbreak of hostilities with the US, the Dai-Ichi Kaigun Kōkū Gijutsu-shō would study such efforts in an attempt to produce fast flying aircraft.

Form drag is the component caused by the shape of the body moving through the air. Therefore, when designing an aircraft the form and shape of the plane is one of the most important factors a designer has to consider. The wider the cross section, the more drag is produced. Having significant form drag results in lower speeds because the faster the aircraft moves through the air, the more drag force is applied to the aircraft. Therefore, in order to realise higher air speeds, the designer must take steps to reduce drag and thereby lower the amount of drag force slowing the aircraft down.

Before World War 1 some aircraft designers appreciated the need to reduce drag. This often took the form of fuselages that had clean lines in an attempt to remove protrusions and also to streamline propeller hubs to help them cut through the air more efficiently. The best example would be the 1912 Deperdussin that won the Gordon Bennett race in Chicago, Illinois, which became the first airplane to exceed 161km/h (100mph) (in 1913 a later model of the plane would achieve 205km/h (127mph).

At the beginning of World War 1, few of the major combat aircraft utilised significant drag reducing methods. Exhaust stacks, radiators, protruding machine guns, wire bracing, struts and engines only partially cowled predominated. One of the few exceptions was the Morane-Saulnier N 'Bullet'. Nevertheless, the rapid pace of combat aircraft development during World War 1 saw designers looking for ways to increase speed as a means to get the edge over the enemy. The Albatross D series and the Roland 'Walfisch' would epitomise those efforts.

Following World War 1, the resurgence in air racing such as the Schneider Trophy in Europe and the National Air Races in America saw rapid advances in aerodynamics and drag reduction to produce fast flying racing aircraft for competition. Aircraft such as the Curtiss R2C-1 Navy Racer, the Adolphe Bernard 'Ferbois' (capturing the world speed record of 451km/h (280mph) in 1924), Gloster III, Supermarine S.5, Kirkham-Williams Racer (which, unofficially, flew to a speed of 519km/h (322mph) in 1927) and the Savoia-Marchetti S.65 typified high performance race aircraft. The benefits of these innovations were not lost on military aircraft designers.

With the war clouds looming on the horizon, the seeds planted by the air racers of the 1920s and early 1930s were germinating in the aircraft used by the air forces of the major powers. Designs by Curtiss for the US Army Air Force were influenced by the Curtiss racers while the retractable landing gear of the 1920 Dayton Wright RB racer would become

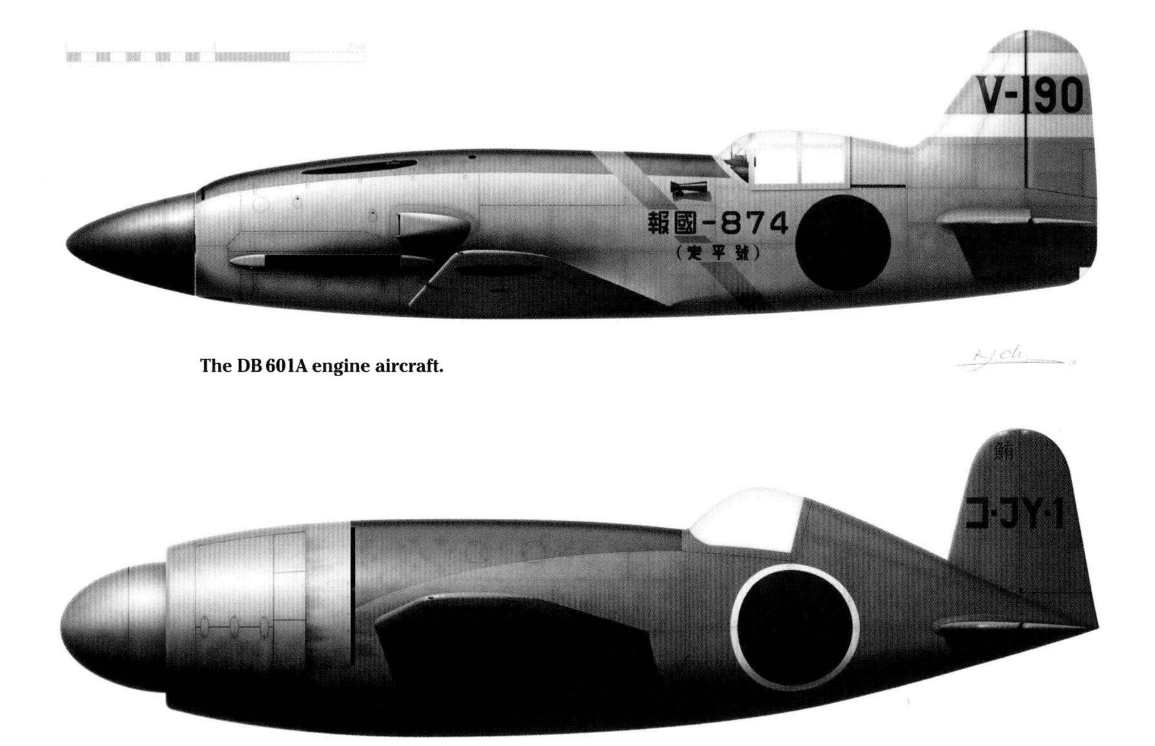

The DB 601A engine aircraft.

The NK1B engine design.

RONNIE OLSTHOORN

a hallmark of Grumman aircraft such as the F2F. In Great Britain, R. J. Mitchell would draw heavily from his experience designing Schneider Trophy racers to build the Supermarine Type 300 which would eventually evolve into the Spitfire. In Italy, Mario Castoldi, lead designer for Macci, would turn his skills in constructing racing aircraft to producing fighters for the Regia Aeronautica with types such as the Macci C.202 Folgore.

Japan, like other countries, sought to produce racing aircraft and planes designed to beat world speed records. An early example was the Emi 16 Fuji-go built by Itoh Hikōki Kenyusho (Itoh Aeroplane Research Studio), which from 1920 was used in Japanese competitions, and the contemporary racing aircraft from Shirato Hikōki Kenkyusho. Kawanishi was not far behind with the K-2 speed racer which, despite extreme measures to minimise drag, suffered from a drag-inducing radiator mounted on top of the fuselage. The K-2 achieved an unofficial speed of 258km/h (160mph) in a flight made on 31 July 1921. Other refinements in aerodynamics could be seen in the Kawasaki Ki-28 of 1935 which, despite its advantages in speed, climb and acceleration, was not successful in attracting IJA contracts.

In 1938, a group of designers sought to produce a high-speed aircraft to challenge the world air speed record. Once war had broken out this aircraft, called the Ken III, was soon taken over by the IJA. Redesignated the Ki-78, its development was continued under Kawasaki. During this time, it may have been the IJN who decided to conduct its own studies of high speed aircraft with Kūgishō assigned the task of doing so. Whether the studies were initiated in response to the IJA's own high-speed aircraft project is unknown but the prevalent aircraft design philosophy of both the IJN and the IJA prior to the war was of speed, agility and range at the expense of firepower, durability and protection.

Kūgishō examined over half a dozen aspects of aerodynamics in order to produce data on what would be needed to realise an aircraft capable of significant speed. One area of research was the main wings. The shape of a wing is one of the more critical aspects of aircraft design. Factors such as wing loading, expected air speeds, angles of attack and the intended use of the aircraft all influence how the wing is shaped. For high speeds, a low aspect ratio wing is often considered. Typically, these are short span wings with the benefits of higher manoeuvrability and less drag. In addition, having a backward sweep to the wing also lowers drag. The drag most associated with wings is termed induced drag, which is caused by wing tip vortices that change how the air flows over the wings. This change results in less and less lift which then requires a higher and higher angle of attack to compensate and, from this, induced drag results. Elliptical wings offer less induced drag than more conventional straight wings. However, low aspect ratio wings are more prone to larger vortices because they cannot be spread out across a longer wing. Kūgishō's study on wing shapes was the likely result of testing various airfoils in a wind tunnel to determine their effectiveness and record the results.

Another aspect Kūgishō engineers reviewed were the merits and flaws of using either an inline or a radial engine and how each type reduced the form drag. In both cases the engineers drew up two concept aircraft and each made use of streamlining. Streamlining is the process of shaping an object, in this case, a fuselage, to increase its speed by reducing the sources of drag. One concept used the 1,159hp Daimler-Benz DB 601A, a 12-cylinder, inverted-V, liquid-cooled, inline engine. This engine would be licence built for the IJN as the Aichi AE1 Atsuta (the 'A' stood for Aichi, 'E' for liquid-cooled and '1' for first liquid-cooled engine; Atsuta was a holy shrine in Aichi Prefecture) and for the IJA as the Ha-40 before it was renamed the [Ha-60] 22. The second concept aircraft used a 1,000hp Nakajima NK1B Sakae 11 which was a 14-cylinder, air-cooled, radial engine. This engine was a licence version of the Gnome-Rhône 14K Mistral Major (in engine nomenclature, the 'N' was for Nakajima, 'K' for air-cooled, '1' as the first air-cooled engine, while the 'B' was for the second version of the NK1; Sakae means prosperity in Japanese).

Kūgishō would use the same basic airframe for the engine study. It consisted of a well streamlined fuselage with the pilot mounted in a cockpit set behind the wing and just forward of the vertical stabiliser. This style was found in a number of racing aircraft such as the American GeeBee R1 and Geebee Z. Both used a standard tail-sitter configuration for the landing gear. The concept equipped with the DB 601A engine had a fuselage shape that was not unlike the Kawasaki Ki-61 Hien (meaning Swallow; codenamed *Tony* by the Allies) which would appear in prototype form in December 1941. The wings were mounted low on the fuselage. The fuselage appearance was due to the inverted-V engine which, by design, offered lower height, weight and length when compared to more conventional motors. By contrast, the concept using the NK1B had a more ovoid fuselage shape, the result of the height of the radial engine. To maintain the aerodynamic streamlining a large spinner was used. Also, in contrast to the DB 601A equipped design, the wings were mounted mid-fuselage.

Kūgishō would not produce any direct prototype aircraft from either concept. Instead, the results of the various studies were likely kept available as reference for engineers to access as a means of obtaining data on the aerodynamic problem. Perhaps Kūgishō in hindsight considered themselves fortunate to not have expended additional expense and effort in producing working prototypes given the failure of the IJA's Ki-78, a program that lingered on into 1944 and never met its design goals.

The DB 601A engine aircraft is shown in the colours originally used on a Mitsubishi A6M3, serial 3032, tail code V-190 of the Tainan Kōkūtai. It was found on Buna Airfield on 27 December 1942 in disrepair. It was a presentation aircraft donated by Sadahei, a civilian volunteer group. The Hukuko number was 874. The NK1B engine design is painted in the standard training orange used on prototypes and trainer aircraft.

Kūgishō High-Speed Aircraft Project – data

Contemporaries
Messerschmitt Me 209 (Germany)

Type High-Speed Aircraft
Crew One

Powerplant One Daimler-Benz DB 601A, 12-cylinder, inverted-V, liquid-cooled, inline engine developing 1,159hp or one Nakajima NK1B Sakae 11 14-cylinder, air-cooled, radial engine developing 1,000hp

Dimensions

Span		N/A	
Length	(DB 601A)	6.91m	22.7ft
	(NK1B)	6.97m	22.9ft
Height		N/A	
Wing area		N/A	
Wing loading		N/A	
Power loading		N/A	

Weights (approximate)

Empty	(DB 601A)	1,600kg	3,527.3 lb
	(NK1B)	1,289kg	2,841.7 lb
Loaded	(DB 601A)	1,900kg	4,188.7 lb
	(NK1B)	1,659kg	3,657.4 lb
Fuel & oil weight	(DB 601A)	215kg	473.9 lb
	(NK1B)	270kg	595.2 lb

Performance

Max speed	N/A
Range	N/A
Climb	N/A
Ceiling	N/A

Armament None

Deployment
None. Both Kūgishō designs existed on paper only.

Kūgishō MXY6

The development of the Kyūshū J7W Shinden was an ambitious undertaking. Captain Masaoki Tsuruno, the man behind the Shinden, needed to confirm the handling characteristics of a canard aircraft before proceeding further with the plans and construction of the J7W itself. To do this, he commissioned Kūgishō to design and build three gliders that were based on his J7W1 aircraft plans. The result was the MXY6.

Kūgishō drew up the design of the MXY6 with the assistance of Captain Tsuruno. Constructed entirely of wood, the MXY6 featured a slightly swept wing, vertical stabilisers fitted inside of the wing ailerons and canards mounted along the nose of the fuselage. The braced tricycle landing gear was fixed and provided with suspension. Once the MXY6 was finalised, construction was entrusted to Chigasaki Seizo K.K. and they had completed the three gliders by the fall of 1943. Flight trials got under way soon thereafter and the MXY6 was found to have good handling characteristics which provided verification to the concept of the J7W.

For further testing, one of the three gliders was modified by having a small engine installed in the rear of the fuselage in the same pusher configuration as the proposed J7W. The engine, a Nihon Hainenki Semi 11 ([Ha-90] 11), allowed the handling under power to be studied as opposed to unpowered flight only. Following the conclusion of the testing of both the unpowered and powered MXY6, the validation of the canard design provided the needed proof of concept and as such the IJN instructed Kyūshū to proceed with the J7W Shinden.

Kūgishō MXY6 – data

Contemporaries
Hamburger Ha 141-0 (Germany), FGP 227 (Germany), Göppingen Gö 9 (Germany), Horton Ho IIIB and Ho IV (Germany), Berlin B 9 (Germany), Junkers Ju 49 (Germany), Lippisch DM-1 (Germany), DFS 194 (Germany)

Type	Proof of Concept Glider	
Crew	One	

Powerplant Unpowered except for one modified with a Nihon Hainenki Semi 11 ([Ha-90] 11) 4-cylinder, air-cooled engine developing 22hp and driving a two-bladed, fixed stroke wooden propeller

Dimensions		
Span	11.12m	36.5ft
Length	9.63m	31.6ft
Height	4.20m	13.8ft
Wing area	20.49m²	220.6ft².

Weights		
Loaded	640kg	1,410 lb

Performance	
Max glide speed	N/A

Armament	None

Deployment
None. The MXY6 was purely a proof of concept glider.

The profile shown is based on one of the MXY6 gliders found at Atsugi in September 1945. The paint is training orange as normally used on experimental and training aircraft.

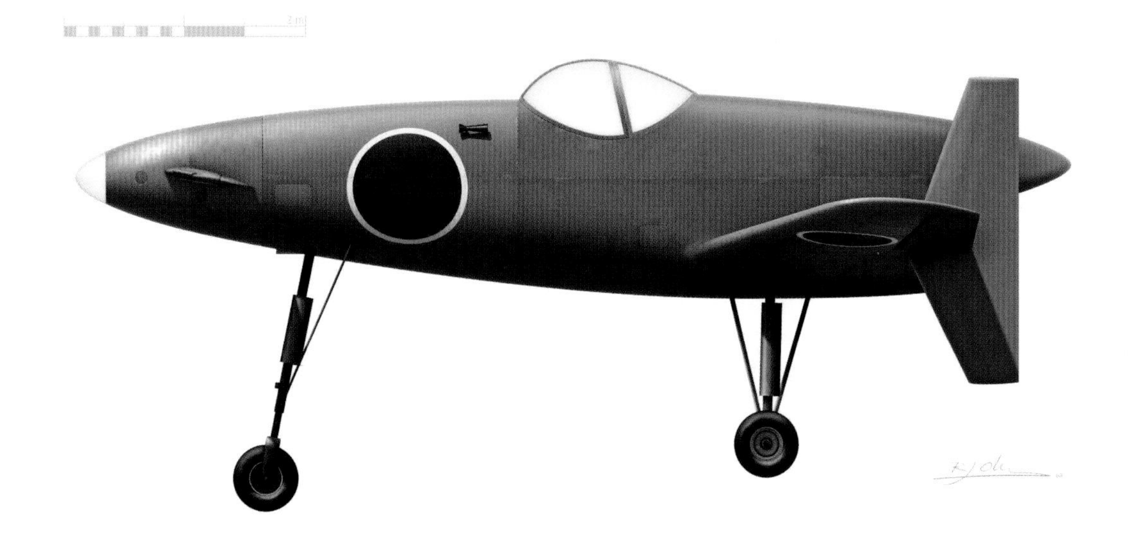

RONNIE OLSTHOORN

Kūgishō MXY7 Ōka

The Ōka Model 11 depicted here uses markings commonly seen on deployed aircraft.

Ōka Model 11 – data

Type	Special Attacker	
Crew	One	
Powerplant	Three Type 4 Mark 1 Model 20 solid fuel rockets, each developing 267kg (588 lb) of thrust, for a total of 801kg (1,764 lb)	
Dimensions		
Span	512m	16.8ft
Length	6.06m	19.9ft
Height	1.15m	3.8ft
Wing area	5.99m²	64.5ft²
Wing loading	356.90kg/m²	73.1 lb/ft²
Power loading	2.67kg/hp	5.9 lb/hp
Weights		
Empty	440kg	970 lb
Loaded	2,140.5kg	4,718 lb
Useful load	650kg	1,433 lb
Performance		
Max speed	649km/h at 3,505m	403mph at 11,500ft.
Dive speed	927km/h	576mph
Cruise speed	462km/h at 3,500m	287mph at 11,482ft
Max range	37km	23 miles
Ceiling	8,250m	27,066ft
Armament	1,200kg (2,646 lb) Tri-Nitroaminol explosive warhead	

'No longer can we hope to sink the numerically superior enemy carriers through ordinary attack methods. I urge the use of special attack units to crash dive their aircraft and I ask to be placed in command of them.'

These words by IJN Captain Eiichiro Jyo, commander of the carrier *Chiyoda*, reflected a mood he had observed in some of his pilots and men. Their feelings were that to carry on with conventional tactics was doomed to failure. While death in combat was worthy, a death that did no good was shameful and would not serve the Emperor or Japan. Jyo's words, written in a memo to Rear Admiral Soemu Obayashi and Vice Admiral Jisaburo Ozawa, would be the catalyst for the formation of special attack units and from this a new weapon would arise that would become the only purpose-built special attack aircraft to see operational combat service during World War 2: the Kūgishō MXY7 Ōka.

Vice Admiral Takijiro Onishi is most often credited with officially forming and organising the special attack units, the first of which became operational in October 1944. A pivotal man in the formation of the IJN's Rikusentai (airborne troops), Onishi was also eccentric which did not always endear him to his superiors and so, prior to his assuming command of the IJN land air forces in the Philippines, he served as a supply officer. Speaking to the officers of the 201st Air Group, Onishi stated that because of the limited resources only a Mitsubishi A6M Reisen with a 250kg (551 lb) bomb that was crashed into enemy ships would suffice in slowing the US fleet. From this began the rise of the IJN special attack force, the Shimpū Tokubetsu Kōgekitai. Their story, as well as that of the IJA's Shimbu Tokubetsu Kōgekitai, is beyond the scope of this book (however, for those interested there is a wealth of material available on the subject such as David Brown's *Kamikaze* and Earl Rice's *Kamikazes*).

The majority of the shimpū missions were flown using types already in service. In addition to the Reisen, the Kūgishō D4Y Suisei (meaning 'Comet' but known to the Allies as *Judy*), Kawasaki Ki-48 (*Lily*), Nakajima Ki-49 Donryu (meaning 'Storm Dragon' but called *Helen* by the Allies), Aichi D3A (*Val*) and many others were modified, sometimes heavily, and used against the Allies, but none were specifically built from the ground up for shimpū (suicide) operations. It would be IJN Ensign Mitsuo Ōta, a transport pilot flying with the 405th Kōkūtai, who put forward a design for a piloted glide bomb.

Ōta's concept was not the only one that called for a dedicated shimpū aircraft. Other ideas were considered such as the Showa Toka (see elsewhere in this book on the Nakajima Ki-115 Tsurugi for more information), but what set Ōta's idea apart was that he wanted to have the explosive payload carried internally as opposed to fitting an external bomb. Also, the aircraft had to be carried and released by a parent plane and rocket boosters would be used to speed the approach and terminal dive onto the target.

Ōta did not have any aeronautical engineering experience and would not have been able to present a definitive plan for his aircraft. In order to help his cause, Ōta sought and received assistance from the Aeronautical

Research Institute of the University of Tōkyō. Professor Taichiro Ogawa headed the study of Ōta's concept while Hidemasa Kimura provided the basic design of the aircraft and even produced models that were wind tunnel tested. Within weeks, the proposal for Ōta's design was drafted, the design illustrated and performance estimates presented along with the data obtained from the wind tunnel testing.

In August 1944, Ōta brought his proposal to the attention of Lieutenant Commander Tadanao Miki. Miki was the department head of the aircraft design section of the Dai-Ichi Kaigun Kōkū Gijutsu-shō. It is said that when Miki reviewed Ōta's concept he was taken aback and shocked at the idea of putting men into piloted bombs. However, by this time the policy of shimpū tactics had been approved and regardless of how Miki felt personally he could not deny the submission. Miki placed the design before the Naval General Staff on 5 August 1944. Air Staff Officer Minuro Genda, after looking over Ōta's plan, approved the concept and instructed chief of staff Admiral Koshiro Oikawa to set the wheels in motion for turning the design into reality. Perhaps it was ironic that the task of starting the development of the aircraft fell to Miki. Kūgishō was the organisation that would develop the aircraft, which was given the initial designation MXY7. Miki assembled a team of engineers led by three men, Masao Yamana, Tadanao Mitsugi and Rokuro Hattori, and they began drafting and refining the MXY7 design.

The MXY7 was essentially a glider bomb with a pilot providing the guidance. There were several specific factors involved in the MXY7, most of which were out of necessity. In order to conserve war materials, the MXY7 was to be constructed using wood as well as non-critical metals such as aluminium, if necessary. It was expected that pilots with minimal skill would be required to fly the machine and therefore the aircraft had to possess good handling and manoeuvrability to ensure a successful strike. Not surprisingly, instrumentation for the MXY7 was kept to the bare minimum. The aircraft also had to be simple to construct so as to allow rapid mass production by semi-skilled and unskilled labour.

The MXY7's primary mission was anti-ship. The flight profile began with the MXY7 being carried aloft by a modified Mitsubishi G4M bomber. At the point where it was within range of the target, the G4M would release the MXY7 which would then glide towards the intended victim. During the approach the pilot would ignite the rocket motors in the rear of the plane to increase its speed and close in to the target as quickly as possible. This would minimise the chances of interception and present a fast moving target to defending anti-aircraft gunners.

Miki and his team completed the design of the MXY7 in weeks and by the end of September 1944 ten MXY7 had been completed and were ready for testing. The aircraft was then renamed the Ōka Model 11, Ōka meaning 'Cherry Blossom'. A 1,200kg (2,646 lb) explosive charge was fitted into the nose and five fuses were installed, one in the nose and the remaining four on the rear plate of the charge. The fuses were armed by the pilot from inside the cockpit and they could be set to explode on impact or the detonation could be delayed by up to 1.5 seconds to allow the Ōka to penetrate the target (such as a ship hull) and explode inside. The carrier for the Ōka was the Mitsubishi G4M, known to the Allies as *Betty*. A number of G4M2a Model 24B and 24C bombers were modified by having their bomb bay doors removed to be replaced by the required shackles to hold the Ōka. These modified carriers were redesignated G4M2e Model 24J. However, the Ōka's loaded weight of 2,140kg (4,718 lb) far exceeded the bomber's standard load of 1,000kg (2,205 lb) and as a consequence the G4M2e suffered from poor handling and performance.

As the Ōka did not take-off on its own nor was it anticipated that it would fly at speeds under 322km/h (200mph), the wings were kept very short. For propulsion, three Type 4 Mark 1 Model 20 solid fuel rockets were installed in the tail of the fuselage. Each rocket could produce up to 267kg (588 lb) of thrust for a total of 801kg (1,764 lb). The pilot could activate them as he saw fit and could fire them one by one or all three at once. Total burn time for each rocket was 8-10 seconds. Given that the Ōka would have to fly through significant anti-aircraft fire as it approached its target as well as the possible aerial interception by Allied fighter cover, the pilot was afforded protection through armour plate. A 19mm strip of plating was fitted along the underside of the fuselage near to the pilot's feet while his bucket seat had between 8mm and 15mm of armour, the majority protecting his back.

As discussed above, the instrumentation was kept to a minimum. The instrument panel contained the altimeter, compass, attitude indicator (artificial horizon), airspeed indicator, arming handle for the fuses and the rocket motor ignition switches.

With the ten available MXY7 prototypes, flight testing was to commence in October 1944. However, the IJN did not want to wait for the results of the tests and in September, Rear Admiral Jiro Saba, director of the Kūgishō Naval Aeronautical Research Laboratory, went to Lieutenant Commander Yokei

Ōka Model 21 – data

Type	Special Attacker	
Crew	One	
Powerplant	Three Type 4 Mark 1 Model 20 solid fuel rockets, each developing 267kg (588 lb) of thrust, for a total of 801kg (1,764 lb)	
Dimensions		
Span	4.11m	13.5ft
Length	6.88m	22.6ft
Height	1.12m	3.7ft
Wing area	3.99m²	43ft²
Wing loading	399.78kg/m²	81.9 lb/ft²
Power loading	1.99kg/hp	4.4 lb/hp
Weights		
Empty	535kg	1,179 lb
Loaded	1,600kg	3,527 lb
Useful load	915kg	2,017 lb
Performance		
Max speed	642km/h	399mph
	at 4,000m	at 13,125ft
Cruise speed	443km/h	275mph
	at 4,000m	at 13,125ft
Max range	111km	69 miles
Ceiling	8,500kg	27,887ft
Armament	600kg (1,322 lb) explosive warhead	

Ōka Model 22 – data

Type	Special Attacker	
Crew	One	
Powerplant	One Tsu-11 thermojet developing 200kg (440 lb) of thrust	
Dimensions		
Span	4.11m	13.5ft
Length	6.88m	22.6ft
Height	1.12m	3.7ft
Wing area	3.99m²	43ft²
Wing loading	401.82kg/m²	82.3 lb/ft²
Power loading	7.98kg/hp	17.6 lb/hp
Weights		
Empty	545kg	1,201 lb
Loaded	1,450kg	3,197 lb
Useful load	965kg	2,127 lb
Performance		
Max speed	445km/h	276mph
	at 4,000m	at 13,125ft
Cruise speed	427km/h	265mph
	at 3,500m	at 11,482ft
Max range	160km	99 miles
Ceiling	8,500m	27,887ft
Fuel capacity	290 litres	76.6 gallons
Oil capacity	10 litres	2.6 gallons
Armament	600kg (1,322 lb) explosive warhead	

Ōka Model 33 – data

Type	Special Attacker		
Crew	One		

Powerplant

One Ne 20 axial-flow turbojet developing 475kg (1,047 lb) of thrust or one Ne 12B jet engine developing 320kg (705 lb) of thrust

Dimensions			
Span		4.99m	16.4ft
Length		7.19m	23.6ft
Height		1.15m	3.8ft
Wing area		5.99m²	64.5ft²
Wing loading		382.78kg/m²	78.4 lb/ft²
Power loading		4.76kg/hp	10.5 lb/hp

Weights			
Empty		N/A	
Loaded		2,300kg	5,070 lb
Useful load		N/A	

Performance			
Max speed		643km/h	399mph
	(Ne 20)	at 4,000m	at 13,125ft
Cruise speed		N/A	
Max range		212km	132 miles
Ceiling		N/A	
Fuel capacity		250 litres	66 gallons
Oil capacity		N/A	

Armament

800kg (1,763 lb) explosive warhead

Ōka Model 43A – data (estimated)

Type	Special Attacker		
Crew	One		

Powerplant

One Ne 20 axial-flow turbojet developing 475kg (1,047 lb) of thrust

Dimensions		
Span	8.99m	29.5ft
Length	8.16m	26.8ft
Height	1.12m	3.7ft
Wing area	12.99m²	139.9ft²
Wing loading	193.83kg/m²	39.7 lb/ft²
Power loading	5.30kg/hp	11.7 lb/hp

Weights		
Empty	N/A	
Loaded	2,520kg	5,555 lb
Useful load	N/A	

Performance		
Max speed	596km/h	370mph
	at 4,000m	at 13,125ft
Cruise speed	N/A	
Max range	200km	124 miles
Ceiling	N/A	
Fuel capacity	400 litres	105.6 gallons
Oil capacity	16 litres	4.2 gallons

Armament

800kg (1,763 lb) explosive warhead

Matsurra at the Munitions Ministry to sort out the arrangements for opening production of the Ōka. Matsurra, who shared a similar distaste of the suicide concept to Miki, saw to it that much of the production was handled by military contractors to maintain secrecy and not by the private aviation industry. As such, Kūgishō would build the Ōka at Dai-Ichi Kaigun Kōkū Gijutsu-shō as well as at Dai-Ichi Kaigun Kokusho, and two sub-contractors, Nippon Hikōki K.K. in Yokohama and Fuji Hikōki K.K. in Kanegawa, would provide wing and tail assemblies. It was expected that 100 Ōka aircraft would be ready by November 1944.

The first unpowered flight tests of the Ōka began at the Sagami Arsenal located in Sagamihara in Kanagawa Prefecture. To begin with, unmanned, unpowered flights were conducted to assess the Ōka's flight characteristics and these were followed soon afterwards by unmanned, powered flight tests. All of the Ōka drops were made from the G4M2e bombers with the Ōkas being directed out into Sagami Bay. Flight testing was then moved to Kashimi in Saga Prefecture which was near the IJN base in Sasebo in Nagasaki Prefecture. At Kashimi, the first manned flight of an Ōka took place on 31 October 1944 with Lieutenant Kazutoshi Nagano (other sources have his last name as Nagoro) at the controls. The particular Ōka that Nagano was to fly was the prototype for the Ōka K-1 trainer. In place of the warhead and the three rocket motors were tanks holding water as ballast that simulated the combat weight of the Ōka. Since there was no room for a conventional landing gear, a central landing skid was fitted to the underside of the fuselage and under each wing tip were rounded skids to protect the wings and prevent them from digging into the ground on landing. Prior to landing, the water was to be jettisoned which slowed the landing speed to 223km/h (138mph). For Nagano's flight, a rocket booster was fitted to the underside of each wing. At 3,505m (11,500ft) Nagano was released from the G4M2e bomber and entered a good, stable glide. A few minutes into the flight, Nagano activated the booster rockets and almost immediately the Ōka began to yaw. Nagano quickly jettisoned the rockets and the problem disappeared. The remainder of the flight went perfectly, Nagano bringing the Ōka down without mishap after releasing the water ballast. Subsequent investigation showed that uneven thrust from the rockets caused the yawing and Nagano is said to have stated that the Ōka handled better than a Reisen.

As flight testing and production of the Ōka got underway, 721st Kōkūtai was formed at Hyakurigahara Airfield on 1 October 1944 under the command of Commander Motoharu Okamura with Lieutenant Commander Goro Nonaka and Lieutenant Commander Kunihiro Iwaki as his operations officers. The unit was nicknamed the Jinrai Butai, translating as 'Thunder God Corps'. Through October the unit received hundreds of volunteers. Those who were too old, married or were only sons, or those with significant family responsibilities, were rejected for the Jinrai Butai, leaving 600 pilots to be accepted into the unit. The 721st Kikōtai consisted of the 708th Hikōtai and the 711th Hikōtai, each with 18 G4M2e bombers. The 306th Hikōtai and the 308th Hikōtai were assigned the task of escorting the Ōka carrying bombers, each squadron maintaining 36 Mitsubishi A6M Reisen fighters. The unit's initial 10 Ōka aircraft were supplemented by some 40 Mitsubishi A6M5 Reisens fitted with 250kg (551 lb) bombs.

Flight testing of the Ōka continued throughout November. These tests showed that when dropped from 5,944m (19,500ft) at a downward glide angle of 5.5° the Ōka could achieve a range of 60km (37 miles) at a speed of 317km/h (230mph). In a nearly vertical dive it was clocked at over 966km/h (600mph). However, under combat conditions the Ōka could manage 25 to 29km (15 to 18 miles). Based on the tests and flight experience, a mission profile was developed for the Ōka's deployment. Flying at a height between 6,096m and 8,230m (20,000ft and 27,000ft), the G4M2e would release the Ōka when it was within 17 to 33km (10 to 20 miles) of the target. The pilot would then enter a shallow glide with an airspeed of between 371km/h and 451km/h (230mph and 280mph). At a point about 8 to 12km (5 to 7 miles) from the target, and from an altitude of approximately 3,505m (11,500ft), the pilot would activate the rocket boosters increasing the speed to 649km/h (403mph). Prior to striking the target, he would put the Ōka into a 50° dive that would take the speed up to nearly 934km/h (580mph). At the last moment, the pilot would pull up the nose to strike the ship at the waterline.

Ōka pilot training was soon underway. Typically, the pilot would use a Reisen to practice the Ōka attack routine flying the fighter with the engine switched off. For many, they only had the opportunity to become familiar with the Ōka while it sat on the ground. A few were fortunate to make an unpowered flight using one of the MXY7 trainer prototypes. As expected, accidents occurred and on 13 November 1944, the Ōka claimed its first casualty. Lieutenant Tsutomu Kariya executed a perfect drop from 2,987m (9,800ft)

RONNIE OLSTHOORN

Ōka Model 22 in the colours of the example found at the close of the war and now on display at the Smithsonian Air and Space Museum.

and was bringing the Ōka down for a landing. He inadvertently released the water ballast from the nose tank, leaving the rear tank full. This immediately caused the nose to pitch up, putting the Ōka into a stall that Kariya was unable to recover from, the plane crashing into the ground. Kariya was pulled from the wreckage but within a few hours had died from his injuries.

By December 1944, Kūgishō had produced 151 Ōkas and the Dai-Ichi Kaigun Kokusho production was also well under way. Attempts were made to deploy the Ōka to units outside of the Japanese home islands. Fifty were dispatched to the Philippines aboard the carrier *Shinano*, but on 29 November 1944 the ship was sunk en route. Only a handful would reach other bases, notably in Okinawa and Singapore, and none would see combat. Even though the 721st had yet to see combat, there were some who realised that the G4M2e bomber would be easy targets for enemy fighters and the odds of actually reaching the target were small. Consequently, morale dropped as the Ōka was seen as a waste of a pilot who could be used to better effect elsewhere. The vulnerability of the G4M2e was vividly displayed when the 721st went into battle for the first time on 21 March 1945. Attacking US Task Group 58.1, all 18 bombers (of which 15 were Ōka carriers) were shot out of the sky by US Navy fighters along with their fighter escort before they could get within attack range. Again, the story of this and subsequent Ōka missions are beyond the scope of this book but the interested reader can find many excellent sources of information on the topic.

Following the Ōka's disastrous debut, reviews of gun camera footage from the US Navy fighters and from pilot debriefings revealed the existence of the new weapon for the first time to the Allies. At first it was thought that the Ōka was simply a large, anti-ship bomb. This would change when four to six examples were captured near Kadena Airfield after the Allied victory at Okinawa. Only then was the aircraft's true nature made known to Allied intelligence. The Ōka was subsequently given the codename *Baka* by the Allies, the word baka meaning 'fool' in Japanese.

Production of the Ōka Model 11 ceased in March 1945 with the Dai-Ichi Kaigun Kōkū Gijutsu-shō having built 155 and the Dai-Ichi Kaigun Kokusho constructed a total of 600. One Ōka Model 11 was fitted with sheet steel wings made by Nakajima but no other examples were produced with this feature. To help improve the training regimen, once the Dai-Ichi Kaigun Kōkū Gijutsu-shō had completed their run Ōka production was switched to the Ōka MXY7 K-1 trainer. In all, 45 of the K-1 would be completed and placed into the pilot training program.

Clearly, the G4M2e carrier aircraft was too slow and easy prey for defending Allied fighter protection. In addition, the short range of the Ōka Model 11 compounded the problem. Consequently, Kūgishō decided to utilise the superior Kūgishō P1Y Ginga (Allied codename *Frances*) as the carrier aircraft and also to give the Ōka a longer range. This adaptation was called the Ōka Model 22.

The primary change in the Ōka Model 22 was the use of the Tsu-11 thermojet engine in

Ōka Model 43B – data (estimated)

Type	Special Attacker	
Crew	One	

Powerplant One Ne 20 axial-flow turbojet developing 475kg (1,047 lb) of thrust; one Type 4 Mark 1 Model 20 solid fuel rocket, developing 256kg (565 lb) of thrust

Dimensions		
Span	8.99m	29.5ft
Length	8.16m	26.8ft
Height	1.12m	3.7ft
Wing area	12.99m²	139.9ft²
Wing loading	174.79kg/m²	35.8 lb/ft²
Power loading	5.48kg/hp	12.1 lb/hp
Weights		
Empty	1,150kg	2,535 lb
Loaded	2,270kg	5,004 lb
Useful load	1,120kg	2,469 lb
Performance		
Max speed	556km/h at 4,000m	345mph at 13,125ft
Cruise speed	N/A	
Max range	277km	172 miles
Ceiling	N/A	
Fuel capacity	300 litres	79.2 gallons
Oil capacity	16 litres	4.2 gallons

Armament
800kg (1,763 lb) explosive warhead

Ōka Model 53 – data (estimated)

Type	Special Attacker	
Crew	One (or none)	
Powerplant		
One Ne 20 axial-flow turbojet developing 475kg (1,047 lb) of thrust; one Type 4 Mark 1 solid fuel rocket, developing 267kg (588 lb) of thrust		
Dimensions		
Span	6.43m	21.1ft
Length	7.77m	25.5ft
Height	1.43m	4.7ft
Wing area	8.99m²	96.8ft²
Wing loading	N/A	
Power loading	N/A	
Weights		
Empty	N/A	
Loaded	N/A	
Useful load	N/A	
Performance		
Max speed	N/A	
Cruise speed	N/A	
Max range	277km	172 miles
Ceiling	N/A	
Fuel capacity	400 litres	105.6 gallons
Oil capacity	16 litres	4.2 gallons
Armament		
600kg (1,322 lb) explosive warhead		

Ōka K-1 – data

Type	Trainer	
Crew	One	
Powerplant	None	
Dimensions		
Span	5.12m	16.8ft
Length	6.06m	19.9ft
Height	1.12m	3.7ft
Wing area	6.00m²	64.6ft²
Weights		
Empty	730kg	1,609 lb
Loaded	2,120kg	4,673 lb
Useful load	150kg	330 lb
Performance		
Max speed	N/A	
Cruise speed	147km/h	91mph
Landing speed	200km/h	124mph
Armament	None	

place of the rocket boosters. This consisted of a 100hp Hitachi Hatsukaze [Ha-11-11] 11 4-cylinder, inverted inline engine driving a single-stage compressor. Fuel was injected into the compressed air that was then ignited, producing up to 200kg (440 lb) of thrust. To compensate for the weight of the engine and fuel, the warhead had to be reduced to 600kg (1,323 lb). Finally, as the P1Y was smaller than the G4M2e, it was necessary to reduce the wing span by 1m (3.2ft), although the length of the Ōka Model 22 was increased by .8m (2.6ft). These changes improved its range of up to 129km (80 miles), although 65km (40 miles) or less was considered achievable under combat conditions. A rocket booster could be fitted to the underside of the fuselage to increase speed during the terminal dive.

Once the design of the Ōka Model 22 was finalised, Kūgishō began a production run of 50 aircraft even before flight testing was underway. Aichi Kokuki K.K. was contracted to construct a further 200 Model 22 aircraft, but due to US B-29 bomber raids Aichi's production lines would never enter operation. Once the first handful of Ōka Model 22 aircraft had been made available their testing began. Thanks to its short wings, a high stall speed of 334km/h (207mph) and high landing speed made a soft landing impossible. Test pilots were instructed to abandon the Ōka rather than make a landing. Lieutenant Kazutoshi Nagano took the Ōka Model 22 up for the first time on 26 June 1945. The flight would also be his last. After being released from a modified Kūgishō P1Y1 at 3,658m (12,000ft), the Ōka went out of control (another source states that the wing rocket boosters fired accidentally, causing the Ōka to crash into the Ginga, damaging the Ōka's controls). With no ability to regain level flight from the plummeting Ōka, Nagano was able to extract himself from the stricken aircraft but his parachute only partially opened before he hit the ground and was killed. A second test model was ready in August 1945 but the war ended before it could fly. Although fifty Ōka Model 22s were built, the carrier, the Kūgishō P1Y3 Model 33, would never leave the drawing board. The completed Ōka Model 22 were retained in Japan for use against the expected Allied invasion force.

Kūgishō continued to investigate ways to improve the performance of the Ōka and a series of models were planned around the Kūgishō Ne 20 turbojet. The first was the Ōka Model 33 which was simply the Ōka Model 22 enlarged to accept the Ne 20 (or as one source states using the Ne 12B jet engines that had been built prior to the shift to the Ne 20 development). For a carrier, Kūgishō planned on using the Nakajima G8M1 Renzan (known as *Rita* to the Allies) but with the failure of the Renzan to enter production, the Ōka Model 33 was quickly shelved without any prototype being constructed. This was followed by the Ōka Model 43A. Larger in dimensions in comparison to the Ōka Model 22, the Ōka Model 43A was designed to be launched from submarines such as the Sen Toku class. To facilitate storage on such boats the wings were foldable, but with the Allies in complete control of the seas the Ōka Model 43A was soon put aside and work begun on the Ōka Model 43B instead.

This version was designed to operate from caves and launched by a catapult. It retained the folding wings to allow the production lines to be set up in cramped, underground sites or caves as well. Unlike the previous models, the Ōka Model 43B was all metal, used a central skid and in order to better facilitate target penetration the pilot could jettison the wing tips. Like the Ōka Model 22, a rocket booster could be carried under the fuselage. A full scale wooden mock-up was completed in June 1945 and was promptly approved for production. Aichi were tasked with construction of the Ōka Model 43B at their Gifu and Oyaki factories but the war ended before the first prototype was completed. However, a catapult ramp was built at Takeyama, near Yokohama, and pilots destined for the Ōka Model 43B were being given instructions on catapult launching as they waited for their aircraft to be delivered.

A hybrid Ōka was considered which was called the Ōka Model 21. The Tsu-11 engine was to be removed from the Ōka Model 22 to be replaced by the standard rocket booster system as used on the Ōka Model 11. This may have been contemplated as production of the Tsu-11 engine was slow and was not keeping pace with the Ōka Model 22. The proposal, however, never proceeded past a single prototype.

Whereas all previous Ōkas, with the exception of the Models 43A and 43B, required modified bombers to carry them aloft and launch, the Ne 20 turbojet equipped Ōka Model 53 was designed to be towed into the air. As such any aircraft, with the addition of a tow line and having enough power, could be used to tow the Ōka Model 53 into the air. Nothing came of this design due to the end of the war. However, it is worth noting that some contemporary illustrations show the Ōka Model 53 without a cockpit, which would turn the type into a glider bomb. For guidance, it is speculated that upon release from the tow aircraft, it was either radio controlled from a parent plane or used infrared or acoustic homing to guide itself to the target. This concept has not been verified in wartime Japanese sources and could be post-war conjecture.

A derivative of the MXY7 K-1 was planned and this was known as the Ōka Model 43 K-1 Kai Wakazakura (meaning 'Young Cherry' in Japanese). This was to be the definitive trainer for pilots destined for operational Ōka models. A second cockpit was installed in the nose in place of the warhead, flaps were fitted to the wings to help with landing and, like the K-1, the Model 43 had a central landing skid with wing bumpers. It also included a single Type 4 Mark 1 Model 20 rocket in the tail to allow the student to get a taste of powered flight. By the close of the war only two of the Wakazakura trainers had been completed.

Perhaps one of the more unusual uses for the Ōka occurred in Singapore. The handful of Ōka Model 11 aircraft that were received by units in Singapore were, for the most part, grounded because they did not not have their G4M2e parent aircraft. In order to get some use from the Ōkas, mechanics planned to fit them with floats cannibalised from unserviceable or available floatplanes such as the Aichi E13A (known as *Jake* to the Allies). It is not known exactly how the floats were to be installed but crude fittings could have been fabricated to attach a float under each wing. It is believed that the float equipped Ōkas were to be positioned along the Straits of Johor that separate Johor from Singapore and be used in conjunction with Shinyo special attack boats. Another unknown is how they would have performed given the short burn time of the rocket boosters let alone handling qualities across water. It can be surmised that performance would have been very poor. By comparison, the German Tornado attack boat used two floats from a Junkers Ju 52/3mg5e and was powered by an Argus 109-014 pulse-jet. Trials would prove a failure as the boat could not operate on anything but calm seas without capsising.

Ōka 43 K-1 Kai – data

Type	Trainer	
Crew	Two	
Powerplant		
One Type 4 Mark 1 solid fuel rocket, developing 261kg (576lb) of thrust		
Dimensions		
Span	5.12m	16.8ft
Length	6.06m	19.9ft
Height	1.12m	3.7ft
Wing area	N/A	
Weights		
Empty	644kg	1,419lb
Loaded	810kg	1,785lb
Useful load	166kg	365lb
Performance		
Max speed	N/A	
Cruise speed	129km/h	80mph
Landing speed	N/A	
Armament	None	

DANIEL UHR

DANIEL UHR

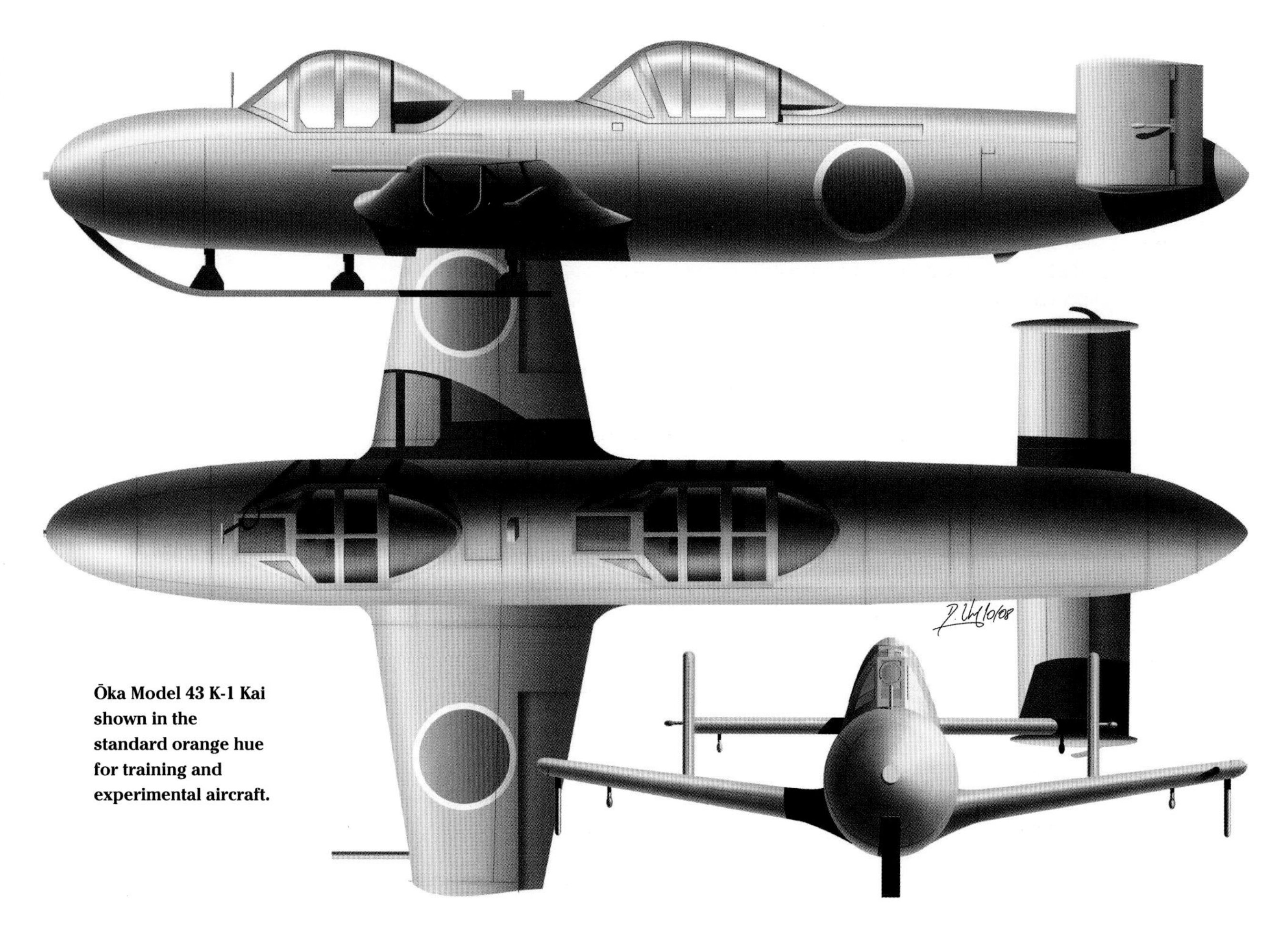

Ōka Model 43 K-1 Kai shown in the standard orange hue for training and experimental aircraft.

K-1 Kūgishō MXY7 Ōka – data

Contemporaries Daimler-Benz Projekt E and Projekt F (Germany), Messerschmitt Me 328C (Germany)

Deployment
Varied. The Ōka Model 11 and MXY7 K-1 saw operational service. The Ōka Model 22 was deployed but did not see action. The Ōka Model 21 remained a single prototype. The Ōka Model 43B prototype was incomplete at war's end. The Ōka Model 33, 43A and 53 remained designs only. The Ōka Model 43 K-1 Kai was too late to be issued to training units.

Survivors
Kūgishō MXY7 Ōka (FE-N50)
The 'N' is assumed to signify 'Navy' as in the US Navy, thereby denoting the US Navy was evaluating this particular aircraft. This MXY7 was listed on a 10 March 10 1946 report allowing it to be released to aviation industry. On 1 August 1 1946, an inventory reported it at MAMA and by 18 September 1946 was slated for the museum and storage at Park Ridge. No further trace of the MXY7 is known.

Kūgishō Ōka Model 11 (no tail number assigned)
One of a number of Ōka aircraft taken to the US, this one, serial number 1049, was obtained by Edward Mahoney. It was restored and remains on display at his Planes of Fame Museum in Valle, Arizona.

Kūgishō Ōka Model 11
Bearing the serial 1018, this Ōka is currently on display at the Marine Corps Base Quantico, near Triangle, Virginia.

Kūgishō Ōka Model 11
Originally this Ōka was in the collection of the Victory Air Museum located in Mundelein, Illinois. It closed its doors in 1984 and the aircraft was sold off. It was last obtained by the Yanks Air Museum in Chino, California.

Kūgishō Ōka Model 11
Shipped to India in September 1947 by the No.4 Squadron of the Indian Air Force following their duties in Japan as part of the British Commonwealth Occupation Forces, the Ōka is currently on display in the Indian Air Force Museum at Palam Air Force Station, New Delhi, India.

Kūgishō Ōka Model 11
Another Ōka in England, this time displayed at the Fleet Air Arm Museum in Yeovilton, Somerset, UK.

Kūgishō Ōka Model 11
This example of the Ōka is in the collection of the Museum of Science and Industry in Manchester, UK, with the registration number of L1996.53.10. Since 1961, this Ōka has passed through a number of museums before it reached its current location.

Kūgishō Ōka Model 11
This Ōka is housed in the collection of the Defence Explosive Ordnance Disposal School. The school is currently located in Chattenden, Kent, but is to be relocated to St. George's Barracks, Bicester in Oxfordshire, UK.

Kūgishō Ōka Model 11
The fourth Ōka in the British Isles is on display at the Royal Air Force Museum at Cosford in Shropshire. Prior to this, it was housed at the Rocket Propulsion Establishment in Westcott, Buckinghamshire.

Kūgishō Ōka Model 11
This, the only known genuine Ōka in Japan (a replica is used at the Yasukuni Shrine in Chiyoda, Tōkyō as well as the Ōka Park in Kashima City, Ibaraki Prefecture), is currently housed at Iruma Air Base, a Japanese Air Self-Defence Force facility in Iruma, Saitama Prefecture. During the war it was at the IJA base Irumagawa Airfield.

Kūgishō Ōka Model 22
Restored and on display at the Smithsonian Air and Space Museum.

Kūgishō MXY7 K-1
With a serial number of 5100, the MXY7 K-1 is housed in the Navy Museum at the Washington Navy Yard in Washington, D.C.

Kūgishō MXY7 K-1
This trainer is currently on display at the National Museum of the United States Air Force, located on the property of the Wright-Patterson Air Force Base in Riverside, Ohio, which is just outside of Dayton, Ohio. At one time it was painted as an operational Ōka but has since been returned to the orange colour scheme of a trainer.

Kūgishō Ōka Model 43 K-1 Kai
At present, this trainer bearing the serial number 61 is in storage and unrestored at the Paul E. Garber facility.

(Note: The Kūgishō Ōka Model 11 displayed at the Wings of Eagles museum in Horseheads, NY, is a replica.)

Kūgishō MXY8 and MXY9

The design and development of the Mitsubishi J8M1 Syūsui presented a challenge. Despite the information available to the Japanese on the Messerschmitt Me 163B, upon which the J8M1 was based, the concept of a tailless fighter, let alone a rocket powered one, was new and untested. What was required was a means to verify the design of the J8M1 and in doing so provide a way to train pilots who would be flying a plane that was unlike any they had ever flown before.

Therefore, Kūgishō was given the task of creating a glider that was to be a copy of the J8M1. The main purpose was to assess the flight characteristics of the tailless fighter given that the Japanese did not have extensive experience with such aircraft. Data collected from flying the glider would in turn be reviewed and applied to the J8M1 fighter prior to series production. In addition to serving as a proof of concept vehicle, the glider would provide the means to train new pilots in flying the aircraft since it was like no other fighter then in service in the IJN and IJA. By using the glider as a trainer, pilots could better transition to the J8M1 and therefore minimise operational mistakes.

Kūgishō assigned the glider construction, called the MXY8 Akigusa (meaning 'Autumn Grass'), to engineer Hidemasa Kimura. Kimura utilised wood with some cloth covered surfaces in the design of the MXY8 and ensured that the glider was a near exact replica of the J8M1 in order to provide the most accurate flight data once testing got under way. By the close of 1944, the first MXY8 was finished and another two were nearing completion.

In December, the first MXY8 was taken to the airfield located in Hyakurigahara, which is about 79km (49 miles) northeast of Tōkyō. It was here that the IJN's Hyakurigahara Air Group was stationed, operating in the defence of Tōkyō. Also at the airfield was the 312th Kōkūtai, a newly formed unit that was to be equipped with the J8M1 once it entered production. As such the 312th Kōkūtai was the perfect group to begin testing the MXY8. The first flight, scheduled for 8 December 1944, was given to Commander One. Unfortunately, One was taken ill and was unable to fly so the mission was assigned to Lieutenant-Commander Toyohiko Inuzuka. On the day of the flight, Inuzuka climbed into the cockpit of the MXY8 and once secure, a Kyūshū K10W1 of the 312th Kōkūtai took the glider into the sky. At altitude Inuzuka was released from the tow plane and began his descent. After successfully bringing the glider down, Inuzuka gave the MXY8 high marks, having found the handling and flight characteristics to be very acceptable.

The IJA, who were also slated to fly the J8M1 as the Ki-200, was provided with the second MXY8. Delivered to the Rikugun Kokuyijutsu Kenkyūjo, the pilot selected to test the MXY8 for the IJA was Colonel Aramaki, and like Inuzuka, he felt that the MXY8 performed well. The only notable deficiency to be found by both Inuzuka and Aramaki was the tendency for the MXY8 to nose over into a dive. The third MXY8 to be built was delivered to the Naval Air Force.

The first MXY8 did not match the combat weight of the J8M1. To this end the IJN wanted to modify the MXY8 so that it incorporated ballast tanks which could hold enough water to fully simulate the combat weight of the J8M1 and be the definitive production model for use in training pilots. With the completion of the initial three MXY8 gliders by Kūgishō, a number of manufacturers were organised to begin the production of the revised 'heavy' MXY8 glider to meet the training needs of the 312th Kōkūtai and other units that would be flying the J8M1 and Ki-200. Maeda Kōkū Kenkyūjo was tasked with producing the MXY8 for the IJN and the MXY8 was to be built for the IJA by Yokoi Kōkū K.K. as the Ku-13.

Further flight testing by the 312th Kōkūtai found that the MXY8 experienced aileron flutter at speeds above 295km/h (183mph) (as a side note, the same problem was encountered in the Messerschmitt Me 163A V1 first prototype during testing). This and other minor problems were noted, analysed and corrected, and the flutter issue was resolved by closing the gap between the wing and the aileron (the Me 163A V1 was rebalanced). In the meantime, the MXY8 was being flown by Naval Air Force pilots at the Kashiwa airfield in Chiba Prefecture. However, the pilots were less enthusiastic on the design, especially after a crash involving one of the gliders that severely injured the pilot. Regardless, the Kaigun Koku Hombu assessed all of the data from the test flights and formally approved the MXY8 on March 1945 and work proceeded with full production of the MXY8 and Ku-13 that continued until the end of the war.

Kūgishō MXY8 – data

Contemporaries Messerschmitt Me 163S, Heinkel He 162S (Germany)

Data is for the MXY8. The specifications also apply to the Yokoi Ku-13. No specific data is available on the MXY9 Shuka.

Type	Proof of Concept/Training Glider	
Crew	One	
Powerplant	None	
Dimensions		
Span	9.50m	31.2ft
Length	5.82m	19.1ft
Height	2.46m	8.1ft
Wing area	17.65m²	190ft²
Weights		
Empty	905kg	1,995 lb
Loaded	1,037kg	2,286 lb
Performance		
Max glide speed	Unknown	
Max tow speed	295km/h	183mph
Armament	None	

Deployment Kūgishō built the three prototype MXY8 gliders, Maeda constructed 44 to 54 MXY8 trainers while Yokoi produced 6 Ku-13 trainers. A number of MXY8 gliders were operated by the 312th Kōkūtai. No MXY9 was constructed and the project remained a design only.

Another version of the glider was investigated by the IJN. Whereas the MXY8 was unpowered, the new version would have some means of propulsion. Designated the MXY9 Shuka (meaning 'Autumn Fire'), the new design was to be an advanced trainer which, because it had the means to propel itself when it was airborne, would provide training with a modicum of power and offer longer flight times. It was envisioned that once training in the MXY8 was completed, pilots would transition to the MXY9 for advanced training before moving to the J8M1 or Ki-200. The propulsion method proposed was the Tsu-11 thermojet. This was the same engine as used in the Kūgishō Ōka Model 22 (see Page 70). However, the MXY9 was never realised.

KELCEY FAULKNER

MXY8 shown in the orange colouration as used on trainers and experimental aircraft.

Kūgishō R2Y Keiun

RONNIE OLSTHOORN

Given the expanse of the Japanese empire by 1942, the IJN found that they had a need for a long range reconnaissance aircraft that could operate from land bases and fly at high speed to render it immune to interception. In the same year, the IJN issued a 17-shi specification for just such a plane and Kūgishō looked to provide the response.

The 1942 17-shi specification called for the aircraft to have a maximum speed of 667km/h (414mph) at 6,000m (19,685ft) along with a mission profile of long range reconnaissance. The speed requirement stemmed from the need to be able to avoid interception; the intelligence it gathered would be useless if the aircraft was shot down before it could return to base. The initial design, the R1Y1 Gyoun (meaning 'Dawn Cloud'; other sources use Seiun, meaning 'Blue Cloud'), bore the designation Y-30 and was to be developed around a new Mitsubishi, 24-cylinder, liquid-cooled engine that was projected to produce 2,500hp. However, delivery of the engine was not expected to be rapid and in order to proceed with the R1Y1, Kūgishō decided to utilise two Mitsubishi MK10A radial engines. In so doing, the R1Y1 took on the appearance of the Kūgishō P1Y1 Ginga and with the use of two radials and the resulting drag imposed by them the R1Y1's calculated performance was projected to fall below the 17-shi specification. Consequently, all work on the R1Y1 ended and the project was abandoned.

Even as Kūgishō was working on the R1Y1, they were developing another design, the Y-40, which was the result of an evaluation of the Heinkel He 119, two examples being purchased from Germany in 1940.

The He 119 was an attempt to create a fast, unarmed reconnaissance aircraft whose high speed would enable it to avoid interception and elude pursuit. To accomplish this, the He 119 used radical concepts to minimise drag and thus enhance speed performance. A pair of Daimler-Benz DB 601 engines coupled together drove a single propeller shaft. The engines were placed in the rear of the He 119 fuselage with the shaft running forward, through the middle of the cockpit, spinning a four-bladed propeller in the nose. To cool the paired powerplants, the He 119 used a wing surface evaporation system in which steam from the engines was circulated through the wings where it cooled and condensed back to liquid where it was pumped back to the engines. To cool the engines when on the ground or during take-off and landing (due to the lack of sufficient airflow across the wings at such times), a supplementary radiator was installed under the forward fuselage. The He 119 V1 first prototype attained a top speed of 565km/h (351mph) at 4,500m (14,765ft). Unfortunately, Heinkel was forced into adding armament to the He 119 but this was done in a very minimal fashion. The V2, with a full functional bomb bay, was able to reach speeds of up to 585km/h (363mph) at 4,500m (14,765ft). The V4 was used as a record breaker, briefly holding the record for speed with a 1,000kg (2,205 lb) payload on a closed 1,000km (621 mile) circuit with the average speed of 504.97km/h (313.78mph). Later the V4 was wrecked in a crash during an attempt to better that time. The record was set on 22 November 1937 and the successful aeroplane was listed as the 'He 606'. The V3 was built as a float-plane, intended to best the 1,000km (621 mile) seaplane speed record. Ultimately, the V5 through to the V8 would be the last He 119 aircraft built because the Luftwaffe showed no further interest in the aircraft.

Following testing in the summer of 1938, a delegation from the IJN was able to inspect the He 119 at Marienehe in Germany. The Japanese were most impressed by the range offered by the He 119 as well as its speed. Of interest were the coupled DB 601 engines. After reporting their positive findings, nine technicians from the Dai-Ichi Kaigun Kōkū Gijutsu-shō flew from Japan to Germany to study the He 119 further. Commander Hideo Tsukada arranged to obtain the manufacturing licence for the He 119 and also the purchase of the He 119 V7 and V8. Both aircraft were crated for shipment and sent to Japan arriving in May 1940. Reassembled at Kasumigaura, Kūgishō began flight trials under the leadership of Major Shōichi Suzuki. During the brief trials, one He 119 was lost to landing gear failure (the He 119 used a special, retracting telescopic oleo leg in order for the long landing gear to fit into the wings). In the end plans to manufacture the He 119 in Japan did not come to fruition.

Although the He 119 was rejected, the study of this aircraft resulted in the development of the Y-40. Like the He 119, the Y-40 was to be a fast, unarmed two-seat reconnaissance aircraft using coupled engines placed within the fuselage behind the cockpit and driving a propeller via an extension shaft. The IJN's 18-shi specifications for a long range reconnaissance aircraft were based on the Y-40.

The Y-40 project, by now called the R2Y1 Keiun (meaning 'Beautiful Cloud'), was led by Commander Shiro Ōtsuki and his design team made good progress. The Keiun was to be equipped with two Aichi Atsuta 30 engines coupled together in a combination known as the Aichi [Ha-70] 10. The 24-cylinder, liquid-cooled [Ha-70] 10 was rated at a maximum of 3,400hp and drove, via the extension shaft, a 6-bladed propeller. The Keiun did not use the same method of cooling as the He 119. Instead, it relied on air intakes and a radiator bath underneath the fuselage, and it also differed from the He 119 in that the Keiun used a tricycle landing gear system and was not a tail sitter.

By the fall of 1944, the war situation for Japan was deteriorating. With the loss of territory to the advancing Allies, the IJN no longer saw a need for a long range reconnaissance aircraft. Following the defeat of the Japanese in the Marianas Islands (following Operation Forager), the fate of the Keiun was all but sealed. The IJN had no need for such a plane as existing designs would be adequate for the dwindling Japanese holdings. In addition, the need for fighters and bombers was rather more urgent than reconnaissance aircraft.

But Ōtsuki and Kūgishō did not let the Keiun fall by the wayside. In late 1944, Kūgishō approached the IJN and informed them that the R2Y1's airframe was readily adaptable to other roles, including that of a fast attack bomber. To heighten the interest, it was proposed that the [Ha-70] 10 engine be replaced with two Mitsubishi Ne 330 axial-flow turbojets, each of the engines being slung under the wings in nacelles. The fuselage space vacated by the Aichi engine would be replaced with fuel tanks. For weapons, the aircraft would carry one 1,800kg (764 lb bomb) and have a cannon armament in the nose. With the introduction of the Ne 330 engines, the maximum speed was expected to be 495mph, superior to the projected 720km/h (447mph) top speed of the Aichi engine model. With these advantages in mind, the IJN approved that work should begin on designing the R2Y2, the turbojet powered Keiun which was sometimes referred to as the Keiun-Kai, as well as permitting the R2Y1 to be completed as an airframe demonstrator to test the handling characteristics.

In April 1945, the first prototype of the R2Y1 was completed and moved to Kisarazu in Chiba Prefecture to begin flight testing. Initial taxi trials, conducted by Kūgishō test pilot Tereoka, showed that the nose wheel had a bad shimmy when in motion and the Aichi engine was prone to overheating. The latter was either due to a lack of airflow through the radiators and inlets during taxi tests or through a poorly designed cooling system. Nevertheless, despite the problems testing of the Keiun continued.

On 8 May 1945, Lieutenant-Commander Kitajima, another Kūgishō test pilot, took the Keiun on its first flight. Kitajima noticed that the oil temperature was rising rapidly and he cut short the flight, landing the Keiun before the engine suffered damage. Mechanics and engineers continued to try and solve the cooling problems, but a few days later the engine caught fire during ground testing, completely destroying the power unit. Then before the Keiun could be returned to Kūgishō to receive a new engine, the aircraft was destroyed by a US bombing raid.

Even before the destruction of the first R2Y1, a second was being constructed and design work for the R2Y2 was underway. Contemporary sources show no less than four versions for how the R2Y2 may ultimately have appeared. The first had the Ne 330 engines in underwing nacelles. The second version showed the two engines buried within the fuselage with wing root air intakes and narrow jet nozzles. The third removed the wing intakes and replaced them with a nose intake, but it retained the narrow nozzles. Finally, the fourth was similar to the third save that the engine nozzles were larger. The first design is considered by most to be the initial R2Y2 concept while the other three are subject to debate. In part, this is due to the fact that the Japanese had very little time to explore various installations of turbojets in airframes. The easiest means to place turbojets on aircraft was by using nacelles and this was seen in the Nakajima Kitsuka, Nakajima Ki-201 Karyū and proposed Kūgishō Tenga and Kawanishi K-200.

Even the Germans with their turbojet experience did not fully understand the effects of a long nose intake feeding a high performance jet buried in a combat fighter's fuselage. Messerschmitt, when they began to study how to start the P.1101 second generation jet fighter, catalogued the obstacles that needed to be overcome. They included the effects of engine operation on the fuselage integrity, ensuring the nose intake was properly positioned and shaped for maximum airflow, making sure the intake tube was made as smooth as possible to minimise air restrictions, how to protect the rear of the aircraft from the heat generated by the exhaust thrust, the effects of reduced airflow on thrust due to flight angles and more. The Germans were at least able to devote some time to investigating these problems and providing solutions to them. This was time however, that the Japanese simply did not have. Up until the construction of the P.1101 V1 and the planned Focke-Wulf Ta 183, all of the wartime jet designs flown by the Luftwaffe had nacelle mounted turbojets. The Japanese may not have been made fully privy to the latest German jet engine technology as it pertained to long intakes before the war ended. It is within reason to suggest that the R2Y2 with the wing root intakes could have been under consideration since it would be a logical development, especially since such intake arrangements were not entirely new. The third and fourth designs may or may not have been post-war conjecture.

Unfortunately for Kūgishō and the IJN, the R2Y2 would never be brought to full production. With the end of the war, the second R2Y1 prototype remained incomplete and the R2Y2 would forever remain a design board aircraft.

Kūgishō R2Y Keiun – data

Contemporaries
Messerschmitt Me 509 (Germany), Tupolev Tu-91 (NATO codename *Boot*) (Russia), Messerschmitt P.1100 (Germany)

The specifications in parenthesis are for the R2Y2 with the underwing turbojets.

Type	Long range reconnaissance aircraft (attack aircraft)
Crew	Two

Powerplant One Aichi [Ha-70] 10, 24-cylinder, liquid-cooled engine developing 3,400hp at take-off and 3,100hp at 3,000m/9.845ft, driving a 6-bladed metal propeller (two Ne 330 axial-flow turbojets developing 1,320kg/2,910 lb of thrust each)

Dimensions

Span		13.99m	45.9ft
	(R2Y2)	13.99m	45.9ft
Length		13.04m	42.8ft
	(R2Y2)	13.04m	42.8ft
Height		4.23m	13.9ft
	(R2Y2)	4.23m	13.9ft
Wing area		33.99m²	365.9ft²
	(R2Y2)	33.99m²	365.9ft²
Wing loading		238.26kg/m²	48.8 lb/ft²
	(R2Y2)	269.99kg/m²	55.3ib/ft²
Power loading		2.35kg/hp	5.2 lb/hp
	(R2Y2)	3.22kg/hp	7.1 lb/hp

Weights

Empty		6,015kg	13,261 lb
	(R2Y2)	5,700kg	12,566 lb
Loaded		9,400kg	20,723 lb
	(R2Y2)	9,950kg	21,935 lb
Fuel capacity		1,555 litres	411 gallons
	(R2Y2)	3,218 litres	850 gallons

Performance

Max speed		720km/h	447mph
		at 10,000m	at 32,810ft
	(R2Y2)	797km/h	495mph
		at mean sea level, estimated	
Cruise speed		464km/h	288mph
		at 4,000m	at 13,125ft
Landing speed		166km/h	103mph
	(R2Y2)	158km/h	98mph
Range		3,139km	1,950 miles
	(R2Y2)	1,269km	788 miles
Climb		10 min to 10,000m (32,810ft)	
	(R2Y2)	7 min to 10,000m (32,810ft)	
Ceiling		11,700m	38,385ft
	(R2Y2)	10,700m	35,104ft

Armament
None (one 800kg/1,764 lb bomb and a battery of forward firing cannon)

Note
Concerning the three other R2Y2 jet variants with internal engines, little is documented and much is open to conjecture. In some instances, the wing span, length, height and wing area are listed as being the same for the R2Y1 but the speed is given as being a maximum of 800km/h (497mph).

Deployment
None. One prototype of the R2Y1 was built and flown while the second R2Y1 prototype was unfinished by the end of the war. The R2Y2 stayed on the design board.

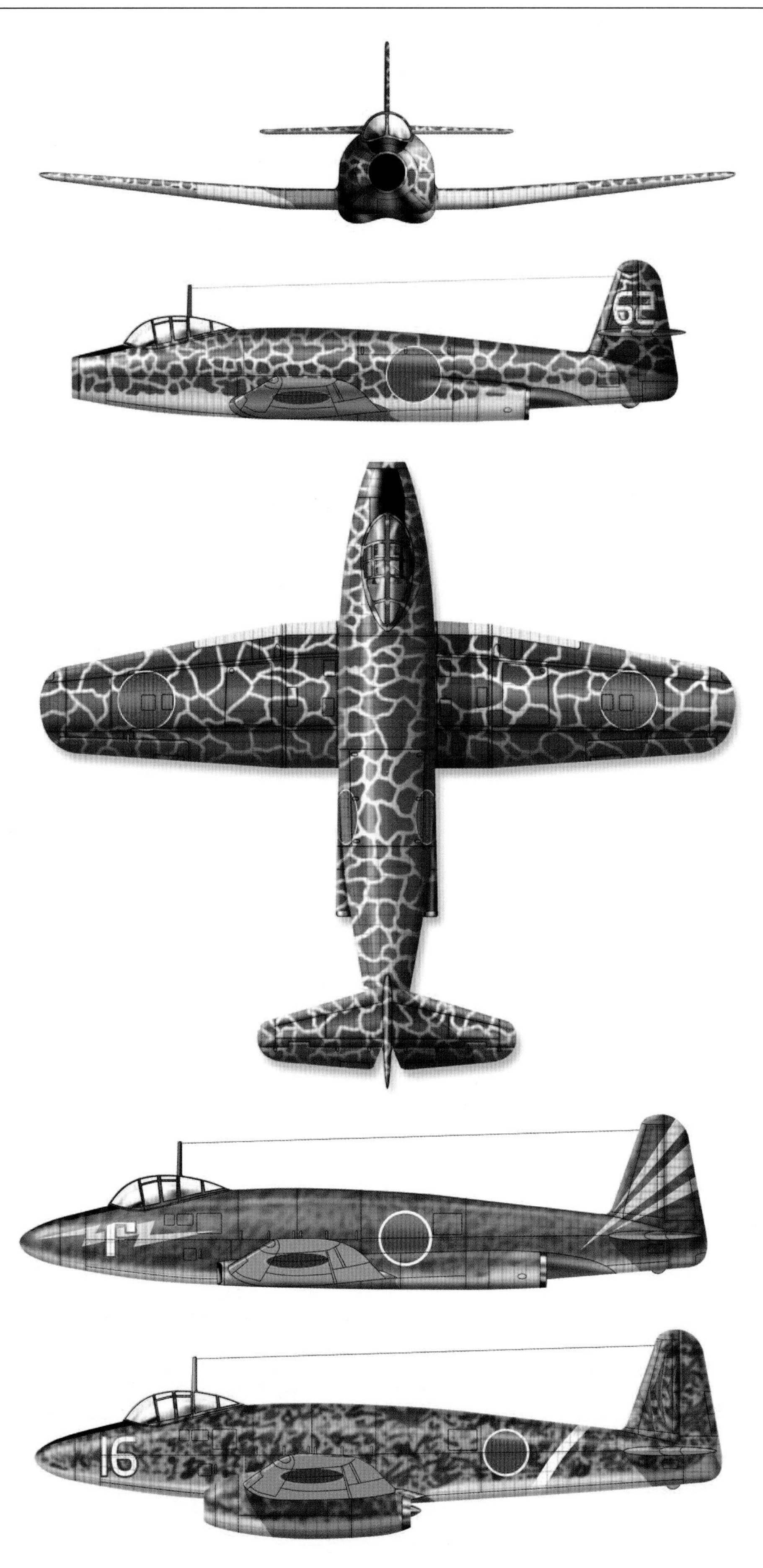

PETER ALLEN

Kūgishō Tenga

Of the many Japanese experimental aircraft of World War 2, perhaps none is more of a mystery than the Kūgishō Tenga. The Tenga (which can mean the Milky Way as one translation of the kanji) was to be a first for Japan: a turbojet powered bomber. To realise this ambition as quickly as possible, the Japanese intended to use one of their latest and best bomber designs – the Kūgishō P1Y Ginga ('ginga' also means Milky Way) – as the basis for the Tenga.

If one examines the aircraft available to the Japanese during the war, the distinct lack of a medium bomber quickly becomes evident. Whereas most of the warring powers operated medium bombers (for example, the Martin B-26 Marauder, the Junkers Ju 88 or the Vickers Wellington), the Japanese were very late in bringing such aircraft to the front. The IJA brought the Ki-67 Hiryū medium bomber into service in 1944 and so the IJN looked to the Kūgishō P1Y Ginga as their answer to the need for a medium bomber.

Development of the Ginga began in 1940 as the Dai-Ichi Kaigun Kōkū Gijutsu-shō's attempt to meet a 15-Shi specification for a medium bomber capable of high speeds, the ability to conduct low-level bombing and torpedo missions, and the capability to perform dive bombing. With Tadanao Mitsuzi and Masao Yamana at the helm the Y-20, as the Ginga was called at this stage, emerged as an aerodynamically clean, mid-wing, twin-engine design. Despite its relatively small size, the Ginga had fourteen fuel tanks (of which only eight had some protection from battle damage), a modicum of armour for the pilot (which consisted of a 20mm thick plate behind his head), a light defensive armament of a 7.7mm machine gun in the nose and in the rear of the cockpit, and the ability to carry a single 800kg (1,764 lb) torpedo or two 500kg (1,102 lb) bombs. With the two Nakajima Homare 11 18-cylinder, air-cooled radial engines developing 1,280hp each, speed was estimated at 556km/h (345mph).

The first prototype was completed in August 1943 and flight testing began shortly afterwards. Test pilots found that the Ginga possessed excellent speed and also displayed good handling qualities. Ground crews on the other hand had anything but good things to say about the aircraft. The Homare 11 engines and the hydraulic system used in the Ginga were a constant maintenance hassle, requiring far more time and effort to maintain than was considered reasonable. So bad were the problems, the IJN postponed its acceptance of the aircraft.

Despite the problems production got moving and design changes saw the machine guns replaced with Type 99 Model 1 20mm cannons and 13mm Type 2 machine guns. Other changes included revised engine cowlings, replacing the retractable tail wheel with a fixed wheel, moving from flush riveting to flat-head riveting, incorporating a bullet-proof panel in the windshield and also replacing the Homare 11 engines with the Homare 12 which could produce 1,825hp.

After these modifications, the IJN finally accepted the P1Y1 Ginga bomber into service. But the type was still nagged by problems, notably the Homare 12 engines which rarely produced the horsepower they were rated for. Such issues delayed the Ginga entering combat until the spring of 1945. Even though the Ginga would see battle for a mere six months the design nevertheless proved to be a capable medium bomber and one which the Allies respected when they encountered it. When the Allies first heard of the plane they thought it was a heavy fighter and assigned the codename *Francis* to it (after Francis 'Fran' Williams of the Material Section of the Directorate of Intelligence, Allied Air Forces, Southwest Pacific Area). However, when the Ginga was finally spotted after 1943, it was realised that it was a bomber and the name was changed to the feminine version of Francis – *Frances*.

The Ginga was developed into several variants and there were plans to use the bomber as a carrier for the Ōka Model 21 and Ōka Model 22 suicide aircraft. Kawanishi built a night-fighter/intruder version as the P1Y2-S, which entered service with the IJN as the Kyokko (meaning 'Aurora') in the summer of 1944. The Kyokko was fitted with Mitsubishi Kasei 25a 1,850hp, 14-cylinder radials because the Homare 12 could not be assembled fast enough to meet demand. Weapons included two forward oblique mounted 20mm Type 99 Model 2 cannons firing upwards and the nose cannon was removed. First flown in July 1944, it was found that the Kyokko did not perform well at the high altitudes where the Boeing B-29s roamed. This revelation was so disappointing that the upward firing cannons were removed and the Kyokko returned to its bomber role as the Ginga Model 16 (P1Y2). Nakajima also built a similar night-fighter version as the P1Y1-S Byakko (which meant 'White Light'). The Byakko fared little better than the Kyokko and did not see service. Other modifications and plans included upgrading the engines to the Homare 23, Kasei 25c or the Mitsubishi MK9A, the idea of an attack model with ten to sixteen forward firing 20mm cannons and using steel and wood in the aircraft's construction. The most interesting was the P1Y3 Model 33. This version was to be built from the ground up to carry the Ōka and would have had a special bomb bay to accept the Ōka Model 21 or 22 with increased wing span and an enlarged fuselage. The P1Y3 never left the drawing board.

With the Ginga's success in terms of performance, it's easy to see why there was interest in converting it to turbojet power. The concept of the Tenga was certainly real. But outside of the name and the basic intent to replace the radial engines with turbojets, nothing else is known. Therefore, one has to review other designs to make assumptions on what kind of task the Japanese might have faced in making the Tenga a flying reality.

The first point to consider would be that the Kūgishō Ne 20 turbojets, then in production for use in the Nakajima Kitsuka, would not have been sufficient to provide the Tenga with any meaningful speed if mounted one per wing. One Ne 20 produced 487kg (1,074 lb) of static thrust and two could propel the Kitsuka to 623km/h (387mph), which was not particularly significant over conventional high-performance propeller driven aircraft. The Kitsuka was a much lighter aircraft and a twin turbojet Tenga using Ne 20s would not have been feasible.

It would have needed some of the projected advances in the Ne 20's development to come closer to reality to provide the Tenga with a meaningful system of propulsion. The Ne 30 turbojet was expected to generate up to 850kg (1,873 lb) of thrust (better than the German BMW 003 turbojet rated at 800kg/1,763 lb) while the Ishikawajima Ne 130 was projected to produce 900kg (1,984 lb) of static thrust, comparable to the Junkers Jumo 004 engine. The Nakajima Ne 230 and the Mitsubishi Ne 330 were estimated to be able to produce 885kg (1,951 lb) and 1,300kg (2,866 lb) of thrust respectively with the Ne 230 sacrificing thrust for a lighter weight.

It is said that the Ne 30 would have been the initial choice to power the Tenga had it been available. In comparison, the German Arado Ar 234B jet bomber used two Jumo 004 engines. It was similar in size to the P1Y1, the notable differences being a smaller wing span, the loaded weight was nearly 680kg (1,500 lb) lighter and the Ar 234B had far less wing area. Together, the two Jumo 004 engines could move the Ar 234B at speeds up to 742km/h (461mph). Certainly, two Ne 30 engines would not have provided such a speed when mounted to the P1Y1 but it would have been the logical starting point. Quite possibly, RATO units may have been needed to boost the Tenga off the ground. Clearly the Ne 130 would have been a better selection and with the Ne 330, the Tenga would have enjoyed a noticeable speed improvement. Problems with the development of the Ne 30 engine are cited as a reason for the Tenga project being cancelled. Indeed, the Ne 30, an off-shoot from the Ne 12 program, never advanced, being surpassed by the Ne 20, Ne 130, Ne 230 and Ne 330 developments.

But could the basic airframe of the Ginga be used with radial engines replacing with turbojets? It may have been attempted had the Tenga advanced in design. Even changing the radials for turbojets would have necessitated fairly significant adjustments in the wings to accommodate them but at least redesigning a wing to accept turbojets is a simpler task than redesigning the entire aircraft.

However, if one examines the history of combat aircraft, you would be hard pressed to find a conventional combustion engined bomber switching to jet power merely by changing the engines and adjusting the wings. For instance, not even among the dozens of jet bomber projects undertaken by the Germans did a piston-engined bomber switch its engines for turbojets without heavy modifications, if at all. One such example was the Messerschmitt Me 264 which used four Junkers Jumo 9-211 radial engines when the first prototype was flight tested. However, the proposed four turbojet engined version bore little resemblance to the original design.

Perhaps the only notable propeller to turbojet design created by adaptating an existing airframe was the Russian Tupolev Tu-12 whose heritage was owed to the Tu-2, one of the premiere Soviet light bombers. Built from 1941 through 1948, the Tu-2 possessed fast speed, excellent agility and had a substantial weapon fit and bomb carrying capacity. When Tupolev answered the call to produce a jet bomber, he took the Tu-2 as the basis for his Tu-12. He used the fuselage, wings and tailplane of the Tu-2 and adapted them to suit the installation of two Rolls-Royce Nene-1 turbojets and the higher speeds that would result. Although one can certainly see the lineage of the Tu-2 in the Tu-12, the aircraft still required a general redesign to cope with the new engines and the associated handling characteristics and was not simply a case of swapping the radial engines for turbojets. The design of the Tu-12 began in 1946 and the first flight took place in June 1947.

It is not unreasonable to conclude that the initial Tenga designers may have tried to utilise as much of the Ginga as possible, offering the benefit of an airframe already in production with proven airworthy characteristics. This would have reduced development time when the need for such a bomber was most urgent. It would have also served as a starting point for aerodynamic testing. Still, when one reviews the jet bomber proposals of other nations, the number of piston engine to jet engine concepts can be counted on a single hand. For the majority, the jet bomber was designed from the ground up instead of being adapted from an exisiting aircraft. The designers of the Tenga may have come to the same conclusion had they had the opportunity to continue their work. If so, the final Tenga design and prototype may have borne little resemblance to the Ginga with which it shares its name.

Kūgishō Tenga – data

Contemporaries
Arado Ar 234 Blitz (Germany), Heinkel He 343 (Germany), North American B-45 Tornado (US), Ilyushin IL-22 (Russia)

There is no exact information available on the specifications for the Kūgishō Tenga. The data provided below is based on the Tenga having used the P1Y Ginga airframe pretty much verbatim, apart from the change of engines (as the Tenga is often depicted). Even then, information is fragmentary and subject to guesswork.

Type	Medium Bomber
Crew	Three

Powerplant (planned)
Two Ne 30 turbojets producing 850kg (1,873 lb) of thrust each

Dimensions		
Span	19.99m	65.6ft
Length	14.99m	49.2ft
Height	4.29m	14.1ft
Wing area	55.00m²	592ft²
	(likely to be different with turbojets)	

Weights	
Empty	N/A
Loaded	N/A

Performance	
Max speed	N/A
Range	N/A
Climb	N/A
Ceiling	N/A

Armament
Two 20mm cannons or 13mm machine guns, one in the nose, the other rear firing; one 800kg (1,764 lb) torpedo or between 1,000kg to 1,560kg (2,205 lb to 3,525 lb) of bombs

Deployment
None. The Tenga existed only as a paper design.

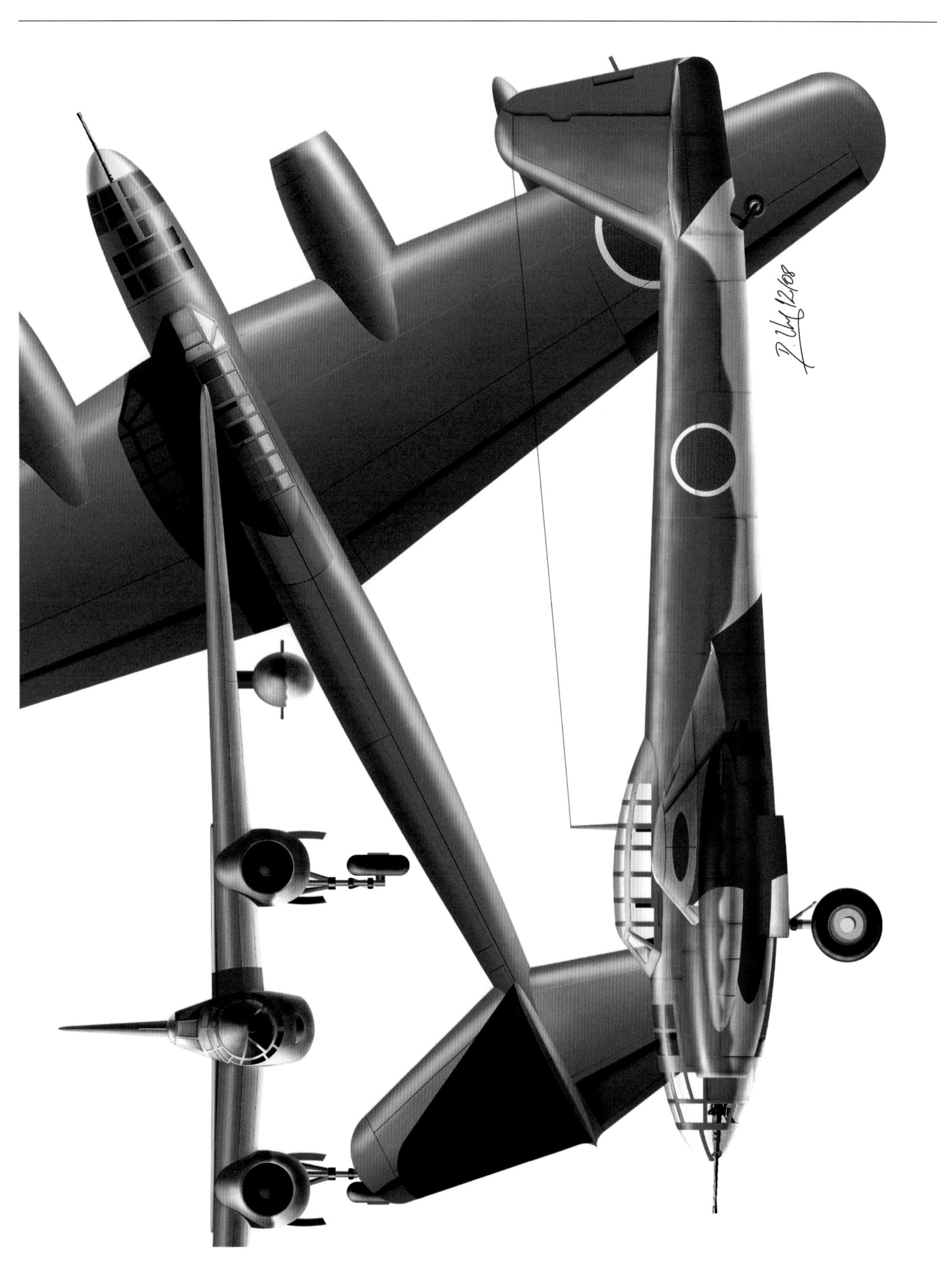

DANIEL UHR

Kyūshū J7W Shinden

In 1943, the IJN issued an 18-shi specification that included the requirement for a new interceptor. Japanese aircraft tasked with interception roles had by this time begun to be eclipsed by the newest Allied fighters and the IJN sought to ensure their edge was maintained. Three contenders submitted their designs and it would be Kyūshū's that was the most radical of them all: the J7W Shinden.

The man behind the Shinden ('Magnificent Lightning') was Captain Masaoki Tsuruno, a member of the Technical Staff of the IJN. Tsuruno conceived an interceptor that made use of a configuration rarely seen at the time of his design work, a design with canard foreplanes. Canards were not a new concept, even in 1943. They were seen as far back as 1910 with a Gabriel and Charles Voisin design and later a Bleriot tail-first aircraft had incorporated canards. (Both planes used the term 'canard' which in French means 'duck' – the 1910 Canard Voisin and the 1911 Blériot 'Canard'). Canards would sporadically appear in experimental aircraft right up to World War 2, examples being the 1929 Raab-Katzenstein Rakate, the 1931 Focke-Wulf Ente (the 'Duck') and the 1937 Beltrame Colibri. Tsuruno felt canards could offer a number of advantages such as reducing the chances of stalling, improved controllability and manoeuvrability and easing some construction concerns such as the engine installation and control linkage arrangements.

Besides the canards, Tsuruno introduced another feature in the Shinden that was certainly new to the Japanese – the use of a turbojet to power the aircraft. Of course, Tsuruno understood that a more conventional piston-engine would have to be used until such time as a suitable turbojet became available, but a turbojet was incorporated into his original design to ensure that the transition would not present any difficulties. At this time, the Shinden was known as the X-18.

By the time Tsuruno's initial layout for the Shinden was complete the IJN had already issued its late 1943 18-shi specifications for three classes of aircraft. The first of these covered an air superiority fighter (18-shi Ko), the second for an interceptor (18-shi Ōtsu) and the third for a night fighter (18-shi Hei). For the 18-shi Ōtsu competition, both Nakajima and Kawanishi had submitted designs: the single-engine J6K1 Jinpu ('Squall') and the twin-engine J5N1 Tenrai (or 'Heavenly Thunder') respectively. These entries were based on the rather sparse directives of the specification which called for a top speed of 665km/h (413mph), a climb to 8,000m (26,246ft) in nine minutes and the ability to carry at least two 30mm cannons. To go with these two projects, Tsuruno introduced the Shinden to the IJN as a third competitor.

Despite some opposition to the design, the IJN was intrigued enough to accept the Shinden proposal. However, the design had to show promise and the canard configuration needed to be proven before the IJN would authorise further development. Therefore, Tsuruno designed a glider based on his Shinden concept as a means to test the canard properties and handling. Kūgishō was commissioned to build three gliders which were called the MXY6. Further details on MXY6 development can be found on page 69. The initial, positive results achieved with the MXY6 convinced the IJN to move forward with the Shinden project even before the completion of the glider testing by authorising two prototypes of the J7W1.

The IJN gave the Shinden project to Kyūshū Hikōki K.K. even though Kyūshū had no experience with high performance aircraft, let alone one like the Shinden. Unlike other major manufacturers however, Kyūshū's research facilities, personnel and production capacity were not heavily taxed by the needs of the Japanese war machine. To assist Kyūshū, the IJN placed a team from the Dai-Ichi Kaigun Kōkū Gijutsu-shō as well as Tsuruno himself at the disposal of Kyūshū engineers and managers to bolster their capability in handling the program.

With everything in position work commenced on the first prototype in June 1944. The heart of the J7W1 was the Mitsubishi MK9D ([Ha-43]) 12 18-cylinder radial engine boosted by a supercharger. Although Tsuruno wanted to use a turbojet he rejected the Ne 12B (TR-12) as insufficient in terms of thrust production. And since further turbojet developments were projected to show improved performance, the Shinden would use this radial engine until such time as a suitable turbojet was available. The Mitsubishi engine and its supercharger were mounted in the rear of the fuselage. A six-bladed, metal Sumitomo VDM propeller was mated to the engine through an extension shaft and placed in a pusher configuration. If required the propeller could be jettisoned to effect pilot bail-out. On each side of the fuselage were air intakes for cooling the engine. The main wings were swept and on each was mounted a vertical stabiliser situated in approximately the middle of the wing. The pilot sat in a cockpit in the centre of the fuselage while the canards were mounted on the nose. A tricycle landing gear was employed, the front tyre being 550x150mm and the two main tyres being 725x200mm in size.

The Shinden would carry four Type 5 30mm cannons. The Type 5, while heavier than the earlier Type 2 30mm gun, possessed a higher rate of fire at 500 rounds per minute and had a higher muzzle velocity. Each cannon was provided with 66 rounds. With less than eight seconds of 30mm rounds per gun, one hit would be sufficient to cripple and shoot down a fighter or bomber, therefore there was little ammunition to waste. Therefore, there were two Type 1 7.92mm machine guns, one on either side of the gun camera, in front of the nose. The purpose of these guns was not offensive but to serve as a ranging weapon for the cannons. Upon lining of his target, the pilot would fire a short burst from the machine guns. If the rounds struck the target, he would fire a burst from the cannons and be reasonably assured of a hit, thereby conserving the precious cannon ammunition. Each Type 1 was provided with 75 rounds of ammunition in a saddle drum magazine. It should be noted that sources often list the two Type 1 weapons for training purposes, i.e. for practice and gunnery training, not gun laying. While certainly possible, gun laying would seem more plausible due to the rapid ammunition consumption of the Type 5 cannons and in training there is no real reason why machine guns would be used as a substitute for cannons. For payload, the Shinden had a modest bomb carrying capacity of 120kg (264 lb).

By September 1944, a model of the Shinden was being tested in a wind tunnel to assess its aerodynamic properties of the shape and planforms. With the results deemed acceptable, the first metal was cut on the prototype at the Kyūshū Haruda factory located in Fukuoka City. By May 1945, the Shinden was nearly complete although it lacked the canopy, landing gear fairings, much of the main wings and other components. As the MK9D ([Ha-43]) 12 was already installed, testing of the powerplant commenced and trials showed that a cooling problem existed, probably in part because no airflow was reaching the engine during static testing.

In June 1945, the first prototype was finished but the armament was not fitted. Instead, weights simulating the Type 5 cannons were installed in the nose. Flight testing was to commence immediately although the problem with the engine cooling would delay the first flight until 3 July. Tsuruno would be the first to fly the Shinden. The aircraft was to

MUNEO HOSAKA

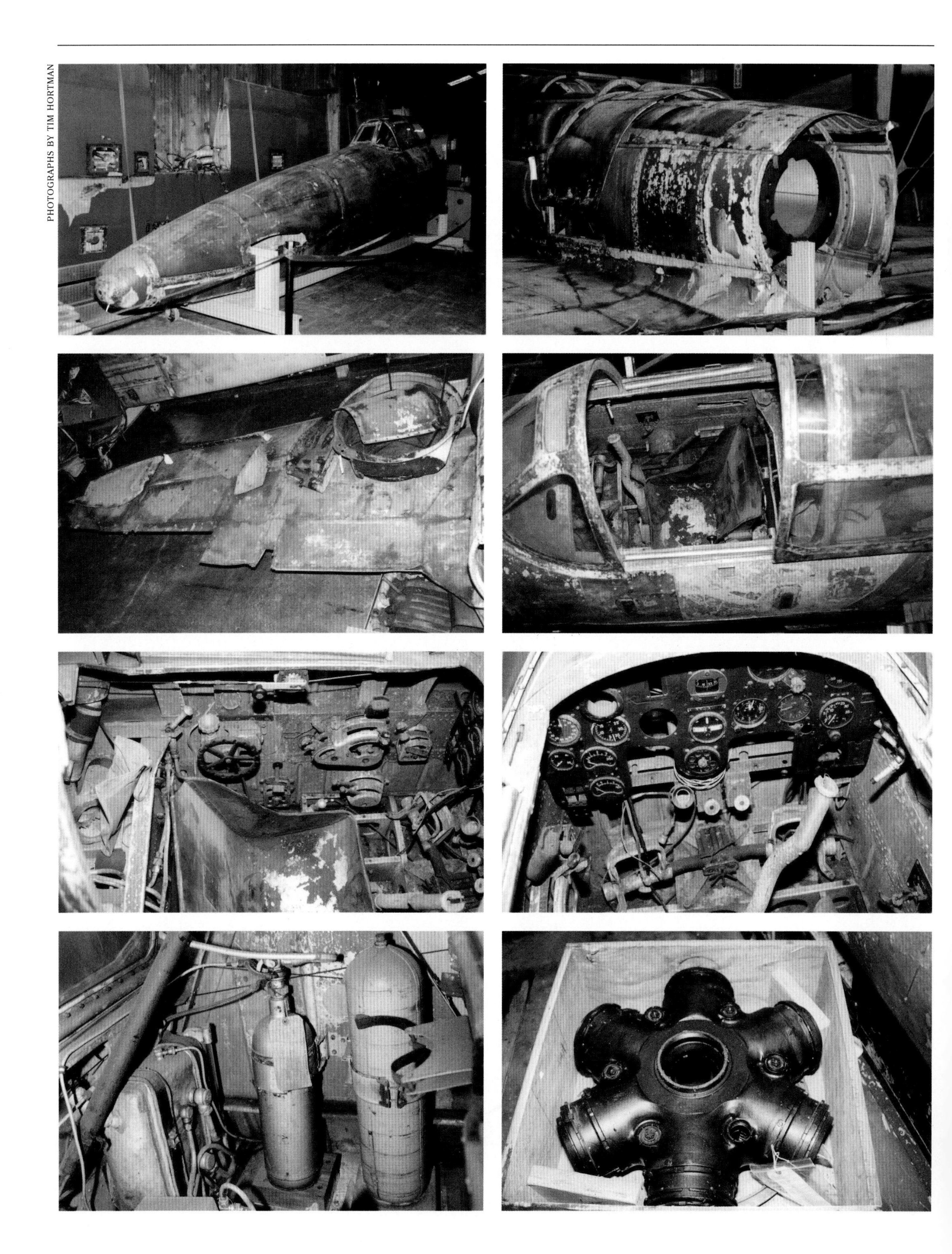
PHOTOGRAPHS BY TIM HORTMAN

MUNEO HOSAKA

take-off from the Mushiroda Airport in Fukuoka City. The engine was started and Tsuruno climbed into the cockpit. On releasing the brakes and commencing to taxi, the Shinden showed an unexpected heavy torque pulling to the right. Surprised, Tsurano was unable to stop the plane swerving off the runway where the propeller touched the ground bending several of the blades by as much as 28cm (11 inches). In addition, a portion of the right wing's vertical stabiliser was also damaged. The accident would delay flight testing for nearly a month while repairs were made. To prevent the propeller from striking the ground, tail wheels, as used on the Kyūshū K11W Shiragiku trainer, were fitted to the bottom of the vertical stabilisers.

On 3 August 1945, the Shinden was prepared for flight. Only 38 litres (10 gallons) of fuel were loaded with 80 litres (21 gallons) of lubricating oil. The weights simulating the cannons remained. The flight would be made by Kyūshū's Yoshitaka Miyaishi. With the torque now a known issue, Miyaishi was able to compensate and the Shinden successfully took to the air for the first time. The flight was for a very short duration and the aircraft was not taken above 400m (1,312ft). On landing Miyaishi reported that the take-off was relatively easy but rudder rise was experienced at 185km/h (115mph) with the plane lifting off the ground at 193km/h (120mph). As he climbed pushing the speed to 222km/h (138mph), the pull to the right caused by the torque from the propeller was very noticeable. After levelling off at 400m (1,312ft) and at a maximum speed of 161mph, the pull was still a problem. He also found the landing to be a tricky process. The Shinden was found to have a relatively fast landing speed at 240km/h (149mph) and because of the torque pull and the inclination of the nose, bringing the Shinden down was not a simple task.

A second flight was made on 6 August 1945 with Miyaishi at the controls. Manoeuvrability was the main focus of the test, though the aircraft was flown up to 491m (1,610ft). The pilot found that during the climb the nose wanted to dip. Again, the pull to the right was evident and during landing if a slight rudder up position was applied the nose would pop up just before touchdown. It was also discovered that the oil temperature rose as the flight went on and a means to rectify the problem would have to be found.

On 8 August 1945, the third and final flight of the Shinden took place with Miyaishi at the controls. At 193km/h (120mph), the nose wheel left the runway and at 203km/h (126mph) the plane lifted off. Miyaishi noted that the nose tended to drop regardless of how fast or slow the engine revolutions were. He also found that even with the nose down, the Shinden still flew horizontally with a level track and slight application of the rudder. Landing speed was again 240km/h (149mph).

In total, the first Shinden logged between 30 and 45 minutes in the air. In addition to the problems already noted, Miyaishi complained of strong vibrations in the fuselage, in part due to the engine torque and from the extension shaft that mated the propeller to the engine. With the flight results, Kyūshū engineers set about the process of solving the torque and vibration problems as well as the cooling concerns.

However, even before the Shinden took flight the IJN was desperately in need of a high performance interceptor. The Kawanishi J6K1 Jinpu failed to show any improvement over the Kawanishi N1K2-J Shiden-Kai

Kyūshū J7W Shinden – data

Contemporaries

Curtiss-Wright XP-55 Ascender (US), Henschel P.75 (Germany), Gotha Go P.50/I (Germany), Henschel P.87 (Germany), Messerschmitt P.1110 Ente (Germany), Miles M.35 and M.39B Libellula (UK), Mikoyan-Gurevich MiG-8 Utka (Russia), Ambrosini SS.4 (Italy)

The specifications in parenthesis are for the J7W2 Shinden-Kai in which the standard J7W1 airframe is used.

Type Interceptor

Crew One

Powerplant One Mitsubishi MK9D ([Ha-43]) 12, 18-cylinder, air-cooled radial engine, developing 2,130hp at take-off, 2,020hp at 1,180m/3,870ft and 1,160hp at 8,700m/28,545ft, driving a six-bladed, alternating stroke propeller (one Ne 130 axial-flow turbojet developing 900kg/1,984 lb of thrust)

Dimensions

Span		11.09m	36.4ft
	(J7W2)	11.09m	36.4ft
Length		9.63m	31.6ft
	(J7W2)	9.63m	31.6ft
Height		3.90m	12.8ft
	(J7W2)	3.90m	12.8ft
Wing area		20.49m²	220.65ft²
	(J7W2)	20.49m²	220.65ft²
Wing loading		241.19kg/m²	49.4 lb/ft²
	(J7W2)	240.21kg/m²	49.2 lb/ft²
Power loading		2.40kg/hp	5.3 lb/hp
	(J7W2)	5.44kg/hp	12.0 lb/hp

Weights

Empty		3,525kg	7,771 lb
	(J7W2)	3,465kg	7,639 lb
Loaded		4,950kg	10,912 lb
	(J7W2)	4,930kg	10,868 lb
Max loaded		5,272kg	11,622 lb
Useful load		1,425kg	3,141 lb
	(J7W2)	1,465kg	3,229 lb

Performance

Max speed		750km/h	466mph
		at 8,700m	at 28,545ft
		800km/h	497mph
	(J7W2)	at 10,000m	at 32,808ft
Cruise speed		424km/h	263mph
		at 4,000m	at 13,125ft
		449km/h	279mph
	(J7W2)	at 6,000m	at 19,685ft
Landing speed		240km/h	149mph
Take-off length		560m	1,837ft
Landing length		580m	1,902ft
Range		851km	529 miles
Endurance		2.5 hours	
Climb		10 min 40 sec to 8,000m (26,245ft)	
Ceiling		12,000m	39,370ft

Armament

Four Type 5 30mm cannons with 66 rounds per cannon, two Type 1 7.92mm ranging machine guns with 75 rounds per weapon with the capacity to carry two 60kg (132 lb) bombs or four 30kg (66 lb) bombs

Deployment

None. Two J7W1 Shinden aircraft were produced. Although the aircraft was ordered into production, no further examples had been constructed by the end of the war. The J7W2 remained a design only.

Survivors

Kyūshū J7W1 Shinden (FE-326)

This was the second Shinden prototype and was captured at Kyūshū's main factory. It was listed on the aviation industry release report on 10 March 1946 and to undergo restoration at MAMA by 1 August 1946. FE-326 was moved to Park Ridge in September 1946. Of note is the Shinden was provided with a stipulation that it should be housed in such a way that it could be quickly removed from storage if an engine and other parts were to be obtained to bring it to flight status. This never happened but the Shinden was fortunate enough to escape the cutting torch and was moved to the Paul. E. Garber facility where it currently remains in pieces and unrestored (see page 86).

(meaning 'Violet Lightning', known to the Allies as *George*) and the Nakajima J5N1 Tenrai was proving to be a disappointment by the time flight trials commenced in July 1944. With the failure of these two entries for the 18-shi specification, the IJN ordered the J7W1 Shinden into production in May 1944 and in so doing made the type the only canard configuration aircraft to achieve this status during World War 2. By September 1944, the production plans had been formulated with Kyūshū's Zasshonokuma factory expected to turn out 30 Shindens per month while Nakajima's Handa plant would produce 120 Shindens each month. In light of the war situation, such production numbers would have been very difficult to meet. As it was, the war ended before production could get going.

In addition to the first prototype, the second machine was also completed but it did not fly before the end of hostilities. The war's end meant that the modifications required to correct the problems found during ground and flight testing were never made. As a side note, nearly four decades later Colonel Bob Thacker would construct a radio controlled flying model of the Shinden. His initial prototype showed the same pull problem as the original Shinden resulting in two crashes that required the complete rebuilding of the model each time. To solve this problem, Thacker placed the front canards at 7.5° positive incidence, adjusted the centre of gravity and pointed the extension shaft for the propeller 3° to the right and 4.5° down from the zero thrust line. The pull problem was successfully eliminated by these adjustments and the Kyūshū engineers may have found the same solution had they had the time to implement it.

The Shinden was not an easy aircraft to fly. Given the configuration of the aircraft, it would have required a skilled pilot to use in combat and Japan's forces were low on experienced pilots by the time the Shinden would have entered service. The same problem would plague the Germans when their high performance turbojet fighters were coming into operational use.

The end of the war also spelled the end of the J7W2 Shinden-Kai. This was to be the turbojet-equipped version of the Shinden. The use of the radial engine had been a stop gap until a suitable turbojet was available. The Ne 12B was rejected as its power was considered too low to effectively propel the aircraft. In any case, work was by this time under way on the Kūgishō Ne 20 turbojet that was based on the German BMW 003A engine, the only turbojet built and flown in a Japanese aircraft: the Nakajima Kitsuka (page 114). The J7W2 was to use the Ne 130 turbojet, also based on the BMW 003A, which was being developed by Ishikawajima-Shibaura. The Ne 130 was to have produced nearly double the thrust of the Ne 20; however, the Ne 130 would not be ready by the close of the war and as such the J7W2 remained a design board aircraft. There is speculation concerning what the J7W2 would have looked like. One suggestion is that the J7W2 would have been the J7W1 with the Mitsubishi radial replaced with the Ne 130 turbojet. A second suggestion concerns the fact that without the need for propeller clearance the Shinden could dispense with the tall landing gear, thus lowering the height of the aircraft. Aside from modifying the landing gear, the vertical stabilisers, fuselage and canopy shape may also have required adjustment. It is likely that had development of the J7W2 commenced with the availability of the Ne 130, a J7W1 airframe would have been adapted to accept the engine and testing conducted on this, with other modifications coming into play as a production J7W2 was standardised.

GINO MARCOMINI

GINO MARCOMINI

Mitsubishi G7M Taizan

RONNIE OLSTHOORN

The illustration of the G7M1 provided in this book is based upon Kijiro Takahashi's design. It is shown in the colours of the Yokosuka Kōkūtai.

Prior to the start of World War 2, there were men who foresaw the need for long range strategic bombers capable of striking across vast distances. Men like Generalleutnant Walter Wever of Germany who pushed with urgency the need for such bombers despite the veritable wall of opposition to such endeavours. This was also the case in Japan where it was clear that aggression against the United States would require the capability of hitting the US. Therefore in 1941, the Kaigun Koku Hombu issued its 16-shi specification for a long range bomber.

A review of bombers in service with the IJN by 1941 showed that none were capable of crossing the Pacific to attack distant targets. At the time, the Mitsubishi G3M (codenamed *Nell* by the Allies) was being phased out to be replaced by the Mitsubishi G4M (known as *Betty* to the Allies and Hamaki or 'Cigar' to the Japanese). Although the G4M1 had a range of 6,043km (3,749 miles) this was insufficient to attack targets in the United States or, if required, deep into Russia. Following this review, the Kaigun Koku Hombu put forth the 16-shi specification for an attack bomber. Only two key specifications were stated. The first was that the maximum speed had to be at least 580km/h (361mph) and the second was a maximum range of at least 7,340km (4,598 miles). Mitsubishi set about the task of designing a bomber capable of meeting these requirements.

Initially, Mitsubishi engineer Kiro Honjo (who designed the G3M and G4M) proposed that the 16-shi bomber should be of a four engine design. Within Mitsubishi the bomber was known as the M-60. His proposal, however, was flatly rejected by the Kaigun Koku Hombu. Instead, another Mitsubishi engineer, Kijiro Takahashi, put forward his own design for the 16-shi bomber which upon review was allowed to proceed.

Takahashi's version of the M-60 was to use two 'Nu' engines. The Nu engine was a 24-cylinder, horizontal-H, liquid-cooled engine. Simply put, a horizontal-H engine is two flat engines placed one on top of the other and geared together (a flat engine is one in which the pistons move horizontally). Despite having a poor power to weight ratio, they offer the advantage of being more compact and, because of this, Takahashi elected to use them on his bomber. Each engine was rated at 2,200hp at 5,000m (16,404ft).

In appearance, Takahashi's bomber bore a strong resemblance to the Heinkel He 177 Greif (German for 'Griffon') heavy bomber that first flew on 19 November 1939. The nose

Mitsubishi G7M Taizan – data

Contemporaries

Bristol Buckingham (UK), Lockheed P2V Neptune (US), Junkers Ju 88H-1 and H-2 (Germany), Junkers Ju 288A (Germany)

The specifications for the G7M1 Taizan are based on the design dimensions and estimated performance of the final G7M1 proposal as derived by Mitsubishi.

Type	Long-Range Bomber
Crew	Seven

Powerplant Two Mitsubishi MK10A (Ha-42-11) 18-cylinder, air-cooled radial engines developing 2,000hp for take-off, 1,810hp at 2,200m (7,217ft) and 1,720hp at 5,400m (17,716ft); each engine drove a metal, four-bladed, alternating stroke propeller with a 4.5m (14.7ft) diameter

Dimensions		
Span	25.00m	82.0ft
Length	20.00m	65.6ft
Height	6.09m	20.0ft
Wing area	N/A	
Wing loading	N/A	
Power loading	3.99kg/hp	8.8 lb/hp

Weights		
Empty	10,600kg	23,368 lb
Loaded	16,000kg	35,273 lb
Useful load	5,400kg	11,904 lb
Bomb load	800kg	1,764 lb maximum

Performance		
Max speed	544km/h at 5,000m	344mph at 26,246ft
Normal range	2,799km	1,739 miles
Max range	7,400km	4,598 miles
Climb	10 min to 10,000m (32,808ft)	
Ceiling	N/A	
Fuel capacity	4,497 litres	1,188 gallons

Armament

Six 13mm Type 2 machine guns, two mounted in each of two upper fuselage turrets (one forward, one aft of the wings) and two in a ventral, rear firing position; two 20mm Type 99 Model 2 cannons, one mounted in the nose, the other in the tail

Deployment

None. A wooden mock-up was built before the Taizan project was cancelled.

was rounded and fully glazed, a style unlike any Japanese bomber then in service. The wings were mounted mid-fuselage, each wing sporting the Nu engine in a well-streamlined nacelle. On top of the fuselage, fore and aft of the wings, was a turret for a portion of the defensive armament. A fairly spacious tail gunner position was fitted beneath the vertical stabiliser on the underside of the fuselage with a rear facing ventral gun station. A relative rarity in Japanese bomber design was the tricycle landing gear. Takahashi's performance estimates put the normal operational range at 6,412km (3,984 miles) which, with a lighter payload, could meet the 16-shi specification. The maximum speed would have been 555km/h (345mph) with a relatively light defensive weapon armament of two Type 99 20mm cannons and two Type 97 7.7mm machine guns.

Unfortunately for Takahashi, Operation Barbarossa, the German invasion of the Soviet Union on 22 June 1941, would prevent the required machine tools and equipment to produce the Nu engine from being exported to Japan. Without the powerplant, the design was doomed. With Takahashi's proposal having fallen by the wayside, Kiro Honjo resumed control of the M-60 project. This time, instead of a four-engine bomber, Honjo would utilise two engines and base his design heavily on the G4M.

The G7M Taizan (meaning 'Great Mountain') as the design was later designated was to use two 18-cylinder, air-cooled radial engines, the Mitsubishi MK10A (Ha-42-11), developing 2,000hp each. The wings were mounted midway on the fuselage and the aircraft was to be constructed of metal with fabric covering the ailerons and rudders. It was anticipated that the Taizan would carry the same 800kg (1,764 lb) bomb load as the G4M1 but unlike the Hamaki, the Taizan would have a far more potent defensive armament as the bomber would operate far from fighter protection. This step also took into account the shortcomings in the G4M1's protection. Of course, using less powerful engines and a heavier weapon fit caused a revision in performance when compared to Takahashi's design. A 31 October 1942 performance estimate gave the G7M1 a range of 5,559km (3,454 miles) at a speed of 518km/h (322mph) at 5,000m (16,404ft) with a weapon fit of two Type 99 20mm cannons, two Type 2 13mm machine guns and two Type 1 7.9mm machine guns. However, as work on the G7M1 proceeded and the design underwent further testing, these estimates would continue to be revised. Unfortunately for Mitsubishi, the revised estimates did not see any expected improvements to the performance but rather some deterioration.

By 1942, Mitsubishi had completed the bomber's design and were ready to construct a full size wooden mock-up of the G7M1 Taizan, which was in due course completed. Unfortunately, the Kaigun Koku Hombu had now issued a 17-shi specification for a bomber that Kawanishi was developing as the K-100 (which some sources designate as the G9K Gunzan, meaning 'Mountain Group', but this has never been verified; other sources have the G9K as a 1944 19-shi bomber project). Mitsubishi was instructed to halt all further work on the G7M1 until the K-100 could be evaluated.

Kawanishi completed the initial design of the K-100 bomber and the Kaigun Koku Hombu reviewed it along with the G7M1 in the summer of 1943. By this time, the G7M1 had suffered further range performance reductions, dropping from a proposed normal range of 3,705km to 2,778km (2,302 miles to 1,726 miles). This was caused in part by the heavier armament compared to the initial fit, removing the two Type 1 machine guns and adding three more Type 2 machine guns to make a total of six Type 2s. This was, to a degree, tempered by a higher speed of 544km/h (344mph) at 5,000m (16,404ft).

Based on the projected performances of both aircraft, it was felt that neither design would be suitable either for the 16-shi or the 17-shi specifications. The Kaigun Koku Hombu was critical of the G7M1's design for concentrating much of the defensive weaponry in the frontal arc of the bomber, thereby reducing the aircraft's defences in the side and rear arcs. In addition, it was considered that the actual performance of the G7M1 would likely have been little, if at all, better than the operational G4M1. Another nail in the coffin for the G7M1 was the fact that the Kaigun Koku Hombu was looking to four-engine bombers as the real means to achieve the necessary range (at least 8,816km/5,478 miles, allowing for a one way trip from Tōkyō to Los Angeles). In fact as early as 1938 the IJN had asked Nakajima to produce a four-engine bomber, the G5N Shinzan ('Mountain Recess') which was based on an imported Douglas DC-4E.

With the Kaigun Koku Hombu showing no interest in the G7M, Mitsubishi shelved all further work on the bomber. Ironically, the G5N Shinzan would prove a failure and had a worse range than the G4M. Only with the construction of the four-engine Nakajima G8N1 Renzan ('Mountain Range') which first flew in October 1944 would the original 16-shi range specification be met. By then, the need for such bombers had passed as attention had turned to defending Japan and fighters/interceptors were required.

Mitsubishi J4M Senden

MUNEO HOSAKA

The concept of the J4M Senden ('Flashing Lightning') was born of the need for a high performance interceptor that could operate at high altitude. The main catalyst for this was the American Boeing B-17 Flying Fortress. The bomber, in action in the Pacific Theatre from 1941 to 1943, proved to be difficult to intercept since it normally flew at heights that operational Japanese fighters could not reach or attain with difficulty. Even if an interception was achieved, the B-17 carried a formidable defensive armament with which to protect itself. To a lesser extent, the Consolidated B-24 Liberator was also a factor when it began to replace the B-17s still remaining in the Pacific. In 1942, two companies, Mitsubishi and Kawanishi, were given a 17-shi Ōtsu specification by the Kaigun Koku Hombu to develop an aircraft to meet the need for a high altitude, high performance aircraft.

Mitsubishi Jūkōgyō K.K.'s response to the 17-shi Ōtsu directive was anything but conventional when compared to Kawanishi's design, the J3K1. The proposed plane, known within the company as the M-70, was a monoplane pusher design that featured twin booms connected to vertical stabilisers by a low mounted horizontal stabiliser. The booms were slung under the low, fuselage mounted wings. The heart of the aircraft was to be the Mitsubishi [Ha-43] 12 MK9D turbocharged, radial engine. Rated at 1,650hp at 8,000m (26,246ft), it was projected that this engine would push the Senden to a top speed of 704km/h (437mph) via its six bladed propeller. For weapons, there was a Type 5 30mm cannon and two Type 99 20mm cannons. All three were arranged in the fuselage nose with the Type 5 being centrally mounted and the two Type 99 cannons on either side of the fuselage. If required, the aircraft could carry a small bomb load of up to 120kg (264 lb). Mounted across the top of the fuselage behind the cockpit were inlets to feed air to the turbocharger and engine. The purpose of the turbocharger was to boost the manifold pressure on the engine over and above operating pressures at sea level as a means to maintain and improve performance at altitude. For landing gear, the Senden had a tricycle arrangement with the nose gear retracting into the fuselage and the main wheels being housed in the booms. The pilot sat in the glazed nose of the aircraft in a cockpit that was blended into the fuselage. The majority of the Senden was constructed of metal with fabric being used on the rudders and ailerons.

The Senden came in two versions. The first was the project described above while the second variation replaced the blended cockpit with a bubble canopy to improve the pilot's radius of vision. It also removed the protruding inlets and replaced them with two bands of flush inlets that wrapped around the fuselage, the first being directly behind the cockpit and the second around the engine area just past the wings. Finally, the horizon-

Mitsubishi J4M Senden – data

Contemporaries
Focke-Wulf mit BMW 803 (Germany), Vultee XP-54 'Swoose Goose' (US), Belyayev EOI (Russia), Bell XP-59 (US)

Specifications in parentheses refer to the J4M4 Project 2 Senden only.

Type	Fighter/Interceptor
Crew	One

Powerplant One Mitsubishi (Ha-43) MK9D 18-cylinder, air-cooled radial developing 2,100hp at engine start, 1,900hp at 2,000m (6,561ft) and 1,650hp at 8,000m (26,246ft), driving a alternating stroke, six bladed propeller with a 3.2m (10.5ft) diameter

Dimension			
Span		12.49m	41ft
Length		12.98	42.6ft
	(J4M4)	12.49m	41ft
Height		3.47m	11.4ft
Wing area		22.00m^2	236.8ft^2
	(J4M4)	24.69m^2	265.8ft^2
Wing loading		199.69kg/m^2	40.9 lb/ft^2
	(J4M4)	197.73kg/m^2	40.5 lb/ft^2

Weights			
Empty	(J4M4)	3,400kg	7,495.7 lb
Loaded		4,400kg	9,700.3 lb
	(J4M4)	4,486kg	9,889.9 lb
Max loaded	(J4M4)	5,255kg	11,585.2 lb

Performance			
Max speed		756km/h	470mph
		at 8,000m	at 26, 246ft
		703km/h	436mph
	(J4M4)	at 8,000m	at 26, 246ft
Cruise speed		462km/h	287mph
	(J4M4)	499km/h	310mph
Landing speed	(J4M4)	147km/h	91mph
Endurance		2.2 hours	
Climb		15 min to 8,000m (26, 246ft)	
	(J4M4)	10 min to 8,000m (26, 246ft)	
Ceiling		12,000m	39,370ft
	(J4M4)	11,000m	36,089ft

Armament
One Type 5 30mm cannon with 100 rounds of ammunition and two Type 99 20mm cannons with 200 rounds of ammunition each; provision for two 30kg (66 lb) bombs or two 60kg (132 lb) bombs

Deployment
The Senden did not advance past a wind tunnel model.

MUNEO HOSAKA

tal stabiliser was moved to the top of the vertical stabilisers. The remainder of the aircraft was basically the same between the two versions. The blended cockpit version is credited as the J4M1 Project 1 while the second, with the bubble canopy and modified inlets, is sometimes referred to as the J4M4 Project 2.

After analysing the two designs, Mitsubishi selected the original configuration, the J4M1, to develop further. To confirm their initial projections, a full scale model was constructed in 1943 and put to the test in a wind tunnel. Unfortunately for Mitsubishi, the tests proved to be a disappointment. Performance projections based on the testing were below the initial calculations and problems with the MK9D in terms of not reaching its horsepower rating only added to the concerns.

However, the Kaigun Koku Hombu and the IJN ensured that Mitsubishi would not have to concern themselves further with the Senden. In 1943 as Mitsubishi was working on the Senden, the Kaigun Koku Hombu issued an 18-shi Ōtsu specification. From it, the Kyūshū J7W Shinden resulted (page 84 for details). With the 18-shi Ōtsu requirements being similar to the 17-shi Ōtsu specifications and with the J7W showing far more promise and having the support of the IJN, Mitsubishi were told to cease work on the Senden and instead further develop the Mitsubishi A7M Reppū ('Hurricane') to meet the 17-shi Ōtsu standards. The result was the A7M3-J Model 34 Rifuku (Land Wind) that had not advanced beyond the design phase before the war ended.

Despite the fact that the J4M Senden did not progress past a wind tunnel model, US air intelligence was aware of the design mainly through captured documentation. In the January 1945 issue of the *US Recognition Journal*, the J4M Senden was announced as a possible adversary in the coming weeks of the war. No artist renderings of the Senden were included in the article. The J4M was given the codename *Luke* in anticipation of Allied pilots encountering the aircraft in combat, something which was never to occur.

As a note, although there are artist impressions of a jet-powered Senden (as shown here) there is no evidence to support the notion the J4M was ever revived or considered for turbojet power as there were other designs being considered (for example, the J7W2 and the Ki-201) which offered better prospects and capability.

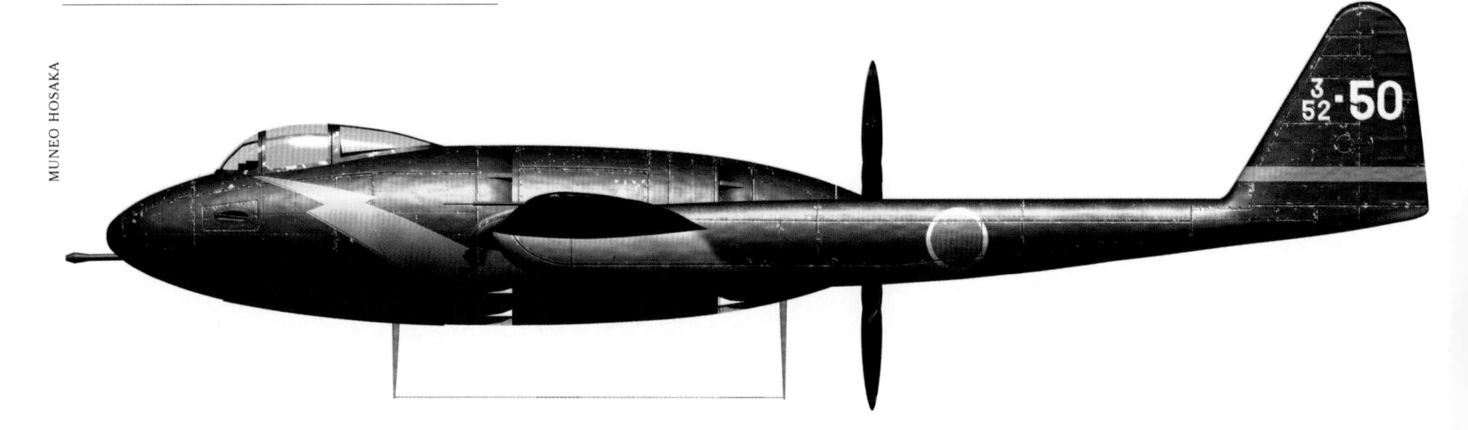

MUNEO HOSAKA

MUNEO HOSAKA

Mitsubishi J8M Syūsui

MUNEO HOSAKA

In 1943, the Japanese were only too well aware of a threat looming on the horizon. That threat was the Boeing B-29 Superfortress. With the development of the B-29 starting in 1939, the Japanese were in no doubt that once the bomber entered production it would eventually appear over Japan. The problem for the Japanese was that they did not have an effective countermeasure against the B-29 and feared they would not be able to have one ready in time for its anticipated arrival. Fortunately, the answer was found in one of the most radical fighters ever to achieve operational status.

Towards the middle of 1943, representatives of the Japanese military in Berlin were notified of the development and progress of the Messerschmitt Me 163, a point defence interceptor powered by a rocket engine. Interest was expressed immediately. In short order Japanese attachés from the IJN and the IJA visited Bad Zwischenahn in Germany where Erprobungskommando 16 was stationed. This unit had been created earlier in 1943 to develop Me 163 combat tactics, deployment and training as well as the coordination of the various contractors and test centres involved in development and production of the Me 163. During the tour EKdo 16 personnel explained to the Japanese the temperamental nature of the Walther HWK 509A rocket motor and the dangerous and explosive properties of the two fuels the motor used. This did nothing to dissuade the Japanese who saw the answer to their needs right before their eyes. To them, the benefits of an interceptor able to climb rapidly and possessing a very high speed overrode any concerns about the fuels or the engine. The Japanese wasted no time in entering negotiations to obtain the Me 163B.

However, not everyone was in agreement about the value of the Me 163. Detailed reports had been sent to Japan from Germany regarding the findings of the attaches which overall were positive; nevertheless, some argued that it would not be possible to produce the fuels the aircraft required in sufficient quantity to support operational requirements. Others criticised the unorthodox nature of the Me 163 and that developing such a plane and its engine would consume much needed resources. Despite these objections, the supporters for the Me 163 won out.

The Japanese swiftly and successfully negotiated the licences to manufacture both the Me 163B as well as its HWK 509A rocket motor. The motor licence alone cost the Japanese 20 million Reichsmarks. In addition to the two licences, Germany was to provide complete blueprints for the Me 163B and the HWK 509A, manufacturing data for the aircraft and engine, one complete Me 163B, three HWK 509A motors, and two sets of subassemblies and components by no later than 1 March 1944. Also, Japanese military attachés in Berlin were to be notified of any improvements to the Me 163 design so changes could be incorporated into the Japanese version. The Japanese also requested to oversee the manufacturing processes for the Me 163B and the rocket motor as well as being allowed to study and review Luftwaffe operational procedures for the fighter. Three submarines were tasked with shipping the materials to Japan – the RO-500, RO-501 and I-29.

RO-500 was still named U-511 when it departed from Lorient in France on 10 May 1943 bound for Penang, Malaysia. Aboard were four Japanese including Vice Admiral Naokuni Nomura and Major Tam Ōtsu Sugita of the IJA medical service. Also aboard was the data for the Me 163B. During the transit, U-511 was named Satsuki 1 ('satsuki' meaning the month of May). On 16 July, U-511 reached Penang where Nomura, Sugita and the other Japanese passengers disembarked and returned to Japan by air. U-511 departed Penang for Kure, Japan, on 24 July 1943 and arrived in Kure on 7 August 1943 where the submarine was presented to the IJN as the RO-500.

RO-501, a Type IXC/40 submarine, was formally U-1224. On 15 February 1944, U-1224 was handed over to the IJN who gave it the name Satsuki 2, and on February 28, it was commissioned into the Imperial Navy as RO-501 with Lieutenant Commander Norita as captain. On 30 March 1944, RO-501 departed from Kiel, Germany, with the manufacturing data and blueprints for the Me 163B among other cargo. At 7.00pm on 13 May 1944, north west of the Cape Verde Islands, the USS *Francis M. Robinson*, a Buckley class destroyer escort, reported a sonar contact 755m (825 yards) from the ship. The *Francis M. Robinson* immediately initiated an attack, launching 24 Mark 10 Hedgehog bombs and five salvos of Mark 8 depth charges. Sonar reported four explosions signifying the death of the RO-501.

I-29 of the Imperial Japanese Navy departed from Lorient, France, on 16 April 1944. She carried on board a HWK 509A rocket motor, the fuselage of a Fieseler Fi 103 and a Junkers Jumo 004A turbojet, again with other cargo. Technical Commander Eiichi Iwaya, a passenger, carried with him the plans for the Me 163B and Me 262 while another passenger, Captain Matsui, had plans for accelerators used for rocket launching. Between the two of them, they also had plans for a glider bomb and radar equipment. On 14 July 1944, the I-29 arrived safely in Singapore. Here, Iwaya and Matsui disembarked, along with a portion of their documents, and continued on to Tōkyō by air. On 15 July, Allied code breakers intercepted a message from Berlin to Tōkyō regarding the cargo that the I-29 carried and on 26 July 1944 at 5:00pm near the western entrance of the Balintang Channel, Luzon Strait, the USS *Sawfish* spotted the I-29 on the surface. She fired four torpedoes and three struck the Japanese submarine. I-29 sank almost immediately and only one sailor survived who swam to a nearby Philippine island and reported the loss.

Technical Commander Eiichi Iwaya, upon leaving the I-29, did not take all of the documentation he had for the Me 163B (or the Me 262) and the loss of the I-29, along with that of the RO-501, delivered a major blow to the development program. However, the information Iwaya had preserved, combined with what was received from the RO-500, was enough to keep the project alive and in July 1944 the IJN issued a 19-shi specification for a rocket powered interceptor. This decision was based on the analysis of the documentation on hand for the Me 163B and the current construction capacity and capability of the air industry, and also down to the drive of Vice Admiral Misao Wada who supported the development of the rocket aircraft.

Upon issuing their 19-shi specification, the Kaigun Koku Hombu assigned the project to Mitsubishi. Mitsubishi were initially reluctant to accept the design, but further consideration and the need to adapt the Me 163B design to Japanese production capability saw the manufacturer agree. Even though the IJN was behind the aircraft, the IJA would also be involved in the development of both the aircraft and rocket motor. The Japanese rocket interceptor was to be called the J8M1 Syūsui (which means 'Autumn Water') and in IJA service the Syūsui was to be designated Ki-200.

On 27 July 1944, all personnel involved met to discuss the Syūsui and it was agreed to follow the design plan of the Me 163B as much as possible. The key reason was that the design was proven and worked and thus critical time could be saved. The same applied to the rocket motor. A second reason for adhering to the Me 163B design was that Japanese fabricators had almost no experience with the type of aircraft that the Me 163B was. But not everyone was in full agreement.

The IJA saw flaws in the Me 163B and felt that Japanese industry could not fully produce the Syūsui to the specifications of the German aircraft. Modifications to meet the current capabilities of the Japanese aviation industry would be required to both the rocket motor and the aircraft which, as a consequence, would force changes to the design. As such the IJA argued that in the end a new design would be required anyway. The IJN, however, would hear none of it and was adamant that the Me 163B design would be followed.

Mitsubishi forged ahead with assembling a team to develop the J8M1. The project was led by Mijiro Takahashi at Mitsubishi's Nagoya plant. Under Takahashi was Tetsuo Hikita who would be the lead designer for the airframe. In addition to the Mitsubishi men, representatives of the Yokosuka Kōkūtai were involved, namely Captain Kumamoto and Commander One, who was tasked with test flying the J8M1 upon completion. Technical Commander Eiichi Iwaya was also a part of the overall development team given his familiarity with the Me 163B acquired during his time in Germany. One last meeting was held on 7 August 1944 to finalise the development of the Syūsui and then work began.

The first stage was the wooden mock-ups. On 8 September 1944, the full scale mock-up of the cockpit was completed and on 26 September 1944, the mock-up of the Syūsui was completed. Both the IJN and the IJA inspected them and suggestions were made for possible alterations to the design. These changes were incorporated and Takahashi's team laboured day and night to produce the detailed blueprints for the J8M1. Three prototypes were to be built; the first would be for load testing while the remaining two would be used for the flight test program. As the rocket motor was not yet available, two of the prototypes would be weighted to simulate the motor and fuel. To hasten construction, when one portion of the aircraft was drafted and finalised, a copy was sent to the assembly shop assigned to construct the component so work could begin without delay.

Externally, the J8M1 was unmistakable in its lineage but Takahashi and his group had to make modifications as they adapted the Me 163B design. For example, the Me 163B used two MK 108 30mm cannons which were heavier and shorter than the 30mm cannons the Japanese were to use. Fuel capacity was similar to the German aircraft and so were the dimensions, although the J8M1 was slightly longer due its more pointed nose and had a wider span and smaller wing area. (The Syūsui unlike the Me 163B did not use a nose-installed generator, the space being used for radio equipment.) The wing thickness was also increased. The main difference, however, was the weight: the Syūsui was 363 to 408kg (800-900 lb) lighter than the Me 163B. This was not due to any effort to purposely lighten the Syūsui as it lacked armour protection for the pilot and carried less ammunition for its cannons than the German interceptor. For weapons, the J8M1 was to be equipped with two Type 5 30mm cannons in the wings while the IJA's Ki-200 would use two Ho-155 30mm cannons or two Ho-5 20mm cannons.

Because the Japanese lacked the experience in flying tailless aircraft, Kūgishō was tasked with creating a glider version of the Syūsui. In part, the glider would provide performance data, findings from which could be incorporated into the Syūsui, but would also serve as a trainer for rocket aircraft pilots. Therefore, the MXY8 Akigusa and MXY9 Shuka were developed, as described elsewhere in this book on page 77.

While work was underway on the first three prototypes, a production plan for the fighter was put together and was completed by October 1944. By March 1945, 155 Syūsui were to be produced with another 1,145 built by September 1945. Ultimately, by March 1946 at least 3,600 Syūsui were anticipated to be in service.

In addition to developing the Syūsui, Mitsubishi was also assigned the task of creating the Japanese version of the Walther HWK 509A rocket motor and both the IJN and the IJA were involved in the motor program. To assist the engineers in Mitsubishi's engine department, personnel from the IJA's First Army Air Arsenal engine section were assigned to the firm. The resulting motor was called the KR10 but was also known as the Toku-Ro.2. Components for the KR10 were constructed by four companies: Hitachi, Ishikawajima, Mitsubishi and Washimo. Washimo, for example, was responsible for the fuel flow control mechanisms and the relief valve for the Ko fuel tank.

Mitsubishi faced several problems in building the KR10, the main issue being that the HWK 509A used a nickel-chromium alloy in the fuel injector atomiser, regulating valves and relief valves. Since the Japanese did not have access to this alloy they had to use plain chromium steel. It was expected that the KR10 would be ready for testing by October 1944, but the first prototype exploded immediately when it was started for the first time, partly believed to have been caused by the metal used. A deviation was made from the original HWK 509A plan in that the KR10 motor used wider supports and included a bearing in the middle for the Ko fuel compressor. This revision in the KR10 resulted in the KR12 but the addition of a second version of the motor risked compounding any production problems. Indeed, testing of the KR12 also resulted in an explosion. Mitsubishi engineers discovered that a bearing seal had failed that allowed the Ko fuel to leak into the motor and then come into contact with the bearing lubricant with catastrophic results. Given that it offered no real advantage, the KR12 was shelved and work focused solely on the KR10. These accidents, their subsequent investigations and the resulting revisions put the KR10's development further and further behind.

For fuel, the Syūsui used two ingredients which, when combined, provided the combustion and resultant thrust. The first, Ko, was the Japanese version of the German fuel T-Stoff formed from eighty per cent hydrogen peroxide with the remainder Oxyquinoline and pyrophosphates to act as stabilisers. Ko was the oxidising fuel. The second, Ōtsu, was the Japanese equivalent of C-Stoff. Ōtsu was the reductant fuel and was composed of thirty per cent hydrazine hydrate with the remainder being methanol, water and potassium-copper cyanides. Together, Ko and Ōtsu were a hypergolic fuel combination, which meant that when the two fuels were combined they spontaneously ignited. The problem with Ko and Ōtsu was that they were colourless and, of course, when they came together, the result was explosive. This required strict handling procedures and containment methods. Both fuels were stored in special ceramic pots. To produce both fuels, three chemical companies were contracted. They were the IJN's First Fuel Arsenal, Mitsubishi Kasei and Edogawa Kagaku. In the Syūsui, the fuels were stored in wing and fuselage mounted tanks. The pilot sat between two 91 litres (24 gallons) tanks of Ko while behind him in the fuselage was a 961 litres (254 gallons) tank and a 8 litre (2 gallon) tank of Ko. Each wing housed two tanks of Ōtsu, the capacity of each tank in each wing being 64 and 197 litres (17 and 52 gallons) in the two tanks respectively.

By December 1944, the second and third J8M1s had been completed but as no engines were ready for installation, ballast was used to simulate the weight of the KR10 with full fuel tanks. Earlier, the first J8M1 had been completed and load tested on 1 December 1944. However, the 7.9 magnitude Tonankai earthquake that struck the Tokai region of Japan at 1.30pm on 7 December 1944 destroyed the aircraft and the testing facility that housed it. The remaining J8M1 aircraft were transferred to the IJN's First Naval Air Technical Arsenal. From there, the aircraft were shipped to Hyakurigahara, located about 79km (49 miles) northeast of Tōkyō. December would also see delays due to the increasing B-29 bomber raids. Attacks against Mitsubishi's Nagoya facility resulted in the KR10 program being moved to the Dai-Juichi Kaigun Kokusho complex at the Hiro Naval Arsenal in Kure, Hiroshima. Here, work continued on the motor supervised by Professor Kasai of the Kyūshū University (although another source states the entire engine development group was moved to an underground facility in Natsushima in Yokosuka prefecture, overseen by the Dai-Juichi Kaigun Kokusho).

During testing, the KR10 delivered less thrust than the HWK 509A. Although the Syūsui was lighter than the Me 163B, when Takahashi and Hikita completed performance calculations for the Syūsui based on the thrust rating of the KR10, they found that the lighter weight did not totally offset the lower thrust. Regardless, the estimated speed and climb rate was considered exceptional.

On 8 January 1945, a Nakajima B6N1 (known as *Jill* to the Allies) towed the Syūsui into the air from the Hyakurigahara airfield and after a successful flight the design was validated. Work quickly proceeded on further production of the Syūsui, this time with the KR10. However, the motor program was at least three months behind schedule and it was not until 11 April 1945 that the KR10 was sufficiently developed to enable it to function with some measure of reliability. With the possibility of powered flight, Captain Shibata, commander of the 312 Kōkūtai due to be equipped with the J8M1, sought to speed up the process for testing. In discussions with the Syūsui development team it was decided that if the KR10 could produce thrust for at least two minutes without mishap, the motor should be fitted to the Syūsui so that powered flight testing could commence. 22 April 1945 was set as the deadline for the first powered flight.

Meanwhile, Germany made another attempt to send more material to Japan including documents and parts for the Me 163. These items and other cargo were loaded onboard U-864 that departed from the Bruno U-boat pen located in Bergen, Norway, on 5 February 1945. However, having past Fedje the submarine developed a misfire in one of her two MAN diesel engines and it was necessary to return to Bergen to effect repairs. The British submarine HMS *Venturer*, dispatched to deal with U-864, spotted the German submarine's periscope on 9 February 1945. Korvettenkapitän Ralf-Reimar Wolfram realised he was being followed and began to take evasive action, moving in a zigzag fashion. James S. Launders, *Venturer*'s captain, decided to press home the attack and fired all four of his loaded torpedoes in a spread pattern. U-864 crash dived, dodged three of the torpedoes but turned into the fourth which struck the submarine. The resulting explosion split U-864 into two.

Unfortunately for the Syūsui, the deadline for the KR10 would not be met. In exhaustive testing, another motor detonated after having achieved two minutes of burn time. In addition, fears of B-29 raids saw the KR10 team being moved to the Yamakita factory complex in Hakome prefecture while the Mitsubishi Syūsui development group was relocated to the IJA research and development centre in Matsumoto in Nagano Prefecture. These moves consumed precious research time throughout April and May 1945. Both groups were eventually able to continue work on the KR10 in an attempt to enhance its reliability and, in June, success was achieved. A KR10 from the Yamakita group functioned for four minutes while the Mitsubishi group in Matsumoto managed three minutes. With these motors now meeting the two minute requirement, plans were swiftly prepared to install the Yamakita KR10 into a J8M1 while the Matsumoto motor was to be placed into another airframe that would be completed as a Ki-200.

The J8M1's installation was completed first in the second week of June 1945 at Mitsubishi's Number One Plant in Nagoya. The Syūsui lacked much of its operational equipment including weapons and was transported to Yokoku airfield. This site was favoured because it was situated along a shoreline, which meant that if the pilot had to ditch the aircraft he could do so into the ocean, offering a better chance for survival as well as possibly lessening the damage to the Syūsui. The Syūsui arrived at Yokoku at the beginning of July and ground testing began immediately. Secured to the tarmac, the tail of the Syūsui was removed exposing the KR10 and motor running tests commenced. It was found that the motor did not burn fuel evenly, generating plumes of light red smoke from the combustion chamber as it ran. By 5 July 1945, technicians and engineers had corrected the burn problem to the point that the KR10 was deemed ready and the Syūsui's first powered flight was scheduled for 7 July 1945.

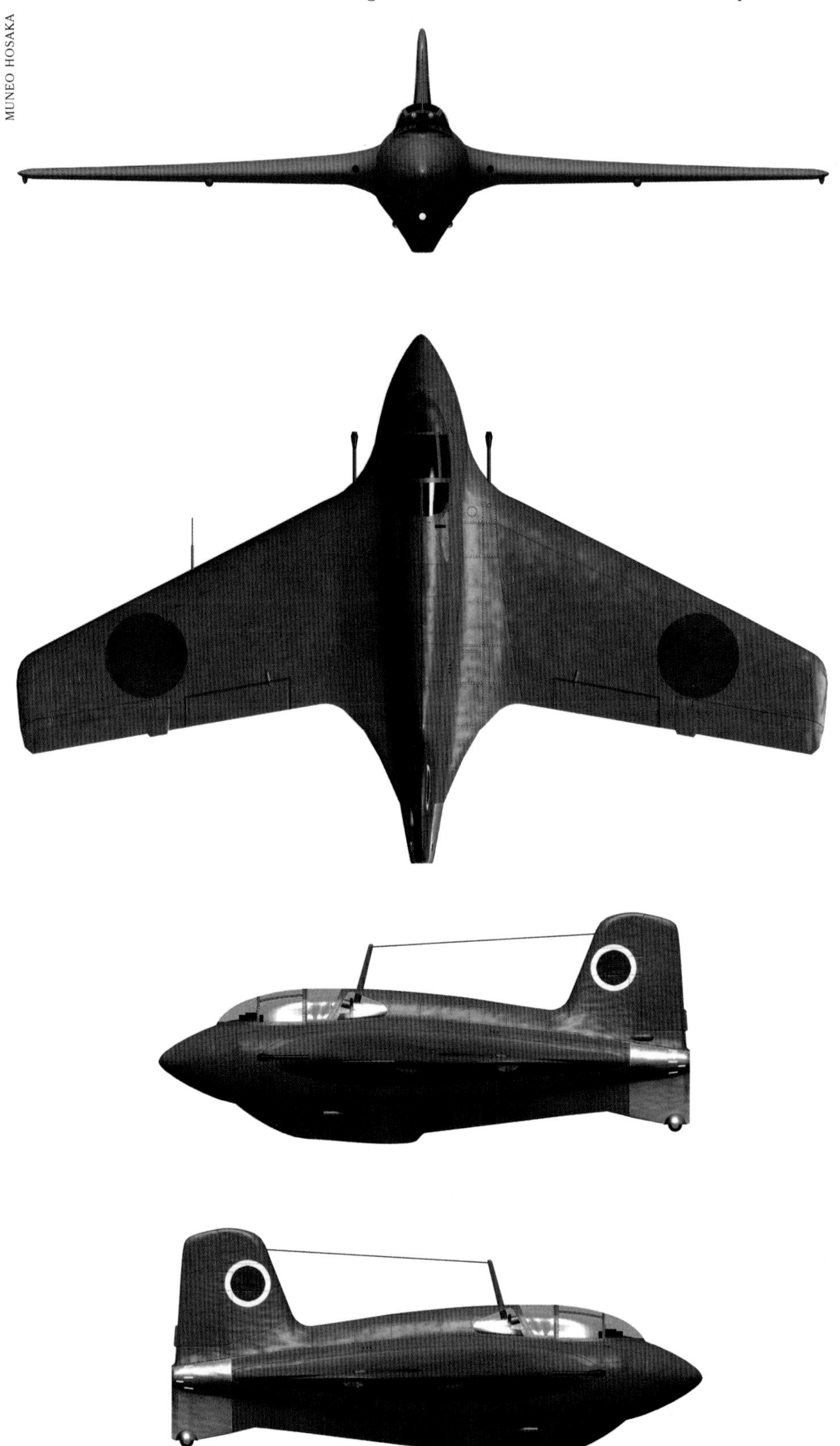
MUNEO HOSAKA

In front of a crowd of onlookers, the Syūsui was moved to the start of the 1,200m (3,937ft) runway, the longer of the two at Yokoku. It was then fuelled with 568 litres (150 gallons) of Ko into the fuselage tanks and 159 litres (42 gallons) of Ōtsu into the wing tanks as the mixture ratio was approximately 10 to 3.6. At 4:55pm, the pilot, Lieutenant-Commander Toyohiko Inuzuka, fired the engine and within 11 seconds and after only 320m (1,049ft) of runway, the Syūsui lifted off the ground and into the air, Inuzuka releasing the dolly and raising the nose to provide a 45° angle climb. Then, at 350m (1,148ft), a puff of black smoke issued from the motor, sputtered and went out. The speed that had been built up carried the Syūsui up to 500m (1,640ft) where Inuzuka levelled off and banked to the right ready to return to the runway and land. As Inuzuka continued his right hand bank, the Syūsui began to drift and airspeed rapidly dropped off. As he approached the runway, Inuzuka raised the nose of the Syūsui to try and avoid colliding with a building but it was too late. A wing clipped the side of the building, putting the Syūsui into a crash so forceful that it broke apart, scattering pieces across the south-west edge of the airfield. Both wings were ripped away and the front of the aircraft was completely destroyed. Inuzuka survived the impact and was extracted from the wreckage. However, the extent of his injuries was so severe that he died the following day.

No time was wasted in trying to find the cause of the motor failure. Mechanical issues were ruled out and it was surmised that the puff of smoke and the subsequent loss of power from the KR10 was due to fuel being cut off from the motor. Miraculously, the fuel tanks did not explode on impact and it was found that at least half of the fuel loaded prior to take-off remained. It was determined that the culprit was the fuel line from the Ko tank. Due to poor design, when the Syūsui went into its climb the fuel in the tank shifted away from the line which starved the motor of the needed oxidiser and thus the KR10 cut out. While the investigation was being carried out, bench tests of two additional KR10 motors (one each at Matsumoto and Yamakita) resulted in both exploding. This left a single KR10, the one slated for the Ki-200.

Flight testing of the Syūsui was suspended until the problem with the fuel system could be resolved. A further four Syūsui aircraft had been completed by Mitsubishi by the time a solution was found. These changes were incorporated into the KR10 engines then under development and flight testing was scheduled to resume in late August 1945. However, on 15 August 1945, Japan surrendered. All further work on the Syūsui ceased and no further flights were made. At the end of the war the Ki-200 remained engineless, its KR10 never having been installed. Aside from the seven J8M1 aircraft built – including the one to be finished as the Ki-200 – another six were in various stages of completion. A further four KR10 motors had been completed with another two nearly finished. Enough components had been constructed to assemble a further twenty motors.

Another variant of the J8M had been planned which was called the J8M2 Syūsui-Kai. The J8M2 lost one of the Type 5 30mm cannons/ammunition to be replaced by additional fuel tankage. It was hoped that this would increase the endurance of the aircraft. The end of hostilities would see the J8M2 remain only a preliminary design though production of the J8M2 was a certainty had it been completed. As mentioned earlier, the IJA was not pleased with the Ki-200 and it would undertake development of its own version of the J8M, the Ki-202 Syūsui-Kai, to right the wrongs it felt were evident in the Syūsui. For more details, please see the chapter on the Ki-202 (page 40).

A note regarding the use of Syūsui as the name for the J8M. The kanji for the aircraft (Syū and Sui) translate as 'Autumn Water'. However, Shūsui has been used in many sources with translations ranging from 'Sword Stroke' or 'Swinging Sword' to 'Rigorous Sword', but the name Shūsui is not correct. The use of Shūsui evolved from the metaphor that Syūsui represents – the wavy pattern on the metal blade of a highly sharpened sword as well as the brightness of the polished metal which reminds one of the waves on a body of clear water.

Mitsubishi J8M Syūsui – data

Contemporaries
Messerschmitt Me 163B Komet (Germany)

Specifications in parenthesis pertain to the J8M2 only and are based on Mitsubishi's estimated data.

Type	Interceptor/Fighter
Crew	One

Powerplant
One Toku-Ro.2 (KR10) bi-fuel rocket motor developing 1,500kg (3,307 lb) of thrust

Dimensions

Span		9.47m	31.1ft
Length		6.03m	19.8ft
Height		2.68m	8.8ft
Wing area		17.72m²	190.8ft²
Wing loading		219.22kg/m²	44.9 lb/ft²
	(J8M2)	219.70kg/m²	45 lb/ft²

Weights

Empty		1,445kg	3,185 lb
	(J8M2)	1,510kg	3,328 lb
Loaded		3,000kg	6,613 lb
	(J8M2)	3,650kg	8,046 lb
Maximum		3,870kg	8,531 lb
	(J8M2)	3,900kg	8,598 lb
Useful load		1,545kg	3,406 lb
	(J8M2)	2,140kg	4,717 lb

Performance

Max speed	900km/h	559mph
	at 10,000m	at 32,810ft
Cruise speed	699km/h	434mph
Landing speed	150km/h	93mph
Range	3 min 6 sec of powered flight	
	at 599km/h	372mph
Max range	5 min 30 sec of powered flight	
Climb	40 sec to 2,000m (6,561ft)	
	2 min 8 sec to 4,000m (13,123ft)	
	3 min 8 sec to 8,000m (26,246ft)	
	3 min 50 sec to 10,000m (32,808ft)	
Ceiling	12,000m	39,370ft
Fuel capacity	1,181 litres (312 gallons) of Ko and 522 litres (138 gallons) of Ōtsu	

Armament
Two Type 5 30mm cannons with 53 rounds of ammunition per gun (one Type 5 cannon with 53 rounds of ammunition)

Deployment
None. A total of seven J8M1 aircraft were completed with one to be finished as a Ki-200. The 312 Kōkūtai were to receive the J8M1 had it entered production. No J8M2 was ever built nor were any Ki-200 aircraft.

Survivors
Mitsubishi J8M1 Syūsui (FE-300)
One of three brought from Yokosuka on 3 November 1945, this Syūsui is aircraft No.403 and is thought to have been captured at Mitsubishi's No.1 plant in Nagoya. Appearing on the 10 March 1946 report for aircraft releasable to the aviation industry, the Syūsui would be made available for display purposes on 1 August 1946 appearing to the public in Hollywood, California. The aircraft was later obtained and restored by Edward Maloney for display at the Planes of Fame Museum in Chino, California, where it remains to this day.

Mitsubishi J8M1 Syūsui (tail number 24)
After being received at NAS Patuxent River, the aircraft was moved to NAS Glenview in Glenview, Illinois (a suburb of Chicago, Illinois), where it was on display by 3 October 1946. This Syūsui eventually reached a derelict state and was scrapped.

Mitsubishi J8M1 Syūsui (tail number A-25)
Nothing is known about this particular Syūsui other than it likely ended up as scrap.

Mitsubishi J8M1 Syūsui
Mitsubishi has recently restored a J8M1 and it is currently on display at the company's Komaki Plant Museum. A portion of the restoration contains components from a badly damaged J8M1 fuselage found in a cave but it still required significant custom fabrication of new parts to finish the project. Prior to Mitsubishi obtaining the fuselage, the remains had been on display on the grounds of the Japanese Air Self-Defence Force's Gifu Air Base.

Ki-200 – data (estimated)

Type	Interceptor/Fighter
Crew	One

Powerplant One Toku-Ro.2 (KR10) bi-fuel rocket motor developing 1,500kg (3,307 lb) of thrust

Dimensions

Span	9.47m	31.1ft
Length	5.88m	19.3ft
Height	2.68m	8.8ft
Wing area	17.69m²	190.5ft²

Weights

Empty	1,505kg	3,317 lb
Maximum	3,870kg	8,531 lb

Performance

Max speed	800-900km/h	497-559mph
	at 10,000m	at 32,808ft
Cruise speed	351km/h	218mph
Range	2 min 30 sec of powered flight	
Max range	7 min of powered flight	
Climb	3 min 40 sec to 10,000m (32,808ft)	
Fuel capacity	1,181 litres (312 gallons) of Ko and 522 litres (138 gallons) of Ōtsu	

Armament
Two Ho-155 30mm cannons (or two Ho-5 20mm cannons)

Mitsubishi-Payen Pa.400 and Suzukaze 20

When Allied intelligence discovered an illustration of the Suzukaze 20 in a Japanese magazine, it was unlike anything so far seen in Japanese aviation design. Despite the radical appearance, it was felt the Suzukaze 20 was a bona fide aircraft and might be encountered in action. As it was, the plane was a work of fiction and so the Suzukaze 20 was later stricken from the publications on Japanese aircraft identification and coding. However, Allied intelligence may or may not have been aware of the very real inspiration for the artist of the Suzukaze 20.

At the time, because of the relative difficulty in obtaining information on Japanese military matters, intelligence services relied on various publications such as newspapers and magazines as a means to glean data on the Japanese military machine. In April 1941, the Japanese magazine *Sora* (translated as 'Sky') published a number of illustrations of various aircraft in a section entitled 'Dreams of Future Designers'. Included in the selection of artwork was the rendition of the Suzukaze ('Cool Breeze') 20. The 25 December 1941 issue of the US magazine *Flight* would also feature the Suzukaze 20, along with three other aircraft: the Nakajima AT27 (codenamed *Gus*), the Mitsubishi T.K.4 Type 0 (codenamed *Frank* then *Harry*) and the T.K.19 (codenamed *Joe*). The Suzukaze 20 would receive the codename *Omar*.

The illustration of the Suzukaze 20 depicted a single-seat fighter with the striking feature of having a cockpit blended into the vertical stabiliser that was itself in the form of a half-delta. Another notable feature was the use of two radial engines, one mounted behind the other, driving two, contra-rotating propellers. Armament appeared to be heavy with four weapons fitted in each wing. Its speed was given as 769km/h (478mph), loaded weight 2,858kg (6,300 lb), wing area 13.37m² (144ft²) and wing loading 214.82kg/m² (44 lb/ft²).

As the war dragged on it became evident that the Suzukaze 20, along with the other three aircraft illustrated with it, were works of fantasy and thus all four were removed from Japanese aircraft intelligence bulletins, the last of them disappearing by June 1943. Despite the Suzukaze 20 being a fictional aircraft, there was a kernel of truth behind it that perhaps germinated in the mind of the artist that drew the Suzukaze 20. The kernel could have been the works of the French aircraft designer, Nicholas Roland Payen.

Payen was born in France in 1914 and became interested in aviation early in life. By the 1930s, he had begun to focus on the use of delta planforms as well as canards and ogival (bullet shaped) flight surfaces. Throughout his life, Payen would design a large number of aircraft in a wide array of configurations but, despite the prolific nature of his studies, only two were built before the end of World War 2. Both used Payen's Flechair (an English contraction of *avion fleche* or 'arrow aircraft') configuration that consisted of a trapezoidal fore-wing that housed the ailerons and a rear delta wing which contained the horizontal control surfaces. Payen had to rely on his salesmanship to gain access to material, wind tunnel time and other resources to build his aircraft as he had little money of his own to fund projects. Of course, the nature of his designs often made it a hard sell to the more conservative aviation industry. The Payen Pa.100 Fleche Volante ('Flying Arrow') was his first aircraft to be built and was intended to be a racer to compete in the Coupe Deutsch de la Meurthe. Payen was able to borrow a 180hp Regnier R6 but the engine was later returned. He was then able to acquire a larger engine, a 380hp, 7-cylinder radial Gnome-Rhône 7KD Titan Major, but was too large for the Pa.100. Payen had to seek donations (which he received) and rebuilt the Pa.100 around the 7KD to create the Pa.101. Unfortunately for Payen, the Pa.101 failed to meet expectations. It finally took to the air on 17 April 1935, but on 27 April a hard landing broke the port landing gear and a fire broke out in the resulting crash gutting the Pa.101. The accident saw Payen's flight insurance revoked and so he went to work at the Bloch factory constructing a mock-up of the Pa.112 fighter that used two 150hp Salmson engines in tandem buried in the fuselage. The outbreak of World War 2 saw the French military show no interest in this design.

The second aircraft was the Pa.22 which was the test bed for Payen's proposed Pa.112 fighter. Originally to be powered by a ramjet, no such engine was available and a 180hp Regnier R6 engine was used instead. Payen constructed the Pa.22 in 1939 and the Germans would later capture it after the invasion of France on 12 June 1940. The Germans, showing some interest in the design, test flew it on 18 October 1941 and found modifications were needed to correct poor longitudinal stability. The aircraft was moved to Rechlin in Germany and after adjustments had been made to the cockpit position and the vertical stabiliser had been rebuilt the Pa.22 flew in the summer of 1942. After a number of short flights, the aircraft was wrecked in a crash landing. The Pa.22 was returned to France for repairs and was consequently abandoned by the Germans.

Prior to the outbreak of war, the Japanese had civilian and military personnel in France who studied and reviewed French aviation progress for possible use by Japan. This practice went as far back as 1919 when Japan invited French military aviation instructors to teach the fledgling Japanese Army air force. The French also brought with them some of the latest aircraft that their country had available. This training would forge a link between Japan and France that would last for many years, and it was by these means that the Japanese would learn of Payen's work.

In 1938, Payen received a letter from Mitsubishi expressing an interest in his designs, notably the delta wing so often used in his aircraft concepts. A meeting was held between Payen, Commander Koshino and the captain of the IJN corvette *Sumikawa* to talk about the Pa.112. During the discussions the IJN inquired as to whether the Flechair design could be adapted to that of a two-seat, carrier borne, light bomber. The specifications required the aircraft to have the ability to take-off from and land on a deck space 80m (262ft) long, to have a range of at least 800km (497 miles), be capable of carrying a 800kg (1,763 lb) torpedo or bomb and be fitted with up to 180kg (396 lb) of armament.

Payen took the specifications and worked up a study to meet the IJN requirements. The design was called the Payen-Mitsubishi Pa.400. This would have used two 670hp radial engines mounted one behind the other driving two, two-bladed, contra-rotating propellers. For weapons, in addition to carrying the required torpedo or bomb, a nose mounted cannon (firing through the propeller hub), two machine guns per rear wing and a tail mounted machine gun were proposed. Endurance was to be 11-12 hours with a maximum speed of 580km/h (360mph). Unlike his other Flechair designs, Pa.400 used staggered wings (his earlier offerings had the two wings level with each other). The study was reviewed and Payen was asked by Japanese representatives to obtain from the French government the authorisation to export the technical information for the Pa.400 study. This would have allowed the Japanese to further develop the Pa.400 in Japan. The authorisation was granted on 28 September 1938, signed by the head of the cabinet of the Ministry of Air. However, with the cloud of war on the horizon, Payen decided not to send the requested documents to Japan and it would appear the Japanese did not follow this up. To

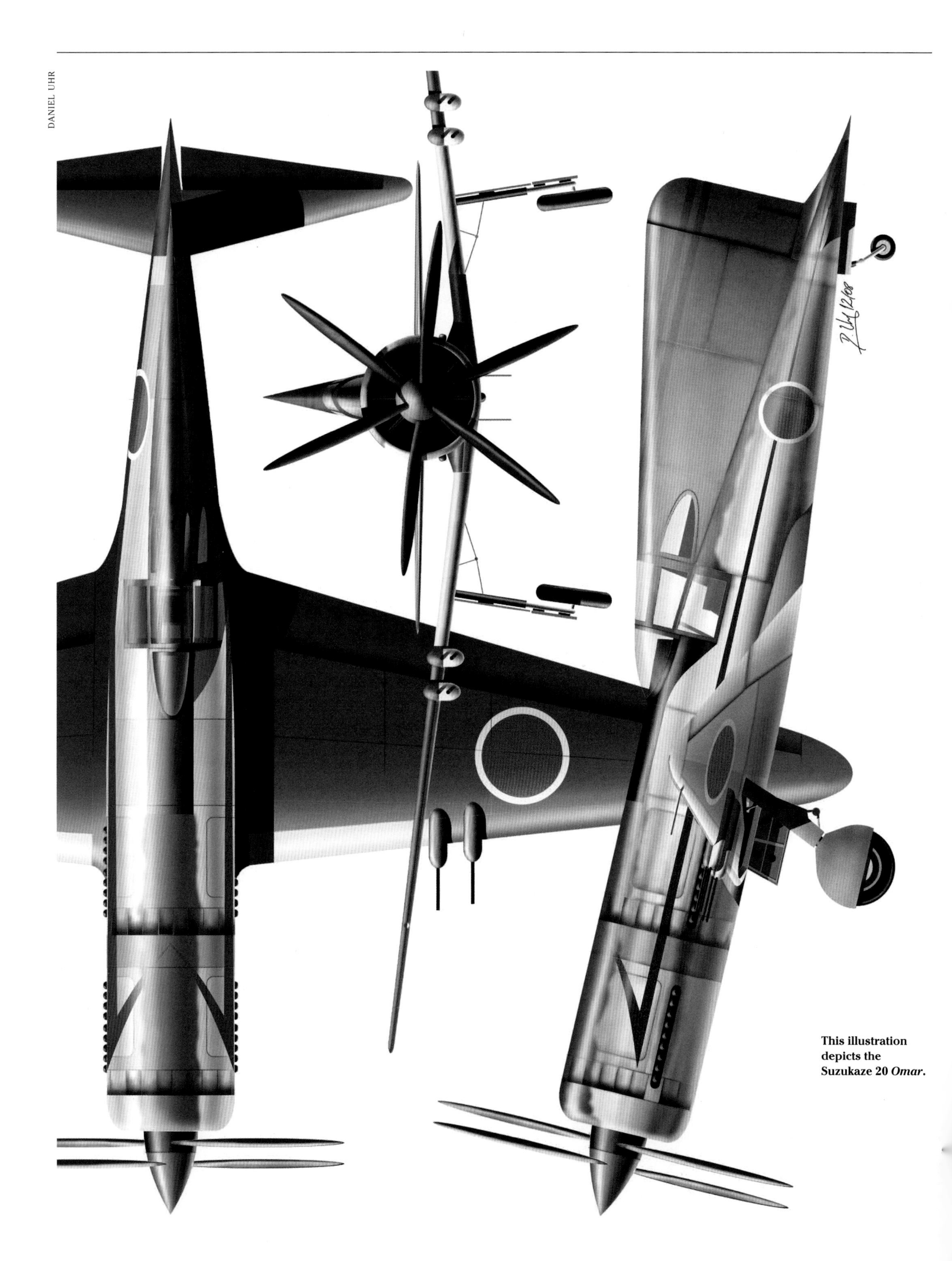

This illustration depicts the Suzukaze 20 *Omar*.

all intents and purposes, the Japanese seemed to have lost interest in the Pa.400.

Why would the Japanese show an interest in the Pa.112 and the Pa.400 only to abandon it on the brink of receiving the technical information? There were several factors which the Japanese may have become aware of upon further review of Payen's initial Pa.400 study. The first was that Japanese radial engines of the time did not have sufficient horsepower and, more importantly, were not of the correct size to fit into the Pa.400's fuselage. Thus, the Japanese would have had to either construct a new radial engine or adapt the Pa.400 to use a Japanese engine, radial or not. A more pertinent problem was the use of tandem radial engines. To make such an arrangement workable required a considerable feat of engineering and such designs making it to prototype form were exceedingly rare. Another factor concerned the poor visibility afforded the pilot given that the cockpit was situated far back in the fuselage which made landing a challenge at the best of times, let alone landing on a moving and rolling aircraft carrier. The rear wings and the long nose blocked side and downward vision, a serious liability in aerial combat, and the relatively short wingspan of the Pa.400 would not have offered much agility, a trait favoured by Japanese pilots and designers. In addition, the Japanese may have learned that the Pa.101 was a flawed design and since the French military paid Payen no attention may have concluded there was nothing worth pursuing where the Pa.400 was concerned. Finally, it may have been the radical design of the Pa.400 that saw more conservative IJN officials directing Mitsubishi to focus their efforts on more conventional aircraft projects.

Enter the Suzukaze 20. A photograph of what was likely the Pa.101 appeared in Japan in a printed document in the late 1930s. The caption for the photograph read 'French Brand New Model Pey-yan 266th. Airplane No-mu 400 Horse Power'. The 'Pey-yan' was the phonetic spelling in Japanese of Payen while 'No-mu' was the phonetic spelling for Gnome. How it got to Japan is open to speculation but the two prevailing theories are that Payen, in trying to drum up funds for his work, made it available to a French diplomat to take to Japan to shop around to Japanese industry. Alternatively, the photograph was given to the IJN by Payen during the discussions over the Pa.400.

The photograph – and perhaps other sources because Payen's aircraft were shown in publications such as *Bill Barnes: Air Adventurer* (from April 1935) – likely played a part in the rendering of the Suzukaze 20. The similarities to Payen's designs cannot be ignored. For one, the Suzukaze 20 utilised two radial engines in tandem driving two, contra-rotating propellers. Also, the Suzukaze 20's cockpit was blended into the large, half delta-shaped vertical stabiliser, another Payen trait seen in the Pa.100/Pa.101 and Pa.22. The artist likely removed the rear delta wing and slid the forward wings back and enlarged them since their shape is reminiscent of the Pa.400. With the exception of the nose, the fuselage shape of the Suzukaze 20 was similar to that of the Pa.400. Even the horizontal stabilisers of the Suzukaze 20 had a delta shape, perhaps a nod to the Pa.101. However, whether or not the artist based the Suzukaze 20 on Payen's designs may never be known for certain.

The Pa.400 depicted here is in the colours and markings as used on a Nakajima B5N2 torpedo bomber (known as *Kate* to the Allies) flown by Petty Officer First Class Toshio Takahashi from the carrier Hiryū during the attack on Pearl Harbor.

Mitsubishi-Payen Pa.400 – data

Contemporaries
Horton Ho X (Germany), Messerschmitt P.1106 (Germany), Lippisch P13a (Germany), BMW 803 engine (Germany), Wright R-2160 Tornado engine (US), Pratt & Whitney R-4360 Wasp Major engine (US), Butler-Edwards 'Steam Dart' (UK), Scroggs 'Dart' (US)

For the Mitsubishi-Payen Pa.400, based on the design study conducted by Payen.

Type	Light Carrier Bomber
Crew	Two

Powerplant
Two Gnome-Rhône 14 M4/5 radial engines, each developing 670-680hp maximum, driving two contra-rotating, two-bladed propellers

Dimensions		
Span	6.58m	21.6ft
Length	10.00m	32.8ft
Height	2.68m	8.8ft
Wing area	25.00m²	269ft²

Weights		
Empty	2,179kg	4,784lb
Loaded	5,860kg	12,919lb

Speed		
Max speed	570km/h	360mph
	at 4,950m	at 16,240ft
Max speed (one engine)	447km/h	278mph
	at 4,950m	at 16,240
Landing speed	89km/h	55mph
Endurance	12-14 hours	
Ceiling	4,950m	16,240ft

Armament
Five machine guns, two in each wing and one in the tail; one cannon firing through the propeller hub; one 800kg (1,764lb) torpedo or bomb

Deployment
None. The Suzukaze 20 was a fictional aircraft while the Pa.400 remained a design only.

RONNIE OLSTHOORN

Mizuno Shinryū II

DANIEL UHR

In June 1944, the first Boeing B-29 Superfortresses appeared over Japan. It was the start of a bombing campaign that would see key Japanese cities, infrastructure and industries reduced to ashes through conventional and firebombing raids. With the aircraft industry being a priority target, the Kaigun Koku Hombu looked to ways to combat the B-29 menace. One concept was a point defence interceptor that could quickly rise to meet the bombers and so the Mizuno Shinryū II was born. However, the development of the Shinryū II (Shinryū meaning 'Divine Dragon') began with designs for a far more conventional craft.

In November 1944, the Kaigun Koku Hombu looked into the possibilities of an aircraft to undertake shimpū missions. While the mission was not unique, the fact that the aircraft being investigated would be a glider was. The Kaigun Koku Hombu envisioned that gliders would be launched with rocket boosters from caves or shore positions and pilots would guide the aircraft and the 100kg (220 lb) explosive payload inside it into Allied ships or tanks should the Japanese home islands be invaded.

The Kaigun Koku Hombu assigned the Dai-Ichi Kaigun Kōkū Gijutsu-shō at Yokosuka the task of turning the glider into reality. The project was led by Shigeki Sakakibara who staffed a number of teams that would each be responsible for one part of the glider. The different sections were the wings, the fuselage, control surfaces, aerodynamic testing and test flights once the prototype was complete. The Kaigun Koku Hombu gave instructions that the glider must be built from as much wood as possible. This restriction was imposed for two reasons. The first was that in using wood and keeping the use of metal to an absolute minimum, the glider could be manufactured in any small shop using only wood working tools, and secondly, as a consequence, what metals were available would be conserved for other military uses.

Much of the glider's design was conceived by Yoshio Akita. A number of concepts were discussed and sketched and after much deliberation among Akita and his teams the design was complete by May 1945, and Mizuno, a small aircraft manufacturer, had almost finished the prototype. The glider was very simple and used a high-wing monoplane form. The straight and flat wings were wide but had a short span and were designed to ensure that the glider was easy to handle given that inexperienced pilots would be at the controls. Also, the planform would be able to accommodate the rocket engines that were to be used to boost the glider into the air. The pilot sat in an open cockpit.

The design was sent to the Kaigun Koku Hombu for review. Sakakibara studied the plans and projections and after his analysis it was felt the glider was flawed and changes were necessary. After these had been made the design was approved. Work began on the revised Jinryū as the glider was now called by the middle of June 1945. To hasten the construction, the finalised blueprints and work plans for the Jinryū were drawn up even as the components for the first prototype were being built. Construction of the Jinryū was again given to Mizuno. Working around the clock, the company completed two prototypes with such speed that wind tunnel testing of the design was still underway. In fact, the first flight of the Jinryū occurred even before the results of the testing had been provided to Tonsho and Sakakibara.

Tashiichi Narabayashi was the pilot who flew the maiden flight in mid-July 1945 at the airfield in Ishioka, a city located in Ibaraki prefecture, about 90km (56 miles) northeast of Tōkyō. The Jinryū was towed into the air by a Tachikawa Ki-9 (known to the Allies as *Spruce*) piloted by Saburō Fujikura, a man known for his skill in flying gliders prior to the beginning of the war.

For the first test, Narabayashi assessed the Jinryū's handling. On landing, his opinion was that the glider was stable and possessed good handling characteristics. For the second flight Narabayashi would investigate the Jinryū's diving capability and after a few bounces on the ground the Ki-9 and the Jinryū took off. At a height of 2,300m (7,545ft), Narabayashi went to cast off from the Ki-9 but found that the tow rope release had stuck; however, he was able to cut the rope and proceed with the test flight. When Narabayashi put the Jinryū into a dive and had reached 300km/h (186mph), the glider began to vibrate to such a degree that he was unable to read the gauges. Pulling the nose up to bleed off speed, Narabayashi discovered that the vibrations ceased. During his descent Narabayashi examined the vibrations and after landing the issue was reviewed. The conclusion was that the tail was not sufficiently reinforced and the vertical stabiliser was too small. The Jinryū was modified by adding some strengthening in the tail and the fitting a second stabiliser. The changes were later validated both in the air and in the wind tunnel testing of the modified Jinryū model. Interestingly, before flying the Jinryū, Narabayashi had suspected that the aircraft would have stability problems which, as was seen, proved to be the case.

With the handling and flight characteristics of the Jinryū proven, the testing moved to the next phase – that of powered flight. The glider was relocated to an airfield in Kasumigaura, about 19km (12 miles) north of Ishioka. Here, the Jinryū was modified to accept a group of three Toku-Ro 1 Type 1 rocket engines that together would produce 661 lb of thrust during a 10 second burn. Testing of the rocket array showed two serious flaws. The first was the quality of the rockets that resulted in a number of failures. The second was the inconsistency of the burn times. Narabayashi noted his concerns and forwarded them to Major Suganuma who had been placed in charge of the Jinryū project. In addition to expressing his doubts about the rocket engines, he also stated that the Jinryū would be unsuited for shimpū missions because, despite the changes made to the glider to improve the flight characteristics, it was a challenging aircraft to fly. Narabayashi suggested that instead of being used for shimpū operations the glider should be modified to take six rocket engines each with a 30 second burn time. He estimated that at maximum burn the Jinryū could attain a speed of 750km/h (466mph), and for weapons he envisioned that it could carry ten explosive charges adapted from artillery shells used by the IJA in their 100mm guns (likely the Type 92). Not only did Narabayashi agree that the Jinryū could be used against tanks and ships but added that it could also be used to attack US B-29 bombers. Despite the issues with the rockets work continued on preparing the Jinryū for powered flight.

Major Suganuma, however, would become the catalyst for the Shinryū II's continued development. Taking Narabayashi's concerns onboard, Suganuma formed a team to revise the Jinryū and produce a design for an interceptor rather than a glider; Suganuma was especially interested in this idea since he had access to rocket engines that promised 32 second burn times. Two people were retained from the Jinryū project: Sakakibara, the lead designer, and Yoshio Tonsho who would oversee the construction of the prototype. Yūjirō Murakami was tasked with the aerodynamic testing of the Shinryū II. All of those assigned to develop the Shinryū II were ordered by Suganuma to maintain the utmost secrecy.

Unlike the Jinryū, the Shinryū II was to be built from the outset as an interceptor. Sakakibara would use a canard design that made this the second Japanese aircraft to be developed during the war with such a feature (the first was the Kyūshū J7W Shinden on page 84). In addition, the main wings had a planform similar to a cropped delta. These design features were included as a means of ensuring stability in flight as well as good handling characteristics. Since the average Japanese pilot had little experience with canard equipped aircraft, the Shinryū II had spoilers fitted into the top of each main wing. Each spoiler was able to rotate between 60° and 90° and if the mechanism for controlling the spoilers was damaged, they would automatically return to the closed position. The pilot was provided with a canopy covered cockpit.

For power, the Shinryū II was to use four Toku-Ro 1 Type 2 rocket engines located in the rear of the fuselage. Each engine provided a 30 second burn time and all together up to 600kg (1,322 lb) of thrust could be delivered. Two rockets would be used to get the Shinryū II airborne while the other two engines would be used when making the attack. There was a concern regarding the operating temperatures of the Toku Ro rockets and two methods of cooling the engines were considered. The first would have utilised an air-cooled combustion chamber that would have required an air inlet using a bayonet mechanism in order to maintain air flow across the chamber. It also would have required specific positioning of the fuel injectors so as not to have the air flow disrupt the injection process. The second method would use injectors which sprayed a water and alcohol mixture onto the rocket nozzle, cooling it. In reviewing the two solutions for cooling, it was determined that the water/alcohol system would be the simplest to implement.

No provision was made for a wheeled landing gear system and design skids were used. A nose skid was provided with a basic spring suspension to absorb the landing forces. Under each wing was a non-sprung skid arrangement supported by two struts. For take-off the Shinryū II was to use a two-wheeled dolly similar to the one used by the

Mitsubishi J8M Syūsui. Once airborne the pilot could jettison the dolly. In addition to conventional runway take-off procedures, other methods for launching the Shinryū II were considered but what exactly these were is not known. It can be speculated that towing the Shinryū II aloft was one consideration. Another may have been air dropping the Shinryū II in the same manner as the Kūgishō MXY7 Ōka. In both cases this may have preserved two of the rocket engines which would have been used up had the Shinryū II taken off from the ground.

In order to combat the B-29, which could operate at altitudes up to 10,241m (33,600ft), the Shinryū II was to be equipped with a pressurised cockpit or, if such a cockpit proved problematic, the pilot would wear a pressure suit. For weapons, the Shinryū II was to be armed with eight rockets. Attached to the inside of the rear landing skid arrangement were four tubes, one on top of the other and angled downwards, which contained the rockets.

There has been some conjecture as to the mission objective of the Shinryū II. Some sources make the case that the Shinryū II was to be used like the Ōka while others come to the conclusion that the Shinryū II was to attack armoured ground targets such as tanks. In both cases these sources state that the nose of the Shinryū II contained an impact fused explosive warhead and once the rocket armament was expended, the pilot would crash the aircraft into his final target using the warhead to deliver the coup de grâce. However, analysis of the Shinryū II shows that neither mission was likely. The aircraft would have been far more complex to build than the Showa Toka or Ōka and the Shinryū II was constructed for manoeuvrability, high altitude operation and the means to land. In addition, using the Shinryū II for shimpū missions against tanks makes little sense when there were other simpler and more effective means (both already in service and under development) to eliminate armour. Perhaps this is a case of the Jinryū glider's role being applied to the Shinryū II, or an assumption based on the fact that, like the IJN's other special attack aircraft such as the Nakajima Kitsuka, Kawanishi Baika and Showa Toka, the Shinryū II possessed no letter/numerical designation. So, by extension, the Shinryū II must also have been a special attack weapon. This, of course, is not to say that the pilot could not choose to use the Shinryū II as a shimpū aircraft.

As an interceptor, the Shinryū II had a similar role to the Mitsubishi J8M Syūsui and the German Bachem Ba 349 Natter for which the Japanese were aware of and obtained data on (although the plans never made it to Japan). Like the J8M and Ba 349 and due to the limited range afforded by the rocket engines, the Shinryū II would have to be positioned close to targets that were likely to be bombed. And like the J8M, the Shinryū II would have used a jettisonable wheeled dolly to take-off while firing a pair of its rocket engines. Unlike the J8M which burned up all of its fuel at once, the Shinryū II had a second set of rocket engines which could be used to sustain flight endurance or to increase speed during the attack. In the same way as the Ba 349, the Shinryū II would be armed with rocket projectiles, likely fired as a group to affect a spread pattern, to bring down the bomber target. Finally, akin to the J8M, once the fuel and ammunition were expended, the Shinryū II would glide back to its base to be recovered, refuelled and rearmed.

The Shinryū II would never be built because the end of the hostilities in August 1945 terminated any further work on the design. Likewise, the Jinryū glider would never fly under power. After the failure of the rocket motors during ground tests, the war came to a close before more suitable and reliable motors could be acquired and tested. Mizuno completed a total of five Jinryū gliders. As a note, Jinryū is the known name for the first Mizuno glider. For the purposes of this text, the author used Shinryū II to differentiate the interceptor from the glider. The kanji is the same for both spellings but is pronounced differently. Both translations of Jinryū and Shinryū mean 'Divine Dragon'. Shinryū II is also used in contemporary texts and as such, is used here for recognition purposes. Whether the interceptor would have carried the same name as the glider is unknown.

Mizuno Shinryū II – data

Contemporaries
Blohm und Voss BV 40 (Germany), Zeppelin Fliegende Panzerfaust (Germany), Heinkel P. 1077 Julia (Germany), Junkers EF 127 Walli (Germany), Messerschmitt Me 163B (Germany), Bereznyak-Isayev BI (Russia)

Specifications in parenthesis are for the Shinryū II and are estimates only.

Type Special Attack Glider (Interceptor)
Crew One

Powerplant Three Toku-Ro Type 1 rockets with a total combined thrust of 400kg (881 lb) with a burn time of 10 seconds (Four Toku-Ro Type 2 rockets with a total combined thrust of 600kg/1,322 lb with a burn time of 30 seconds)

Dimensions		
Span	7.00m	22.9ft
Length	7.60m	24.9ft
Height	1.80m	5.9ft
Wing area	11m²	118.4ft²
Wing loading	N/A	(N/A)
Power loading	N/A	(N/A)

Weights		
Empty	N/A	(N/A)
Loaded	N/A	(N/A)
Maximum	N/A	(N/A)

Performance		
Max speed	300km/h	186mph
Cruise speed	110km/h	68mph
Range	4km	2 miles
Endurance	(Shinryū II) 1.3 minutes	
Ceiling	400m	1,312ft

Armament 100kg (220 lb) of explosive (8 unguided rockets)

Deployment None. A total of five protoptype Jinryū gliders were built by Mizuno. The Shinryū II remained a design board aircraft.

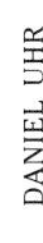
DANIEL UHR

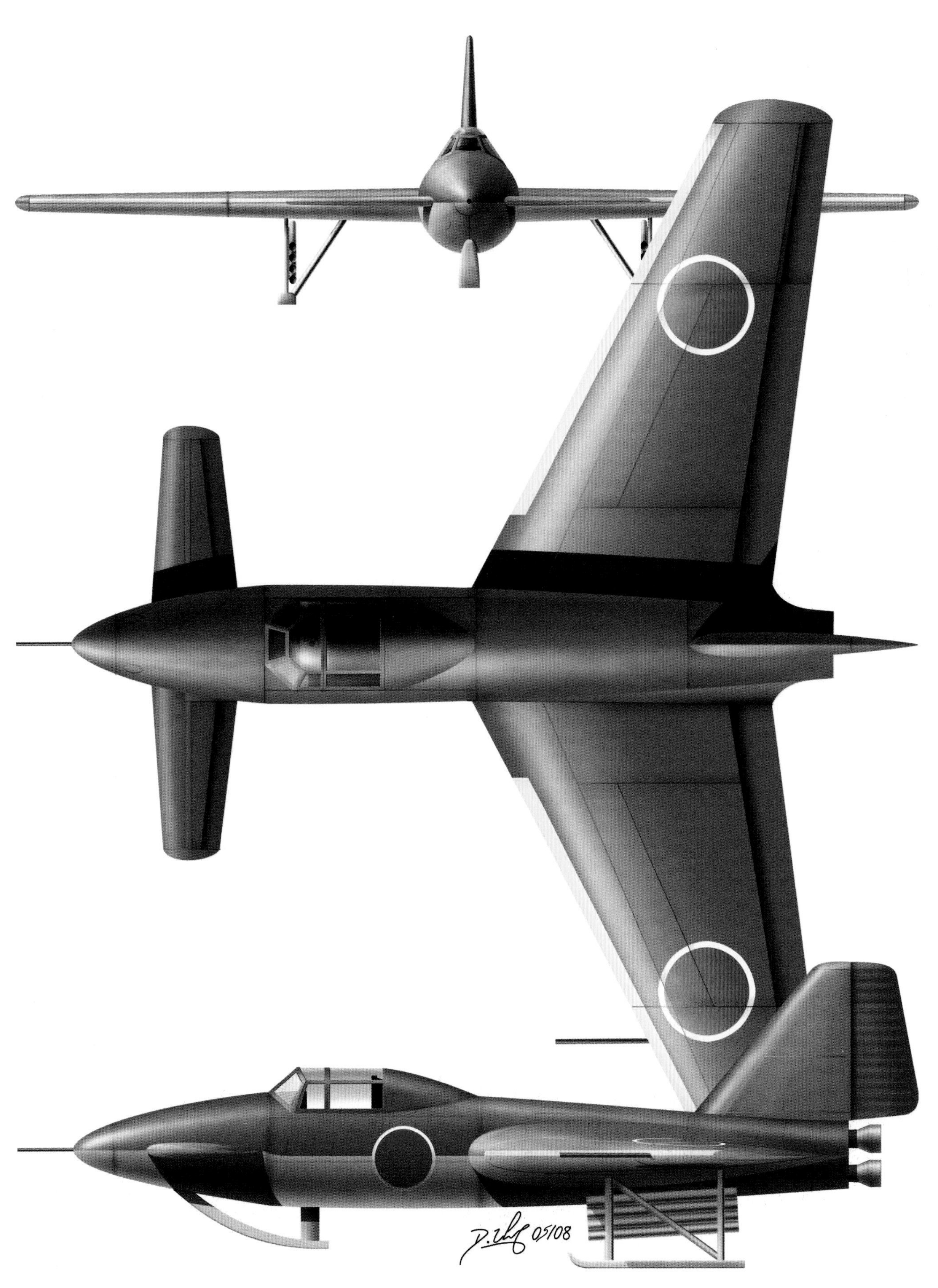
05/08

Nakajima Fugaku

MUNEO HOSAKA

Japan shared a fundamental flaw with Germany in regards to not developing a bomber capable of long range missions. The lack of this capability is considered by some to be a pivotal nail in the coffins of each country during the war. In both cases, efforts to develop such a bomber came too late to affect the outcome of the conflict. Although the Japanese had considered the need for such a bomber at the outset of hostilities – as had the Germans with the disastrous Heinkel He 177 Greif – very little happened until the need was dire, and by then the noose was tight, choking any hope for putting a long range bomber into service.

The main cause of this apathy was the early success in the Pacific theatre where the short and medium range bombers then in use by the Japanese were adequate to fulfil the needs of the IJA and IJN. With the entry of the United States into the war a formidable problem arose. Geography put the military machine of the US far out of reach of Japan. When the tide of war turned against the Japanese, it was soon realised that some means to attack the US mainland had to be acquired, not only to destroy the war industry of America but to ravage the civilian population centres to reduce morale and bring the war to the US doorstep. In consequence, the US would have to allocate or divert resources to increase the defence of the homeland which would affect the war on other fronts. As history was to show, the Japanese did succeed in launching attacks against America, but only in the form of the Fu-Go balloon bombs and isolated attacks on the west coast from submarine-launched float planes. None had much of an effect.

There were some early attempts to produce a long range bomber – for example, the Mitsubishi G7M1 Taizan (a 16-shi project) – plus designs that were actually built such as the Nakajima G5N Shinzan and Nakajima G8N Renzan. The Shinzan was not a success and the Renzan failed to reach operational service as a combat aircraft, let alone reach America and return.

It was to be Nakajima who would attempt to provide a strategic long range bomber capable of bringing the war to America. The man behind the project was Chikuhei Nakajima, chairman and engineer of Nakajima Hikōki K.K. Motivated by his fears over the inability of the Japanese to reach and destroy US industrial capacity, Chikuhei tried to convince the IJN and the IJA of the need for a strategic bomber. However, officials from both services refused to consider his ideas. Thus, without official sanction or request, Chikuhei invested a portion of Nakajima's resources to draft designs for a bomber that could take-off from Japanese bases, cross the Pacific, attack targets on the West Coast of America and return to either their original bases or elsewhere in Japanese or Axis held territory. Nakajima gave the design work the name 'Project Z'.

On 29 January 1943, Nakajima began the task of assembling drafts and studies for the design of the bomber, along with reports which studied the feasibility and problems of production. On the completion of this stage in April 1943, he again pitched the concept to both the IJA and the IJN. This time, neither service turned Nakajima away. However, despite the information Nakajima had assembled for the proposed bomber, and despite both services now accepting the need for such an aircraft, the IJA and the IJN also produced their own ideas. Not surprisingly, the two services had differing opinions on the requirements for the bomber. The IJA desired a type that could operate at 9,998m (32,800ft) and carry a heavy defensive armament. By contrast, the IJN wanted a bomber capable of flying at a height of 14,996m (49,200ft), an altitude where interception would be minimal and thereby allowed a lighter defensive weapon load to be carried. Furthermore, the IJN wanted the bomber to take-off from Japan, bomb any target within the US, then utilise bases in Germany or German held territory to land, as opposed to making a round trip.

Though there were a number of variations of the aircraft during the Project Z development, three basic designs of what became the Fugaku emerged. The project presented by the IJA used a 'tail sitter' undercarriage, featured dual vertical stabilisers and bore some resemblance to German designs. It also had a rounded off nose similar to the Boeing B-29 Superfortress and Messerschmitt Me 264 'Amerika' bomber. The IJN's proposed design used a tricycle landing gear arrangement and rounded nose but utilised a single vertical stabiliser. Nakajima's proposal kept the single vertical stabiliser but had a stepped nose much like that used on the G5N Shinzan which the company had previously worked on.

By June 1943, Nakajima had received plans from the IJA and IJN, reviewed them and begun work on drafting a final design. To continue the research and further development and study the Project Z aircraft, the Army and Navy Aviation Technical Committee was formed on 9 August 1943. The IJA delegation was headed by Captain Andō. Later in August, Chikuhei Nakajima prepared a thesis entitled 'Strategy for Ultimate Victory'. Chikuhei used his personal clout to make sure his document reached not only IJA and IJN officials, but also politicians and even Prime Minister Hideki Tōjō. His thesis was laid out in six chapters and contained Chikuhei's plan for defeating the US as well as defending Japan. The key component was the Project Z bomber which he proposed could be used to destroy US airfields as a means to deny the US the ability to launch raids against Japan. This suggestion was in part due to his belief that Japanese air forces were not strong enough to repel a bombing raid. Another facet of the thesis was the use of the bomber to attack the US war industry. Without materials and oil, the US could not produce aircraft, tanks and other weapons. More importantly, he added, the Japanese should use the bomber to destroy the Soviet military industry as a means to support Germany. This implied that Nakajima could provide Germany with such long range bombers.

The Project Z bomber would employ an all metal structure with the wings mounted in the mid-fuselage position. The plane was envisioned to be powered by the Nakajima Ha-54, 36-cylinder radial engine, also known as the D.BH. The Ha-54 was, in fact, two Ha-44 18-cylinder radials paired together. It was projected that the Ha-54 engine could produce up to 5,000hp and that six of these would be sufficient to propel the bomber to a generous maximum speed of 679km/h (422mph). Each engine would drive two contra-rotating, three-bladed propellers with a 4.5m (14.7ft) diameter. The Ha-54 engine, however, would not be ready for some time (and as events turned out, by war's end it was still only a prototype engine and problems with cooling the power unit through the use of a ducted cowling were never solved). Therefore, Nakajima had to settle for the experimental NK11A (Ha-53) which, while also in development, was expected to be ready for trials. The drawback was that the NK11A was expected to muster only 2,500hp and this would certainly have lowered the performance estimates. The introduction of the NK11A meant that a revision of the Project Z airframe became necessary.

The bomber's ceiling was estimated to be 15,000m (49,212ft) and it was believed that a heavy defensive armament was not necessary as the high altitude would offer protection from fighter opposition. To a lesser extent the projected speed would also reduce vulnerability. Consequently, the bomber would carry at least four Type 99 20mm cannons, but contemporary illustrations of the bomber often show a much heavier armament. This may be a result of having to settle for the less powerful NK11A and any speed/altitude advantage would have been lost, so an increased weapon load would have been necessary to protect the aircraft. Typically, illustrations show two cannon mounted in the tail, two in the nose, two twin-cannon turrets placed in the front and rear of the fuselage top and at least one belly turret. Variations included waist gunner stations. For a normal bomb load, the bomber was expected to carry up to 20,000kg (44,092 lb) of

Nakajima Fugaku – data

Contemporaries

Convair B-36 Peacemaker (US), Convair XC-99 (US), Messerschmitt Me 264 and Me 264B (Germany), Junkers Ju 390 (Germany), Junkers EF100 (Germany), Messerschmitt Me P 08.01 (Germany), Tupolev Tu-4 (NATO codename *Bull*) (Russia), Tupolev Tu-85 (NATO codename *Barge*) (Russia), Tupolev Tu-70 (Russia), Vickers-Armstrong Victory Bomber (UK)

Specifications in parentheses refer to the Fugaku specifically. All other specifications refer to the primary Nakajima Project Z design.

Type	Long range strategic bomber
Crew	Six to ten (seven to eight)

Powerplant Six Nakajima Ha-54 36-cylinder, air-cooled radials developing 5,000hp at engine start, each driving two alternating stroke, contra-rotating three bladed propellers of 4.5m (14.7ft) diameter/Six Nakajima NK11A [Ha-53] 18-cylinder, air-cooled radials developing 2,500hp at engine start and each driving a alternating stroke, four-bladed propeller of 4.8m (15.7ft) diameter

Dimensions

Span		64.98m	213.2ft
	(Fugaku)	62.97m	206.6ft
Length		44.98m	147.6ft
	(Fugaku)	39.98m	131.2ft
Height		8.77m	28.8ft
	(Fugaku)	8.77m	28.8ft
Wing area		352.01m²	3,766.8ft²
	(Fugaku)	330.00m²	3,552ft²
Wing loading,		348.60kg/m²	71.4 lb/ft²
normal	(Fugaku)	126.94kg/m²	26 lb/ft²
Wing loading,		456.99kg/m²	93.6 lb/ft²
loaded	(Fugaku)	211.89kg/m²	43.4 lb/ft²
Power loading,		5.44kg/hp	12 lb/hp
normal	(Fugaku)	3.76kg/hp	8.3 lb/hp
Power loading,		7.21kg/hp	15.9 lb/hp
loaded	(Fugaku)	6.30kg/hp	13.9 lb/hp
Aspect Ratio		12.1	(N/A)

Weights

Empty		65,000kg	143,300 lb
	(Fugaku)	33,800kg	74,516 lb
Loaded		122,000kg	268,963 lb
	(Fugaku)	42,000kg	92,594 lb
Max loaded		160,000kg	352,739 lb
	(Fugaku)	70,000kg	154,323 lb

Performance

Max speed		679km/h	422mph
		at 10,000m	at 32,808ft
		779km/h	484mph
	(Fugaku)	at 10,000m	at 32,808ft
Take-off run	(Fugaku)	1,020m	3,347ft
Range		16,499km	10,252 miles
	(Fugaku)	16,499km	10,252 miles
Max range		17,999km	11,184 miles
	(Fugaku)	19,400km	12,054 miles
Ceiling		15,000m	49,212ft
	(Fugaku)	15,000m	49,212ft

Armament

Four Type 99 20mm cannons (up to 12 cannons depending on the source) and a maximum bomb payload of 20,000kg/44,092 lb

Deployment

None. The 'Project Z' and Fugaku aircraft existed only as paper designs.

bombs, but in the case of anti-shipping missions, torpedoes could be carried (see below). For attacks on the United States, the bomber would carry only up to 5,000kg (11,023 lb) of bombs.

As work continued on the Project Z, plans were made to assemble and house the bomber's production line. By the fall of 1943, these plans had been completed and construction of the new facility had begun. By January 1944, the Project Z moniker was dropped and changed to the Fugaku which means 'Mount Fuji'.

As it was, more pressing demands on Nakajima resulted in less and less work being done on the Fugaku. To compound the problem, by the time the design was nearing completion, Japan was on the defensive and chances of producing the Fugaku, let alone using it to attack America, were about nil. The IJA believed that there was no probability of the Fugaku being built and therefore abandoned the project, leaving the IJN as the sole remaining party involved. Even the Gunjushō (the Ministry of Munitions) felt the Fugaku was impossible to realise and ordered Kawanishi to design a new long range bomber. Unfortunately, the Gunjushō failed to inform the IJA, IJN and Nakajima about the Kawanishi bomber, which was known as the TB. When the new bomber project was discovered, a hail of protests and arguments erupted that hampered not only the development of the Fugaku but all long range bomber projects including the TB which was soon cancelled.

However, it was the fall of Saipan in 1944 that sealed the Fugaku's fate. The Japanese air forces no longer had need of a super long range bomber and demanded more pertinent aircraft to protect the mainland. As such, all work on the Fugaku was stopped and the plans, calculations and drafts were shelved. Work on the production facility was halted prior to completion and left unfinished. With the Japanese surrender, all documentation for the Fugaku was to be destroyed to prevent the information being handed over to the Allies. Papers on the Fugaku that survive to this day, including a number of drafts for various Project Z/Fugaku proposals, were mislaid or kept for safe-keeping by individuals. Since the war it has been claimed that the Misawa Air Base would have been used by Fugaku bombers to launch raids against the US. While Misawa was used by the IJA and operational IJA bombers flew from this facility, there has been no definitive evidence to support or refute Misawa being considered as a Fugaku base.

Bombing was not the only mission that was envisioned for the Fugaku and during the Project Z brainstorming three other concepts arose and later formed part of Chikuhei's thesis. The first was an attack design that had 400 Type 97 7.7mm machine guns crammed into the aircraft. The front and the back of the bomber would accommodate 40 machine guns arranged in ten rows. The intention was to rain thousands of rounds of bullets down on to enemy ships with the theory that a swath of destruction 45m (148ft) wide and 10km (6.2 miles) long could be achieved by 15 Fugaku aircraft. Once the decks of these ships were swept of personnel, nine Fugaku bombers, each with twenty 907kg (2,000 lb) bombs or torpedoes, would deliver the coup de grâce, covering a path 200m (656ft) wide and 1km (0.62 miles) in length with high explosive.

Another version had the Fugaku loaded with 96 Type 99 20mm cannons. The front and the back of the aircraft would contain 12 cannons arranged in eight rows while another 36 cannons were fitted on each side of the aircraft. This particular variant was to target enemy bombers flying missions against Japan and would use hidden bases untouched by the Japanese airfield bombing campaign. By flying over the enemy bomber formation and unleashing a withering fusillade of cannon fire, it was speculated that ten of the cannon equipped Fugaku could bring down 100 bombers, the area covered by the cannons from one plane being 2.5m (8.2ft) and 3km (1.86 miles) long. A system of ground radar stations would give advance warning of the incoming enemy bomber force, allowing time for the Fugaku to intercept and destroy the bombers before they reached Japan. This was all very impressive on paper but had it been put into practice the results were likely to have been less than stellar, especially when considering the failure of the Mitsubishi G6M1 heavy escort fighter (a G4M converted into a gunship to provide cover for bomber formations). Finally, the Fugaku was considered as a transport which would have provided a significant heavy lift capability. It was estimated that one Fugaku transport would be able to carry 300 soldiers with full equipment, about equal to one infantry rifle company with a heavy weapon platoon. Chikuhei envisioned a grand scheme of a raid against America where four hundred transports would deposit 120,000 men (equivalent to a Japanese Army, which equates to a US and British Corps) on US soil to take over the Seattle-Tacoma airport located in Washington. After landing the troops would move overland to attack and destroy Boeing's B-29 producing Renton Factory in Renton before returning to Japan.

There is no evidence to suggest any of these concepts made it to the final Fugaku designs. However, if any of the three ideas were supported, a transport may have topped the list for possible consideration given the late war need for aircraft capable of bringing raw materials into Japan to feed the war industry that was slowly being starved. As a note, although the designations G10N and G10N1 have been used in print for this aircraft for many years, there has been no confirmation in historical sources that confirms this was the case.

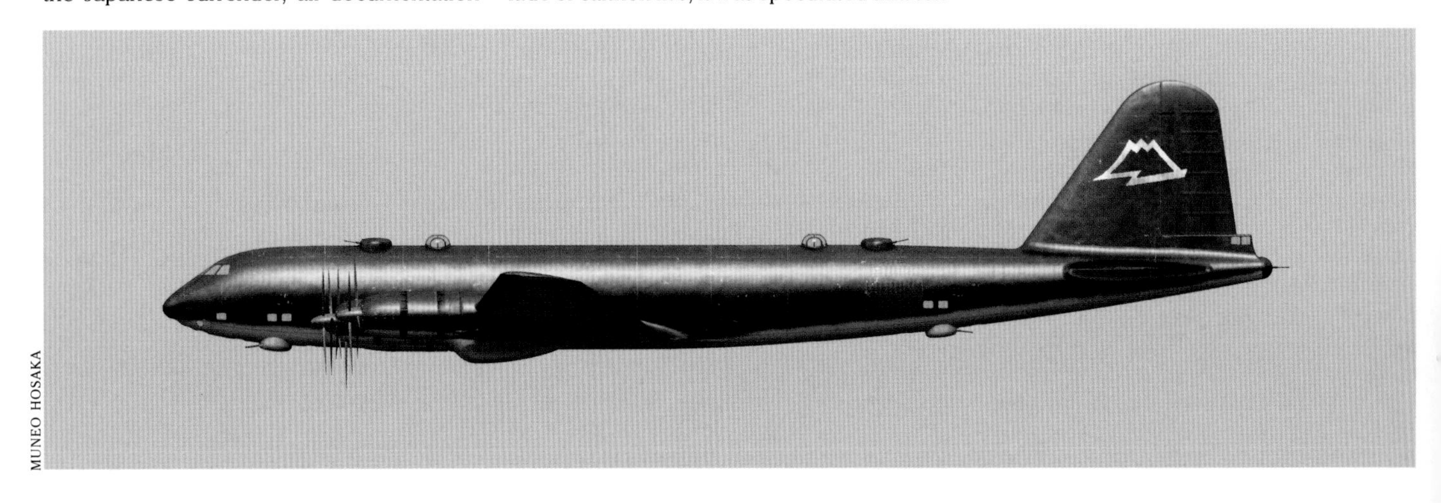
MUNEO HOSAKA

MUNEO HOSAKA

Nakajima J1N Gekkō

In the spring of 1938, the IJN issued a 13-shi specification for a long range fighter. This came about as a result of combat experience in China that showed that Japanese fighters did not have the range to escort bombers on missions deep into Chinese territory, the result of which were high losses. What Nakajima produced to answer the specification would have been a complete failure had it not been for one redeeming feature.

The 13-shi specification was a very strict one with a number of very demanding criteria. Nakajima's Katsuji Nakamura would produce the initial prototype. It was an aerodynamically clean 3-seat monoplane with low mounted wings. Each wing housed a Nakajima Sakae radial, developing 1,130hp. However, one wing was fitted with a Sakae 21 engine, the other with the Sakae 22, and their propellers rotated in opposite directions to reduce torque. To complement the nose armament, twin remote controlled barbettes, each with two 7.7mm Type 97 machine guns, were placed behind the pilot's cockpit. Designated the J1N1, the first two prototypes were delivered and put under test. A myriad of problems were noted – the plane was overweight, the novel propeller arrangement caused numerous difficulties, the hydraulic system was too complex, the barbettes were too difficult to aim and the entire arrangement was too heavy. To top it all off, manoeuvrability was poor and all the J1N1 had going for it was its range.

Rejected as a heavy fighter, the J1N was given new lease of life as a reconnaissance aircraft. Nakajima stripped the aeroplane of its weapons and the barbettes, cut the fuel capacity (which, in part, was made up by using drop tanks) and replaced the Sakae 22 engine with another Sakae 21 powerplant. The armament was a single, rear firing 12.7mm Type 2 machine gun to be was used by the radio operator. Now called the J1N1-C, following successful trials the aircraft received approval and entered service with reconnaissance units from August 1942. On encountering it in combat, the Allies codenamed the plane *Irving*, thinking it was a fighter. The IJN renamed the plane J1N1-R, equipping some examples with a turret mounting a 20mm Type 99 Model 1 cannon.

In early 1943, Commander Yasuna Kozono, who led the 251st Kōkūtai operating from Vunakanau Airfield in Rabaul, Papua New Guinea, believed that the J1N1-C would make an excellent night fighter. Mechanics replaced the observer's station and installed two 20mm Type 99 cannons that fired upward and forward at a 30° angle and two additional cannons firing downward and forward at a similar angle. Called the J1N1-C Kai, the field modification proved a success and with that success, the IJN became interested.

In short order, Nakajima was instructed by the IJN to produce a dedicated night fighter version of the J1N. By August 1943, the assembly of the first model, the J1N1-S Gekkō (meaning 'Moonlight'), had begun at Nakajima's Koizumi plant. The main changes saw the glazing over the crew compartment reduced and the step removed. The ring exhaust collector was also removed and the engines used individual exhaust stacks. In addition, it was realised that the downward firing cannons were ineffective and in the J1N1-Sa were removed. Both the J1N1-S and J1N1-Sa were sometimes fitted with a centimetric radar in the front of the aircraft, the external antenna for the set being situated on the tip of the nose. Others had a searchlight in the nose while a number lacked the radar and searchlight to be replaced by a single forward-firing 20mm Type 99 cannon.

In combat, the Gekkō proved satisfactory against the Consolidated B-24 Liberator, but against the faster Boeing B-29 Superfortress was hard pressed to make a single attack. Therefore, it should not be surprising that the J1N was considered as a candidate to be equipped with two turbojets. Successful as a reconnaissance platform as well as a night fighter, replacing the radial engines with turbojets would have provided the J1N with a superior speed that would have served it well in either role. A contemporary illustration of the turbojet equipped J1N shows the fuselage of a J1N1-Sa. The illustration lacks the upward firing cannon and radar which suggests it was equipped with the nose mounted cannon as its armament. Perhaps it may have worked in conjunction with radar and/or searchlight equipped J1N1-S and J1N1-Sa during combat missions, or it may have been considered as a fast special attacker fitted with two 551 lb bombs (as surviving J1N aircraft were at the end of the war). The wings seem to have been unaltered outside of the required modifications to fit the nacelles for the turbojets. As to what jet engines were to be introduced is not known. The Kūgishō Ne 20 was certainly a candidate as was the Nakajima Ne 230. The adaptation of the J1N to jet power would likely have been an easier task than that faced by Kūgishō in adapting the P1Y1 Ginga into the turbojet bomber Tenga.

Exactly when the proposal to modify the J1N to a turbojet aircraft was made is unknown. What is known is that it did not progress past the drafting board.

Nakajima J1N Gekkō – data

Contemporaries
Curtiss XP-87 Blackhawk (US), Messerschmitt P.1099 (Germany)

No exact specifications are known for the turbojet powered J1N. The specifications given below are for the J1N1-S.

Type	Night Fighter
Crew	Two

Powerplant
Two Nakajima NK1F Sakae 21 14-cylinder, air-cooled radial, each rated at 1,130hp for take-off, 1,100hp at 2,850m (9,350ft) and 980hp at 6,000m (19,685ft), driving a three-bladed, constant speed metal propeller

Dimensions		
Span	16.97m	55.7ft
Length	12.74m	41.8ft
Height	4.54m	14.9ft
Wing area	40.00m²	430.5ft²
Wing loading	175.27kg/m²	35.9 lb/ft²
Power loading	3.62kg/hp	8 lb/hp

Weights		
Empty	4,840kg	10,670 lb
Loaded	7,010kg	15,454 lb
Maximum	8,184kg	18,043 lb

Performance		
Speed	507km/h at 5,840m	315mph at 19,160ft
Cruise speed	333km/h at 4,000m	207mph at 13,125ft
Climb	9 min 35 sec to 5,000m (16,405ft)	
Range	2,544km	1,581 miles
Max range	3,779km	2,348 miles
Ceiling	9,330m	30,610ft

Armament
Two upward firing 20mm Type 99 cannons and two downward firing 20mm Type 99 cannons installed in the fuselage

Deployment
None. The turbojet powered J1N remained a paper project.

DANIEL UHR

Nakajima Kitsuka

MUNEO HOSAKA

Even though the genesis of the turbojet began long before World War 2, it would take the war to accelerate the development of this new powerplant to the point that by the close of hostilities jet aircraft had been blooded in battle. Germany can, by some, be considered the leader in turbojet technology during the war, but the US and Britain were not far behind. Japan, too, was not idle in producing its own turbojet but it would take German knowledge to give their industries a boost. One such results was was an historic aircraft in the annals of Japanese aviation history: the Nakajima Kitsuka.

Because the Kitsuka (which in Japanese means 'Wild Orange Blossom') was probably the most important Japanese aircraft to use a jet engine as its powerplant, it seems apt to provide a general overview of Japanese turbojet development in this section. The first axial-flow turbojet was patented in 1921 by Frenchman Maxime Guillaume. However, the technology of his day was not enough to realise a working model. In 1930, Englishman Frank Whittle designed a turbojet using a centrifugal compressor and, despite relatively little interest being shown in it, he patented his concept. In 1933, German Hans von Ohain designed a turbojet similar to Whittle's but it would not be until 1936 that Ernst Heinkel took an interest in the engine and hired von Ohain to continue his work. By March 1937, this resulted in the Heinkel HeS 1, the first German jet engine although in fact a hydrogen demonstrator. The following month Whittle tested his first jet engine, the WU or Whittle Unit.

Around this time, Rear Admiral Kōichi Hanajima became aware of Whittle's work as well as that of Secondo Campini, an Italian who began work on a thermojet and an aircraft to use it: the Campini Caproni N.1 in 1934. This rekindled his interest in jet propulsion and using his position as head of the engine division of the Dai-Ichi Kaigun Kōkū Gijutsu-shō, saw to it that studies were conducted in such engines. Hanajima reached out to the Tōkyō Imperial University and Mitsubishi Jūkōgyō K.K. and together all manner of rocket and jet engines were investigated such as ramjets. To Hanajima's disappointment, little official interest was generated from the results.

1938 saw German firm BMW begin their research into turbojets and the Heinkel He 178 V1 prototype was built to test the HeS 3 turbojet that was being developed from the earlier HeS 1. In late 1938, Messerschmitt started work on what would become the world's first jet fighter to enter squadron service, the Me 262. In Japan, and despite the lack of interest being shown in jet propulsion, Captain Tokiyasu Tanegashima was appointed as the head of the Engine Test and Field Support Shop of Kūgishō. He was issued with a meager sum to fund jet engine research although, with the assistance of Professor Fukusaburō Numachi, he would initially focus his efforts on turboprops. Both men were able to source the Ishikawajima-Shibaura Turbine Company and Ebara Seizō K.K. to help build a number of test engines that used compressors and gas turbines, but these labours did not bear fruit.

By 1939, BMW had tested its first axial-flow turbojet design and on 27 August of that year the He 178 V1 made its first flight, the first turbojet powered aircraft to fly. In February 1940, the British Air Ministry ordered two examples of the E.28/39 research aircraft from the Gloster Aircraft Company to serve as testbed aircraft for Whittle's engines. 1940 also saw the Italian N.1 fly for the first time and Heinkel began gliding tests of the He 280 jet fighter prototype as it waited for its two HeS 8 turbojets now under development (the He 280 did not enter production). November would see Junkers test the Jumo 004 turbojet and Gloster's jet fighter proposal, the Meteor, was ordered in February 1941. Also in November, Lockheed commenced work on the L-1000 axial-flow turbojet, the first American jet. Finally, in December, Whittle's W.1X turbojet, a flight ready engine, was tested for the first time.

Japan though, was not idle in 1940. Early in the year, Tanegashima, with the help of the Mitsui Seiki Kogyo K.K., created a free piston compressor for a gas turbine based on a Junkers design, but it was not a success as a means for aircraft propulsion. Another attempt was tried by a different department. Under the leadership of Lieutenant Commander Osamu Nagano, head of the Kūgishō aircraft engine division, and Masanori Miyata, who led the Kūgishō electric parts section, built a tiny free piston compressor gas turbine, generating one tenth of a horsepower at 12,000rpm that drove a magneto that lit a lamp. Despite this measure of success, apathy on the part of the IJN continued to stymie progress. Tanegashima soon realised that the Japanese industry was not capable of constructing a free piston engine and switched his studies to axial flow jets.

On 15 May 1941, the Gloster E.28/39 flew for the first time, but previously in April, Heinkel's He 280 V1 had flown under jet power on its maiden flight, the first jet fighter to fly. 1942 saw the Junkers Jumo 004 under test while BMW focused efforts on the BMW 003 Sturm. Heinkel was instructed to concentrate on developing the HeS 011, a turbojet that was to power the second generation of German jets. On 18 July, the Messerschmitt Me 262 flew under turbojet power, becoming the second jet fighter to fly, and on 2 October, the American Bell XP-59 Airacomet jet fighter made its maiden flight. By this time, Japanese engineers and scientists had learned of the flight of the He 178 as proof that an aircraft powered by a jet engine was feasible. This was just the boost the flagging Japanese jet engine research desperately needed.

As a result two different paths were taken with renewed vigour. The first employed the principle of the thermojet (as used by Secondo Campini) and was called the Tsu-11. While this engine was to be selected for use in the Kūgishō Ōka Model 22, it was found to be unsuited as a powerplant for a jet aircraft. The second route, that of a pure jet engine, was pursued further. Kūgishō's Vice Admiral Misao Wada was the man who oversaw the development of a turbojet and the first result was the TR-10. This had a single stage, centrifugal compressor with a single stage turbine and was, in essence, built by adapting a turbosupercharger. The engine was constructed by Ebara Seizō K.K. When the TR-10 was first tested in the summer of 1943 its performance did not meet expectations. The TR-10 was renamed the Ne 10 and the engine was further developed by adding four axial stages in front of the engine inlet. This reduced the load on the centrifugal compressor, lowered the engine RPM and produced more thrust. The revised jet engine was designated the Ne 12. The problem with the Ne 12, however, was its great weight and so steps were taken to lighten the engine, which resulted in the Ne 12B.

1944 was an ominous year for Japan. When the Mariana Islands of Saipan and Tinian were wrestled from the Japanese by US forces in July and August, Japan found herself well within striking distance of the Boeing B-29 Superfortresses. Prior to this, B-29 raids had to fly from remote bases in China and India and so the bombing of Japanese targets was relatively rare. Staging from Saipan and Tinian, B-29s were far closer, could be more active and the Japanese were only too aware of this. In addition, it was surmised that it would only be a matter of time before the main Japanese islands were targeted for invasion. In August 1944, the Kaigun Koku Hombu called for a meeting to discuss changes in air strategy to combat the air and land threat as well as to consider the aircraft that would be used. The Kaigun Koku Hombu invited aircraft designers from both Nakajima and Kawanishi to attend and the outcome of this meeting was the proposal for three classes of aircraft termed Kōkoku Heiki (one literal translation being 'Empire Weapon'). The first class, or Kōkoku Heiki No.1, was the adaptation of current aircraft to accept a 800kg (1,760 lb) bomb with which their pilots would undertake shimpū missions and target enemy invasion ships. If the bomb overloaded the carrying capacity of the aircraft, then RATO (Rocket Assisted Take-Off) units would be used to get them airborne. Kōkoku Heiki No.3 was to be a conventional, radial engine aircraft designed by Kawanishi as the Tokkō-ki, which would be used for shimpū missions, but this project was soon abandoned (perhaps because the IJN was to build the similar Nakajima Ki-115 as the Showa Toka). It would be Kōkoku Heiki No.2 which provided the seed for the Nakajima Kitsuka. This 'Empire Weapon' was to be an aircraft that used the Tsu-11 and, when available, the Ne 12 turbojet.

However, three months prior to the meeting, efforts were underway to obtain the Me 262 from Germany. In May 1944, the Japanese negotiated for the manufacturing rights to the Me 262 and the Germans initially agreed to the release. However, the deal was not concluded due to the large number of modifications that the design was found to require after its flight testing. It was not until July 1944 that orders were given to provide the Japanese with blueprints of the Me 262 fighter and the Junkers Jumo 004 and BMW 003 turbojets.

On 22 July 1944, Reichsmarschall Hermann Göring authorised the licensing of the Me 262 to Japan and the delivery of one sample aircraft. However, the Japanese submarine I-29 had left Lorient, France, on 16 April with a sample Junkers Jumo 004 turbojet and plans for the Me 262 and BMW 003 turbojet among its cargo. Also aboard the submarine was Technical Commander Eiichi Iwaya who carried on his person a portion of the documentation on the German fighter and turbojets. By 14 July, the I-29 had arrived in Singapore. Iwaya, seeking to reach Japan as soon as possible, disembarked from I-29 and took only a portion of the German documentation. From Singapore, Iwaya flew to Tōkyō. On 26 July, Allied code intercepts pinpointed the location of I-29 and the USS *Sawfish* sent her to the bottom near the Balintang Channel in the Luzon Strait, taking the precious cargo with her.

When Iwaya arrived in Japan, all he possessed of the German files with regards to the Me 262 and turbojets was a single copy of a cross-section of the BMW 003A turbojet. The subsequent news of the loss of I-29 was a crushing blow, but not a fatal one by any means. In studying the BMW 003A document, the Japanese found it to be of a similar design to the Ne 12 but instead of the centrifugal compressor the German engine used an eight stage axial-flow compressor. It was adjudged that this method was superior to the Ne 12 and as such, efforts should be concentrated on building the Japanese equivalent to the BMW 003A. Despite the decision against it, work on the Ne 12B continued. Four companies were involved in the development of the new turbojet. Each was to be provided with a copy of the BMW 003A cross-section and other available data and to build their own versions. Ishikawajima-Shibaura Turbine Company was to develop the Ne 130, Nakajima Hikōki K.K. the Ne 230, Mitsubishi Jūkōgyō K.K. the Ne 330, and Kūgishō would move forwards with the Ne 20.

Following the August conference with the Kaigun Koku Hombu, Ken'ichi Matsumura, chief designer for Nakajima and with the assistance of Kazuo Ōno, produced a number of concept drawings for the Kōkoku Heiki No.2. Within Nakajima, the new aircraft was given the codename Maru-Ten. On 14 September 1944, IJN representatives met with Nakajima at their Koizumi plant to discuss the concepts which had been put forward. The design that stood out was based on a description of the Me 262 as provided by Technical Commander Eiichi Iwaya who, while in Germany, was able to view and study the German jet. Thus, Matsumura's drawing bore an outward resemblance to the Me 262. After reviewing the concept, the design was approved as the Kōkoku Heiki No.2. In keeping with the shimpū mission of the aircraft, the initial design had no landing gear and was to be launched from catapult ramps, boosted with RATO units. The calculated range was a mere 204km (127 miles) due to the designated engine, the Ne 12, which burned fuel at a rapid rate. At sea level the estimated speed was 639km/h (397mph). A single bomb fixed to the aircraft was the only armament. Another feature was the inclusion of folding wings to allow the aircraft to be hidden in caves and tunnels and protected from bombing attacks.

On 8 October, Kūgishō ordered Kazuo Yoshida, plant director for Nakajima, to have a wooden mock-up of the aircraft completed and ready for inspection by the end of the month. In addition Nakajima was told to have the initial structural plans finished by the same date. This was ordered so that production of the aircraft could begin without delay. Unfortunately, delays would be a major problem. The IJN promised that the Ne 12 would be ready for testing by November 1944 and in short order thereafter, production engines would be available. Based on this assumption, Nakajima was to construct thirty aeroplanes by the end of December 1944. Because of the rush to produce the aircraft, a myriad of problems arose with the design which necessitated changes. A major issue was the lack of critical war materials which required the use of substitutes and brought additional delays. To compound the problem, Nakajima was concerned that the Ne 12B would not be ready despite the IJN's promises.

Meanwhile, Kūgishō proceeded with the Ne 20. The engineers were forced to use alloys which were not to the standards of the German engine and would be a source of problems during testing. The design of the Ne 20 was smaller than the BMW 003A but it retained the combustion chamber shape of the German engine. While it used the same size of burner as the BMW 003A, it only used twelve instead of sixteen due to the smaller size. Kūgishō would draft and refine the design of the Ne 20 through December.

On 9 December 1944, the IJN called a meeting to discuss the progress and outlook of the Kōkoku Heiki No.2. Based on the problems Nakajima were having with the aircraft, not to mention the doubts about the Ne 12, the production schedule was revised. Nakajima were requested to produce the first prototype by February 1945 for use in static testing. It was also during this meeting that the aircraft's specifications underwent a revision. Instead of a fixed bomb, the bomb could now be released by the pilot. The role of the aircraft was also changed. No longer was it to be used for a shimpū mission but instead for close air support, the aircraft acting as a fast attack bomber. As a consequence of these changes, the design had to incorporate a landing gear. The IJN issued its specifications for the new jet, which was now called the Kitsuka, and the documents requested:

Span: no more than 5.3m (17.3ft) with the wings folded

Length: no more than 9.5m (31.1ft)

Height: no more than 3.1m (10.1ft)

Powerplant: Two Ne 12 jet engines

Maximum Speed: 513km/h (319mph) with 500kg (1,102 lb) bomb

Range: 204km (127 miles) with a 500kg (1,102 lb) bomb or 278km (173 miles) with a 250kg (551 lb) bomb

Landing Speed: 148km/h (92mph)

Take-off Run: 350m (1,148ft) using two 450kg (992 lb) RATO bottles

Manoeuvrability: The aircraft had to be highly manoeuvrable, have a short turn radius and be stable at speed to facilitate target tracking

Protection: Shatter proof glass for the canopy. Front windscreen to have 70mm of bullet proof glass. 12mm of steel armour plate below and behind the pilot. Fuel tanks to be 22mm sandwich types

Basic Instrumentation: Tachometer, altimeter, artificial horizon, airspeed indicator, Model 0 Type 1 flux gate compass, fuel pressure gauge, oil pressure gauge, oil temperature gauge, tail pipe temperature gauge and a pitot tube electric heater

Basic Equipment: Type 0 parachute, automatic fire extinguisher, Type 3 dry battery, Type 3 radio receiver, Type 1 life raft and a reserve weight of 30kg (66.1 lb)

1945 would open with more misfortune for the Japanese war machine. Japanese troops were pushed out of Burma from 5 January and B-29s would bomb Tōkyō the next day. Two days earlier, Matsumura and Ōno, along with others involved in the Kitsuka project, discussed the possibility of using the Ne 20 turbojet in place of the Ne 12. In the debate, some suggested that the Ne 20 was not as far in development than the Ne 12 and would delay progress if used. On the other hand, some argued that the Ne 12 was not achieving significant results. In the end, the consensus was that the Ne 12 should remain as the powerplant only because it was projected to be ready before the Ne 20.

On 28 January 1945, the wooden mock-up of the Kitsuka was finally ready for inspection at Nakajima's Koizumi plant. Vice Admiral Misao Wada and his staff visited the plant and inspected the mock-up with both Matsumura and Ōno in attendance. It was made clear to the Kūgishō inspectors that the Kitsuka was a very simple aircraft that could be constructed in 7,500 man-hours. By comparison, it took 15,000 man-hours to build a Mitsubishi A6M Reisen. Following the inspection, Nakajima was told to make two slight adjustments to the Kitsuka. The first involved the windscreen. Originally, the front windscreen was rounded but now it was desired that it should be flat panelled. This change may have been suggested to allow for the future installation of a reflector gun sight because such a sight requires flat panels to avoid sighting problems due to canopy distortion. The second alteration was to make the canopy slide to the rear instead of opening to the side. At the conclusion of the meeting, Nakajima was told to cease all work on the Nakajima J5N1 Tenrai and the company was also informed that they could expect the Nakajima G8N1 Renzan to be terminated as well. These changes in production and development were done to speed the coming production of the Kitsuka. The close of January also saw the final design draft of the Ne 20 completed and almost immediately work began to build the first engine. Kūgishō's Aero Engine Division provided 400 machine tools and engineers and labourers began to toil day and night to realise the Ne 20.

February 1945 opened with the Japanese naval docks in Singapore targeted and destroyed by B-29 bombers along with continued fighting in the Philippines. A second inspection of the Kitsuka was called for on 10 February. Present at the inspection, among the other engineers and Kūgishō personnel, were Technical Commander Iwaya and the man who was destined to fly the Kitsuka, Lieutenant Commander Susumu Takaoka. The Kitsuka was given final approval and production was to commence at once, even before the Kitsuka had been flight tested. The first five Kitsuka aircraft, No.1 through No.5, were to serve as prototypes and none would be fitted with armour plating or self-sealing fuel tanks. In addition the first two aircraft would not to be equipped with the bomb carrying apparatus. February would also see the Ne 12B tested for the first time.

Unfortunately for the Kitsuka, US bombing ensured that production did not go smoothly. Due to the ever increasing number of strikes against the industrial centres of Japan, it was felt that it was only a matter of time before the Nakajima Koizumi plant would attract the attention of US bombers. Therefore, on 17 February, engineering staff for the Kitsuka was moved to Sano in Tochigi Prefecture. Despite the move, a sizable portion of the Kitsuka component construction remained at Koizumi while the wings, tail assembly and the centre and aft portion of the fuselage were constructed by Kūgishō in Yokosuka. In the face of further bombing attacks, production was dispersed among silkworm factories and buildings in Gunma Prefecture (northwest of Tōkyō).

March arrived in a blaze of smoke and fire as the US ramped up their incendiary bomb campaign against Japan's cities. Tōkyō and Nagoya were particular targets, the burning cities lighting the night sky. On March 26, the first Ne 20 engine was successfully test run from a cave set into a cliff in Yokosuka. With the success of the Ne 20, the Kitsuka engineering team began to seriously consider replacing the Ne 12B with the Ne 20. It was clear that the Ne 20 outperformed the Ne 12B and, based on the higher thrust potential, it was decided that the Kitsuka should use the Ne 20 even if it meant a longer delay while the engine became available. Although the current Kitsuka production did not yet involve the engine mountings, a revision of the aircraft design plans was required to accommodate the Ne 20. By March 31, these revisions were complete and the Kitsuka program entered a stage of finality.

With the revised Kitsuka, some of the specifications were adjusted as follows:

- **Maximum Speed:** 620km/h (385mph) with a 500kg (1,102 lb) bomb at sea level
- **Range:** 351km (218 miles), at sea level, at full power
- **Take-off Run:** 500m (1,640ft) with two 450kg (992 lb) RATO bottles
- **Landing Speed:** 92km/h (57mph)
- **Bomb Load:** 500kg (1,102 lb) as normal with the ability to carry a 800kg (1,763 lb) bomb; a Type 3 rack would be used for the larger bomb
- **Protection:** Reduce the bullet proof glass thickness to 50mm and add 12mm of armour to the front of the cockpit, while the fuel tanks would incorporate an automatic fire suppression system

Engineers working on the Ne 20 found that, although the initial test of the engine was a success, there were many issues to solve. At first, the blades were prone to cracking but this was soon overcome. An electric starter was fitted into the compressor spinner that could spin the engine at 2,250rpm; the engine would reach maximum RPM within 10-15 seconds of engine start. Gasoline was used to start the engine and once running the fuel was switched to a pine root distillate using 20-30 per cent gasoline. What was becoming a problem was how to position the tail cone. Lieutenant Commander Osamu Nagano and his team, along with Captain Tokiyasu Tanegashima, laboured to refine the Ne 20. The worsening bombing situation saw the Ne 20 team moving to Hadano in Kanagawa Prefecture, a three hour drive from Yokosuka.

Set up in warehouses belonging to a tobacco factory, the Ne 20 group comprised 10 officers and 200 men. Here, two bench testing stations were created and Ne 20 development and testing continued. The process revealed numerous flaws. At one stage the pressure of the axial-flow compressor was found to be too low. Nagano came to the conclusion that the camber of the stators was not correct and so he took them out, bent them on an anvil and then reinstalled them. These were tested in the second Ne 20 to be built. Yet another difficulty arose with the thrust bearings on the compressor which was burning out very quickly. Nagano solved the problem by revising the bearings and bearing rings. One problem that reappeared was blade cracking. The blades were made from manganese-chromium-vanadium steel and not the more suitable nickel alloy. These blades were then welded to the disk and, as such, the blades did not have the strength to withstand the operating stresses of the motor. After one to two hours of operation, cracks would appeare on the blade roots at the point where they connected to the disk. The solution was to thicken the blades but this lowered the efficiency of the engine. However, the Ne 20 was able to run for four or five hours before cracks appeared and while the engine could have run longer, there was no guarantee when blade failure would occur. With these improved results, work began to produce a small number of engines.

25 April 1945 would see the first Kitsuka fuselage completed. This was then subjected to stress and load testing which began on 20 May, but with the stipulation that the fuselage was not to be damaged during tests. Nakajima was scheduled to produce 24 Kitsuka aircraft by June 1945 and with the availability of six Ne 20 engines. On the surface, the Kitsuka project looked to be moving along. The reality was a far different story.

On 13 June, Vice Admiral Wada held a meeting to discuss the Kitsuka. Wada addressed a number of issues that were becoming problematic. Nakajima's G8N1 Renzen program had to be stopped in order to free up production capacity for the Kitsuka as both a special attack aircraft and an interceptor. More troubling was that unless the stock of aluminium was conserved the supply would be exhausted by September 1945. At best, even with conservation, by the close of 1945 there would be no more aluminium available. As a result, only steel and wood would be left and to use such materials would, again, have caused a revision to the Kitsuka design. The final blow was that high grade aviation fuels would only be available for the Homare series of radial engines. All other engines, including the Ne 20, would have to make do with poorer quality fuel. This, coupled with defeat after defeat for the Japanese military, cast a very serious cloud over the Kitsuka project and some no longer saw value in continuing with the aircraft. Others however, had a strong desire to see the Kitsuka taken to completion because it would put Japan into the jet age.

On 25 June 1945, the first Kitsuka was completed but without its engines. Although externally the Kitsuka bore a resemblance to the Me 262, that was as far as it went. The wings of the Kitsuka had a total of 13° sweepback, the centreline of the wings being at 9°. Wing tip slots eliminated the tip stall discovered during wind tunnel testing and split flaps and droop ailerons were fitted to compensate for the heavy wing loading. Nakajima K series airfoils were used – a K 125 airfoil at the wing root and a K 309 airfoil at the wing tip. The wings were

Interceptor initial concepts – data

The specifications in parenthesis refer to the modified wing variant.

Type Interceptor
Crew One

Powerplant Two Kūgishō Ne 20 axial-flow turbojets, each developing 490kg (1,080 lb) of thrust

Dimensions			
Span		10.00m	32.8ft
Length		9.23m	30.3ft
Height		3.04m	10ft
Wing area		13.19m²	142ft²
	(modified)	14.51m²	156.2ft²
Weights			
Empty		3,920kg	8,642.1 lb
	(modified)	2,980kg	6,569.7 lb
Loaded		4,152kg	9,153.5 lb
Useful load	(modified)	945kg	2,083.3 lb
Fuel capacity		725 litres	191.5 gallons
with drop tanks		1,450 litres	383 gals
Performance (estimated)			
Max speed		698km/h	434mph
		at 6,000m	at 19,685ft
		684km/h	425mph
	(modified)	at 6,000m	at 19,685ft
Range		608km	378 miles
		at 6,000m	at 19,685ft
		594km	369 miles
	(modified)	at 6,000m	at 19,685ft
Service ceiling		12,100m	39,698ft
	(modified)	12,300m	40,354ft

Armament
One Type 5 30mm cannon with 50 rounds of ammunition

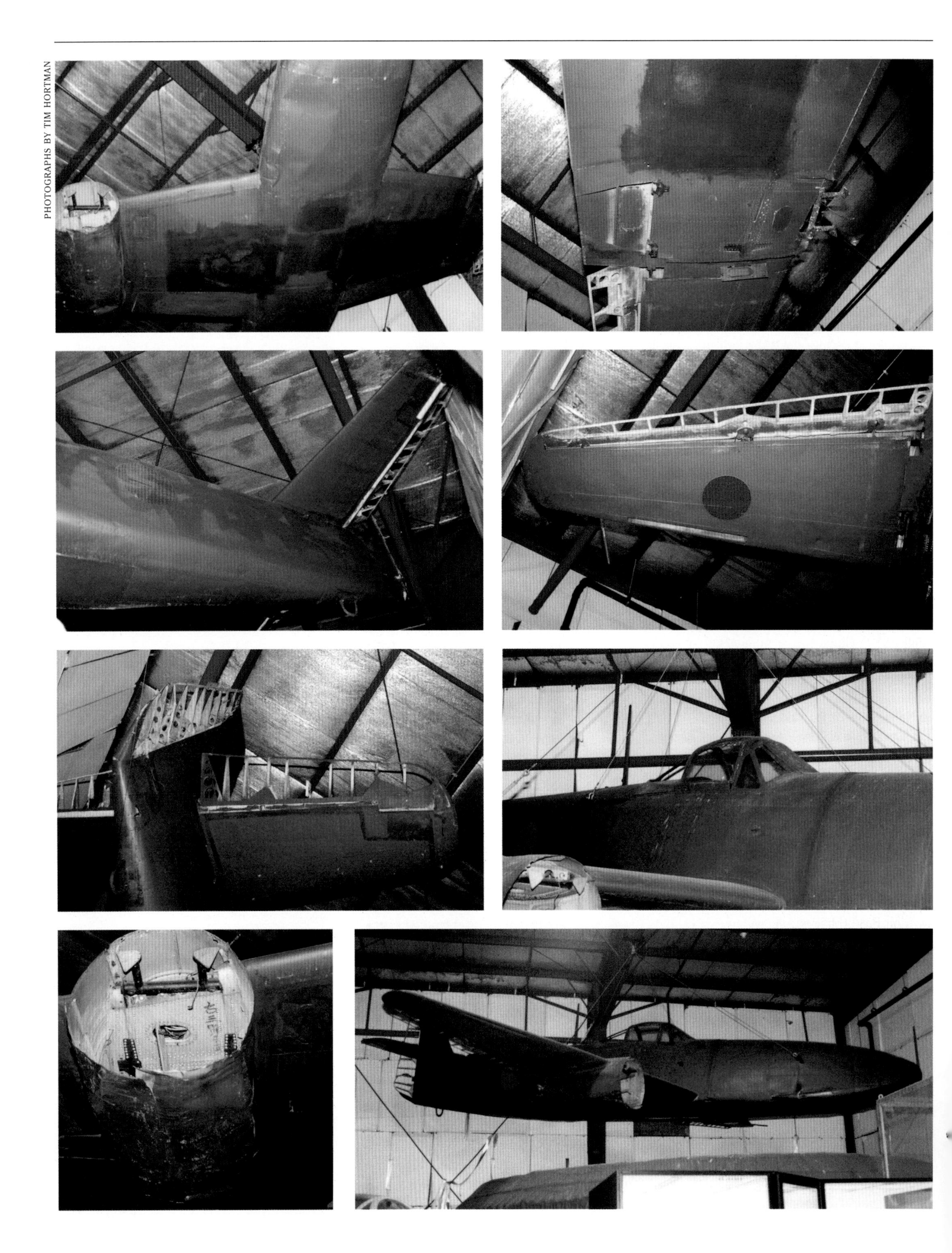

PHOTOGRAPHS BY TIM HORTMAN

of double spar construction with nine main support ribs, all covered with steel and duralumin skinning. Mitsubishi A6M Reisen flap hinges were used on the trailing edge flaps and the wing tips were fabricated from wood and steel sheeting. The outer wing folded upwards. The Kitsuka had a slight gull wing form thanks to 5° dihedral of the centre span and 2° dihedral of the outer wing. All control surfaces were fabric covered. The fuselage had a slight triangular shape, being composed of three sections (nose, centre section and aft). The centre section had the centre wing span built into it and much of this and the other two sections were constructed from sheet steel due to the unavailability of duralumin in quantity. Twenty-four bulkheads were contained within the complete fuselage with two bulkheads coming together where each section met, which were then bolted together to complete the fuselage. Two fuel tanks were fitted, one in front of and the other behind the cockpit. The tail of the Kitsuka was fairly conventional and the aft fuselage line was kept high so that the stabiliser would not be effected by the jet efflux. For the tricycle landing gear, the main gear (to include the brake system) from a Mitsubishi A6M Reisen was modified to suit the Kitsuka and the 600mm x 172mm-sized wheels retracted into the wing. The 400mm x 140mm-sized nose wheel was taken from the tail wheel of a Kūgishō P1Y Ginga and it retracted into the rear of the nose.

After being assembled the Kitsuka was then broken down, loaded into trucks, and moved to Nakajima's Koizumi plant where two Ne 20 engines awaited it. By 27 June, the Kitsuka had been put back together and the engines installed, and two days later weight and balance checks had been completed. The Kitsuka was then declared ready for flight testing. On 30 June 30 1945, both Ne 20 engines on the Kitsuka were started and run for a short time. Flight testing could not be conducted at the airfield at Koizumi because the runway was too short and had many approach restrictions. Misawa Air Base (Misawa Hikōjō), in Aomori Prefecture 684km (425 miles) north of Tōkyō, was also considered since it had open approaches and was rarely visited by Allied long range fighters. However, because of the great distance it was ruled out. Finally, it was settled that the airfield at Kisarazu Air Base (Kisarazu Hikōjō) would be the location for the first flight because it was far closer to Yokosuka than Misawa. Once more the Kitsuka was disassembled, loaded into trucks, and moved to the Kisarazu airfield, adjacent to Tōkyō Bay.

On arrival, the Kitsuka was reassembled and made ready for its first flight. Unfortunately, on 14 July, during engine testing, a loose nut was ingested which completely shattered the blades in one of the compressors. The damage to the engine was so extensive that repairs were simply not possible and replacement the only option. This delayed the flight for many days. As the Kitsuka was being repaired, the personnel for the 724 Kōkūtai, which had been designated a special attack unit and which would fly the Kitsuka in service, had been assembled at Yokosuka after its formation on 1 July 1945. On 15 July, the new unit moved to Misawa Air Base where it began training using Aichi D3A1 and D3A2 carrier bombers (known as *Val* to the Allies), which had been relegated to the training role.

On 27 July, Lieutenant Wada conducted some successful taxi tests with the Kitsuka. High speed taxi tests, however, were prepared by appointed Kitsuka test pilot Lieutenant Commander Susumu Takaoka. Two days after the initial taxi tests, Takaoka ran the Kitsuka up to 129km/h (80mph) and then applied the brakes to test their effectiveness. He found that their stopping power was not adequate, though he felt the problem was not so severe that flight testing had to be stopped. Ground testing was finally completed on 6 August, the same date that Hiroshima was devastated by the 'Little Boy' atomic bomb dropped from the B-29 'Enola Gay'. News of this strike soon reached the Kitsuka crews, technicians and engineers.

7 August 1945 would see excellent flying conditions and the Kitsuka was made ready for flight. Weather reports stated a 24km/h (15mph) southwest wind and a crosswind blowing from the right across the 1,692m (5,550ft) length of Runway 20 that pointed towards Tōkyō Bay. The Kitsuka was only given a partial fuel load to keep the weight to 3,150kg (6,945 lb); this allowed for approximately 16 minutes of flight time. No RATO bottles were fitted so that the take-off characteristics of the aircraft could be assessed. Takaoka climbed into the cockpit and made ready to take-off. On his signal the Ne 20 turbojets were started and he was soon taxiing out to the start of the runway. Once there, he extended the flaps to 20° and kept the brakes set. So as not to cause a compressor stall, Takaoka slowly eased the engine throttles forward and when both had reached 11,000rpm, he released the brakes and the Kitsuka began to roll. Twenty-five seconds later and after a run of 725m (2,378ft), the Kitsuka was airborne and went into the history books as the first Japanese jet to fly.

At 610m (2,000ft), Takaoka levelled off. He was instructed to not retract the landing gear nor exceed 314km/h (195mph). As a test pilot he was used to hearing the roar of a conventional aircraft engine and used such noise as a means to detect problems. However, Takaoka was not prepared for the whine of the turbojets

Kitsuka Special Attacker – data

Specifications in parenthesis refer to the rail launched version.

Type	Special Attacker		
Crew	One		

Powerplant Two Kūgishō Ne 20 axial-flow turbojets, each developing 490kg (1,080 lb) of thrust

Dimensions			
Span		10.00m	32.8ft
Length		9.23m	30.3ft
Height		3.04m	10ft
Wing area		13.19m²	142ft²
Wing loading	(Rail)	270.00kg/m²	55.3 lb/ft²
Weights			
Empty		2,300kg	5,070.6 lb
Loaded		3,550kg	7,826.4 lb
	(Rail)	4,080kg	8,994.8 lb
Performance (estimated)			
Max speed		676km/h	420mph
		at 6,000m	at 19,685ft
		888km/h	552mph
	(Rail)	at 10,000m	at 32,808ft
Landing speed	(Rail)	171km/h	106mph
Range		583km	362 miles
		at 6,000m	at 19,685ft
	(Rail)	814km	506 miles, max
Climb	(Rail)	11 min 50 sec to 6,000m (19,685ft)	
Ceiling		10,700m	35,104ft
		12,100m	39,698ft

Armament One 250kg (551 lb) bomb, one 500kg (1,103 lb) bomb, or two Type 99 20mm cannons

Trainer Kitsuka – data

Type	Trainer		
Crew	Two (Student and Instructor)		

Powerplant Two Kūgishō Ne 20 axial-flow turbojets, each developing 490kg (1,080 lb) of thrust

Dimensions		
Span	10.00m	32.8ft
Length	9.23m	30.3ft
Height	3.04m	10ft
Wing area	13.19m²	142ft²
Weights		
Loaded	4,009kg	8,838.3 lb
Performance (estimated)		
Max speed	721km/h	448mph
	at 6,000m	at 19,685ft
Landing speed	166km/h	103mph
Range	66km at	414 miles
	6,000m	at 19,685ft
Ceiling	12,000m	39,370ft
Service ceiling	10,700m	35,104ft

Armament
Likely to carry the payload as per the Kitsuka

Reconnaissance Kitsuka – data

Type	Reconnaissance	
Crew	Two (Pilot and Observer)	

Powerplant Two Kūgishō Ne 20 axial-flow turbojets, each developing 490kg (1,080 lb) of thrust

Dimensions		
Span	10.00m	32.8ft
Length	9.23m	30.3ft
Height	3.04m	10ft
Wing area	13.19m²	142ft²

Weights		
Loaded	4,241kg	9,349.8 lb

Performance (estimated)		
Max speed	721km/h	448mph
	at 6,000m	at 19,685ft
Landing speed	169km/h	105mph
Range	666km	414 miles
	at 6,000m	at 19,685ft
Ceiling	12,000m	39,370ft
Service ceiling	10,700m	35,104ft

Armament
None (possibly two Type 5 30mm cannons)

Interceptor definitive version – data

Type	Interceptor	
Crew	One	

Powerplant Two Ishikawajima Ne 130 or two Mitsubishi Ne 330 axial-flow turbojets, each developing 900 or 1,300kg (1,984 lb or 2,866 lb) of thrust respectively

Dimensions		
Span	10.00m	32.8ft
Length	9.23m	30.3ft
Height	3.04m	10ft
Wing area	13.19m²	142ft²
Wing loading	302.71kg/m²	62 lb/ft²

Weights		
Empty	3,060kg	6,746.1 lb
Loaded	4,232kg	9,329.9 lb
Useful load	940kg	2,072.3 lb

Performance (estimated)		
Max speed	713km/h	443mph
(Ne 130)	at 6,000m	at 19,685ft
Landing speed	154km/h	96mph
Range	594km	369 miles
	792km	492 miles at cruise
speed		
Climb	11 min 18 sec to 6,000m (19,685ft)	
Ceiling	12,300m	40,354ft

Armament
Two Type 5 30mm cannons or two Ho-155 30mm cannons (IJA); one 500kg (1,102 lb) or 800kg (1,763 lb) bomb (if used as a fighter-bomber)

that told him almost nothing outside of what his instruments reported. He circled Kisarazu airfield, keeping it in sight in case of a failure and because the airspeed kept rising, Takaoka had to constantly throttle back to keep from exceeding the gear down speed limit. A brief test of the control sensitivity showed that the rudder was stiff, the ailerons were heavy but were working and the elevators were overly responsive. When his flight time was up, Takaoka was wary of how he would land. He did not want to drop the turbojets to below 6,000rpm since that risked a flameout from which he would likely not recover in time. Therefore, he chose a long, shallow drop, lowered his flaps 40° and brought the turbojets down to 7,000rpm. On touchdown, he only needed moderate braking to bring the Kitsuka to a stop using only a little under 610m (2,000ft) of runway. Takaoka brought the Kitsuka back to the ramp amid throngs of cheering men. The total flight time was 11 minutes. In his immediate report on the flight, Takaoka stated he had experienced no problems with the engines and had no recommendations for improving the aircraft. During his debriefing, technicians had removed the cowlings to the Ne 20 turbojets and examined each engine. They found no faults and so gave the Kitsuka clearance for another flight, scheduled for 10 August 1945.

For the second flight, more fuel was to be stored and RATO bottles used; this would allow for a longer flight and test the RATO units as boosters. Takaoka would again pilot the Kitsuka. Prior to the flight Takaoka examined the RATO bottles which were fitted to the underside of the fuselage and found fault with the angle at which they were set. However, to adjust them would have taken too much time and so instead of 800kg (1,763 lb) of thrust, the bottles were reduced to 400kg (881 lb) each.

On the day of the second flight, Allied air power was highly active and any flight attempt was bound to be spotted putting the Kitsuka at risk. Consequently, it was decided to wait until the following day on 10 August. However, it would be remembered for the drafting of the Imperial Rescript on the Termination of the War by the Japanese cabinet at the behest of Emperor Hirohito, though the populace had no knowledge of this.

11 August 1945 shared a similar weather pattern to the day the Kitsuka had first flown. The difference was that several IJN and IJA officials of high rank had arrived to witness the second flight. Once more Takaoka climbed into the cockpit, signalled for engine start and taxied out to the runway. As before he extended the flaps 20°, and after receiving the signal to take-off, he slowly opened the throttles until the engines had reached 11,000rpm before releasing the brakes and the Kitsuka rolled forwards. At four seconds into the take-off roll, Takaoka activated the RATO units. Immediately, the acceleration caused the nose of the Kitsuka to pop up, the tail slamming onto the runway. Takaoka fought to get the nose down by jamming the stick forwards but he received no response from the aircraft's elevators. The two RATO units burned for a total of nine seconds and during eight of those seconds Takaoka was helpless and unable to correct the nose up condition. One second prior to the units burning out, the elevators finally took effect and the nose came down so hard Takaoka was sure the front tyre had blown when it contacted the runway. Takaoka felt a sense of deceleration as the Kitsuka reached the halfway point on the runway – his speed at that point was 166km/h/103mph. A second later, with the feeling of deceleration still present, Takaoka decided to abort the take-off and he cut the power to the engines. Unfortunately, the brake issue Takaoka had discovered during high-speed taxi tests now came back to haunt him.

Despite maximum application of the brakes, the Kitsuka showed no signs of slowing and Takaoka was rapidly running out of runway. As he neared one of the taxiways, Takaoka held the left brake in an attempt to make the Kitsuka bring its left wing down into the ground to bleed off speed (known as a ground loop). The Kitsuka's nose turned slightly but this then put the aircraft on a crash course with a group of hangars and buildings. Takaoka reversed the braking, holding the right brake. The Kitsuka came back around onto the runway and despite Takaoka working the brakes, it was to no avail. The aircraft ran out of tarmac and crossed the 100m (328ft) of grass overrun before the landing gear caught in a drainage ditch and collapsed. The Kitsuka slid along its belly until finally coming to a halt by the edge of the water of Tōkyō Bay. The damage to the Kitsuka was extensive. In addition to the mangled landing gear, the two Ne 20 engines were badly damaged, having been jarred from their mounts but still remaining attached to the wings. Initial assessments suggested that the damage was so severe the Kitsuka could not be repaired. On the positive side, the aircraft did not catch fire and causes of the accident were swiftly looked into. IJN Captain Itō, who was present for the flight, was thankful that the Kitsuka did not become airborne with the nose high attitude during the RATO burn. Had that happened and once the RATO bottles cut out, the Kitsuka would have most likely crashed into the ground. A motion picture camera captured the flight and the film developed to see if it could shed any light on the crash.

On 15 August, the film of the ill-fated flight was studied but proved inconclusive as to whether or not the Kitsuka was airborne once the RATO bottles were exhauasted, as was suspected. This would have explained the heavy impact of the front landing gear on the runway and the sense of deceleration experienced by Takaoka. In any case, the Kitsuka would never fly again for at 12.00pm the Imperial Rescript on the Termination of the War was broadcast on the radio bringing World War 2 to a conclusion.

The end of the war would see none of the Kitsuka production plans realised. Nakajima, by the close of December 1945, was to have produced 200 Kitsukas. In reality, Nakajima completed only one with a further 22 under construction. The Kyūshū Hikōki K.K. was, also by the end of the year, to have turned out 135 Kitsuka aircraft but was only able to begin construction of two aircraft, started in July 1945, which remained unfinished by the close of hostilities. A third producer, the Sasebo Naval Arsenal (Sasebo Kaigun Kōshō), was scheduled to have begun production of the Kitsuka in September 1945 with 115 completed by the close of December. The fourth production line was to be at the Kasumigaura Naval Air Arsenal with the commencement of Kitsuka construction scheduled for October 1945; 80 aircraft were to have been completed by the end of December.

A number of variants of the Kitsuka were planned, none of which would see completion come the capitulation. One of these was a two-seat trainer. Given the nature of the Kitsuka, it was appreciated that a trainer would be required to help the conversion of pilots used to conventional piston engined aircraft to the peculiarities of a turbojet powered aircraft. Five of the Kitsuka airframes under production by Nakajima were modified by including a second cockpit for the instructor. Outside of the inclusion of the additional cockpit, it is unknown exactly what other changes were made in the Kitsuka to accommodate it. If there were a parallel to the German Me 262B-1a two-seat trainer, the rear fuel tank would have been removed to make room for the instructor's cockpit. The German solution to the loss of fuel was to utilise the two front bomb racks for drop tanks. Whether Nakajima considered the use of drop tanks (as the Kitsuka could use them) or simply accepted the reduced endurance for the sake of expediency is not known. The two-seat trainer would be the only variant of the Kitsuka to reach the production phase.

It was planned that some of the two-seaters were to be modified for reconnaissance roles. The instructor's cockpit was to be removed and replaced with a crew position for an observer. He was to have a Type 96 Model 3 radio set at his disposal for use in relaying target information to other aircraft. It is unknown

MUNEO HOSAKA

Nakajima Kitsuka – data

Contemporaries Messerschmitt Me 262A-1a/U3 and Me 262A-5a (Germany), Messerschmitt Me 262A-2a/U2 (Germany), Messerschmitt Me 262B-1a (Germany), Messerschmitt Me 262C-1a, Me 262C-2b, and Me 262C-3 (Germany)

Type	Attack Bomber
Crew	One

Powerplant Two Kūgishō Ne 20 axial-flow turbojets, each developing 490kg (1,080 lb) of thrust

Dimensions

Span	10.00m	32.8ft
	5.24m	17.2ft (wings folded)
Length	9.23m	30.3ft
Height	3.04m	10ft
Wing area	13.19m²	142ft²
Wing loading	268.53kg/m²	55 lb/ft²
Power loading	1.6kg/kg	3.7 lb/lbst

Weights

Empty	2,300kg	5,070.6 lb
Loaded	3,550kg	7,826.4 lb
Max loaded	4,312kg	9,506.3 lb
Useful load	1,249kg	2,753.5 lb

Performance

Max speed	621km/h	386mph at sea level
	679km/h	422mph
	at 6,000m	at 19,685ft
	695km/h	432mph
	at 10,000m	at 32,808ft
Max speed	509km/h	316mph
	at sea level, with 500kg (1,102 lb) bomb	
Take-off speed	148km/h	92mph
	at a weight of 3,950kg (8,708.2 lb)	
Landing speed	158km/h	98mph
	at a weight of 2,570kg (5,665.8 lb)	
Take-off length	504m	1,653.5ft
	with RATO with zero wind at	
	a weight of 4,200m (9,259.4 lb)	
	1,363m	4,471.7ft
	without RATO with zero wind at	
	a weight of 3,950kg (8,708.2 lb)	
Range	583km	362 miles
	at 6,000m	at 19,685ft
	888km	552 miles
	at 10,000m	at 32,808ft
	203km	126 miles
	with maximum bomb load	
	555km	345 miles
	with 551 lb bomb load	
	948km	589 miles at cruise speed
Climb	12 min 16 sec to 6,000m (19,685ft)	
	32 min 42 sec to 10,000m (32,808ft)	
Ceiling	12,000m	39,370ft
Service ceiling	10,700m	35,104ft
Fuel capacity	725 litres	191.5 gallons
	1,450 litres	383 gals with drop tanks

Armament
One 500kg (1,102 lb) or 800 (1,763 lb) bomb

Deployment
None. One finished aircraft was built by Nakajima (two if one counts the airframe completed for load testing) with a further 24 in various stages of construction by war's end.

Survivors
Nakajima Kitsuka (tail number A-103)
With the loss of the only completed Kitsuka following its crash on 11 August 1945, examples captured by the US following the war were from the stocks of incomplete Kitsuka aircraft found in Nakajima and Kyūshū's plants. This particular Kitsuka arrived at NAS Patuxent River and on 18 October 1946 was shipped to San Diego, California. The aircraft eventually found its way back to the Paul. E. Garber facility where it is believed to be the second Kitsuka held in storage there. Some sources have the serial for this Kitsuka as 7337.

Nakajima Kitsuka (tail number A-104)
Also at NAS Patuxent River with A-103, it was later shipped to NAS Willow Grove in Willow Grove, Pennsylvania on 23 October 1946. Following its arrival, no further trace of the Kitsuka is known.

Nakajima Kitsuka (no tail number assigned)
This Kitsuka was received in the US and appeared on a storage manifest in 1950 being housed at NAS Norfolk in Norfolk, Virginia. In 1960, it was shipped to the Paul E. Garber facility. From 1972 until the facility closed to the public, it was on display hanging from the ceiling (see page 118).

if any cameras were to be fitted but it would not be unreasonable to conclude that the observer would at least have had a hand-held camera.

An interceptor version of the Kitsuka was discussed, as previously mentioned, and a number of general arrangements for it were considered. One of these was the inclusion of a single Type 5 30mm cannon with 50 rounds of ammunition installed in the nose. A second design was to feature enlarged and extended wings incorporating flaps and double-edged leading slots. A more definitive interceptor was to replace the Ne 20 engines with either Ne 130 or Ne 330 turbojets. A second cannon was to be added in the nose. Interestingly, it appears that if the IJA had used the Kitsuka, the Type 5 cannons would be replaced with two Ho-155 30mm cannons. This may have been a stopgap or fallback if the IJA's own Ki-201 Karyū failed to materialise. With the heavier weight the structure of the Kitsuka, including the landing gear, would have been strengthened. A fighter-bomber model was envisioned for the definitive interceptor by including a fitting for a single 500kg (1,102 lb) or 800kg (1,763 lb) bomb.

As originally planned, a model of the Kitsuka was proposed for shimpū missions. Similar to the Kitsuka as constructed, this version was to carry either a 500kg (1,102 lb) bomb, a 250kg (551 lb) bomb or two Type 99 20mm cannons. With the latter, it could be assumed the cannons would be used for self-defence and for firing at the target before ramming the aircraft into the victim using any remaining fuel and ammunition as the secondary explosive element. A variant of this Kitsuka was to utilise a 200m (656ft) launch rail that Kūgishō had been designing and which they expected to have ready for testing by September 1945. Using a rocket booster, the Kitsuka would leave the launch rail at 220km/h (137mph) at an acceleration of between three to four 'g'.

In regards to the 724 Kōkūtai, with the end of the war they would never see their Kitsuka aircraft. It was planned that by November 1945 the unit would have been based near Yokosuka at a site along the Miura Peninsula, west of Tōkyō Bay. It was expected that by then the unit would have received sixteen Kitsukas. In addition, the unit was to use one of the handfuls of Kawanishi E15K1 Shiun (meaning 'Violet Cloud'; codenamed *Norm* by the Allies) reconnaissance floatplanes, which were removed from active service following their disastrous combat debut in 1944. The Shiun, operating from a nearby harbour, would locate the shipping targets, mark them and then loiter in the area to broadcast radio signals. The Kitsukas would then be rapidly launched and, by means of the radio signals received through the Kuruku system, attack the ships at low level with bombs and ramming tactics. Had the reconnaissance version of the Kitsuka gone into production, the 724 Kōkūtai was to receive it as a replacement for the far more vulnerable Shiun.

Finally, with the close of the war, none of the projected turbojet successors to the Ne 20 would enter production. One prototype of the Ishikawajima Ne 130 had been completed by June 1945 but testing was unfinished by the time the war ended. Nakajima started development of the Ne 230 in May 1945 and had three under construction by August 1945. However, none of the engines were completed or tested. Mitsubishi was unable to construct a Ne 330 and so it remained on the design board.

A note about the use of the name Kitsuka as opposed to the more commonly used Kikka. Kitsuka is the proper translation of the kanji characters. However, it is pronounced 'kikka'. Kikka was used in post-war reports as phonetically it approximated to Kitsuka and thus has become the accepted name of the aircraft. Neither name is incorrect. Also, some sources use the J9Y1 (or sometimes J9N1) designation for the Kitsuka. While logical for the interceptor version of the Kitsuka, there is no evidence in wartime Japanese sources to support the designation. One may also find the designation J8N1 used but this is not supported.

Other Aircraft

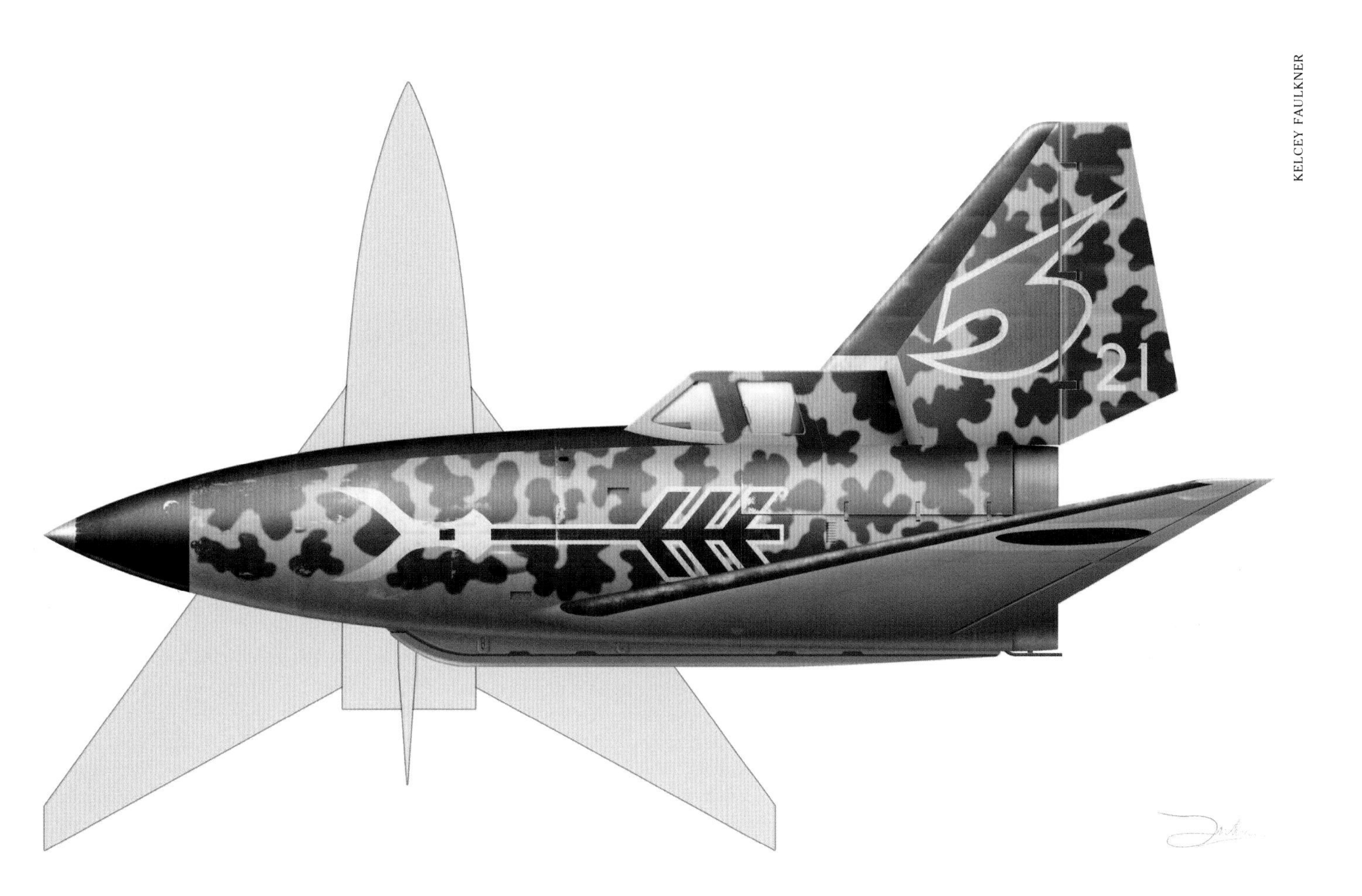

KELCEY FAULKNER

The aircraft depicted here sports the colours and markings of the 53rd Sentai operating in defence of the Japanese homeland.

The Rammer

The practice of tai-atari, which literally means 'body crashing', was not unique to Japan. The deliberate ramming of one aircraft by another aircraft has happened as far back as World War 1 when Imperial Russian Air Force pilot Pyotr Nesterov used his 1912 Morane-Saulnier monoplane to ram an Austrian Albatross B.II on 26 August 1914. In World War 2, the first ramming attack went to Lt. Col. Leopold Pamula who used his stricken PZL P.11c to down a Messerschmitt Bf 109 on 1 September 1939. It would be the Russians, Germans and Japanese who would make ramming a part of their war doctrine.

Whereas the Japanese would simply use available aircraft to conduct ramming or tai-atari attacks, the Germans took it a step further by producing and designing aircraft specific to the task. One operational example was the Focke-Wulf Fw 190A-8/R7. To enable the fighter to penetrate bomber formations the Rammjäger (or Sturmböcke) was fitted with armour plating to enable it to weather defensive fire as well as possibly surviving a successful ram. Sturmstaffel 1 was the first Luftwaffe unit to operate the fighter. As the war went on and US bombers filled the skies, and the Luftwaffe was more and more hard pressed to stem the tide, a number of dedicated rammer aircraft designs appeared. One of them was the Zeppelin Rammer.

The Rammer was a small, single seat aircraft that was towed into the air. As it was designed for ramming, the constant cord main wings were strengthened by the use of three tubular spars along the forward edge of the wings. The remainder of the aircraft was bolstered to allow it to withstand impact forces. A single Schmidding 109-533 solid fuel rocket developing 1,000kg (2,205 lb) of thrust was fitted into the tail and the motor provided a total of twelve seconds of thrust. In the nose were fourteen R4M rockets or a single SG 118 battery. The cockpit was within an armoured tub providing 28mm of armour plate in the front and sides with 20mm in the rear. The glazing was 80mm of bulletproof glass in the front and 40mm thick on the sides. The method of attack was to tow the Rammer within .48km (0.3 of a mile) from the target and release it. The pilot would ignite the rocket motor to boost speed and fire off the nose weapon at the first target before making a ram attack on a second (or the same) target. After engaging in the ram attack, the pilot would glide back down to earth. The Rammer was test flown, without power, in January 1945 and a pre-production batch of sixteen aircraft was ordered. However, Zeppelin's production facilities were destroyed by US bombing before their construction could commence.

The Japanese would use aircraft already in operational service for ramming attacks such as that Kawasaki Ki-45 and even stripped down Kawasaki Ki-61 Hein fighters. It was long thought that Japan never developed a dedicated rammer aircraft of its own but this is no longer the case. Recently discovered in the archives of the Japanese National Institute for Defence Studies is just such a project.

The aircraft was a joint venture between the IJA and the IJN, something that occurred with more regularity towards the close of the war. The design was based on the Syūsui-shiki Kayaku Rocketto (meaning 'Autumn Water'-type ram attack rocket), a project started in March 1945 for a unmanned, remote controlled anti-bomber missile. The plan was to ground launch the missile, guide it remotely towards the target, engage the target via ramming, and then recover the missile (if it survived the collision) for reuse. Design work was carried out by the Kokukyoko (the Aeronautical Bureau) and, although a mock-up was completed, the war ended before finalised production plans could be completed, let alone the missile ever being tested. The missile's design borrowed heavily from the Mitsubishi J8M Syūsui in terms of its shape. Interestingly, the Messerschmitt Enzian anti-aircraft missile had a shape influenced by the company's Me 163 rocket interceptor, of which the J8M was the Japanese version (see page 96).

The piloted version used much the same design as the missile and was a small, tailless aircraft featuring low mounted 45° swept wings. The fuselage was bullet shaped with a large vertical stabiliser into which the cockpit was blended. Located in the back of the fuselage were four Type 4 Mark 1 Model 20 rockets, the same as those used on the Kūgishō MXY7 Ōka which on such a small aircraft pushed the maximum speed to an estimated 1.125km/h (699mph or just over Mach 0.91) – i.e. a transonic speed. With a speed in the transonic range, this aircraft would have presented a formidable challenge to the Japanese given that even the Germans had only just started investigating the problems of high-speed flight when their jet and rocket aircraft began to push into such speeds with the resultant issues of compressibility. It is unknown if the Japanese rammer had swept wings because the designers understood the principles in relation to overcoming compressibility problems at transonic speeds, or if the shape was chosen as a means to provide an angled cutting surface to facilitate ramming attacks, or as a drag reducing planform. The wings were strengthened to withstand the high impact forces experienced when striking the enemy bomber. Even though the rammer could rely on speed as a defence when under power, it still had to contend with the defensive armament of the B-29 and thought the pilot had some measure of armour plating and bulletproof glass to protect him. The aircraft was certainly capable of gliding back to base to be refuelled and relaunched once it had conducted its attacks. Given the small size of the plane, no landing gear was fitted. As such, it is likely the underside of the fuselage was reinforced or had a skid installed. How it was to be launched is unknown – it could have been towed aloft, catapult launched or perhaps even vertically launched.

In a ram attack, typically the tail would be targeted because the loss of the tail assembly would send the bomber out of control. Striking the wings and engines was another focus of ramming attacks. Finally, the aircraft fuselage was the other key area to strike. The probable mission profile of the rammer flying from a ground base would include being positioned within very close proximity of likely bombing targets. With the short burn time of the rockets (8-10 seconds) the aircraft's operational radius would have been very limited. After launching, as bombers came into range the pilot would attempt to ram into either the tail or wing of the target with the objective of severing it from the fuselage. If enough speed momentum remained after the initial hit, another ram attack would be made. Should the aircraft remain in flyable condition and if the pilot did not elect to ram his entire plane into a target, he would return to base where the rockets would be replaced. If the bombers were still close by, he could fly another sortie. If the rammer was towed into the air, the rockets would most likely have been fired on approach and again after hitting a target. This would provide enough power to grant a second pass with sufficient speed to allow for significant damage to be inflicted on the bomber when it struck.

However, the Japanese rammer would remain a paper project only. It is unclear if the design was to be the definitive rammer model or simply a proposed concept.

The Rammer – data

As the design was never built, the specifications are estimates based on the original design sketch and data.

Type Rammer
Crew One

Powerplant Four Type 4 Mark 1 Model 20 rockets with a combined 1,102kg (2,232 lb) of thrust

Dimensions

Span	4.41m	14.5ft
Length	2.89m	9.5ft
Height	N/A	
Wing area	N/A	
Wing loading	N/A	
Power loading	N/A	

Weights

Empty	N/A
Loaded	N/A
Maximum	N/A

Performance

Speed	1,125km/h	699mph
Climb	32 seconds to 10,000m (32,808ft)	
Range	N/A	
Endurance	N/A	
Ceiling	N/A	

Armament
None

Deployment
None. The rammer remained a design draft only.

The Kamikaze Airplane

Kamikaze, which in Japanese means 'divine wind', was not a term used by the Japanese to reference their special attack units but came into common use in the West. Instead, shimpū and shimbu were more often used by both the IJN and the IJA respectively. May 1944 would signal the beginning of dedicated suicide attack missions against the US and her allies. The effect of being on the receiving end of such attacks was horrific and would take its toll on US sailors.

A post-war report by the US Strategic Bombing Survey bluntly stated that kamikaze attacks were effective and given the situation for the Japanese, very practical. Statistics of sunk and damaged US ships during the Philippines campaign (October 1944 to January 1945) showed that kamikaze attacks were far more effectual. Of course, being subjected to such attacks wreaked havoc on morale as well as a surge in mental illness. The US Navy, the focus of the majority of kamikaze attacks, saw such illness rise by 50 per cent in 1944 when compared to 1941. So bad was the problem that during the Okinawa campaign, the US Navy stopped warning crews that kamikaze attacks were to be expected as they only added to the sailor's stress levels. General George C. Marshall wrote in a 1945 report to the US Secretary of War that, 'The American soldier has a very active imagination... and is inclined to endow the death-dealing weapons of the enemy with extraordinary qualities...' And thus the 'Kamikaze Airplane' appears on the scene.

Following the close of World War 2, an illustration of an aircraft appeared in either *Popular Mechanics* or *Popular Science* magazine. The aircraft, labelled a kamikaze plane, was a curious mixture of what appeared to be the tail of a Mitsubishi A6M Reisen, a fuselage not too unlike the Nakajima Kitsuka and a canopy similar to aircraft such as the Kawanishi N1K1 Kyōfu (meaning 'Mighty Wind' but known as *Rex* to the Allies) or the Nakajima Ki-84 Hayate (meaning 'Gale'; *Frank* to the Allies). Even more curious was the fact that the aircraft used air-cooled radial engines, one in each wing, but in a pusher configuration.

The Kamikaze Airplane was said to have been sighted by some US Navy crew members as it flew over their ships. It was from their descriptions that the illustration of the aircraft was created. The result was certainly unlike any plane then in the theatre but there is some precedent in terms of genuine aircraft being misidentified. One example was the 'Kawasaki Type 97 Medium Bomber' that was given the codename *Julia*. Because of very inaccurate illustrations of the plane that were derived from a written description, *Julia* was in fact the Kawasaki Ki-48 (*Lily*). It may very well be that the Kamikaze Airplane was actually a US Grumman F7F-2N Tigercat of which two US Marine Corps squadrons equipped with the plane began operating from Okinawa in September 1945. One was VMF(N) 531 while the second was a photo reconnaissance unit. With the Tigercat being new to the Pacific Theatre, it can be surmised that some sailors and crew mistook the twin-engine fighter for a Japanese plane and subsequently described something other than what was actually seen. However, the Kamikaze Airplane was written off as a spectre of the imaginations of sailors who had borne the brunt of kamikaze attacks.

The Kamikaze Airplane illustrated is derived from the magazine artwork and is shown in the colours of the 18th Sentai, operating from Kashiwa Airfield, Japan, spring 1945.

DANIEL UHR

The Kamikaze Airplane – data

No specifications were provided for the aircraft.

Deployment

None. The Kamikaze Aircraft was strictly fictional.

Mitsubishi T.K.4 Type 0

KELCEY FAULKNER

The illustration provided here is an interpretation of the Type 0 as described in the O.N.I. 249 manual and is shown in the colours and markings of the 3rd Chutai, 26th Sentai.

At the outset of hostilities in the Pacific, American intelligence had very little information on just exactly what aircraft the Japanese were fielding. In part this lack of knowledge sprang from poor intelligence management and censorship of periodicals and other publications by the Japanese authorities. In scrambling to document Japanese aviation, invariably US intelligence officers turned to Japanese magazines as a means of gaining information. However, there were pitfalls to using such sources and the Mitsubishi T.K.4 Type 0 was just one example.

The T.K.4 appeared in a section of the Japanese aviation magazine *Sora* entitled 'Dreams of Future Designers'. The issue was published in April 1941. The T.K.4 was depicted as a twin-engine fighter whose design was rather similar to the German Messerschmitt Bf 110. The aircraft, although a fighter, was shown with a glazed nose along with the expected glazing over the pilot and crew positions. Each of the low mounted wings sported an inline engine in a very streamlined cowling, each motor driving a three-bladed propeller. What weapons the T.K.4 carried was unknown nor was the crew compliment listed, although two or three could be estimated. Also lacking was any data on the performance of the T.K.4.

Information on the T.K.4 would also appear in a US magazine. The 25 December 1941 issue of *Flight* mentioned the aircraft as a twin-engine, twin-tail monoplane fighter. From these sources, the US intelligence determined that the T.K.4 was a bona fide fighter that would be encountered in combat. Major Frank T. McCoy, Jr., the head of the Material Section of the Directorate of Intelligence, Allied Air Forces, Southwest Pacific Area, would assign the T.K.4 the codename *Frank*, taking his own first name. It was McCoy who arrived at the method of assigning names to Japanese aircraft in order to simplify identification.

At some point, the T.K.4 Type 0 fighter took on a completely different appearance. When the Japanese Aircraft Manual, O.N.I. 249 (Office of Naval Intelligence), was first published in December 1942, the Mitsubishi Type 0 was no longer called the T.K.4. Although no illustration was provided in the manual, the Type 0 was described as an army fighter based on the Dutch Fokker D.XXIII. The D.XXIII was a twin-engine fighter that mounted the engines in the fuselage in a push-pull configuration. It was also a twin-boom design that was under development and in flight-testing until the German invasion. The manual stated that the Type 0 used two German BMW engines, each developing 750hp, but that a redesign of the aircraft would see it using two 1,000hp Mitsubishi Kinsei air-cooled radial engines. No further information was made available.

When the original T.K.4 Frank failed to materialise in combat, McCoy removed his name from the T.K.4 and reassigned it to the Nakajima Ki-84 Hayate (meaning 'Gale') which was a fighter very much in use, being first encountered in combat in early 1944. The Type 0, as described in the O.N.I. 249 manual, was given the codename *Harry* after Colonel Harry Cunningham, a friend of McCoy's, who was the intelligence officer for General Ennis Whitehead. At the time it was believed that the Type 0 would eventually be seen in action but, just like the T.K.4, it never would and the Type 0 was dropped from the intelligence publications.

Mitsubishi T.K.4 Type 0 – data

No information on the specifications, if any ever existed, is available for the T.K.4 or the Type 0.

Deployment
None. The T.K.4 existed only as an illustration in a magazine while the Type 0 was a description in a manual.

Nakajima AT27

The T.K.4 was not the only Japanese aircraft uncovered in the pages of *Sora*. The same 'Dreams of Future Designers' article in which that image was unearthed also included the Nakajima AT27. Several months later, the 25 December 1941 issue of *Flight*, a US magazine, would also feature these planes, along with several others, lending credence to the idea that they were genuine aircraft in use by the Japanese.

The AT27 was novel in a number of ways. On the outside, the fuselage was sleek and well streamlined. The wings were low-mounted with a conventional tailplane. Inside, however, the AT27 featured two 12-cylinder inline engines each rated at 1,250hp and was reported to obtain a maximum speed of 660km/h (410mph). One engine was in the nose while the other was situated behind the cockpit. Contra-rotating propellers were used, the rear engine driving its propeller via an extension shaft. To maintain the excellent aerodynamic properties, the engines were reported to have been provided with a 'steam cooling' system. This may have been a surface evaporation system. Such a system took the steam created after the water had passed through the engine and ran it through piping in the wings where the cooler airflow would condense the steam back into water that was cycled back through the engine. The pilot was afforded some protection by the engines in front and behind him but the AT27 could also carry additional armour not only for the pilot but for the engines as well. What type of weapons the AT27 was to carry were not known.

Based on its appearance in the magazines, the AT27 was believed to be a bona fide fighter that could be encountered and thus Allied intelligence gave the AT27 the code-name *Gus*. However, the AT27 would never be seen or met in battle since, as was later discovered, the aircraft was fictitious. *Gus* was soon dropped from the Japanese aircraft intelligence rolls.

Interestingly, the AT27 was very similar to the very real Kawasaki Ki-64 whose development began in October 1940. Both used 12-cylinder inline engines, one in the nose and the other behind the cockpit, driving contra-rotating propellers. In addition, both used a surface evaporation system. Perhaps by sheer coincidence, one of the Japanese illustrations of the AT27 that was published in *Sora* and later in *Flight* showed it sporting the number 64 on the fuselage.

The 3-view illustration of the AT27 is in the markings and colouration of an aircraft of the 244th Sentai operating in the defence of Tōkyō, 1944-1945. The side view below depicts the AT27 as it appeared in *Sora* magazine."

Nakajima AT27 – data

Contemporaries Republic XP-72 (US), Fisher XP-75 Eagle (US)

Type Fighter
Crew One

Powerplant Two 12-cylinder, water-cooled V-engines each developing 1,250hp and each driving a three-bladed propeller

Dimensions		
Span	N/A	
Length	N/A	
Height	N/A	
Wing area	22.01m²	237ft²
Wing loading	239.23kg/m²	49 lb/ft²
Power loading	N/A	

Weights		
Empty	3,629kg	8,000 lb
Loaded	5,262kg	11,600 lb
Usable load	1,633kg	3,600 lb

Performance		
Max speed	660km/h	410mph
Cruise speed	N/A	
Range	2,012km	1,250 miles
Endurance	N/A	
Climb	N/A	
Ceiling	N/A	

Armament N/A

Deployment None. The AT27 was purely a fictional aircraft.

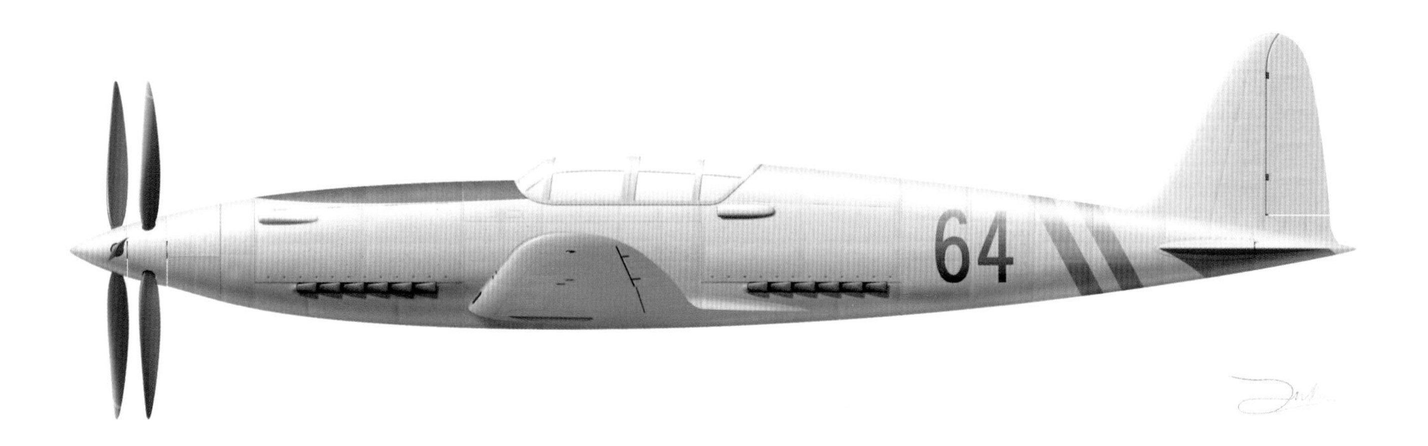

KELCEY FAULKNER

DANIEL UHR

S-31 Kurowashi

As we have already seen, the April 1941 issue of *Sora* misled Allied intelligence over the nature and extent of Japanese aircraft design. As the war continued, none of the four aircraft that feature in the April issue were encountered and subsequently dropped from Allied intelligence publications. However, *Sora* continued and so did the section responsible. How often the 'Dreams of Future Designers' portion of the magazine appeared is not known but one issue from either 1944 or 1945 contained a design that was nothing short of fantastic. This was the S-31 Kurowashi, or Black Eagle.

The Kurowashi was a four-engine heavy bomber concept. What was unique about the aircraft was that all of the engines were housed within the fuselage and the Kurowashi used a push-pull configuration. Both in the front and the rear of the fuselage were two 2,500hp, 24-cylinder, liquid cooled, inline X-engines, driving a pair of contra-rotating, three-bladed propellers via a gearbox. With this powerplant the Kurowashi was to boast a top speed of 689km/h (428mph), but such a powerful engine of this type would not see service with the Japanese air forces. However, this was not for a lack of trying: it may or may not be that the originator of the Kurowashi was aware of the Yokosuka YE3 series of engines.

In 1940, the IJN initiated development of the YE3A, a 24-cylinder, liquid-cooled, X-engine that was to produce 2,500hp. An X-engine is produced by having paired V-block engines horizontally opposed to each other with the cylinders in four banks driving a common crankshaft and thus, when viewed head-on, appearing as a 'X'. The major benefit to using such a configuration is that the engine is more compact than a comparable radial engine or standard V-engine. However, X-engines are far more complex to construct and service and are heavier. It was not be until October 1943 that the first YE3B [Ha-74 Model 01] (also known as the Ken No.1) was completed and tested. The YE3B was designed to be housed inside the wing. A second model, the YE3E [Ha-74 Model 11) (Ken No.2), was rated at 3,200hp and was slated to be completed in March 1944. Unlike the YE3B, the YE3E was designed to be housed within the fuselage. As it was neither engine would see service by the time the war ended. Interestingly, a surviving YE3B engine was fitted with a two-stage reduction gear and a extension shaft that would have been used to drive two, contra-rotating propellers.

With a wingspan of just over 33m (107ft), the Kurowashi was by no means a small aircraft. The plane was just under 21m (70ft) in length and a height just shy of 6m (20ft). These dimensions were very similar to the Boeing B-17 bomber. The Kurowashi sported horizontal stabilisers which ended in ovoid shaped vertical stabilisers.

The Kurowashi was certainly not lacking for weaponry. A total of eight 7.7mm machine guns and four 23mm cannons were carried by the bomber. 7.7mm was a calibre used by both the IJA and the IJN, but on the other hand, the Japanese did not field a 23mm cannon in any form, either in aircraft or on the ground. The IJN did use a 25mm anti-aircraft cannon (Type 96) but did not apply the weapon to aircraft. The IJA also experimented with a 25mm aircraft cannon but abandoned it in favour of the 30mm cartridge. Why the creator of the Kurowashi decided to use 23mm as the calibre for the cannons remains unknown.

What is known is the novel arrangement of the defensive armament. Fitted directly into the leading edge of each wing were two ball turrets. The outer turret contained one 23mm cannon while the inner turret sported two 7.7mm machine guns. Directly opposite these front-facing turrets was another set of ball turrets. As the trailing edge of the wing was too thin to allow the turrets to be internally mounted, each turret was fitted into the end of a nacelle that extended from the back of the wing. Therefore, each wing was fitted with four turrets for a total of two 23mm cannons and four 7.7mm machine guns. To control these turrets the Kurowashi relied on two gunners, the bombardier and co-pilot. Both gunners had positions facing to the rear of the aircraft behind the bomb bay. The first gunner station was in the upper portion of the fuselage while the second was in a ventral station. Weapon sights were provided along with the controls to manipulate and fire the turrets. The bombardier and the co-pilot stations were also provided with a sight and turret controls so that if they were not occupied with other duties they could man the weapons. It is likely that the bombardier and co-pilot had control of the forward facing turrets while the two gunners maintained control over the rear facing weapons.

For its war load the Kurowashi could carry just over 7,257kg (8 tons) of bombs, about 1,814kh (2 tons) less than the Boeing B-29. The bomb bay was divided into two and each section could hold six bombs to give a total of twelve. Beneath the main bomb racks were hinged panels, one per side. Each panel held four bombs for total of eight. When the bomb bay doors opened, the bombs suspended from the panels would be released and the panels swing aside so the remainder of the bombs could drop. This arrangement was created to maximise the payload space available. Situated directly above the bomb bay were fuel tanks and it was likely the wings also housed fuel.

The Kurowashi used a tricycle landing gear system with the nose wheel retracting into the fuselage while the main landing gear went up into the wings. However, because of the heavy tail and to prevent damage to the rear propellers while on the ground or during take-off and landing, a large, retractable tail wheel was fitted to the back of the fuselage.

For its crew the bomber had five men: pilot, co-pilot, bombardier and two gunners. One of the gunners served as the radio operator as the radio station was situated in front of the upper gunner's position.

It may very well be that Allied intelligence was aware of this design and it was also likely that by 1944-1945, intelligence officers were no longer taking aircraft illustrated in the 'Dreams of Future Designers' section in *Sora* magazine at face value. The Kurowashi was a creation that would have been very difficult to execute in reality and may not even have been feasible.

S-31 Kurowashi – data

Contemporaries
Daimler-Benz Schnellbomber mit DB P83 Gruppenmotor (Germany)

Type Heavy Bomber
Crew Five

Powerplant Four 24-cylinder, liquid-cooled X-engines, each developing 2,500hp, each pair driving two, metal 3-bladed contra-rotating propellers

Dimensions		
Span	32.82m	107.7ft
Length	21.09m	69.2ft
Height	5.88m	19.3ft
Wing area	1.33.00m^2	1,431.6ft^2

Weights		
Loaded	17,850kg	39,352 lb

Performance		
Max speed	690km/h	429mph
Cruise speed	589km/h	366mph
Landing speed	145km/h	90mph
Range	5,900km	3,666 miles
Ceiling	15,100m	49,540ft
Fuel Weight	8,000kg	17,636 lb

Armament
Eight 7.7mm machine guns and four 23mm cannons (see text for arrangement); up to 8,000kg (17,636 lb) of bombs

Deployment None. The S-31 Kurowashi was purely a paper, if not impractical, design in a magazine.

The Kurowashi depicted here is in the markings of the 2nd Chutai, 62nd Sentai. Historically, this unit operated Mitsubishi Ki-21 *(Sally)*, Nakajima Ki-49 Donryu *(Helen)* and Mitsubishi Ki-67 Hiryū *(Peggy)* bombers.

RONNIE OLSTHOORN

T.K.19

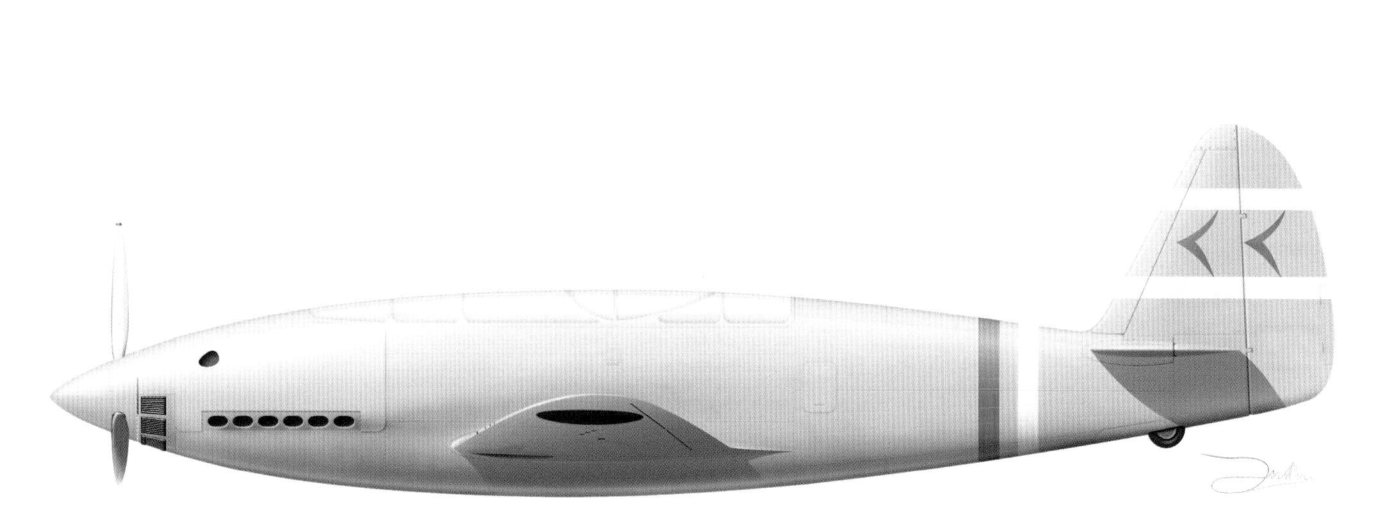

KELCEY FAULKNER

The T.K.19 depicted here is shown in the colours of the 77th Hiko Sentai during operations in Burma, 1941-1942.

It was difficult for the US and her Allies to acquire intelligence about the Japanese war industry as far as HUMINT (HUMan INTelligence) was concerned. This was due to the relative difficulty associated with either turning a Japanese source or inserting a foreign spy into Japan who was capable of avoiding detection. Once it was broken, the PURPLE code (as used by Japanese foreign offices) and the later JN-25 code (as it was labelled by the US) used by the IJN provided a wealth of information and intelligence, but human intelligence and cipher cracking were only a part of the overall processes. One avenue used prior to the war was the gathering of publications such as books and magazines. Besides being relatively innocuous to purchase in Japan, such sources could be obtained outside of Japan and were therefore easier to gather. It was one such publication issued just prior to the start of hostilities that revealed the T.K.19 to intelligence officers.

The illustration of the T.K.19 appeared in the April 1941 issue of the Japanese aviation magazine *Sora* in a section entitled 'Dreams of Future Designers'. The T.K.19 showed a fuselage that was elongated and ovoid in shape. More interestingly, it showed a canopy that could be lowered to fit flush with the top of the fuselage thereby eliminating the drag of a standard canopy. This same concept was seen in the Russian Bisnovat SK and Bartini Stal'-6, both of which were high-speed aircraft whose designers were seeking military applications for their charges. Each wing of the T.K.19 showed what appeared to be three weapon ports, totalling six machine guns or cannons. There were also ducts in each of the wing roots, ostensibly to cool the engine. A radiator bath may have been located in the nose of the aircraft. Given the flush canopy, the T.K.19 may have used a system similar to the Stal'-6 in which for take-off and landing the canopy hood was hinged upwards and the pilot would raise his seat. Whether the T.K.19 used a periscope vision system for the pilot once in flight as was proposed in the Soviet Lavochkin LL fighter was not known.

Like many of the other aircraft in this section, the T.K.19 would later appear in the American magazine *Flight* in the 25 December 1941 issue. The description made no mention of the more striking features of the plane as described and shown in the Japanese magazine. Instead, the article, which contained no illustration, reported the T.K.19 was of orthodox appearance save that the aircraft had a twin row radial engine in the rear of the fuselage and was cooled via ducts. From this, a drawing evolved that took the basic shape of the Japanese T.K.19 and made it more conventional, to the point that it bore a slight resemblance to the Curtiss P-40 Warhawk, a plane that first flew in 1938 and one that Japanese pilots first encountered in combat in late 1941. The changes from the Japanese T.K.19 included doing away with the flush canopy (providing a more standard style seen in many aircraft), moving the wings higher up the fuselage, adding pronounced wing root fairings that extended from the nose of the aircraft to rear of the cockpit (the latter being set behind the wings) and having a main landing gear reminiscent of the Brewster F2A but with landing gear doors. No weapons were shown but air intakes were illustrated in the wing roots.

From reviewing the information, US intelligence made the assumption that the T.K.19 was a bona fide Japanese fighter that was in service or was soon to be in service. Thus, it was codenamed *Joe* after Corporal Joe Grattan, one of the team members responsible for assigning codenames to Japanese aircraft. The T.K.19 failed to appeare in Japanese sources despite remaining in US intelligence bulletins. It eventually became clear that the T.K.19 was nothing more than a fictional aircraft and *Joe* was removed from future intelligence publications.

T.K.19 – data

No information, if any, on the specifications are available for the T.K.19.

Deployment

None. The T.K.19 existed only as an illustration in a magazine.

Weapon Systems

Japanese Missile and Guided Munitions Projects

The aim of tactical missiles, specifically guided munitions, is to increase accuracy. It takes a considerable amount of conventional bombs or torpedoes to strike a ship and inflict enough damage to cripple or sink the vessel. Likewise, anti-aircraft cannons have to put a significant amount of shells into the air to bring down a single plane. Another benefit of using missiles is the measure of protection afforded to the user by way of range. A fighter combating bombers has to attack at such a range that his weapons are effective and therefore within range of the defensive armament of the target. The fighter also has to contend with escorting fighters before he even has a chance to press home an attack on the bomber. The same is true of attacking ships. To improve accuracy, a torpedo or dive-bomber has to be close enough to the ship to ensure a hit. Of course, this also puts the aircraft in the uncomfortable position of being within range of the many anti-aircraft cannons and machine guns carried by the ship, as well as attack by fighters providing cover for the vessel. Guided munitions eliminate some or all of these problems.

Without doubt, the undisputed leader in World War 2 missile development was Germany. Missiles such as the Fieseler Fi 103 (the V-1), EMW A4 (better known as the V-2), Ruhrstahl-Kramer X-1 Fritz X and the Henschel Hs 293A were used operationally with a measure of success. This was just the tip of the iceberg. Many more designs came close to seeing service or were in the latter stages of testing at the war's end. Such weapons included the EMW C2 Wasserfall, Rheinmetall-Borsig Rheintöchter, Henschel Hs 117 Schmetterling, Ruhrsahl-Kramer X-4 and many more. The US was not lacking in missile and guided munition technology of its own. Operational weapons included the ASM-N-2 Bat, GB-1/GB-4 and the VB-1 AZON (AZimuth ONly). Projects included 'Little Joe' (intended as a ship-borne missile to combat kamikazes), the McDonnell LBD-1 Gargoyle and the JB series of missiles. Other Allies, such as the British and the Russians, would not spend nearly as much resources on the subject as did the Germans and Americans. The British would squander the potential of the Brakemine surface-to-air missile and stall the Fairey Stooge while the Russians would only test and reject the promising Korolev Type 212A (built in 1937), waiting until the close of World War 2 to revive its missile development work. In some cases the Soviets used the fruits of German labour as their basis, for example, developing the R-1/SS-1 Scunner from the V-2 missile and the Type 10Ch from the V-1 flying bomb.

An example of the greater accuracy of missiles and guided munitions can be seen in the 27 December 27 1944 mission flown by the US to attack the Pyinmana rail bridge in Burma. Nine VB-1 AZON guided bombs were enough to destroy a bridge that for two years previously had failed to be hit by thousands of conventional bombs. Likewise, the Germans were able to successfully attack shipping targets using the Henschel Hs 293A and Fritz-X using less aircraft and with a higher hit and kill ratio than if the same attacks had been made using conventional bombs and torpedoes.

With these benefits in mind, it is not surprising that Japan also devoted considerable effort to producing such weapons themselves (while Japan did receive some German missile technology, it is unknown how much of it found its way into the IJA and IJN missile programs). Both the IJA and IJN funded the development of missiles as a means to both combat the bombers that tormented the homeland and to attack Allied shipping.

The Funryu (IJN)

The Funryu ('Raging Dragon') was the name given to the IJN's missile program that commenced in 1943. The initial study for the Funryu was conducted by the Kaigun Gijyutsu Kenkyujyo (Navy Technology Laboratory) but three other groups would review the study soon afterwards and they were the Dai-Ichi Kaigun Kōkū Gijutsu-shō, Dai-Ni Kayaku-Sho (2nd Bureau of Gunpowder) and the Kure Kosho (Kure Arsenal). Ultimately, it would be Kūgishō that was given the Funryu project in early 1944. To accomplish the task, Kūgishō formed the Funshin Kenkyu-Bu (Rocket Research Bureau) and was staffed with up to 200 technicians led by a research team made up of 40 officers (all engineers and/or technicians) from the IJN. In all, Kūgishō would investigate and put forward four Funryu designs.

The first was the Funryu 1 and the design was an air-to-surface missile (ASM) whose specific role was anti-shipping. Funryu 1 was much like a miniature airplane. The warhead contained 882 lb of explosive and guidance was via radio control. Testing of the Funryu 1 was conducted with the missile being dropped from a modified Mitsubishi G4M bomber. However, it was seen that the means to effectively control the missile in flight would require a significant amount of time to perfect and with the increase in US bombing raids against Japan, it was decided that efforts should be directed towards surface-to-air missiles (SAMs). Thus, the Funryu 1 was shelved and was to be the only ASM of the Funryu family.

The Funryu 2 was to be a SAM built around a solid fuel rocket using a radio guidance system. Despite three rocket motors being available already (the Ro-Tsu, Ro-Sa and Ro-Ta), it was decided that a new motor was required. This motor was capable of producing 2,400kg (5,291 lb) of thrust during its 3.5 second burn time. The shape of the missile was relatively simple. Four wooden wings were fitted to the body of the missile and each was equipped with an elevon (elevons control both pitch and roll). Four fins, making up the tail, were fitted to the outside of the nozzle for the motor. This final shape and configuration was a result of numerous tests of various missile bodies and wing/fin arrangements in a wind tunnel. The radio guidance system was initially to consist of a single transmitter but a second was fitted to ensure a measure of accuracy. The first transmitter was used for target detection while the second would control and steer the missile to the target. To maintain attitude, the Funryu 2 contained two gyrocompasses and 50kg (110 lb) of explosive was housed in the nose. The basic operation consisted of the Funryu 2 being launched from a rail set at an angle of 80°. Once launched, radio receivers fitted in the wings would receive signals from the ground transmitter, steering the missile onto the target.

The war situation in 1944 was starving Japan of critical war materials and Kūgishō found they were unable to obtain the necessary quantity of duralumin to build the Funryu 2 prototypes. It took theft from a warehouse to obtain the required metals. Using the absconded material, a number of Funryu 2 missiles were constructed with one being used for continued wind tunnel testing and the remainder used for actual field tests, the latter being conducted near Mount Asama (located near Ueda). Testing commenced in the spring of 1945. The first launches of the Funryu 2 were unguided, conducted solely to evaluate the rocket motor performance and the general flight characteristics of the missile. In July 1945, the first test of the Funryu 2 was undertaken using the radio guidance system. With IJN personnel in attendance, the Funryu 2 successfully lifted off from the launch rail and was directed towards a ground target. Using the radio signals, the Funryu 2 was guided to within 20m (65ft) of the target when impact was made. Although a direct hit was not achieved, the test was considered a success. It was to be, however, the last flight of the Funryu 2 because the war ended before any further launches could be made.

The Funryu 2 was 2.2m (7.2ft) long, .28m (0.9ft) in diameter and had a span of .88m (2.9ft). Total launch weight of the missile was 370kg (816 lb) and its maximum ceiling was 5,000m (16,404ft). The maximum speed of the missile at full burn was 845km/h (525mph).

Even as the Funryu 2 was being investigated, a variant of the missile, the Funryu 3, was proposed using a liquid fuel rocket in place of the solid fuel motor. However, initial discussions on the new rocket engine led to the conclusion that there was no time or resources available to study, design, construct and test such a propulsion method. As such, the Funryu 3 was shelved.

With the commencement of flight testing of the Funryu 2, work got underway on another SAM that was to be far more advanced. This missile was designated the Funryu 4. Design work was carried out by engineers from Mitsubishi and from the Aircraft Equipment Factory of Tōkyō, all based in a facility in the Izu Peninsula, west of Tōkyō. The Funryu 4 was to be built around the Toko Ro.2 (KR10) rocket engine, the very same engine used in the Mitsubishi J8M Syūsui rocket fighter. As testing of the Toko Ro.2 was already underway and would soon be put into production, Mitsubishi could devote less time to engine concerns. The Funryu 4 was to use a mixture of the Ko fuels (concentrated hydrogen peroxide) and Ōtsu (hydrazine hydrate solution in methyl alcohol) as used by the J8M. The engine would provide up to 1,500kg (3,307 lb) of thrust and move the Funryu 4 to a maximum speed of 1,099km/h (683mph).

The guidance system selected for the Funryu 4 was far more sophisticated than that used in the Funryu 2. Whereas the latter relied on radio, the Funryu 4 would use radar. Two stations would be used to deliver the Funryu 4 to the target. One station would track the target while the second would track and control the missile. The intention was that the two radar signals would coincide on the target, thus bringing the missile to impact. To control the missile, a radio signal of 1,000MHz was to be used with five frequencies. Each frequency corresponded to controlling the pitch and the roll with the fifth being the detonation command. A variation of this system is used today known at retransmission homing or Track-via-Missile (TVM).

Funryu 4, like the Funryu 2, used two gyrocompasses and carried wing radio receivers for the commands sent to it from the ground. It carried a far heavier warhead of 200kg (440 lb) in comparison to the 50kg (110 lb) warhead of the Funryu 2. The shape of the Funryu 4 was also more streamlined and it only had two of the elevon-equipped wings and two tail fins. Launch would occur from a rail set at a 45° angle.

The Funryu 4 was 4.0m (13.1ft) long, .6m (1.9ft) in diameter and its span was approximately .8m (2.5ft). Fully loaded its weight was 1,900kg (4,189 lb), range 30km (18.6 miles) and ceiling of 15,000m/49,215ft.

Nagasaki Arsenal was tasked with building the Funryu 4 and this did not begin until the late summer of 1945. The first ground test of the missile and its motor commenced on 16 August, but the close of the war prevented the Funryu 4 from being launched or its guidance system fully tested.

To prevent the Allies from learning of the Funryu developments, the IJN forbade any of the personnel involved with the Funryu from discussing the project with anyone. In addition, documents, test data, constructed missiles, the launching apparatus and the facilities in which the Funryu was developed were all burned and destroyed.

The I-Go (IJA)

While the IJN put its focus on SAMs, the IJA's resources went into developing Air-to-Surface missiles (ASMs). The culmination of these developments, begun in 1942 by the Koku Hombu, was the I-Go series of missiles. The majority of the research on the I-Go was carried out by Rikugun Kokugijutsu Kenkyūjo located in Tachikawa. Once the preliminary work for the missiles was completed, the Koku Hombu reached out to Mitsubishi, Kawasaki and the Aeronautical Research Institute of Tōkyō University to commence final development of the I-Go as they saw fit, using the initial data assembled by Rikugun. Sumitomo Communication Industry Co. Ltd. was the provider of the autopilot and the transmitter/receiver system for the first two I-Go missiles with T. Hayashi designing the former and K. Nagamori the latter.

The I-Go-1-A (Ki-147) was the Mitsubishi version of the I-Go. The final design of the Ki-147 was completed by the end of 1943. Work began on the missile using a basic airplane configuration and its construction was made of wood and metal. It was propelled by a rocket engine built by Nissan Jidōsha KK which produced 240kg (529 lb) of thrust with a burn time of 75 seconds, providing a top speed of 550kg (342mph). The warhead was substantial using 800kg (1,764 lb) of explosive triggered by an impact fuse. Guidance was by radio from the carrying aircraft. The first Ki-147 missiles were completed in 1944 and by mid-year unguided test drops had commenced at Ajigaura, Atami and Shiruishi. The carrier aircraft was a modified Mitsubishi Ki-67-I Hiryū bomber. By October 1944, guided test drops of the Ki-147 had begun. Despite the testing, the Ki-147 did not enter production and only fifteen were built. The Ki-147 had a length of 5.8m (18.9ft), a span of 3.6m (11.8ft) and a launch weight of 1,400kg (3,086 lb).

The I-Go-1-B (Ki-148) was the Kawasaki I-Go. Smaller than the Ki-147, the Ki-148 used a HTP rocket motor that developed 150kg (331 lb) of thrust with an 80 second burn time. The wings were constructed of wood while the body and fins were made from tin. As a consequence of the smaller size, the warhead comprised only 300kg (661 lb) of explosive and it used a direct-action fuse. For guidance, the Ki-148 used the same radio system as the Ki-147. Following wind tunnel testing with full- and half-size models, Kawasaki produced a number of missiles at their Gifu factory for testing to begin in late 1944. Ki-148 test launches were made from four modified Kawasaki Ki-48-II Ōtsu bombers at Ajigaura in Ibaraki Prefecture. By December 1944, up to 20 Ki-148 missiles were being launched per week from the bombers. Despite the relatively successful testing, the Ki-148 was never put into production and total deliveries of the pre-production/test Ki-148 missiles amounted to 180. Had the Ki-148 gone into service, the Kawasaki Ki-102 Ōtsu was to be the designated carrier aircraft.

Ki-148 had a length of 4.1m (13.4ft), a span of 2.6m (8.5ft) and a launch weight of 680kg (1,499 lb).

The I-Go-1-C would be the final I-Go project. The Aeronautical Research Institute of Tōkyō University decided to take a completely different approach to guidance. Deciding that anti-shipping would be the main use of the I-Go-1-C, the missile dispensed with the radio guidance method and instead employed a novel system that used the shockwaves produced by naval cannons as the means to direct the missile. In essence, the missile would guide itself to the target by sensing the shockwaves developed in the air by large naval cannons during firing. Since shockwaves travel outwards from the cannon, the missile could determine direction and adjust its flight path accordingly to bring it onto the target. The main benefit of the system was that the missile was a fire-and-forget weapon. As long as naval ships engaged in bombardment, the I-Go-1-C would be able to track and attack them on its own. Testing of the system got under way in 1945 and the initial results showed promise. However, the missile body was never built as the war ended before testing of the guidance hardware was complete. The proposed I-Go-1-C was to be 3.5m (11.4ft) long with a diameter of 1.6ft. Other specifications for the missile, such as its warhead size, rocket motor, performance and weight are still unknown. The I-Go-1-C is sometimes called the Ki-149 but there is no evidence to support the use of this name.

Since the Ki-147 and the Ki-148 achieved flight testing and both used the same radio guidance system, the procedures to launch and control the missiles were basically the same. The Ki-67 and Ki-48 bombers used in the testing were modified to accommodate the missile operator as well as the equipment needed to guide the weapon. Operationally, the missiles would be dropped at an altitude of 1,500m (4,922ft), 11km (6.84 miles) from the intended target. By the time the missile was 5km (3.11 miles) from the target, the altitude varied between 30m to 150m (98ft to 492ft) depending on the preset of the altimeter. The operator would guide the missile via a joystick and just before it passed over the target, the missile would be put into a dive, bringing it down onto its target. The launching aircraft had to remain within sight of the missile and in most cases would be 4km (2.5 miles) from the target when the missile hit. While the handling characteristics of the weapons were found to be good, analysis showed that the missiles tended to fall either 300m (984ft) short of the target or 100m (328ft) past the target. The reason for was that the operator had to rely on his own vision and clear conditions in order to guide the missile. He was not provided with any form of special optics nor did the missile carry a means to mark itself in flight such as using burning flares or smoke which the operator could use to maintain sight of the weapon. The only measure of this kind ever employed was a tail light which was used at night so the operator could track the missile. Had the Japanese given further consideration to the operator's needs, accuracy may have been improved. A factor against the use of the Ki-147 and Ki-148 was that the launch aircraft had to be within 11km (7 miles) of the target and had to remain in the area to proceed with the attack. With the heavy Allied air presence, getting to the launch range would have been a formidable task and this may have been a factor in the Ki-147 and Ki-148 failing to enter service.

OTHER SYSTEMS

Kūrai Aerial Torpedo No.6/No.7

In April 1944, the IJN initiated a design for an air dropped, anti-submarine torpedo. While not a true guided weapon, what made the design unique was that the torpedo was winged and once in the water, entered a circular pattern as it dived down. Work on the torpedo was carried out by the First Technical Arsenal Branch at Kanazawa under Commander Fukuba. The torpedo body was made of wood with the exception of the metal nose. The torpedo had no means of propulsion, either for flight or in the water. The wooden wings, each 1.5m (4.9ft) in length, were glued to the main torpedo body at a 20° upward angle. The wing span was approximately .9m (2.6ft) and the nose carried a 100kg (220 lb) warhead and the total weight was 271kg (597 lb). The wood rudders were fixed at an 8° angle which, once in the water, imparted the counter-clockwise circular path. The rudder was covered with a wood fairing to stop it affecting the freefall glide of the torpedo. Once the torpedo entered the water, the aluminium pin holding the fairing on sheared off and the fairing came free.

The first tests were carried out to evaluate the gliding properties of the torpedo. In all, forty drops were made of which fifteen were complete failures, the torpedo tumbling or spinning out of control. The wings were modified according to the specifications given above, resulting in the Kūrai No.6 which improved the gliding ability but not to a satisfactory level. Underwater testing was conducted by releasing the torpedo from a boat and the results showed a 17° dive angle at a speed of 5-6 knots. Colour dye released from the nose of the torpedo assisted the evaluators in determining how the weapon worked underwater. The maximum depth the torpedo could reach before the pressure overcame it was 100m (327ft). From the tests, it was determined that a form of gyrostabilisation would be required.

The designated carrier plane for the Kūrai was the Nakajima B6N1 and B6N2 Tenzan (known as *Jill* to the Allies). No modification of the plane's torpedo rack was required. In operation, the pilot had to visually sight the target and release the torpedo from a height of 100m (327ft). An air spun vane would arm the weapon after it was released and the torpedo would go into a 20° downward glide. Once in the water, it would enter its circular dive with a diameter of 79m (260ft), making one revolution through a depth of 79m (260ft) after which it would continue to circle and dive until it was crushed under pressure or had struck the submarine before reaching 100m (327ft). A magnetic proximity fuse was to be used on the torpedo.

In all, 100 of the Kūrai No.6 were built with many of them expended in testing. Kūgishō constructed the rudders and the metal components (nose and wing braces) while the Marunimoko Company (located in Futsukaishi, Hiroshima Prefecture) produced the torpedo body and wings.

The poor results of the Kūrai No.6 resulted in slight modifications to the design. The wing span was increased and the rudders made taller and set at 6° rather than 8°, and the nose was thickened to enhance the ability of the torpedo to penetrate a submarine hull. This new model was designated the Kūrai No.7 and in January 1945, eleven test drops were made, but the weapon showed little improvement over the Kūrai No.6. The end of the war brought the entire project to a close, the engineers having run out of time to solve the poor gliding performance and finalise the special fuse.

Two Kūrai No.6 mock-ups were captured and shipped to the US for delivery to TAIC. What their fate was is unknown.

The Ke-Go

As the war progressed the Japanese came to see the invasion of the home islands as a very real threat and various means of attacking the invasion fleet were investigated. One possibility was a bomb capable of homing in on the heat emissions of naval vessels. The plan called for the bombs to be used in night attacks when heat signatures of the ships would not be masked by the sun and other ambient heat sources. The project was undertaken by the IJA and given the name Ke-Go and work commenced in March 1944. The First Military Arsenal's Ōmiya Department in Tōkyō undertook development of the bolometer that would detect heat in the infrared wavelength and bench testing showed that the mechanism was workable. In fact, the sensor could detect the heat from a man's face at 100m (328ft)! For the bomb to carry the bolometer, three different types were investigated: the B-1, B-2 and B-3. Of the three, only the first showed potential and the remainder were abandoned. A myriad of men and departments were assigned to the task of realising the B-1. Under the Military Ordnance Administration Board was Major Fujita who oversaw the gyro and airframe, Major Hizuta who also worked on the airframe research, and Major Sonobe who addressed the amplifier. The Seventh Military Laboratory encompassed Professor Konishi of the Shikan Gakkō in Osaka who handled the mathematical work, Professor Sano of the Osaka Imperial University who conducted the electrical design and Dr. Itakawa of the Aeronautics Research Laboratory who undertook the aerodynamic design studies. All wind tunnel testing was held at Rikugun Kokugijutsu Kenkyūjo.

The first two bomb versions, the Ke-Go 101 and 102, were built in small numbers: ten and five respectively. The hydraulic and mechanical linkages for operating the bomb ailerons, coupled with the use of an electric gyro that interfered with the bolometer (A bolometer is a device used to measure the energy of incident electromagnetic radiation and was invented by Samuel Pierpont Langley in 1878.), saw both of these versions abandoned. Continued study resulted in the Ke-Go 103, 104 and 105. However, none of these designs left the drawing board although the 103 was to use an air gyro instead of an electrical version. The gyro only existed to ensure the bomb did not spin faster than 360° in 50 seconds. The Ke-Go 106 would be the first to be built in numbers, fifty examples in all. Overall length of the 106 was 4.7m (15.5ft) long and the wing span was 2m (6.5ft). Four main fins were fitted 1.7m (5.7ft) down the length of the bomb body with a smaller set of four fins 1.2m (3.9ft) behind the main fins, and the tail of the Ke-Go contained dive brakes. In the nose was the bolometer while the shape charged warhead was contained behind it. Two strikers that protruded out from the nose were tipped with small propellers which spun and armed the bomb after release. The strikers served as the impact fuse, but a delayed fuse was also installed should the bomb strike water, in which case it would explode beneath the waterline of a ship. In short order, the Ke-Go 107 joined the program with a total of 30 bombs. The 107 had similar dimensions to the 106 version and weighed 726kg (1,600 lb).

The Ke-Go was guided in flight by the bolometer. The bolometer was part of a unit that consisted of the bolometer itself, a mirror, motor, distributor, amplifier, relay box and battery. Heat sources passing through the bolometer would strike the mirror that, depending on where it struck, would trigger the amplifier which operated the ailerons, steering the bomb towards the heat source. The use of dive brakes slowed the plummet of the bomb, allowing time for the bomb to make adjustments in flight before impact. The ailerons could move up or down 20°. For a warhead, the Ke-Go carried between 200 to 300kg (440 to 661 lb) of shaped charge explosive, depending on the model. Perhaps in error, a 1946 US Navy report lists the warhead as ranging from 20 to 30kg (44 to 66 lb) of explosive which is very light for the size of the Ke-Go.

With enough bombs ready and available, field testing began without the bombs containing any payload. The test used a floating raft which measured 10m (32.8ft) by 20m (65.6ft) and was anchored in Lake Hamanako (located in Shizuoka Prefecture). On the raft wood and coal in a 4m (13ft) by 4m (13ft) pile was set alight. Both Ke-Go 106 and 107 bombs were released from altitudes varying between 1,524m (5,000ft) and 3,048m (10,000ft) but the results proved very disappointing. In all, around 60 drops were made but only 5-6 of the bombs displayed the zigzag flight path that indicated the bolometer was sensing the heat from the fire and guiding the bomb. The remainder simply veered away from the raft. The dismal results were blamed on faulty equipment although the data collected was not sufficient to properly identify the cause of the failures. It was found that the terminal velocity of the Ke-Go 107 was 539km/h (335mph). In July 1945, further testing ceased, though work continued on improving the bomb.

The Ke-Go 108 was developed but it was with the Ke-Go 109, the last to be designed, in which the Japanese hoped the problems would be resolved and the bomb would finally prove successful. The Ke-Go 109 bomb was 5.5m (18ft long), 5m (1.6ft) in diameter, had a wingspan of 2.9m (9.4ft) and weighed 800kg (1,764 lb). It was estimated that the terminal velocity for the Ke-Go 109 was 579km/h (360mph). It featured a larger wing span because the smaller span was considered to be one of the main causes of the poor performance of the Ke-Go 106 and 107. It was anticipated that the 108 and 109 bombs would be ready for test drops by September 1945. Of course, the end of the war ensured this would never happen and neither bomb was built.

Had the Ke-Go made it into service, the carrier was to be the Ki-67 Hiryū (codenamed *Peggy* by the Allies). The bomb required a special brace that was fitted into the bomb bay, the apex of the brace extending a few inches past the exterior of the doors. The bomb was secured to this and the lower wing could fold to give ground clearance. On take-off, a crewman had to lower the wing and did so by means of a crank that activated a servo in the bomb, which then moved the wing. The bombardier would use bombing tables appropriate for the weight of the weapon and on release the bomb's arming wires were pulled out along with a wire that released the dive brakes. Typically, the bomb would be dropped from 2,000m (6,562ft). After the bomb was away, the Ki-67 saw a 64km/h (40mph) increase in speed.

All of the bombs were built from wood. The only metal components consisted of the nose cap containing the bolometer and the dive brakes. In all cases, the bomb bodies were built by the Atsu Department of the Nagoya Arsenal, the gyroscope by Hitachi Co., the spring/gear parts for the timing mechanism by the Hattori Jewellery Co. and the electrical contacts for the timing mechanism by Sumitomo Communications Branch.

Interestingly, the US would develop a similar weapon, the VB-6 Felix. This was a 454kg (1,000 lb) bomb fitted with an infrared seeker in the nose that controlled the fins and guided the bomb. It was meant for night warfare, notably against ships at sea. The VB-6 was put into production in 1945 but would not see service by the close of hostilities.

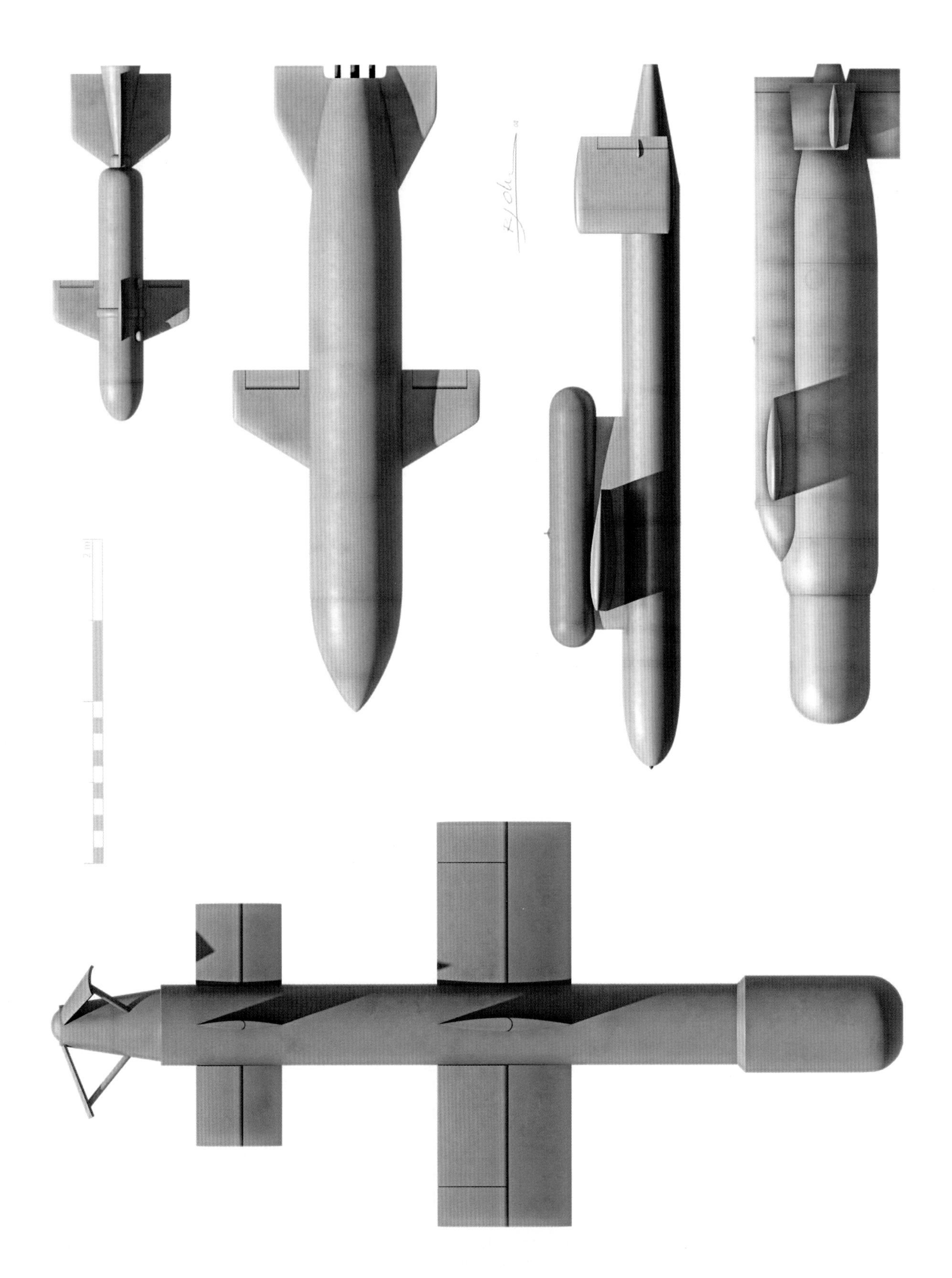

From left to right, the Funryu 2, Funryu 4, Ki-147, Ki-148, and the Ke-Go.

Specialised Bombs

Both the IJA and the IJN developed specialised bomb munitions during the war, some of which remained projects while others saw service. Several were dedicated to the practice of air-to-air bombing in which bombs were used to attack enemy bomber formations. Although not a complete list, the following are some of the more interesting examples.

Ko-Dan

The Japanese expended some effort in developing the Ko bomb. This was developed in response to observations made by one Kobayashi of high-speed photographs of detonations of various experimental shaped charges. The basis of his theory was that the energy produced by an explosion is projected along horizontal lines with the impact surface. By extension, the amount of energy created is proportional to the quantity of the explosive used. To achieve a wider impact area against a target, the Ko bomb had a 2mm thick rubber nose that was mated to a 2mm thick steel case. On impact the nose of the bomb would flatten and expand, thereby enlarging the surface area and increasing the effects of the explosive pellets contained within. The Ko would be used against hard targets such as concrete emplacements. In tests, a Ko bomb with 50kg (110 lb) of TNT and ultropine in an even split mixture could penetrate a 1m (3.2ft) slab of concrete and utterly destroy it. It would take a regular 250kg (551 lb) bomb to accomplish the same effect. A part of this concept is known as the Misznay-Schardin Effect and is in practice today with modern HESH (High Explosive Squash Head) munitions and EFP (Explosively Formed Penetrator) weapons.

Mk. 7 (IJN)

Conceived around 1936 by Dai-Ichi Kaigun Kōkū Gijutsu-shō, the Mk. 7 chemical bomb was not given priority since at the time there was little need for such a weapon and it was thought the work needed to bring it to fruition would be too great. The idea surfaced near the end of the war, the Mk.7 then being denied a second time in favour of guided missiles. The design was based on the 1kg (2.2 lb) practice bomb. It had a rubber nose and within a special tail was a glass bottle of *Bacillus* bacteria, most likely *B. anthracis*, which causes anthrax. It had no fuse or explosive charge, the impact being enough to break the bottle and release the bacteria. The planned colour for the bomb was a purple nose with a purple tail.

Mk.19 (IJN)

This was an air-to-air rocket-propelled bomb design intended for use against bomber formations. It weighed 7.5kg (16.5 lb). Although it was never built, the work eventually resulted in the Mk. 28 rocket bomb.

'Silver Paper Scattering Bomb' (IJN)

This was the Japanese version of the German Düppel, better known as 'Window'. A 2kg (4.4 lb) sheet steel cylinder was packed with 200 pieces of metal coated paper measuring .3m x 8.4m (1ft x 27.5ft). The bomb used a pull fuse that the crewman yanked to arm it and was then thrown out of the aircraft, the subsequent charge expelling the papers into the air to act as false radar targets. This anti-radar weapon was used heavily from 1944-1945.

To-3 (IJA)

Developed and produced from 1941 to 1942, the To-3 was a cluster munition and initially designed to combat aerial targets. However, the To-3 turned out to be more effective against ground targets. Thirty to forty To-3 bomblets could be carried in a dispensing container or modified underwing bomb racks could carry several of the To-3 bomblets. Once released, either from the container or the rack, the To-3's vane would spin, arming the munition. Use of the To-3 was performed on a limited basis and production ended in 1942.

Ta (IJA)

Evolving from the To-3 was the Ta. Each Ta bomb was a 40mm hollow charge weighing .33kg (.74 lb). It used fixed tail fins. When attacking airborne targets, canisters containing between 30 and 76 of the Ta bombs would be released. A burst fuse would open the canisters, usually just after release, to scatter the Ta bombs. The loaded canisters weighed 30kg (66 lb) and 50kg (110 lb) respectively and the Ta was first used operationally in 1943 with Japanese pilots claiming a number of kills using the weapon. Typically, the Ta was far more effective when used against more densely packed bomber formations.

Ta-105 (IJA)

The Ta-105 came from the need to attack Allied shipping during the expected invasion of Japan. The Ta-105 was the Ta bomblet enlarged to carry a more substantial payload. The bomblet had a 100mm hollow charge that was capable of penetrating up to 140mm of armour plate. Unlike the Ta, the Ta-105 used folding tail fins that deployed upon release. Each canister contained 21 Ta-105 bomblets.

Type 2 No.6 21-Go Model 1 (IJN)
This munition was the IJN's version of the Ta. It was a heavier bomblet and weighed 1kg (2.2 lb). A canister would carry up to 40 of the Model 1 bomblets. Like the Ta, a fuse would open the canister deploying the bomblets onto their target.

Type 2 No.6 21-Go Model 2 (IJN)
This was the same bomblet but instead of the hollow-charge in the Model 1, the Model 2 used a solid black powder charge. This change was made because the IJN felt that an armour piercing charge was not necessary against aircraft that were typically unarmoured. This did, however, raise the weight of the Model 2 and a canister could only hold 36 of the bomblets, the total weight of the loaded canister being 49kg (108 lb).

Type 3 No.6 Mk.3 Model 1 (IJN)
This was basically a simplified Type 99 No.3 Mk.3 bomb as it used a wooden nose and did away with the impact fuse. The bomb was 1m (3.3ft) long and weighed 56kg (124 lb). Its design commenced in 1943 and entered service in 1944. Colouration was the same as the Type 99.

Type 3 No.6 Mk.27 Model 1 (IJN)
Development of this anti-bomber rocket bomb began in January 1944. The cone-shaped nose contained 140 iron pellets embedded in 4kg (8.8 lb) of white phosphorous. A 10kg (22 lb) propellant charge moved the bomb to a velocity of 270m/sec (885.8ft/sec). On detonation the pellets were scattered in a 60° radius and the bomb was provided with the fittings for rail launching by fighters. The IJN accepted it for service in February 1945 and final testing was completed in April 1945. Testing was conducted by Dai-Ichi Kaigun Kōkū Gijutsu-shō, the Second Powder Factory Arsenal, and Kashima Bombing Experimental Field. The bomb was 1.4m (4.6ft) long and weighed 60kg (132 lb).

Type 3 No.6 Mk.28 Model 1 (IJN)
Using the Mk.19 as a basis, the Mk.28 was a small, anti-bomber rocket bomb with a .6kg (1.3 lb) explosive warhead A 2kg (4.4 lb) propellant charge moved the bomb to a maximum velocity of 1,312ft/sec. Dai-Ichi Kaigun Kōkū Gijutsu-shō built the bomb and its clearence testing was undertaken by Dai-Ichi Kaigun Kōkū Gijutsu-shō, the Second Powder Factory Arsenal, and Kashima Bombing Experimental Field. Testing was completed late in 1944 but the rocket bomb was not accepted for service. Its length was .7m (2.3ft) and weight 7.3kg (16 lb).

Type 5 No.25 Mk.29 (IJN)
Designed for use by special attacker aircraft, the Mk.29 contained 1,100 pellets packed in 50kg (110 lb) of white phosphorous. After flying into a bomber formation, the pilot would use a pull cord to detonate the bomb while it was still attached to the aircraft. The bomb could also be released where the tail fuse would trigger the bomb explosion. Unlike other pellet dispersing munitions, the Mk.29 flung them at right angles to the bomb casing instead of in a downward cone. Initial testing was begun in 1944 but only one prototype was air dropped and the type did not enter service. The Mk.29 was 1.6m (5.1ft) long and weighed 250kg (551 lb).

Type 99 No.3 Mk.3 Sangō (IJN)
Designed in 1938 and entering service in 1939, this anti-bomber bomb contained 144 white phosphorous-filled steel pellets. Its tail fins were offset to impart spin as it fell and this armed the tail fuse. The fuse would then trigger a burster tube down the middle of the bomb, scattering the pellets. A charge in the tail ensured the pellets were directed downwards. Should the tail fuse fail, an impact fuse was proved in the nose of the bomb. A later modification of the bomb added fins to the body to impart a faster spin. For identification purposes the nose of the bomb was painted silver and the fins red. The bomb was .7m (2.3ft) long and weighed 34kg (74 lb).

Ro-Ta (IJA)
One of the problems the Japanese had with using cluster munitions was that they relied on the attacker having a higher altitude than the target in order to rain the bomblets down upon them. However, many Japanese fighters struggled at the altitudes at which the B-29s usually operated. The IJA sought to solve this dilemma with the Ro-Ta. The same Ta bomblets were used but the canister was essentially a rocket that was launched towards the target. A timed fuse would trigger an explosive charge that scattered the Ta bomblets. In effect, the Ro-Ta was like a buckshot shotgun shell. Because the Ro-Ta could be fired like a rocket, there was no longer a requirement to be above the intended target in order to use the weapon. Luckily for the Allies, the Ro-Ta was still in development when the war ended.

To-2 (IJA)
Even before the To-3 and Ta series of cluster bombs, there was the To-2 parachute bomb. Developed in 1935, the To-2 was a 1.8m (4 lb) bomb that was suspended from a length of steel cable that was itself connected to a silk parachute. Ten To-2 bombs were clustered together, each cluster weighed 50kg (110 lb) and the average single engine fighter could carry up to four clusters. The usual tactic was to drop the To-2 bombs into the path of oncoming bombers. To increase the depth of the bomb spread, some To-2 bombs had a smaller parachute that would result in a faster descent. The bomb was armed with an impact fuse that, regardless of where the bomb struck, would trigger the detonation. Usually the cable would be hit by the bomber with the bomb swinging up and against the plane, exploding the bomb. The To-2, however, was not developed further because the cable was typically cut if hit by a wing, it relied on a high altitude to be effective and the Ta munition showed far greater promise.

Specialised Bombs: Fu-Go

Japan was able to achieve where Germany failed and that was to bomb the US mainland. On 9 September 1942, the Japanese submarine I-25 surfaced west of Cape Blanco, Oregon, and a single Kūgishō E14Y1 floatplane (known as *Glen* to the Allies) was assembled. Pilot Warrant Officer Nobuo Fujita and observer Petty Officer Okuda Shoji climbed into the plane that was loaded with two 77kg (170 lb) incendiary bombs and took off for the US coast, heading towards the Oregon side of the Siskiyou National Forest. Once over the forest, the bombs were released in the hope a forest fire would start. However, recent rains coupled with the bombs having been dropped too low resulted in a few small fires and these quickly put out. The attack would be repeated again on 29 September 1942 but once more the results were disappointing. The first attack marked the only time in history an enemy aircraft bombed the US but another plan was in the works, one far more ambitious and ingenious, but ultimately fruitless.

The plan was called the Fu-Go, 'Fu' being the first kanji of the word 'fusen', meaning balloon. The 'Go' simply meant type. Originally conceived in 1933 by Lieutenant General Reikichi Toda of the Japanese Military Scientific Laboratory, the bomb dropping balloon Fu-Go was part of a series of studies into possible new weapons. Experiments with balloons capable of maintaining a stable altitude were initially allowed to proceed but by 1935 the Fu-Go project was cancelled. However, following the famous Doolittle raid on 8 April 1942, the Fu-Go was revived as a means of exacting retribution for the attack.

The Fu-Go was to have been launched from submarines situated 998km (620 miles) off the US coast. In March 1943, a 6.1m (20ft) diameter balloon was successfully launched and remained aloft for at least ten hours, enough to make the submarine launch plan work. The main problem was the effect of temperature on the hydrogen gas used in the balloon. At night and in cool temperatures, the gas pressure was reduced and the balloon lost buoyancy while by day, in higher temperatures, there was the risk of the gas expanding and rupturing the gas envelope. Because of this launches of the balloons had to take place either by day or by night and not straddle the two times of day. However, the IJN's need for submarines to support operations in the Pacific left no room for launching the Fu-Go and the project was again cancelled in August 1943.

Remaining undeterred, the Fu-Go engineers looked into a solution where the balloon could be launched from Japan, although it would now take 50-70 hours for it to traverse the Pacific Ocean and arrive over the US mainland. General Sueyoshi Kusaba was put in command of the project to tackle the distance issue and put the Fu-Go into operational use.

To overcome the problem of maintaining altitude as the balloon travelled by day and night, a ballast mechanism was designed. This consisted of a cast aluminium ring around which 32 2.5 to 3.2kg (5.5 to 7 lb) sandbags were secured. Fuses were fitted to pairs of sandbags, the fuses powered by a small battery and connected to aneroid barometers. When the balloon sank to an altitude of around 9,144m (30,000ft), the aneroid barometer would trigger a switch. In turn, this triggered a fuse which in turn would fire two small charges that would each release a sandbag, one across from the other to maintain balance. The balloon would then rise to an altitude of around 11,582m (38,000ft) where a gas release valve set into the bottom of the envelope discharged some of the gas to keep the balloon from rising higher. Eventually it would drop again triggering another release of sandbags followed by a rise, vent and the cycle would repeat. By the time the last pair of sandbags was dropped, it was estimated that the balloon should be over the US mainland where its destructive payload would then be released.

The balloon could lift a maximum of 136kg (300 lb) at 9,144m (30,000ft). The typical munition payload was one Type 92 15kg (33 lb) high explosive bomb, one Type 100 5kg (11 lb) incendiary bomb and one Type 97 12kg (26.4 lb) incendiary bomb. A 29m (64ft) fuse was connected to a charge on the gas envelope and once the bombs were dropped, the fuse was lit which, in turn, destroyed the balloon.

The spherical gas envelope could store 538m^3 (19,000ft^3) of hydrogen gas. The diameter at full inflation was 10m (33ft). Early gas envelopes were constructed from rubberised silk but this was too costly to construct and the production Fu-Go used Washi paper made from the kozo bush. While Washi was inexpensive and already produced by hand in paper mills across Japan, there was no means to ensure a constant level of quality. Therefore, the Fu-Go program had to develop mechanical methods to make Washi as well as laminate it. It took four to five layers of Washi to make a gore (a segment) and 38 to 64 gores glued together to make the sphere. The adhesive used, called konnyaku-nori, was made from konnyaku, a potato. As the glue was relatively clear, colouring was added so workers could check for evenness in the application. The glue also served as a sealant to prevent gas leakage as the untreated Washi was porous.

After being brushed with the glue, each gore was inspected for flaws. This was done by laying the gores over a panel of frosted glass beneath which was a light. The glue would appear blue and any uneven applications of the glue showed up as a lighter area. All flaws were marked and patched. Once the gores had passed inspection, they were taken to the final assembly area. A large room was required with sharp objects padded so not to rip the gas envelope. High school girls were often employed for assembly, using the glue to affix the gores together to create the completed gas envelope. Each girl had to ensure her nails were trimmed, that she wore gloves and socks, and that she did not wear hair pins as these could damage the gas envelope. Once the envelope was finished, it was taken to another building, often a sumo hall or theatre (buildings specific for the task were later built), and inflated to check for leakage. After successfully passing the final inspection, the Fu-Go was completed.

The finished Fu-Go had a scalloped waistband around the gas envelope to which the 19 shroud lines, each 14m (45ft) long, were secured. The lines were brought together and tied into two knots from which the bombs and the ballast system were hung.

With the problem of keeping a relatively static altitude solved, the next hurdle was to determine where and when to launch the balloons. Towards the close of 1943 and into the early part of February 1944, the Japanese launched balloons equipped with radios which were tracked so their courses could be monitored. Two stations set up in Hokkaidō and in Chiba Prefecture could track the balloons only through the first portion of their flight, but once over the open ocean all contact was lost. The Japanese were aware that the west-to-east wind speeds were at their peak from November through to March, topping out at 298km/h (185mph). In addition, a shortage of meteorological data on weather patterns over the ocean and at high altitudes limited the ability to plan trajectories for the balloons. While the winds were higher, it was also winter throughout most of the launch window. In addition, the balloons had to be released in clear, cloudless weather with little surface wind. If balloons were sent up in overcast skies with precipitation laden clouds, moisture would collect on the balloons which would freeze at higher altitudes, adding weight resulting in the balloons being unable to reach the US. Three major launch sites were selected: Nakoso (Fukushima Prefecture), Ōtsu (Ibaraki Prefecture) and Ichin Ōmiya (Chiba Prefecture).

On 3 November 1944, the Fu-Go balloon bombing campaign was officially opened. In all, between 9,000-10,000 balloons were available and by 20 November, the first en masse launchings had taken place. Prior to launch, the sandbag release mechanism was set based on the estimated wind speeds to ensure the balloon was over the US before releasing its payload. The gas envelope was only partially filled to allow for expansion of the hydrogen at an altitude of 4,877m (16,000ft). On a good day crews could launch up to 200 balloons. March 1945 would see the highest number of balloons deployed, 3,000 in all, and the final launch was made on 20 April. Typically included in batches of balloon launches would be a radio equipped balloon to allow for tracking.

The first balloon was found on 4 November 1944 by a US Navy patrol boat. It had crashed into the sea 106km (66 miles) southwest of San Pedro, California. Nothing much was made of it until another turned up in the sea two weeks later. Also, balloons were found up in Montana and Wyoming and the US military realised the purpose of the balloons. Federal and state agencies were put on alert (especially forest services as the threat of forest fires from the incendiaries was very real) and steps were taken to prevent news of the balloon bombs reaching the general public. This was done to prevent panic in the populace since no one could be sure when or where a balloon would release its bombs. In addition, by keeping the story from the press, the Japanese would be denied any information on the effectiveness of their attacks. The censorship was very effective and only one story concerning a balloon bomb was published appearing in Thermopolis in Wyoming. This was also reported in a Chinese newspaper. From this, the Japanese judged the Fu-Go campaign was a success and the balloon campaign continued.

The near total shutdown of public information on the balloon bombs had one severe drawback for the Americans and that was that the public had no knowledge of their existence and consequently were not be warned of the dangers. The censorship would be reversed after an inevitable tragedy occurred. On 5 May 1945, near Bly, Oregon, Reverend Archie Mitchell, his wife and five children from his church group were enjoying a picnic in a wooded area. One of the children, Joan Patzke, found a balloon stuck in a tree and tried to pull it down. The subsequent explosion of the bombs it carried killed all but Reverend Mitchell. The deaths would be the only US mainland casualties from enemy action. Following the incident, the censorship was lifted to ensure public safety.

The Fourth Army Air Force was tasked with the detection and interception of the balloons. In addition, Project Firefly was initiated to position aircraft and troops to respond to forest fires. Project Lightening was set up through the Department of Agriculture to be on alert for biological attacks against crops and livestock. Successful interception of the balloons proved difficult owing to the high altitudes at which they travelled, poor ground reporting and inadequate weather reporting (this would also hamper the ability of the US to accurately determine launch points from Japan). In fact, only two Fu-Gos were shot down over the US mainland. Only US Army and US Navy assets in the Aleutian Islands had a higher tally as the balloons often passed over the territory. With the problems in locating the balloons, a final plan, Project Sunset, was initiated to create a web of radar sites across the coastline of Washington State. When balloons were detected, interceptors would be scrambled to engage them. As it turned out, the plan was put into action in April 1945, the same month the Japanese ceased launching the Fu-Go. In any case, radars had a difficult time in detecting the balloons due to their low signal return.

The cost to produce one Fu-Go was approximately 10,000 yen. If the added expense of the design and production of the mechanical equipment to produce Washi and the erection of buildings to inspect the balloons, the price of the Fu-Go project was high in comparison to the results it brought. Still, Japanese propaganda broadcasts played up the Fu-Go prior to the project being cancelled in April 1945.

Ironically, on 10 March 1945, a balloon from one of the last launchings struck a power line, resulting in the loss of power to the nuclear plant in Hansford, Washington. This plant created the atomic material used in the Manhattan Project's atomic bombs, which would ultimately be used against Japan. The loss was barely noticed as back-up systems came online to maintain the reactor. Another irony occurred on 13 March 13 when two Fu-Gos returned to Japan, although they touched down without causing any damage.

In all, 296 balloon sightings or incidents were reported across 17 US states, 5 Canadian provinces and Mexico out of the 9,000-10,000 launched. Hundreds remain unaccounted for and even today, some may still lurk in unpopulated areas or in dense forest presenting a danger to anyone encountering one.

Interestingly, the British would use a similar weapon against Germany. Called Operation Outward, hydrogen filled balloons equipped with a trailing steel chain to short out power lines and three 6 lb incendiary devices to trigger forest fires were launched from two sites in England on 20 March 1942. The balloons were of simple construction, reached a height of 4,877m (16,000ft) and inexpensive at 35 shillings each. More of a nuisance to the Germans, the greatest triumph of the operation was the explosion of the Böhlen power station caused by the failure of an overload switch when a balloon struck a main power line near Leipzig. The last launch was made on 4 September 1944.

Post-war, the US would use Fu-Go technology in the E77 balloon bomb project.

The illustrations depict the following weapons, from left to right: canister for the Ta bomb with a Ta bomb beside it, Ko-Dan rubber bomb, Type 99 No.3 Mk.3 Sangō and the Fu-Go.

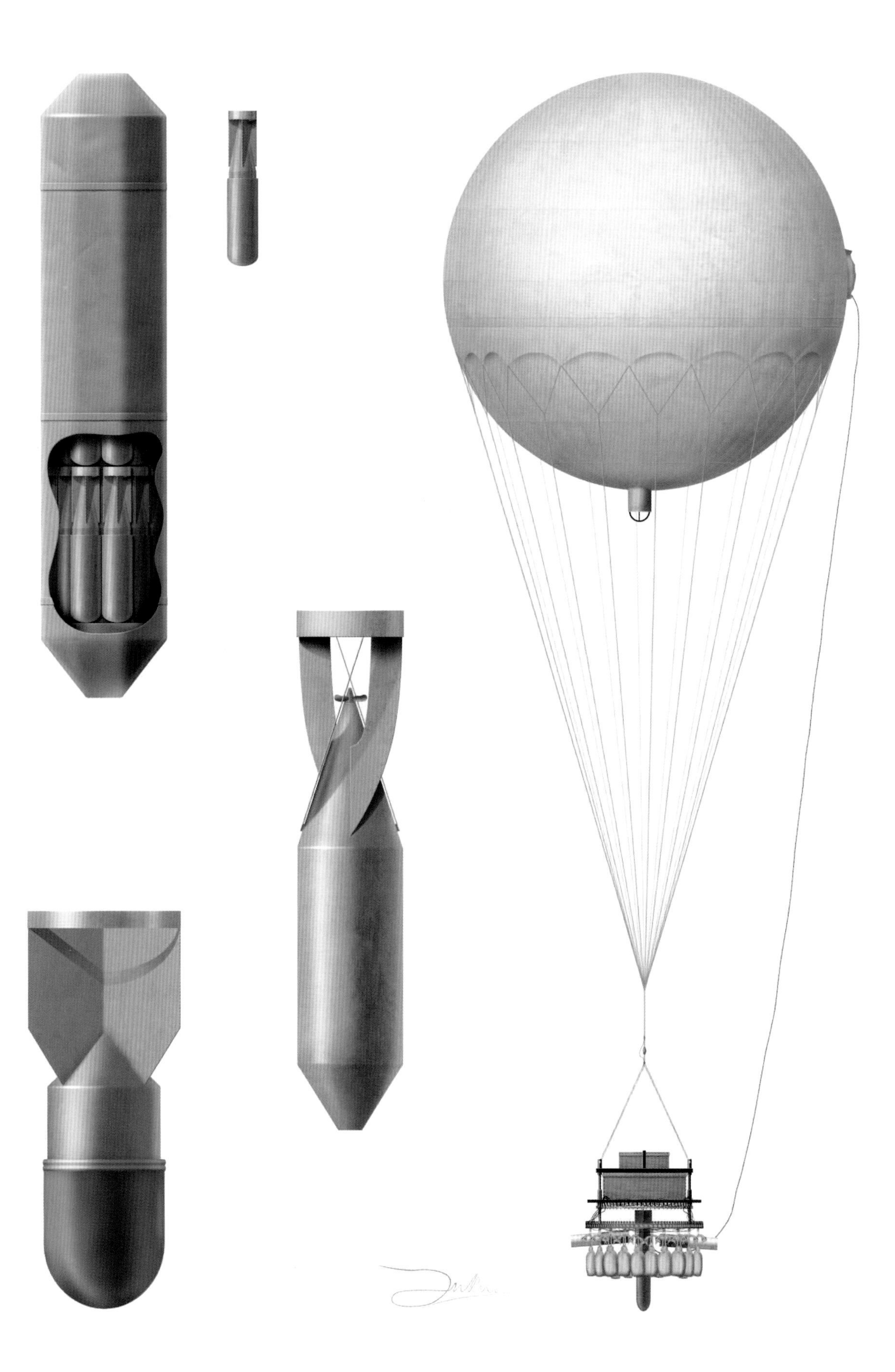

KELCEY FAULKNER

German Technical Exchange with Japan: A Brief Overview

It should not be surprising given Japan was allied to Germany as part of the Axis powers that there were numerous requests for and the exchange of war materials between the two countries. What was perhaps surprising was that the bulk of the exchange would go one way with very little going in the opposite direction.

Japan's relationship with German aircraft and manufacturers went as far back as 1915 when the Isobe Kaizō Rumpler Taube, a copy of the Taube aircraft, was built and flown by the Imperial Flying Association. In the 1920s and 1930s, Heinkel and Junkers were the dominant German firms, both of whose designs were much in demand by the Japanese. Other German firms such as Dornier, Rohrbach and Hansa-Brandenburg also sought to make sales prior to the start of World War 2. Before the war the Japanese military also entertained contacts with British, French and American aviation firms.

However, with the advent of hostilities and Japan having sided with the Axis powers, the country no longer had access to this broad spectrum of aviation companies and aircraft designs. Of course, through their acquisitions of aircraft prior to the war and their subsequent study of aircraft design, the Japanese were capable of producing their own indigenous aircraft with a good measure of success. Prior to the war beginning, and continuing through until 1943, the Japanese obtained a number of German aeroplanes. Some would see series production such as the Bücker Bü 131 Jungmann basic training aircraft, while others were obtained for evaluation or as comparison aircraft to be pitted against Japanese planes.

Formal agreements between Japan and Germany did exist during this time, but it was the signing of the Economic Agreement of January 1943 and, later, the Manufacturing Rights Agreement of March 1944, which paved the way for increased German technical exchange. These agreements, however, restricted Japan to only acquiring technology that Germany's war machine was fielding operationally. This clause denied Japan access to the advanced research being conducted by Germany's war industry. In addition, there were some in the German industrial sector and government who were reluctant to share the fruits of their labours with Japan. Nevertheless, Japan was able to obtain a considerable amount of war material for her army and navy forces. A third agreement, the Patent Rights Agreement drafted in December 1944, was meant to protect technological advancements and prevent confiscation of patents. The Japanese dragged their feet on the agreement and it was never signed.

It would take a decree by Reichschancellor Adolf Hitler in January 1945 to remove the restrictions of the 1943 and 1944 agreements, following which Japan had full access to the German military industry including experimental projects. However, by this time it was too little, too late, because both Germany and Japan lacked the capability to ship material to Japan by sea or by air.

Perhaps surprising given the very long list of technical exchanges that left Germany for Japan is that there was very little that went the other way. Germany was content to receive currency in exchange for the designs and data – Germany needed raw materials for her war industry. One of the very few examples of Japanese technology that was acquired by Germany was a single Nakajima E8N float plane (codenamed *Dave* by the Allies) that, oddly, ended up disguised in British markings and was used by the German merchant raider *Orion*. The only other occasion when Germany attempted to acquire a Japanese aircraft, the Mitsubishi Ki-46 (codenamed *Dinah*), the Japanese ensured that the negotiations with the Luftwaffe for a manufacturing licence went nowhere.

Japan would receive all manner of war goods and data from Germany during the war and it would make for a long list were everything to be included. As such, the list presented here is limited to aircraft and selections pertinent to the experimental nature of the subjects in this book.

Pre-World War 2 German Aircraft Exchange (1914-38)

Dornier Do C transport
In 1927, Kawasaki imported seven aircraft from Dornier including the Do C Komet. Although rejected by the Japanese military, Kawasaki used the Komet to fill an order for three passenger transports from the newspaper service Asahi Shimbun Sha. The three aircraft, known as the Kawasaki-Dornier Komet, were built from imported components. Kawasaki later imported a Dornier Merkur, an updated Komet, leasing the aircraft as the Kawasaki-Dornier Merkur to Asahi Shimbun. However, this Merkur would instead see service with the Army as the Aikoku No. 2 after its conversion to an ambulance. Used during the Manchurian Incident, the Aikoku No. 2 was very active in casualty evacuation and upon retirement became a monument. When the Russians invaded Manchuria in 1945, the plane was burned by the retreating Japanese troops.

Dornier Do J Wal flying boat
In 1929, Kawasaki received an order for a passenger flying boat. As they already had an imported Dornier Wal flying boat from which to source a design, Kawasaki essentially produced their own version using imported components from Dornier. A total of three were built by 1930, being flown as liners for regular passenger services.

Dornier Do N heavy bomber
In 1924, the Army asked Kawasaki to produce a bomber to replace types already in service. To this end, Kawasaki enlisted Dornier and BMW as collaborators on what would become the Type 87 Heavy Bomber. Dornier designed the Do N and the plane was built by Kawasaki, the first completed in 1927. After a year of testing, the bomber, now called the Type 87, was accepted into army service, the last of the 28 bombers being delivered in 1932. Kawasaki produced the BMW VI for the Type 87 under licence. Equipping a handful of bomber chutai, the Type 87 would see brief action during the Manchurian Incident of 1931.

Focke-Wulf Fw 42 bomber
The Fw 42 was a design for a canard-equipped twin-engine bomber. Various revisions of the design were made with wind tunnel models undergoing testing from 1932 to 1933. Once the final revision was settled, a full scale mock-up was built. The Japanese were invited to review the mock-up, Focke-Wulf hoping to entice sales of the bomber or licence rights. The Japanese showed no interest and the Fw 42 was soon cancelled.

Focke-Wulf Fw 200S-1
Announced with a major publicity stunt, the Fw 200S-1 'Brandenburg' took off for Japan from Berlin, Germany, on 28 November 1938 and arrived in Tōkyō in a little under 48 hours. The Japanese were impressed by the Fw 200 and early in 1939 the Dai Nippon Kabushiki Kaisha (Japan-Manchuria Aviation Company) contracted Focke-Wulf for five Fw 200B Condors. Attached to this was an order for a single Fw 200B for the IJN as a maritime reconnaissance aircraft. However, with the outbreak of the war in Europe, none of these orders were fulfilled. The Allies felt, with good reason, that Japan would soon be using the Fw 200 and gave it the codename *Trudy*.

Hansa-Brandenburg float plane
Four were built between 1925 and 1926 as the Aichi Type 15-ko Mi-go. Based on the German plane, Aichi refined the design but failed to win the Navy's competition for a reconnaissance seaplane and so work ceased.

Hansa-Brandenburg W 33 float plane
As part of reparations from World War 1, Germany sent Japan a single W 33 float plane. Highly impressed with the W 33, the IJN requested a copy which resulted in the Type Hansa. 310 were built and served with the IJN from 1926 to 1928 before being retired; many were converted to passenger float planes for civilian use.

Heinkel HD 23 carrier fighter
In 1926, Aichi contracted Heinkel to design a carrier fighter for entry into a Navy competition to replace the Mitsubishi Type 10 fighter then in service. Called the HD 23 by Heinkel, it was known as the Aichi Type-H Carrier Fighter in Japan. Two were built by 1927 and much emphasis was placed on the capability of the plane to ditch at sea, including jettisonable landing gear and the ability for the engine to stop the propeller in the horizontal position. However, performance-wise, the Aichi Type-H Carrier Fighter showed up poorly and lost the competition to Nakajima.

Heinkel HD 25 two-seat float plane
Licence-built in Japan as the Aichi Navy Type 2, this aircraft saw service on a number of heavy cruisers from 1926 onwards, though their service life was short due to the advent of catapult launched seaplanes. The few Aichi Navy Type 2 aircraft were then sold to the civilian market. Later, in 1930, three Type 2 aircraft were converted to transports for civilian use.

Heinkel HD 25 transport
Built as the AB-1, Aichi used the Heinkel HD 25 as the basis for their entry into a 'made in Japan' passenger/transport contest operated by the Aviation Bureau of the Department of Communications. The AB-1 could be converted to a seaplane if required and proved its worth going on to win the contest and seeing several years' service in private hands.

Heinkel HD 26 single-seat float plane
A single example was built by Aichi (also as the Aichi Navy Type 2) while the Navy also acquired a Heinkel constructed HD 26. Both were tested in 1926, but like the two-seater, the model was made obsolete by catapults. Both aircraft were turned over for civilian use.

Heinkel HD 28 three-seat float plane
The Navy purchased one HD 28 from Heinkel in 1926. Tested by the Navy, problems with the Lorraine-Dietrich engine saw the HD 28 failing to meet expectations and in 1928 the Navy withdrew their interest in the design.

Heinkel HD 56 seaplane
To meet a 1929 Navy need for a catapult launched seaplane, Aichi once more turned to Heinkel and imported the HD 56. Meeting the needs of the Navy after modification, it was accepted into service in 1931 as the Aichi E3A1 beginning with the first deliveries out of an eventual total of 12 aircraft. The E3A1 saw combat during the Sino-Japanese conflict, operating from Jintsu-class cruisers. It did not, however, remain in service long, being replaced with superior aircraft. Some E3A1 seaplanes were retained by the Navy as trainers with the remainder released to the civilian market.

Heinkel HD 62 three-seat float plane
Aichi turned to Heinkel to produce a long-range reconnaissance float plane to meet a 1931 request by the Navy for just such a craft. Called the Aichi AB-5, testing showed the design to be sound but with room for further refinement. This would result in the AB-6 of 1932 which, despite being successful, was not accepted into service having been beaten by a Kawasaki design.

Heinkel He 50/He 66
In 1933, the Navy issued requests for a carrier dive bomber. Aichi elected to utilise Heinkel's He 50 which was then entering service with clandestine military air force training units. Called the He 66 for export reasons, Heinkel delivered a single He 66 to Aichi who, after some modifications, submitted it to the Navy. Winning the Navy's competition, the modified He 66 was then licence built in Japan, entering service with the Navy in 1935 as the Aichi D1A1. The D1A1 would see action in China in

1937. The Allies, thinking the D1A1 would be met in battle, assigned it the codename *Susie*. As it was, the D1A1 remained in Japanese service only as a trainer, having long since been withdrawn from frontline service.

Heinkel He 70
light reconnaissance bomber

In the late 1930s, a He 70 was imported to Japan. Few details are available but the wing form of the He 70 would later provide the influence for the wing design of the Aichi D3A1 carrier bomber, known to the Allies as *Val*.

Heinkel He 112B-0 fighter

In 1937, the IJN was seeking new fighters to combat the increasingly modern aircraft being encountered in China. Heinkel was at the time looking to export the He 112, a design which was ultimately rejected by the Luftwaffe. The IJN placed an order for 30 HE 112B-0 fighters, known in Japan as the A7Hel Type He Air Defence Fighter. 12 of the 30 were delivered though Japanese pilots disliked the performance of the plane and mechanics had difficulties maintaining the liquid-cooled engines. As Japanese fighters of improved capability were entering service, the He 112B-0 never saw combat and the Japanese cancelled the remaining 18 aircraft. Serviceable He 112B-0 were used as instructional aircraft and as means to study German manufacturing techniques. Figuring the He 112B-0 was in active service, the Allies codenamed the aircraft *Jerry* although it was never encountered.

Heinkel He 118 dive bomber

With the Luftwaffe uninterested in the He 118, Heinkel found the Japanese receptive to the plane. The IJN placed an order for a single He 118 to be delivered by February 1937 along with the licence to manufacture the He 118 in Japan. The IJA also purchased a single He 118 for delivery by October 1937. Known in Japan as the DXHel, Hitachi Seisakusho was to be the company that would produce the licensed aircraft. The He 118 V4 was shipped to Japan and assembled at Yokosuka for the IJN, but during a test flight it broke up in the air and the IJN abandoned the plane. The IJA received the He 118 V5 months later but it too lost interest and Heinkel received no further orders.

Junkers G 38/K 51 heavy bomber

The Army sought to have their own version of the Junkers massive G 38 airliner and in September 1928, Mitsubishi entered into a contract with Junkers for the design specifications, blueprints, manufacturing data and licence to build the aircraft as a bomber, known as the K 51, the export version of the G 38. Mitsubishi sent designers to Germany in 1928 to study the G 38 and production techniques, and by 1930, the necessary tools, jigs and material were imported and in place. Junkers sent a team of engineers to Japan to assist with the production. The first bomber, the Ki-20, was completed in 1931. A total of six were built from 1931 to 1935. Kept in secret, the general public was not made aware of the Ki-20 until 1940 when three Ki-20s participated in a parade fly-over. The Ki-20 did not see action.

Junkers K 37 bomber

A single K 37 bomber was imported through Sweden and was donated to the Army as Aikoku-1. Used during the Manchurian Incident, the Army was impressed with the K 37 and in 1932 asked Mitsubishi to make a similar bomber. Using the K 37 as a basis and capitalising on experience from the Ki-20, the prototype Ki-1 heavy bomber was completed in March 1933. Despite problems with the engines, the Ki-1 was adopted to replace the old Type 87. The Ki-1-II soon appeared in an attempt to fix issues with the Ki-1 but it was not liked by the crews that flew it. Another aircraft, the Ki-2 light bomber, was also built using the K 37 as a basis. The Ki-2 and later Ki-2-II (both being built from 1933 to 1938) proved very successful, seeing action in China and later as trainers into the late 1930s. The Allies thought the Ki-2-II was still in service when the war began and assigned it the codename *Louise*.

Junkers Ju 90 transport

On 25 July 1938, Mitsubishi entered into negotiations with Junkers on behalf of the IJA to work with the German company to produce a bomber version of the Ju 90 transport. Ten were to be completed and flown to Japan. The IJA even allocated the designation Ki-90 for the bomber. However, Junkers eventually declined Mitsubishi's proposal citing its involvement in filling domestic orders for aircraft.

Junkers Ju 160 transport

The Ju 160 was an improved Junkers Ju 60, the latter having lost to the Heinkel He 70 in the fast, small airliner market. Lufthansa purchased 11 Ju 160A-0 and 10 Ju 160D-0 6-passenger aircraft, putting them into service in 1935-36. Two would end up in Manchuria, registered as civilian aircraft. The IJN pressed them into service as the LXJ.

L.V.G. D.IX

The D.IX provided the inspiration for the Seishiki-1 which used an imported Mercedes Daimler 100hp engine, later licence-built in Japan. The Seishiki-1 was completed in 1916 but the biplane's poor performance resulted in further development being cancelled.

Rohrbach R flying boat

The Navy was very interested in the metal aircraft construction techniques used by the German company Rohrbach. Mitsubishi was asked to study the techniques and the two companies would form Mitsubishi-Rohrbach GmbH in Berlin in June 1925. A total of three Rohrbach flying boats were to be imported, the R-1, R-2 and R-3, known collectively as the Mitsubishi Experimental Type-R flying boats. Although these aircraft would prove to have poor take-off and alighting that denied them military service, they did provide invaluable experience to Mitsubishi when it came to metal stressed skin construction.

Rumpler Taube

The Imperial Flying Association purchased two Rumpler Taube aircraft prior to the outbreak of World War 1. As Japan was part of the Entente Powers, and thus against Germany, the Japanese Army bought the two Taubes from the Association for use in action in the Tsingtao campaign. With no aircraft, the Imperial Flying Association built their own version of the Taube calling it the Isobe Kaizo Rumpler Taube. The solitary aircraft first flew in 1915 before being wrecked in a crash later in the year. The remains were cannibalised and used in the Ozaki Soga-go of 1917.

World War 2 German Aircraft Exchange (1939-1945)

Arado Ar 196 float plane

It was reported by Allied intelligence services that the Japanese received two Ar 196 float planes. However, there is no evidence to suggest this occurred. The Germans operated a submarine facility at Penang, Malaysia, and the unit used the Ar 196 in Japanese colours which may have led to the confusion in the intelligence report.

Arado Ar 234 Blitz jet reconnaissance bomber

The Ar 234 was a twin-turbojet, single-seat reconnaissance bomber that entered service with the Luftwaffe in September 1944. Allied intelligence intercepted a communication between Germany and Japan in March 1944 that confirmed that the Japanese had data on the Ar 234. It was assumed that the data related to the Ar 234A, which was not as advanced as the subsequent Ar 234B models. Another report went so far as to say production plans were in place to build the latest Ar 234 aircraft but this was based solely on the fact another report stated that the FuG 136 Nachtfee visual command indicator equipment (used in the Ar 234P series night fighters) had been delivered to Japan in January 1945. It would become clear that the Ar 234 was never produced in Japan and it is unknown exactly what data Japan did receive on this aircraft.

Bachem Ba 349 Natter rocket interceptor

The Natter (meaning 'Viper' in German) was a rocket powered point defence interceptor – in essence, a manned rocket launched vertically towards enemy bombers where it would use its high speed to avoid enemy fighters and launch a salvo of either 73mm Hs 217 Fohn or 55mm R4M rockets at the attacking bombers. The pilot would then eject from the Ba 349 and return to earth via parachute along with the engine portion of the aircraft. The Ba 349 required little in terms of critical war materials and could be constructed by semi-skilled workers. Several unmanned test flights were flown but the only recorded manned flight ended in the death of the pilot. Despite a handful being deployed, none saw action. Allied intelligence surmised that the Japanese were provided with information on the Ba 349 and they were correct. The RLM ordered Erich Bachem to give the Japanese a complete set of plans for the Ba 349. However, the submarine carrying the data was lost at sea. When this transfer occurred is unknown but it would likely have been late in the war.

GINO MARCOMINI

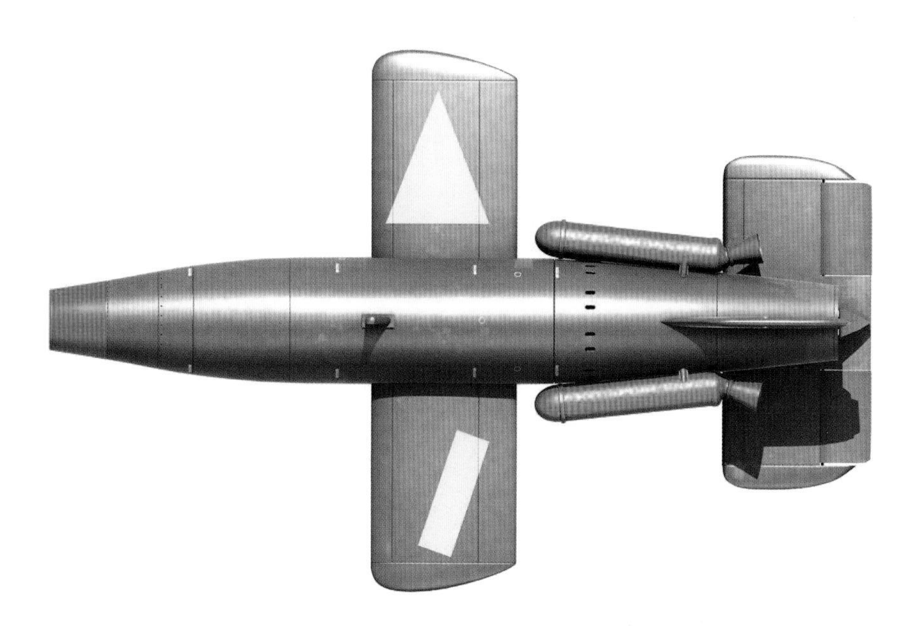

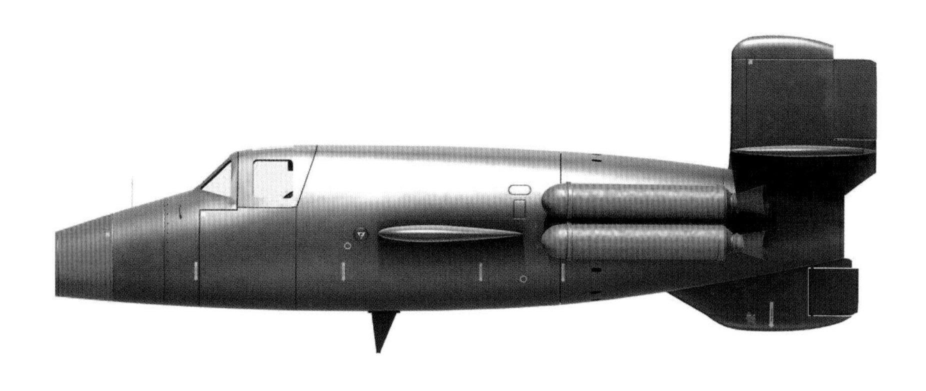

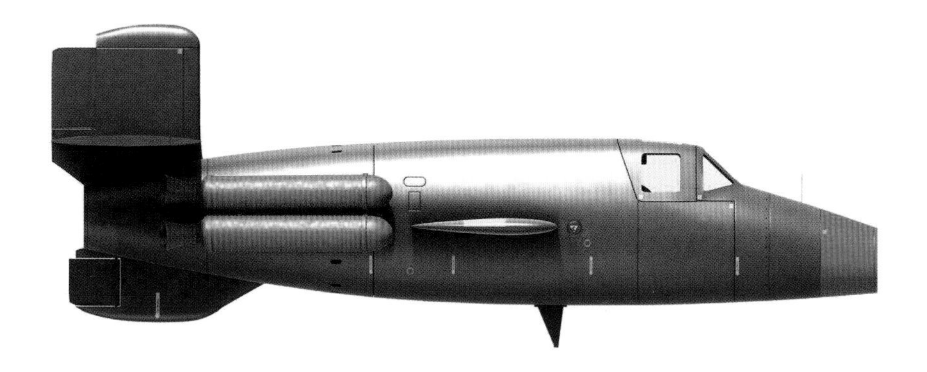

Blohm und Voss Ha 142 heavy bomber
The Ha 142 (later the BV 142) was the land version of the Ha 139 float plane. Unlike the successful Ha 139, the Ha 142 was, ultimately, a failure when converted from a transport to a reconnaissance bomber aircraft in 1940. Despite this, the Blohm und Voss P.48 project was listed as a bomber version of the Ha 142 for Japan. Most likely, this remained a paper concept with no further action being taken as only four BV 142 aircraft were built before the type was withdrawn from service in 1942.

Bücker Bü 131 Jungmann trainer
In August 1942, the Japanese obtained the licence to produce the Jungmann trainer (meaning 'Young Man' in German). The Bü 131 had been demonstrated to the Japanese in 1938 and a total of 22 aircraft were purchased from 1938 to 1939. The Japanese attempted to make their own version of the Bü 131 but the results paled in comparison to the German aircraft and this resulted in the 1942 acquisition of production rights. The Bü 131 was produced for the IJA as the Kokusai Ki-86a and for the IJN as the Kyūshū K9W1 Momiji (meaning 'Maple'). One all-wood Ki-86b was completed in February 1945 but remained a prototype. All told, 339 K9W1 and 1,037 Ki-86a aircraft were built from 1942 through 1945. The Allies codenamed both aircraft *Cypress*.

Dornier Do 217 heavy bomber
It was reported the Japan received two Do 217 aircraft in January 1943, and that by July 1943 the Japanese had purchased the manufacturing licence for the bomber. However, no record exists of any Do 217 being sent to Japan, nor the purchase of the licence, and so the report may have been made in error.

Dornier Do 335 Pfeil fighter bomber
The Pfeil ('Arrow') was a twin engine, puller-pusher fighter and one of the fastest piston-engine fighters of World War 2. Although a number of Do 335s of various makes would eventually be built (and ten Do 335A-0 aircraft were used in the field by Erprobungskommando 335), the type did not enter service with the Luftwaffe. Nevertheless, it was believed that the Japanese were provided with a description of the Do 335 in March 1945 but no substantive information was released to them.

Dornier Do 635
long-range reconnaissance aircraft
The Do 635 was basically two Do 335 aircraft mated together by way of a centre wing section. Conceived in mid-1944, the design of the Do 635 was completed soon afterwards and the RLM ordered four prototypes and six pre-production aircraft. By the close of 1944, the Do 635 was shared with the Japanese who found the design intriguing but outside of their interest. The Japanese made no further moves to obtain the aircraft. Although wind tunnel models were completed and tested and a mock-up of the cockpits were built, the Do 635 was cancelled on 5 February 1945.

Heinkel He 100D-0 fighter
In 1940, Japan paid 2.8 million Reichsmarks for three He 100D-0 aircraft and the manufacturing rights. It was planned to produce the He 100D-0 as the AXHel but the war prevented Heinkel from delivering the required jigs and tools and so production was abandoned. Nevertheless, the Japanese were very impressed with the fighter and the design was a major influence for the successful Kawasaki Ki-61 Hien. Interestingly, Allied intelligence thought that details of a 'He 113' were received by Japan in July 1943. The 'He 113' was actually the He 100. A propaganda ruse using the few He 100s built tried to make it appear that the type was in German service and this succeeded in fooling Allied intelligence who used the 'He 113' designation in their reports.

Heinkel He 119
The Japanese purchased the He 119 V7 and V8 in 1940. See the chapter on the Kūgishō R2Y Keiun for more information.

Heinkel He 162 jet fighter
See the Tachikawa Ki-162 chapter for more information concerning the Japanese acquisition of this fighter in April of 1945.

Heinkel He 177A-7 bomber
The IJN were interested in the He 177 and negotiated to produce the bomber in Japan, with Hitachi building it under licence in Chiba in 1942. The major change was that the Japanese version would use four separate engines to avoid the plethora of problems the Germans encountered with the original coupled engine design. Sample tools were delivered to Japan by submarine but Heinkel was unable to ship the remainder of the machining apparatus and jigs and production was dropped. One He 177A-7 was to be flown to Japan in 1944 to serve as a manufacturing pattern airframe and evaluation aircraft but the bomber lacked the range, even after modification, to make the flight via the route demanded by the Japanese running through Persia and India. Some sources list the proposed plane as the Hitachi 'He-Type' heavy bomber.

Heinkel He 219 Uhu night fighter
The Uhu, meaning 'owl' in German, was perhaps the most advanced night fighter to see operational service in World War 2. The Japanese are believed to have been aware of the He 219 with full access to the relevant design data by July 1944. If this was the case, it is not known what, if anything, the Japanese did with the information.

Heinkel He 277 heavy bomber
The He 277 was, essentially, the He 177 with four separate engines instead of the coupled engines which caused so many problems for Heinkel and maintenance crews. Unlike the He 177, the He 277 would never enter production, being cancelled in July 1944 in favour of more fighters. It was believed that full details of the He 277 were provided to the Japanese in March 1944. One could assume that since the proposed Japanese version of the He 177 would use four separate engines, information on the He 277 would have been of value.

Henschel Hs 129
twin-engine ground attack aircraft
The Hs 129 was a dedicated ground attack platform which, while having problematic engines and poor manoeuvrability, possessed excellent armour and the ability to carry a wide array of armaments. Allied intelligence reported that German sources listed two Hs 129 aircraft for delivery to Japan sometime in 1944. Since none reached Japan, it can be presumed that they were never dispatched and the aircraft were used in German service.

Henschel Hs 130
high-altitude medium bomber
The Hs 130 was the evolution of the Hs 128, the latter a testbed for pressure cabins and high-altitude flight. Initially developed as a reconnaissance platform, the Hs 130 would later evolve into a bomber. Several prototypes were constructed and tested but the type did not enter service and was cancelled in 1944. It was believed by Allied intelligence that the Japanese obtained complete details on the Hs 130 program in July 1944. Recently published photographs showing wartime Japanese notes on the Hs 130, including sketches of the pressure cabin and associated systems, confirm the intelligence.

Fieseler Fi 103R Reichenberg
A US intelligence report stated that the Japanese were aware of the piloted versions of the Fi 103 (V-1) flying bomb and wished to use them. Codenamed 'Reichenberg' by the Germans, 175 Fi 103Rs were built but the unit

tasked with flying them, 5./KG 200 'Leonidas Staffel', would not see combat. The Fi 103R I, II and III were training versions – the Reichenberg I was a single-seater without the Argus pulsejet engine, the Reichenberg II a two-seater with no engine and the Reichenberg III a single seat version but with the engine fitted. In all cases, ballast simulated the warhead weight. The Reichenberg IV was the operational model. It has been suggested that the Reichenberg was the inspiration for the Kawanishi Baika.

Focke-Wulf Fw 190A-5 fighter. Ted S. Nomura/Mid Visions and Antarctic Press

Fieseler Fi 156 Storch army cooperation/observation plane
In June 1941, Japan received one example of the Fi 156 for evaluation. The IJA was impressed with the 'Stork' and desired to have its own version. The result was the Kokusai Ki-76, codenamed *Stella* by the Allies. The Ki-76, despite the obvious similarity to the Fi 156, was not a direct copy as the prototype was completed and flying before the Japanese received their Fi 156. In comparison testing, the Ki-76 was actually found to be superior in all areas except landing distance.

Focke-Achgelis Fa 330 Bachstelze rotorkite
This little engine-less rotorkite (the German name means 'wagtail') was used by a small number of German U-boats as a means to provide increased visibility to observers while the submarines were on the surface. The Fa 330, after being unpacked and assembled, was tethered to the submarine and the wind would turn the three-bladed rotor as the submarine moved forward. Once airborne, the observer could see up to 25 miles instead of the few miles afforded to an observer in the conning tower. One intelligence report suggested that the Japanese may have shown an interest in the Fa 330 had they been made aware of it.

Focke-Wulf Fw190A-5 fighter
In 1943, the Japanese imported one example of this aircraft to pit against Japanese fighter designs and compare their performance. Figuring that Japan would use the Fw 190 in combat, the Allies assigned the codename *Fred* to the aircraft but none encountered.

Focke-Wulf Ta 152 high-altitude fighter
In April 1945, the Japanese purchased the specifications for the Ta 152 as a means to rapidly acquire a high-altitude fighter. However, by this time, there was simply no way for the Japanese to act on the material obtained.

Gotha Go 242 transport glider/ Go 244 transport
In a letter dated 7 February 1944 discovered at Bad Eilsen in May 1945, the Deutsche Mitsui Bussan requested from the Germans design plans for both the Go 242 and the Go 244, the latter being a twin-engine version of the glider. No evidence has surfaced to suggest that either of these craft were sent to Japan. However, it is suggested that they were the inspiration for the Kokusai Ku-7 Manazuru (meaning 'Crane') glider and the powered version of the Ku-7, the Kokusai Ki-105 Ōtori ('Phoenix'). Both the Ku-7 and the Ki-105 were codenamed *Buzzard* by the Allies.

Junkers Ju 52/3m transport
Though the Japanese had no interest in the 'Tante Ju', the Allies thought the Japanese would be using the transport in action. This idea may have stemmed from a May 1939 flight made by a Ju 52/3m to Japan to bolster trade relations. As such, the plane was codenamed *Trixie*.

Junkers Ju 87A 'Stuka' dive bomber
In 1940, a single Ju 87A was sent to Japan for evaluation. By 1939, all A models had been withdrawn from frontline German service, and after flight testing and study the plane was put into the collection of the Tokorozawa museum. However, it was lost when the museum was bombed. The Allies, believing the Japanese would be using the Ju 87, assigned it the codename *Irene*.

Junkers Ju 88A-4 bomber
The Japanese acquired a single example of the Ju 88A-4 in 1940 for the purposes of testing and evaluating the aircraft as well as for the study of the design. The Japanese had no intentions of producing the bomber but nevertheless the Allies thought it likely they would and thus gave the Ju 88 the codename *Janice*. As an aside, one intelligence report states that the Mitsubishi office in Berlin had a number of 'Ju 88K-5' (the export version of the Ju 88A-4) aircraft and parts shipped to Japan, perhaps in 1943, though this has never been verified and only the single Ju 88A-4 is known to have been delivered.

Junkers Ju 290 long range heavy bomber
The Ju 290 was initially a heavy, four engine transport aircraft that was reworked into a long range maritime reconnaissance and bomber aircraft. It was felt that by October 1943, the Japanese were in possession of the complete details of the Ju 290. Even if this was the case, it would appear the Japanese did not act on the information and they may have been more interested in the Ju 390. There is no evidence to suggest that the Ju 290A-7 was ever adapted as a 'nuclear' bomber for the Japanese, especially in light of the fact few A-7 models were ever completed. Some sources suggest that Ju 290 flights were made into Manchuria carrying documents and other intelligence, possibly in exchange for raw materials from Japan, but information has never surfaced confirming these flights and popular opinion in the face of current evidence is that they did not occur.

Junkers Ju 390A-1 reconnaissance bomber
In 1944, the IJA was very interested in the potential of the Ju 390 as a strategic bomber and sought to obtain the rights to the aircraft. In the fall of 1944, the Japanese acquired the manufacturing licence and design plans for the Ju 390A-1 long-range bomber reconnaissance aircraft. By 28 February 1945, Major-General Ōtani of the IJA was to have collected the plans and licence from the Germans but it is unknown if this ever occurred. In any case, the Ju 390 V3, which was to be the prototype for the bomber reconnaissance design, was never built.

Junkers Ju 488 long range bomber
The Ju 488 was a design by Junkers to rapidly produce a long range bomber using components of aircraft then in production. Combining parts from the Ju 388K, Ju 188E, Ju 88A-15 and Ju 288C bombers, construction of two Ju 488 prototypes was begun (V401 and V402), but prior to completion these were destroyed by French resistance forces in July

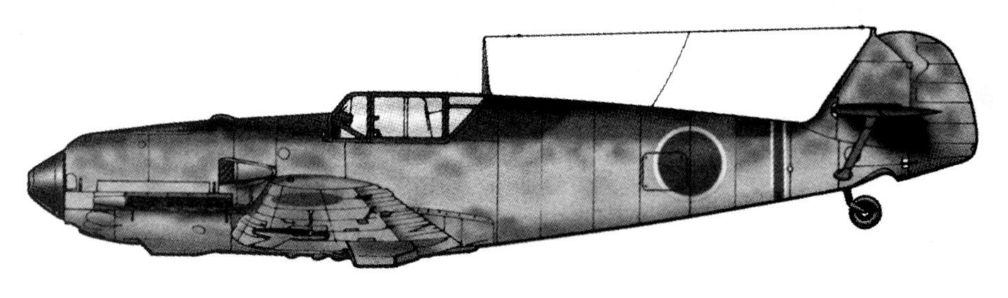

Messerschmitt Bf 109E-7 fighter. Ted S. Nomura/Mid Visions and Antarctic Press

1944. In November 1944, the Ju 488 program was cancelled. In January 1945, the Ju 488 design was offered to Japan but neither the IJA nor IJN took any interest in it. This rejection sealed the fate of the project.

Messerschmitt Bf 109E-7 fighter
In 1941, the Japanese obtained three Bf 109E-7 fighters. These were pitted against various Japanese fighter designs for comparison purposes. Despite the Japanese having no intention of licence building the fighter, the Allies anticipated that they would be encountered in combat and gave the plane the codename *Mike*.

Messerschmitt Bf 110 heavy fighter
Although the Japanese never imported the Bf 110, Allied sources assumed that the aircraft would be seen in combat and gave the Bf 110 the codename *Doc*.

Messerschmitt Me 163B Komet rocket fighter
For details, please see the chapter on the Mitsubishi J8M Syūsui.

Messerschmitt Me 209 fighter
Originally, the Me 209 was designed as a high-speed aircraft capable of breaking the world air speed record. In fact, the Me 209 V1 would set the record at a speed of 755.14km/h (469.22mph) on 16 April 1939. Beginning with the Me 209 V4, the design shifted to that of a fighter. Despite a number of prototypes, the Me 209 was not accepted for service. Still, Allied intelligence was positive that the Japanese knew of the Me 209 and, in fact, a Japanese military attaché in Berlin did recommend in 1943 that the manufacturing rights for the aircraft be acquired as well as a sample aircraft. It would appear this was not acted upon.

Messerschmitt Me 210A-2 heavy fighter
One Me 210A-2, Werk-Nr. 2350, was modified to the standard of the Me 410 (with the exception that it retained the original Daimler-Benz DB 601F engines) and sent to Japan in 1942 for evaluation. After testing, no further interest was shown in the design.

Messerschmitt Me 262A Schwalbe jet fighter
For more details, please see the chapter on the Nakajima Kitsuka and Nakajima Ki-201 Karyū.

Messerschmitt Me 309 fighter
The Me 309 was a failed attempt to create a replacement for the Bf 109. The tricycle landing gear was cause for grief and in comparison testing the Me 309 V1 came up short against the Bf 109. Fully loaded, the Me 309 offered only a marginal increase in speed over the Bf 109 and the latter could out turn the former. With the advent of the Focke-Wulf Fw 190D and the superior performance it offered, the Me 309 was shelved with the remaining prototypes serving as testbeds. Despite the failure of the Me 309, the Japanese attempted to purchase the Me 309 in 1943 prior to the termination of the program. It would appear that with the cancellation of the Me 309, no sales of the remaining aircraft or manufacturing rights were offered to Japan.

Messerschmitt Me 323 Gigant transport
Allied intelligence believed that the Japanese received plans and components for the Me 323 Gigant (meaning 'Giant'), the powered version of the massive Me 321 Gigant transport glider. Although the Japanese were interested in large transports, there is no evidence to suggest they had an interest in the Me 323.

Messerschmitt Me 410 heavy fighter
It was thought by Allied intelligence that the Germans had shared information on the Me 410 with the Japanese in November 1942, with other sources suggesting this occurred closer to the end of 1943. However, no such interest in the Me 410 was shown nor were any aircraft delivered. It may be that some confusion was caused by the one Me 210A-2 that Japan did receive and was configured to the Me 410 standard.

Messerschmitt Me 509 fighter
The Me 509 was a planned derivative of the Me 309, sharing components such as the tricycle landing gear. The Daimler-Benz DB 605B 12-cylinder engine was housed inside the fuselage, behind the cockpit. The propeller was driven via an extension shaft with the cockpit situated well forwards in the nose. The wings were mounted low on the fuselage. The Kūgishō R2Y1 Keiun bears an uncanny resemblance to the Me 509 and it has been suggested that when the Japanese sought the Me 309, information on the Me 509 was also provided to them. No evidence has yet proven this, however.

Other Exchange Items

50mm Bordkanone 5 (BK-5) aircraft cannon
This cannon, used operationally by the Germans in the Me 410A-1/U4 and Me 410A-2/U4 heavy fighters for anti-bomber missions, garnered interest from the Japanese who saw the weapon at a Luftwaffe airfield in Posen in the Warthegau. There is no evidence that an example was sent to Japan.

A4 ballistic missile
Better known as the V-2, the A4 was the first ballistic missile to be used operationally in combat. In an OSS (Office of Strategic Services) report from September 1944, it was said that the Japanese had purchased the design plans for the A4. Another OSS report added that in February 1945 a Doctor Yamada of the Chemical Research Institute brought the plans to Japan. It was surmised that the Japanese were building the missile in Mukden (Shenyang) in Northern China for use against targets in the Philippines and the Chinese interior. However, the OSS reports remained unverified and it was believed by other intelligence agencies that the Japanese would not have had much interest in the A4, let alone that they could construct it. Other sources say the Germans had no intention of releasing information on the A4 to the Japanese.

Blohm und Voss BV 246 Hagelkorn glider bomb
The BV 246 Hagelkorn (meaning 'hailstone' in German) was a radio-guided glider bomb. 1,100 examples of the BV 246 were built from December 1943 through February 1944 before the factory producing them was destroyed by bombing. Using a radio receiver, the bomb also used a smoke generator to assist the operator in guiding the bomb onto the target. Despite good results, it was felt the guidance system could be too easily

jammed and production was not resumed. Allied intelligence believed that information on the BV 246 was made available to the Japanese prior to April 1944.

Donau-60 Bolometer
The Danube-60 was an infra-red detection system used to control coastal guns. It used four thermal sensors in parabolic dish arrangements with a bolometer at each focal point. These dishes would detect the heat given off by ships, for example, through their funnels, and the data was then transmitted to gun layers who would bring the guns to bear on the target. Zeiss produced the system at the rate of 20-30 a month but how widespread it was in service is unknown. That the Japanese may have been interested in this bolometer can be seen in their developments of the Ke-Go (see the chapter on Japanese bombs for more information).

Fieseler Fi 103 guided bomb
Better known as the V-1 or 'buzz bomb' (among many nicknames, German and Allied alike), the Fi 103 was a crude cruise missile first used in action against England. Intelligence reports claim that documentation on the Fi 103 was provided to the Japanese in October 1943, and in November 1944, the Japanese acquired a Fi 103A. These reports also suggest that the Japanese were far more interested in air launching methods than ramps, and data was provided to the Japanese on the methods for air launch techniques as practiced by III/KG 3 and I/KG 53, who fired the Fi 103 from Heinkel He 111H-22 bombers.

Heinkel HeS 011 turbojet
The HeS was to be the next generation of turbojet and was to be the powerplant of choice for a great number of German project designs, and also the first of the second generation jet fighters such as the Messerschmitt P 1101 and the Focke-Wulf Ta 183 'Huckebein'. Only 19 were built before the close of the war and the engine never attained production status. Allied intelligence cited a 12 March 1945 letter from Kurt Lammertz to Director Wolff of Heinkel-Hirth stating that the IJN should be supplied with complete plans for the HeS 011 engine and that it should be transferred via submarine. There is no evidence to show this transfer was completed.

Henschel Hs 293 guided bomb
The Hs 293 was an SC500 bomb onto which wings, a tail and a rocket engine were mated. The Hs 293A-1, which was the only operational model, used radio signals to direct its bomb to the target. Later test versions used wire-guidance as a means to defeat jamming. The weapon entered service in 1943 and, early in that year, a Japanese delegation was given a demonstration of the Hs 293A-1 at a field in Gartz in Germany. The Germans kept information on the improved, wire-guided Hs 293A-2 from the delegation. It is unknown if the Japanese acquired further information on the weapon and Allied intelligence reports suggest that, if they had, the Hs 293 would not have reached service until the fall of 1945. In addition, one report makes the assumption that the Hs 293 was an influence on the Kūgishō MXY7 Ōka in so far as a human operator, in the weapon itself, would have overcome the lengthy research and development of a radio guided munitions.

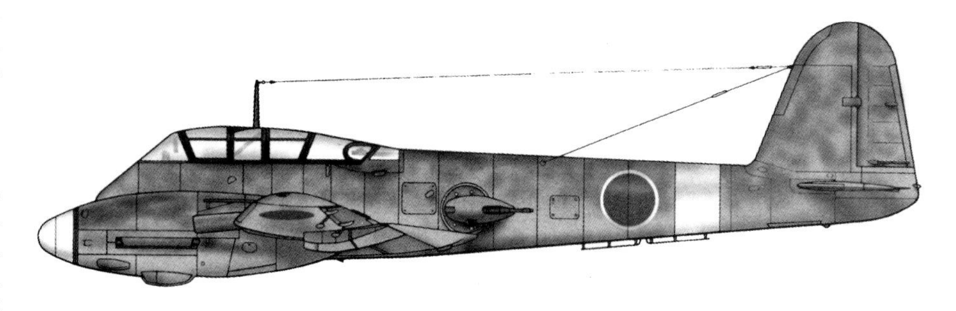

Messerschmitt Me 210 twin-engined fighter. Ted S. Nomura/Mid Visions and Antarctic Press

Henschel Hs 294 guided bomb
This was an improved version of the He 293, incorporating a longer, more pointed nose, heavier warhead and two rocket engines. The Hs 294A used radio guidance, the Hs 294B wire guidance and the Hs 294D used television guidance. The Hs 294 failed to see service. However, in December 1944, IJN representatives met with German Air Ministry officials to discuss the Hs 294 but with what results is unknown.

Rheinmetall-Borsig MK 108 30mm aircraft cannon
Known as the 'pneumatic hammer', the MK 108 cannon was a very successful weapon encompassing heavy hitting power, ease of manufacturing and compactness in one package. Despite having a low muzzle velocity which reduced range, it was used on a number of operational German aircraft and secret projects. The Japanese were very interested in manufacturing the cannon and studied the requirements to produce it. Captured documentation in June 1943 suggested production was soon to be underway as the Japanese had received examples of the MK 108A-2 cannon. The MK 108 was not built in Japan.

Ruhrstahl-Kramer PC 1400X Fritz-X guided bomb
The Fritz-X was a guided munition made from the unguided PC 1400 'Fritz' bomb. Using a cruciform tail arrangement with guidable fins, the Fritz-X was directed to the target via radio signals sent by the operator in the launch aircraft. To help visibility, flares were installed in the tail. The munition saw service from August 1943 to the end of the war in April 1945, being relatively successful in the anti-shipping role. The Japanese were aware of the Fritz-X and information on the bomb was available to Japan in September 1944. It is unknown if any examples were provided or if the Japanese pursued the weapon further.

Ruhrstahl-Kramer X4 air-to-air guided missile
Considered to be the first air-to-air missile to be used successfully in World War 2, the X4 was a short range, wire-guided, rocket-powered AAM that was extensively tested after being conceived at the start of 1943. The X4 was test launched from a number of aircraft such as the Junkers Ju 188L and Focke-Wulf Fw 190F-8 and was envisioned that the Messerschmitt Me 262 would carry the X4 into operational service. Despite 1,300 being built – and suggestions that some were test fired in action against American bombers – no X4 saw active service. Allied intelligence services assumed that the Japanese were aware of the X4 development but no evidence has surfaced to confirm this.

Bibliography

3D CG Japanese Experimental Aircraft. Tōkyō, Futabasha Publishers Ltd., 2003.

Aeronautical Staff of Aero Publishers, Inc. *Kamikaze*. Fallbrook, Aero Publishers, Inc., 1966.

Akimoto, Minoru. *All the Experimental Aircraft in Japanese Army*. Tōkyō, Kantosha Co., 2008.

Baba, Kazuo et al. *General View of Japanese Military Aircraft in the Pacific War*. Tōkyō, Kanto-Sha Co. Ltd., 1958.

Bueschel, Richard M. *Japanese Aircraft Insignia, Camouflage and Markings*. West Roxbury, World War 1 Aero Publishers, Inc., 1966.

Bueschel, Richard M. 'Japanese Army Aircraft.' *Air Pictorial* June-Sept 1956.

Bueschel, Richard M. *Japanese Code Names*. West Roxbury: World War 1 Aero Publishers, Inc., 1966.

Bueschel, Richard M. 'Japanese Navy Aircraft 1940-1945.' *Air Pictorial* Dec 1958-Mar. 1959, July 1959.

Butler, Phil H. *War Prizes*. Leicester, Midland Counties Publications, 1994.

Donald, David. *The Complete Encyclopedia of World Aircraft*. New York, Barnes & Noble Books, 1998.

'Dreaming - The Mitsubishi G7M1: Experimental Model 'Great Mountain'. *Koku Fan* November 1975, pp82-83.

Ethell, Jeffrey and Alfred Price. *World War II Fighting Jets*. Shrewsbury, Airlife Publishing Ltd., 1994.

Famous Airplanes of the World No.24: Army Experimental Fighters. Tōkyō, Bunrin-Do Co. Ltd., 1990.

Famous Airplanes of the World No.129: Kyūshū Navy Experimental Interceptor Fighter Shinden. Tōkyō, Bunrin-Do Co. Ltd., 1982.

Francillon, René J. *Japanese Aircraft of the Pacific War*. Annapolis, Naval Institute Press, 1988.

Gallagher, James P. *Meatballs and Dead Birds*. Mechanicsburg, Stackpole Books, 2004.

Gordon, Yefim and Bill Gunston. *Soviet X-planes*. Leicester, Midland Publishing, 2000.

Gordon, Yefim and Bill Sweetman. *Soviet X-planes*. Osceola, Motorbooks International Publishers & Wholesalers, 1992.

Goodwin, Mike. 'Japanese Interest in Payen Aircraft'. *Arawasi Magazine* October 2005, pp33-37.

Green, William. *Rocket Fighter*. New York, Ballantine Books, 1977.

Green, William. *Warplanes of the Third Reich*. New York, Galahad Books, 1986.

Griehl, Manfred. *Luftwaffe over America*. New York, Fall River Press, 2006.

Gunston, Bill. *The Illustrated Encyclopedia of the World's Rockets & Missiles*. New York, Crescent Books, 1979.

Harmann, Dietmar. *Focke-Wulf Ta 152*. Atglen, Schiffer Publishing Ltd., 1999.

Hasegawa, Tatsuo and Akio Yamazaki. *Vision: Secret Development Record of the High Altitude Fighter Plane Ki-94-B-29 Interceptor*. Tōkyō, Miki Press, 2002.

Herwig, Dieter and Heinz Rode. *Luftwaffe Secret Projects: Ground & Special Purpose Aircraft*. Hinckley, Midland Publishing, 2003.

Herwig, Dieter and Heinz Rode. *Luftwaffe Secret Projects: Strategic Bombers 1935-1945*. Hinckley, Midland Publishing, 2000.

Holt, Lew. 'Flying Tanks that Shed Their Wings'. *Modern Mechanix and Inventions* July 1932.

Horn, Steve. *The Second Attack on Pearl Harbor*. Annapolis, Naval Institute Press, 2005.

Imperial Navy Land Attackers. Tōkyō, Gakken, 2003.

Ishiguro, Ryusuke and Tadeusz Januszewski. *Japanese Special Attack Aircraft & Flying Bombs*. Redbourn, Mushroom Model Publications, 2009.

Ishizawa, Kazuhiko. *Kikka: The Technological Verification of the First Japanese Jet Engine Ne 20*. Tōkyō, Miki Press, 2006.

Januszewski, Tadeusz, and Krzysztof Zalewski. *Japonskie Samoloty Marynarki: 1912-1945, Volume 1 and Volume 2*. Warsaw, Wydawnictwo Lampart, 2000.

'Japan in the Air'. *Flight* 25 December 1941, pp469-470.

Japanese Aircraft Industry in WW2: USAF 1946 Report. London, ISO Publications, 1996.

Japanese Navy Aircraft in the Pacific War. Tōkyō, Airview, 1972.

Jenkins, Dennis. *Warbird Tech Series, Volume 6: Messerschmitt Me 262 Sturmvogel*. North Branch, Specialty Press Publishers and Wholesalers, 1996.

Jones, Lloyd S. *US Fighters*. Fallbrook, Aero Publishers, Inc., 1975.

Kay, Antony L. *Junkers Aircraft & Engines 1913-1945*. Annapolis, Naval Institute Press, 2004.

'Kokusai Ta-Go'. 2004 Corner of the Sky 1 Jan 2009 www.airwar.ru/enc/aww2/tago.html

Matsuoka, Hisamitsu. *Syuusui*. Tōkyō, Miki Press, 2004.

Maru Special Issue: Super Zero Reppu. Tōkyō, Kojinsha, 2008.

Mikesh, Robert C. 'Bombs by Balloon'. *Air Enthusiast International* February 1974, pp79-83.

Mikesh, Robert C. *Japanese Aircraft: Code Names & Designations*. Atglen, Schiffer Publishing, 1993.

Mikesh, Robert C. *Monogram Close-Up 19: Kikka*. Bolyston, Monogram Aviation Publications, 1979.

Mikesh, Robert C. and Shorzoe Abe. *Japanese Aircraft 1910-1941*. London, Putnam Aeronautical Books, 1990.

Mikesh, Robert C. 'The Japanese Giants, Part I'. *Wings* June 1981.

Mikesh, Robert C. 'The Japanese Giants, Part II'. *Airpower* July 1981.

Ministry of the Navy. 1st Section, Science Department, Naval Air Depot. *Study No.6 on High-Speed Machines: Section of Main Wings*. April 1939.

Ministry of the Navy. 1st Section, Science Department, Naval Air Depot. *Study No.7 on High-Speed Machines: General Plan No.2*. April 1939.

Miranda, Justo and Paula Mercado. *Unknown #3*. Madrid: Reichsdreams Research Services, 2004.

'Mitsubishi J8M1 Shusui'. 8 November 2005. Plane-crazy.net. 12 Dec 2008 www.plane-crazy.net/links/j8.htm

Munson, Kenneth G. *Japanese and Russian Aircraft of World War II*. London, Ian Allen Ltd., 1962.

Naruo, Ando. *The Story of the Airplane Plans of the Japanese Army*. Tōkyō, Koku Journal, 1980.

Nohara, Shigeru. *The Xplanes of Imperial Japanese Army & Navy: 1924-1945*. Tōkyō, Green Arrow, 2000.

O'Neill, Richard. *Suicide Squads*. London, Salamander Books Ltd., 1981.

'Roland Payen & His Marvelous Airplanes'. 7 June 2002. Twin Pushers and Other Free Flight Oddities. 3 Dec 2008 http://home.att.net/~dannysoar2/Payen.htm

Rolfe, Douglas. *Airplanes of the World from Pusher to Jet 1490-1954*. New York, Simon and Schuster, Inc., 1954.

Sahara, Akira. *Imperial Japanese Army Prototypes & Paper Plans: 1943-1945*. Tōkyō, Ikaros Publications, Ltd., 2006.

Schick, Walter and Ingolf Meyer. *Luftwaffe Secret Projects: Fighters 1939-1945*. Hinckley, Midland Publishing Limited, 1997.

Smith, J. Richard and E. J. Creek. *Blitz!* Bennington, Merriam Press, 1997.
Takeuchi, Hiroyuki. 'Arado 196 in the Pacific'. J-aircraft.com. 10 Oct. 2008. www.j-aircraft.com/research/stories/yasunaga1.html
Thacker, Bob. 'WW-II Kyūshū Shinden J7W-1'. *Model Builder* August 1984: 14+
Toff, X. 'Forked Ghosts: Twin-Boom Aircraft Projects Designed in 1939-1945'. 22 Mar 2007, Forked Ghosts. 20 Dec 2007. http://cmeunier.perso.infonie.fr/index.htm
Tyson, Ken. 'Setting Sun'. *FlyPast* December 1991, pp28-31.
US War Department. *Handbook on Japanese Military Forces*. Baton Rouge, Louisiana State University Press, 1991.
United States. Division of Naval Intelligence. *German Technical Aid to Japan: A Survey*. 15 June 1945.
United States. US Naval Technical Mission to Japan. *Japanese Bombs*. San Francisco, US Naval Technical Mission to Japan, December 1945.
United States. US Naval Technical Mission to Japan. *Japanese Guided Missiles*. San Francisco, US Naval Technical Mission to Japan, December 1945.
United States. US Naval Technical Mission to Japan. *Japanese Infra Red Devices, Article 1, Control for Guided Missiles*. San Francisco, US Naval Technical Mission to Japan, November 1945.
United States. War Department, Military Intelligence Division. *German Technical Aid to Japan*. Washington, MIS, 31 Aug 1945.
Veronico, Nick and Alan Curry. 'Rising Sun Survivors'. *FlyPast* December 1991, pp22-26.
Wieliczko, Leszek A. 'Manshū (Manpi) K-98' 19 Sept 2004 Samoloty Wojskowe Swiata 1935-1945 15 Jan 2009. www.samoloty.ow.pl/str016.htm
Williams, Anthony G. *Rapid Fire*. Shrewsbury: Airlife Publishing Ltd., 2000.
Wooldridge, E.T. 'Japanese Flying Wings'. 27 Apr 2006. Century of Flight. 2 Apr 2008. www.century-of-flight.net/Aviation%20history/flying%20wings/japan.htm
Yokosuka Naval Air Arsenal 'YE3B (Ha 74 Model 01) or YE3E (Ha 74 Model 11)'. 9 Dec 2008. Aircraft Engine Historical Society. 6 Dec 2008. www.enginehistory.org/Japanese/japanese.htm
Yoshiro, Ikari. *Good-bye, Battleship in the Air: The Dream of Bombing the American Mainland*. Tōkyō, Kougin-sha, 2002.
Zichek, Jared A. 'The Payen-Mitsubishi Pa.400: back to the drawing board'. *Airpower* 1 May 2003.

Online forums:
www.j-aircraft.com
www.secretprojects.co.uk/forum/index.php

Artist Biographies

Peter Allen
A UK-based graphic designer, Peter works in many areas including advertising, graphics for business, watercolour painting and illustrating vehicles, both civilian and military. He has a fondness for secret aircraft projects, from British to Japanese, and many more in between. E-mail: aliensnest@yahoo.com
Website: http://www.flitzerart.com
(http://www.flitzerart.co.uk coming soon)

Muneo Hosaka
Muneo Hosaka received a degree in art and upon graduation entered the business sector as a computer graphics artist. In 1996, he turned freelance. Muneo's 3D aviation artwork has seen print in many Japanese publications over the years, spanning operational aircraft and X-planes. His drive comes from his desire to see project aircraft take to the sky, if only as artwork. Muneo was born on 29 September 1961 and currently resides in Japan, his home country.
Website: http://www.ne.jp/asahi/green/wave/

Gino Marcomini
Born on 16 June 1981 in Pirassununga, Brazil, Gino graduated from the industrial design course at Universidade Estadual Paulista in 2005. He has worked in product and graphic design, being master designer on Coorperdata's Industrial Pole and is a partner of the Brazil based design agency Abissal Design. In addition to design work, Gino teaches technical courses in industrial design, mechanics and mechatronics using Solidworks CAD software and 3DMax as the poly modelling software. He is currently working on his post-graduation studies at the Universidade Federal do Paraná to be concluded in 2009.
Website: http://www.oxygino.com

Ted Nomura
Since 1986, Ted has written and drawn over 100 comics. He is best known for the alternative history comic series 'Families of Altered Wars' which in recent years created a number of comic spin-offs, notably *Luftwaffe: 1946*, *World War 2: 1946* and *Kamikaze: 1946*. In addition, he has produced a number of comic formatted technical manuals on Luftwaffe secret projects, co-authored with Justo Miranda. Ted's work is most often published through the San Antonio, Texas, comic publisher Antarctic Press.

Ronnie Olsthoorn
With over ten years of professional experience and a background in aeronautical engineering, Ronnie's aviation art boasts high levels of realism and accuracy. Every custom artwork is preceded by great amounts of research to ensure the client gets as authentic an image as possible. Yet Ronnie doesn't lose sight of the artistic side of things and each image is a striking visualisation of the real thing.
Ronnie's artwork has featured in and on books, magazines, model kit box tops, computer games and aviation museums. But the most rewarding work he has done were commissions to honour veteran pilots and their families. The positive and often emotive feedback from veteran pilots is the greatest reward any aviation artist could ask for.
To commission custom artwork, contact Ronnie on
ronnie@skyraider3d.com
or alternatively via his website at
www.skyraider3d.com
Prints of his aviation art are available through
www.digitalaviationart.com
Other merchandise such as t-shirts, mugs and mouse pads are available on request.
Daddy's Girl
JAPANESE SECRET PROJECTS
EXPERIMENTAL AIRCRAFT OF THE IJA AND IJN 1939-1945
Edwin M. Dyer, III

3
172
172
Kelcey Faulkner
A founding member of www.phoenix-art.co.uk, producing digital profiles of the finest quality for professional publishing or for the profile enthusiast. Proficient in aircraft of the World War 2 era, but equally confident creating renders of a far wider genre including, aircraft and vehicles, (both in military, civil, historic and modern designs). For commissions and prints at the most competitive rates please visit us at www.phoenix-art.co.uk.
B
AZ
AA722
PHOENIX-ART GRAPHIC REQUISITES
HB
ЗА
РОДИНУ!
PHOENIX-ART
www.phoenix-art.co.uk

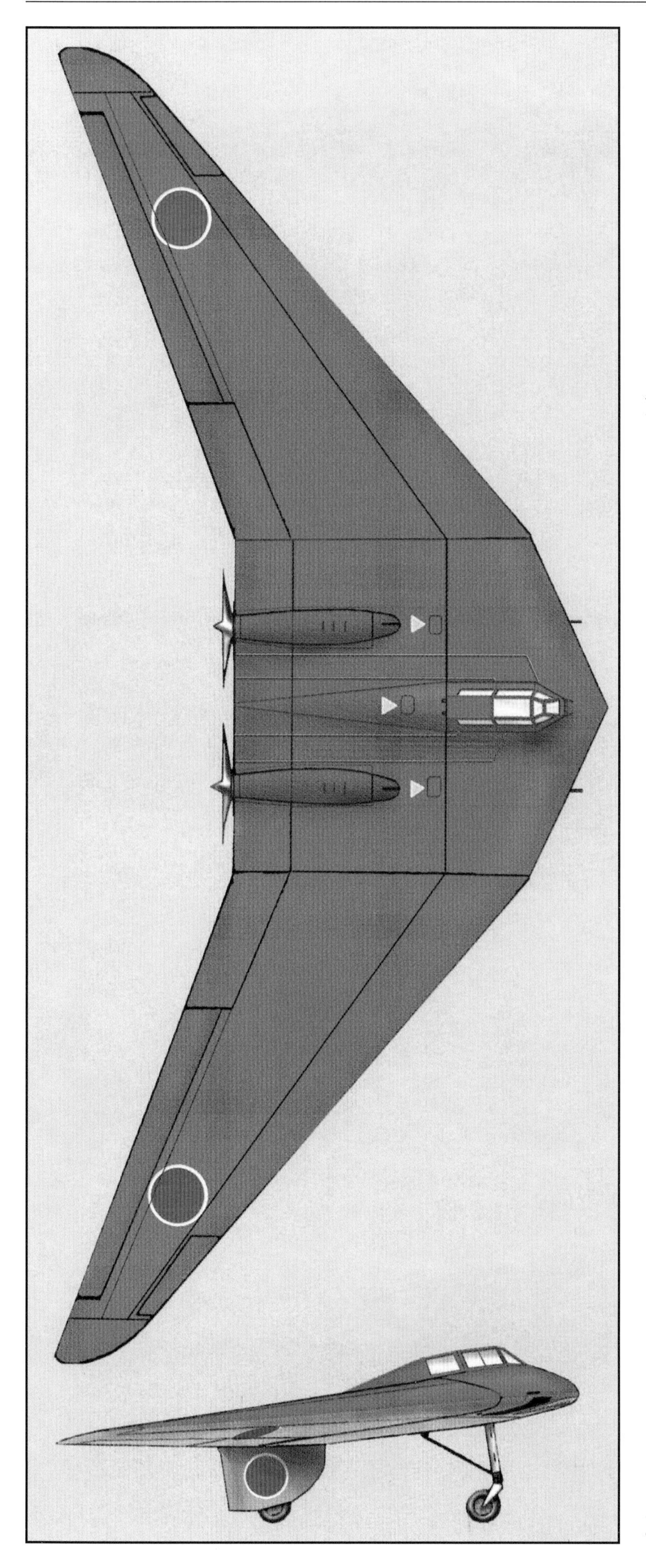

Hypothetical Aircraft Profiles

In 1986, Ted Nomura self-published his comic *Tigers of Terra: Families of Altered Wars* under his Mind Visions label. In 2006, his work celebrated 20 years of alternative military history in visual form. Antarctic Press assumed the printing duties for Nomura's comics, not only continuing *Tigers of Terra* but with spin-offs including the popular *Luftwaffe: 1946*, *Kamikaze: 1946*, and many others, to include several x-plane technical manuals. The latter publications were done with the assistance of Justo Miranda. Nomura's profile artwork in this book come from his many comics and where available, the alternate history he has given them is provided.

Tachikawa Ki-229 as operated by the IJA. This was the Japanese version of the Horten Ho 229. Horten VII trainers were used by the IJA as the Ki-226.
Ted S. Nomura/Mind Visions and Antarctic Press

Nakajima Kitsuka (code named *Linda*), flown by an unidentified Tokkōtai unit. Ted S. Nomura/ Mind Visions and Antarctic Press

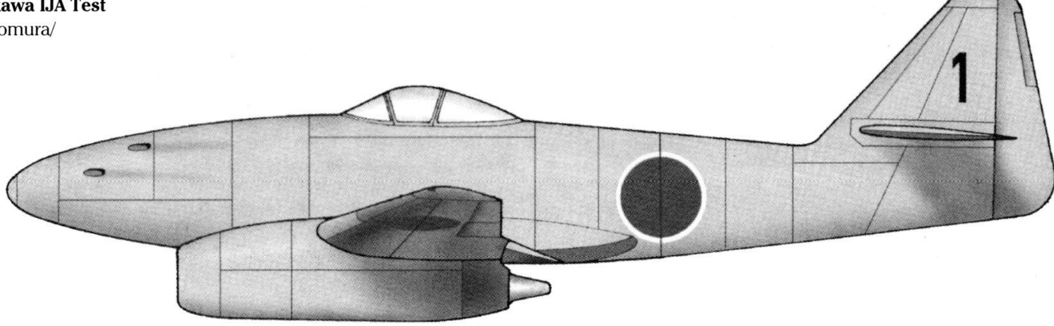

Tachikawa built Ki-201 Karyū (code named *Lee*) prototype, flown by the Fussa/Tachikawa IJA Test Squadron, September 1945. Ted S. Nomura/ Mind Visions and Antarctic Press

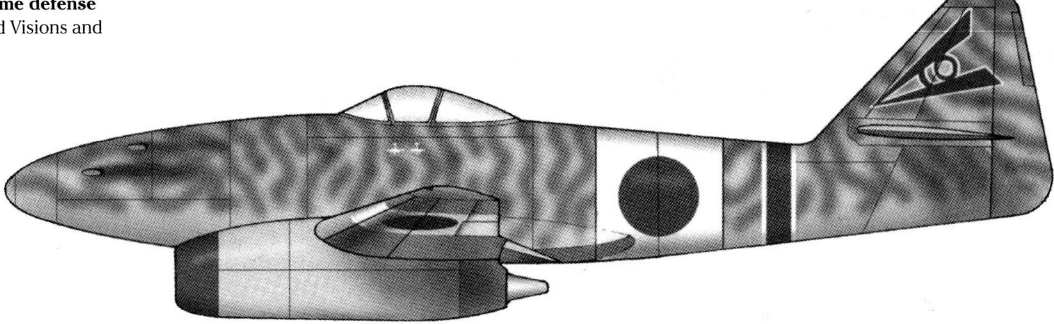

Kawasaki built Ki-201 Karyū (code named *Lee*) flown by a unidentified Japanese home defense unit, March 1946. Ted S. Nomura/Mind Visions and Antarctic Press

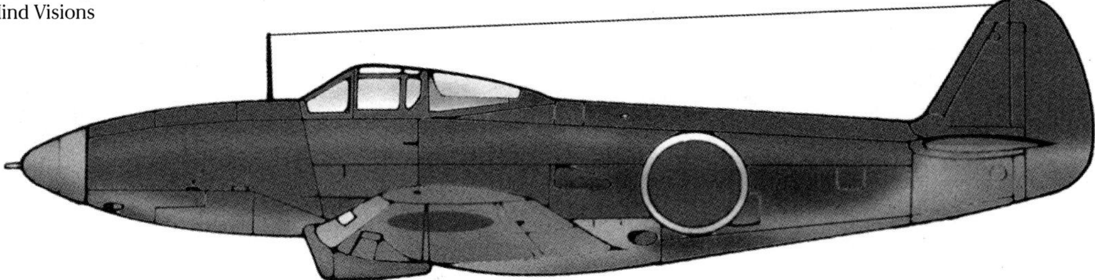

Kawasaki Ki-88 (code named *Bonnie*) as briefly operated by the IJA. Ted S. Nomura/Mind Visions and Antarctic Press

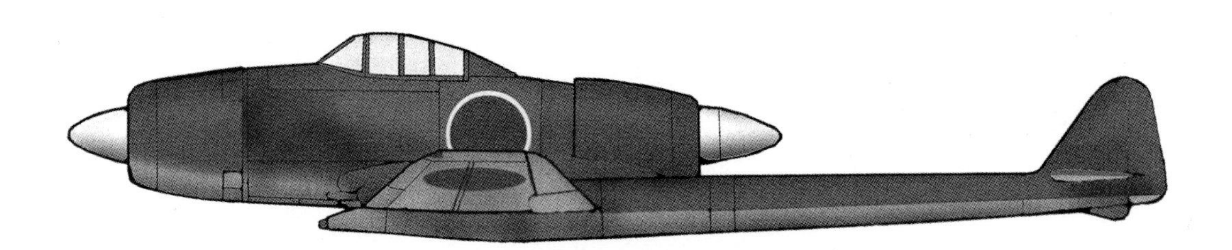

Tachikawa Ki-94-I. Ted S. Nomura/Mind Visions and Antarctic Press

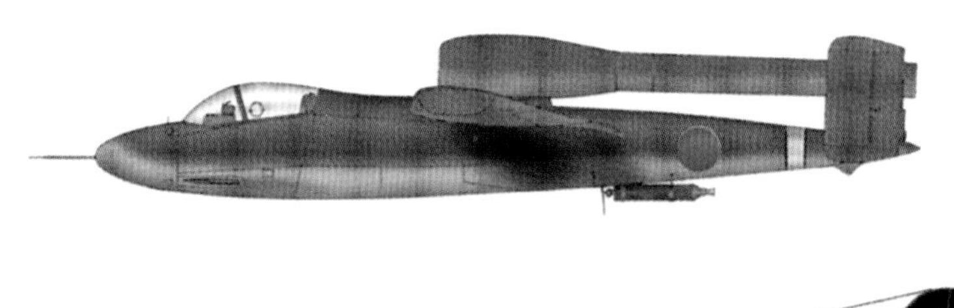

Tachikawa Ki-162 (code named *Jan*), flown by the Fussa/Tachikawa IJA Test Squadron, November 14, 1945. Ted S. Nomura/Mind Visions and Antarctic Press

Messerschmitt Me 262A-2 (code named *Marsha*) flown by the 58th Tokkōtai, December 1, 1945. Ted S. Nomura/Mind Visions and Antarctic Press

Heinkel He111 (code named *Bess*) with Fieseler Fi 103R-IV (code named *Cindy*) as operated by the 47th Tokkōtai, December 7, 1945. Ted S. Nomura/Mind Visions and Antarctic Press

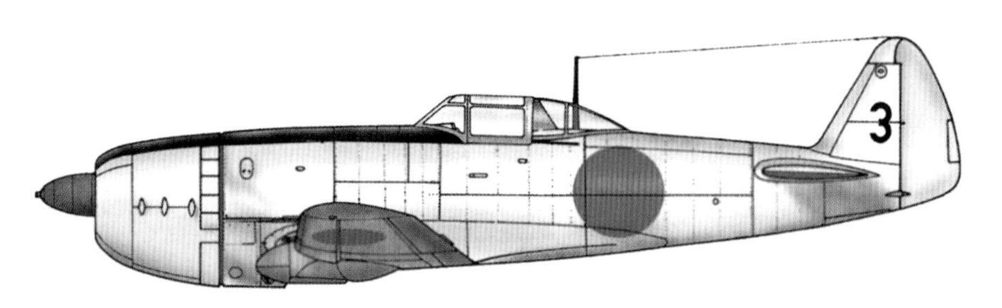

Nakajima Ki-87 (code named *Jeff*) as flown by Major Saburō Kurusu, Fussa/Tachikawa IJA Test Squadron, November 14, 1945. Ted S. Nomura/Mind Visions and Antarctic Press

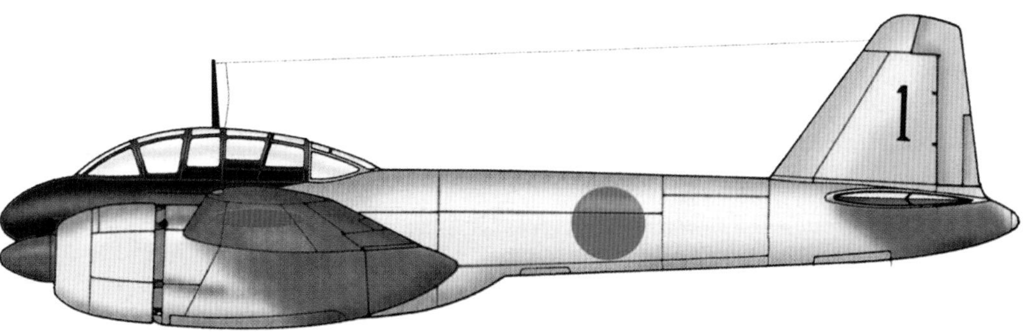

Rikugun Ki-93 (code named *Dora*) flown by Hauptmann Dora Oberlicht of J/KG 200, operating at the Fussa/Tachikawa IJA Test Center, November 14, 1945. Ted S. Nomura/Mind Visions and Antarctic Press

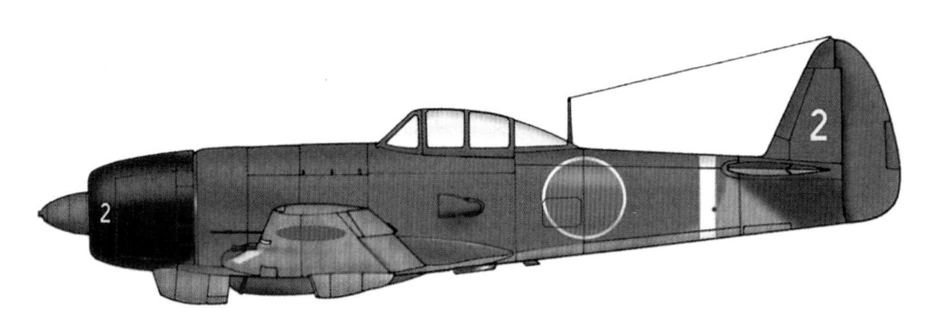

Tachikawa Ki-94-II (code named *Ted*) flown by Lieutenant Colonel Ichirō Mikasa, Fussa/Tachikawa IJA Test Squadron, November 14, 1945. Ted S. Nomura/Mind Visions and Antarctic Press

Index

INDEX OF PERSONALITIES

(rank, professional qualifications and political status are ignored.)

INDEX OF AIRCRAFT

INDEX OF ENGINES

INDEX OF WEAPON SYSTEMS
(as presented in the book)